The Letter of JAMES

DOUGLAS J. MOO

WILLIAM B. EERDMANS PUBLISHING COMPANY
GRAND RAPIDS, MICHIGAN / CAMBRIDGE, U.K.

APOLLOS
LEICESTER, ENGLAND

First published 2000
in the United States of America by
Wm. B. Eerdmans Publishing Co.
2140 Oak Industrial Drive N.E., Grand Rapids, Michigan 49505 /
P.O. Box 163, Cambridge CB3 9PU U.K.
www.eerdmans.com

and in the United Kingdom by
APOLLOS
38 De Montfort Street, Leicester, England LE1 7GP

Printed in the United States of America

12 11 10 11 10 9 8 7

Library of Congress Cataloging-in-Publication Data

ISBN 978-0-8028-3730-1

British Library Cataloguing in Publication Data

A catalogue record for this book is available from the British Library.
ISBN 978-0-85111-977-9

Contents

COMMENTARY ON JAMES

INDEXES

Series Preface

Commentaries have specific aims, and this series is no exception. Designed for serious pastors and teachers of the Bible, the Pillar commentaries seek above all to make clear the text of Scripture as we have it. The scholars writing these volumes interact with the most important, informed contemporary debate, but avoid getting mired in undue technical detail. Their ideal is a blend of rigorous exegesis and exposition, with an eye alert both to biblical theology and the contemporary relevance of the Bible, without confusing the commentary and the sermon.

The rationale for this approach is that the vision of "objective scholarship" (a vain chimera) may actually be profane. God stands over against us; we do not stand in judgment of him. When God speaks to us through his Word, those who profess to know him must respond in an appropriate way, and that is certainly different from a stance in which the scholar projects an image of autonomous distance. Yet this is no surreptitious appeal for uncontrolled subjectivity. The writers of this series aim for an evenhanded openness to the text that is the best kind of "objectivity" of all.

If the text is God's Word, it is appropriate that we respond with reverence, a certain fear, a holy joy, a questing obedience. These values should be reflected in the way Christians write. With these values in place, the Pillar commentaries will be warmly welcomed not only by pastors, teachers, and students, but by general readers as well.

*　*　*

At first glance some might think it rather surprising that the author of one of this century's major commentaries on the Epistle to the Romans should turn his hand to write a sympathetic commentary on James. But that is what Douglas Moo has achieved. More than an enlargement of his well-received little commentary on James in the TNTC series, this volume is a fresh and detailed work that displays, in particular, two great strengths. The first is a deceptive simplicity. Even when he is handling remarkably complex exegetical points, Dr. Moo argues his case with an economy and simplicity of style altogether enviable and sure to be appreciated by every reader. The second is a gentle tone of thoughtful application. Without forgetting that this book is a commentary and not a homily, Dr. Moo expounds the text not only with the cool objectivity of the seasoned scholar but with the warm reflection of the pastor. It is an enormous privilege to work with him as a colleague in the institution both of us serve.

D. A. Carson

Author's Preface

I am very grateful to Don Carson, general editor of the Pillar New Testament Commentary, and to the Eerdmans Publishing Company for the opportunity to write this commentary on the Letter of James. As many readers of this commentary will know, fifteen years ago I wrote a commentary on James for the Tyndale series (*The Letter of James* [Grand Rapids: Eerdmans/Leicester: Inter-Varsity, 1985]). The opportunity to revisit this letter has proved to be very profitable for me and, I hope, for students of James. The Pillar series has enabled me almost to double the space I could devote to commentary on the letter. I have therefore been able to pursue issues of background and theology at greater length. I am more impressed than ever by James's creative use of Hellenistic Jewish traditions in his exposition of practical Christianity. And I remain convinced that the heart of the letter is a call to wholehearted commitment to Christ. James's call for consistent and uncompromising Christian living is much needed. Our churches are filled with believers who are only halfhearted in their faith and, as a result, leave large areas of their lives virtually untouched by genuine Christian values. Nor am I immune to such problems. As I quite unexpectedly find myself in my "middle age" years, I have discovered a tendency to back off in my fervor for the Lord and his work. My reimmersion in James has challenged me sharply at just this point. I pray that it might have the same effect on all readers of the commentary.

In addition to series editor Don Carson and Eerdmans editor Milton Essenburg, I have several others to thank for their help with this volume. My research assistant at Trinity, Stephen Pegler, helped compile bibliography and edit the manuscript. My office assistant, Leigh Swain, keyed my earlier commentary into WordPerfect as a source for this work. She and Trinity doctoral fellow Pierce Yates also helped with the indexes. But most of all I want to thank my wife Jenny, to whom I dedicate this book. She also helped with the indexes; but, more than that, she encouraged me in the work when my self-confidence was at a low ebb.

DOUGLAS J. MOO

Chief Abbreviations

AB	Anchor Bible
ANRW	*Aufstieg und Niedergang der römischen Welt*
AusBibRev	*Australian Biblical Review*
BAGD	W. Bauer, W. F. Arndt, F. W. Gingrich, and F. W. Danker, *Greek-English Lexicon of the New Testament* (2d ed.)
BK	*Bibel und Kirche*
BN	*Biblische Notizen*
BBR	*Bulletin for Biblical Research*
BDF	F. Blass, A. Debrunner, and R. W. Funk, *A Greek Grammar of the New Testament and Other Early Christian Literature*
Bib	*Biblica*
BSac	*Bibliotheca Sacra*
BTB	*Biblical Theology Bulletin*
BZ	*Biblische Zeitschrift*
CBQ	*Catholic Biblical Quarterly*
EvQ	*Evangelical Quarterly*
ExpTim	*Expository Times*
HTR	*Harvard Theological Review*
ISBE	*International Standard Bible Encyclopedia*
JBL	*Journal of Biblical Literature*
JETS	*Journal of the Evangelical Theological Society*
JNES	*Journal of Near Eastern Studies*
JR	*Journal of Religion*
JSNT	*Journal for the Study of the New Testament*
JTS	*Journal for Theological Studies*
KJV	King James Version
LSJ	Liddell-Scott-Jones, *Greek-English Lexicon*

LW	*Luther's Works*
LXX	Septuagint
MM	J. H. Moulton and G. Milligan, *The Vocabulary of the Greek New Testament*
MT	Massoretic Text
NA	Nestle-Aland Greek New Testament (27th ed.)
NAB	New American Bible
NEB	New English Bible
NIDNTT	*New International Dictionary of New Testament Theology*
NIV	New International Version
NJB	New Jerusalem Bible
NLT	New Living Translation
NovT	*Novum Testamentum*
NovTSup	Novum Testamentum, Supplements
NRSV	New Revised Standard Version
NTS	*New Testament Studies*
PL	*Patrologia Latina*
REB	Revised English Bible
ResQ	*Restoration Quarterly*
RSV	Revised Standard Version
SBL	Society of Biblical Literature
SJT	*Scottish Journal of Theology*
SNTSMS	Society for New Testament Studies Monograph Series
TDNT	G. Kittel and G. Friedrich (eds.), *Theological Dictionary of the New Testament*
TEV	Today's English Version
TLZ	*Theologische Literaturzeitung*
TrinJ	*Trinity Journal*
UBS	United Bible Societies Greek New Testament (4th ed.)
WTJ	*Westminster Theological Journal*
ZNW	*Zeitschrift für die neutestamentliche Wissenschaft*

Select Bibliography

I. COMMENTARIES ON JAMES

Adamson, J. B., *The Epistle of James* (Grand Rapids: Eerdmans, 1976).
Bengel, J. A., *Gnomon of the New Testament,* vol. 5 (reprint; Edinburgh: T & T Clark, 1860).
Burdick, D. W., "James," in *The Expositor's Bible Commentary,* vol. 12 (Grand Rapids: Zondervan, 1981).
Calvin, J., *Commentaries on the Catholic Epistles,* trans. J. Owen (reprint; Grand Rapids: Eerdmans, 1948).
Cantinat, J., *Les Épîtres de Saint Jacques et de Saint Jude* (Paris: Gabalda, 1973).
Chaine, J., *L'Épître de Saint Jacques* (Paris: Gabalda, 1927).
Davids, P., *The Epistle of James* (Grand Rapids: Eerdmans, 1982).
Dibelius, M., *A Commentary on the Epistle of James,* rev. by H. Greeven (Philadelphia: Fortress, 1976).
Frankemölle, H., *Der Brief des Jakobus* (Gütersloh: Gütersloher, 1994).
Hiebert, D. E., *James* (rev. ed.; Chicago: Moody, 1992).
Hort, F. J. A., *The Epistle of St. James* (London: Macmillan, 1909).
Huther, J. E., *Critical and Exegetical Handbook to the General Epistles of James, Peter, John and Jude* (New York: Funk & Wagnalls, 1887).
Johnson, L. T., *The Letter of James* (Garden City: Doubleday, 1995).
Knowling, R. J., *The Epistle of St. James* (London: Methuen, 1910).
Laws, S., *A Commentary on the Epistle of James* (New York: Harper & Row, 1980).
Martin, R. P., *James* (Waco, Tex.: Word, 1988).
Mayor, J. B., *The Epistle of St. James* (2d ed.; London: Macmillan, 1913).
Mitton, C. L., *The Epistle of James* (Grand Rapids: Eerdmans, 1966).

Moffatt, J., *The General Epistles of James, Peter and Jude* (London: Hodder and Stoughton, 1928).
Moo, D. J., *The Letter of James* (Grand Rapids: Eerdmans, 1985).
Mussner, F., *Der Jakobusbrief* (4th ed.; Freiburg: Herder, 1981).
Nystrom, D. P., *James* (Grand Rapids: Zondervan, 1997).
Reicke, B., *The Epistles of James, Peter and Jude* (Garden City: Doubleday, 1964).
Ropes, J. H., *A Critical and Exegetical Commentary on the Epistle of St. James* (Edinburgh: T & T Clark, 1916).
Ross, A., *The Epistles of James and John* (London: Marshall, Morgan and Scott, 1954).
Schlatter, A., *Der Brief des Jakobus* (Stuttgart: Calwer, 1956).
Tasker, R. V. G., *The General Epistle of James* (Grand Rapids: Eerdmans, 1956).
Vouga, F., *L'epître de S. Jacques* (Geneva: Labor et Fides, 1984).
Windisch, H., *Die katholischen Briefe* (Tübingen: Mohr, 1951).

II. OTHER WORKS

Baasland, E., "Literarische Form, Thematik und geschichtliche Einordnung des Jakobusbriefes," *ANRW* 2.25.5 (1988) 3,646-84.
Baker, W. R., *Personal Speech-Ethics in the Epistle of James* (Tübingen: J. C. B. Mohr [Paul Siebeck], 1995).
Bauckham, R., *James: Wisdom of James, Disciple of Jesus the Sage* (London: Routledge, 1999).
Blomberg, C. L., *Neither Poverty nor Riches: A Biblical Theology of Material Possessions.* New Studies in Biblical Theology. Grand Rapids: Eerdmans, 1999.
Cadoux, A. T., *The Thought of St. James* (London: James Clarke, 1944).
Cargal, T., *Restoring the Diaspora: Discursive Structure and Purpose in the Epistle of James* (Atlanta: Scholars, 1993).
Cranfield, C. E. B., "The Message of James," *SJT* 18 (1965) 182-93, 338-45.
Crotty, R. B., "The Literary Structure of the Letter of James," *AusBibRev* 40 (1992) 47-48.
Goppelt, L., *Theology of the New Testament* (2 vols.; Grand Rapids: Eerdmans, 1975, 1976).
Hartin, P. J., *James and the Q Sayings of Jesus* (Sheffield: JSOT, 1991).
Hoppe, R., *Die theologische Hintergrund des Jakobusbriefes* (Würzburg: Echter, 1977).
Johnson, L. T., "The Use of Leviticus 19 in the Letter of James," *JBL* 101 (1982) 391-401.
Klein, M., *"Ein vollkommenes Werk." Vollkommenheit, Gesetz und Gericht als theologische Themen des Jakobusbriefes* (Stuttgart: Kohlhammer, 1995).

Maynard-Reid, P. W., *Poverty and Wealth in James* (Maryknoll, N.Y.: Orbis, 1987).

Metzger, B. M., *A Textual Commentary on the Greek New Testament* (New York: United Bible Societies, 1971).

Moule, C. F. D., *An Idiom Book of New Testament Greek* (Cambridge: Cambridge University Press, 1971).

Penner, T. C., *The Epistle of James and Eschatology: Re-Reading an Ancient Christian Letter* (Sheffield: Sheffield Academic Press, 1996).

Popkes, W., *Addressaten, Situation und Form des Jakobusbriefes* (Stuttgart: Katholischer, 1986).

Rendall, G. H., *The Epistle of St. James and Judaistic Christianity* (Cambridge: Cambridge University Press, 1927).

Tamez, E., *The Scandalous Message of James: Faith without Works Is Dead* (New York: Crossroad, 1990).

Turner, N., *Syntax,* vol. 3 of *A Grammar of New Testament Greek,* by J. H. Moulton (Edinburgh: T & T Clark, 1963).

Wessel, W., "The Epistle of James," *ISBE* 2.959-66.

Wuellner, W. H., "Der Jakobusbrief im Licht der Rhetorik und Textpragmatic," *Linguistica Biblica* 44 (1978-79) 5-66.

Quotations of the Apocrypha are taken from *The Oxford Annotated Apocrypha* (ed. B. M. Metzger; rev. ed.; New York: Oxford University Press, 1977), of the pseudepigrapha from *The Old Testament Pseudepigrapha* (2 vols.; ed. J. H. Charlesworth; Garden City: Doubleday, 1983, 1985), and of Philo from The Loeb Classical Library.

Introduction

Few NT books have been as controversial as the Letter of James. Its place in the canon was contested by some early Christians. The reformer Martin Luther called it an "epistle of straw" and relegated it to a secondary status within the NT. And modern theologians often dismiss the letter as a holdover from Judaism that does not truly express the essence of the Christian faith. Yet quite in contrast to the sometimes negative view of the letter among academics and theologians is the status of James among ordinary believers. Few books of the NT are better known or more often quoted than James. It is probably one of the two or three most popular NT books in the church. In the sections of the Introduction that follow we will investigate just why some theologians have had difficulties with James. But why is James so popular among believers generally? Three characteristics of the letter seem to provide the answer.

First, James is intensely practical; and believers looking for specific guidance in the Christian life naturally appreciate such an emphasis. Typical of the letter is 1:22, arguably the most famous command in the NT: "Do not merely listen to the word, and so deceive yourselves. Do what it says" (1:22). James is filled with similar clear and direct commands. In fact, the Letter of James contains a higher frequency of imperative verbs than any other NT book. James's purpose is clearly not so much to inform as to chastise, exhort, and encourage. It is not, as we will show, that James is unconcerned with theology or that he does not have solid theological basis for his commands. It is, rather, that he touches only briefly and allusively on the theology while concentrating on the practical outworking of the theology.

A second factor making James so attractive to believers is his conciseness. He rarely develops the points he makes at any length, being content to make his point and to move quickly on. Interpreters of James are often, indeed, puzzled to figure out a clear organization in the letter. But what troubles interpreters is a virtue for many readers, who can immediately appreciate the point that James is trying to make. Indeed, in this respect James is somewhat similar to OT and Jewish wisdom books, such as Proverbs; and Christians appreciate these books for similar reasons.

Third, James's lavish use of metaphors and illustrations makes his teaching easy to understand and to remember. The billowing sea, the withered flower, the image of a face in a mirror, the bit in the horse's mouth, the rudder of the ship, the destructive forest fire, the pure spring of water, the arrogant businessman, the corroded metal, and moth-eaten clothes — all are images of virtually universal appeal.

Nevertheless, without denying the direct and often obvious point in what James writes, his letter does come from circumstances far removed from ours. To appreciate fully what James wants to communicate to the church of our day, we need to understand these circumstances as best we can. In the sections that follow, we will take up the various facets of James's situation so that we may gain as accurate and detailed a picture as possible of the context in which God used him to communicate his word for his people.

I. THE LETTER IN THE CHURCH

The Letter of James is not addressed to a single church but to "the twelve tribes scattered among the nations" (1:1). This general address led early Christians to categorize James, along with the similarly vaguely addressed 1 and 2 Peter, 1, 2, and 3 John, and Jude, as a "general" or "catholic" (in the sense of "universal") letter. Perhaps because the letters did not find a home in any single church, each of them had something of a struggle to find general acceptance as canonical books. James was not finally recognized by both the eastern and western parts of the church until the fourth century.

The Letter of James was, of course, known and used by many Christians long before then. The letter is first mentioned by name early in the third century. But ancient Christians were in the habit of quoting from books and using their content without naming them. So determining how early James was used in the early church depends on identifying places in early Christian literature where the teaching of James is cited or referred to. But such an identification is not always easy since much of what James teaches is traditional. What might seem to be a reference to James could simply be a reference to a widespread teaching that James shares with many other Jews and early Christians. J. B. Mayor, in his classic commentary on James, takes a maximal approach, identifying allusions to James in many NT books and early Christian writings.[1] But many of these allusions prove to be no more than similarities in rather common language or ideas. A more sober and realistic estimate comes from L. T. Johnson, a recent commentator on James. He thinks a good case can be made that two Christian books from the late first and early second century depend on James: *1 Clement,* a letter written in Rome about A.D. 95, and *The Shepherd of Hermas,* a series of homilies from the early or middle second century.[2] Similarities between James and the Mandates section of *The Shepherd* are particularly striking.

An early Christian writer, Cassiodorus, claims that Clement, head of the catechetical school in Alexandria, wrote a commentary on James. But it has never been discovered, and Clement does not show dependence on James in his other writings.[3] Clement's successor in Alexandria, Origen, is the first to cite James by name. He attributes the letter to James, "the apostle" (*Commentary on John,* frag. 126), and cites the letter as Scripture (*Selecta in Psalmos* 30:6). In the Latin translation of Origen's works, the author is more explicitly identified as "the brother of the Lord," but the reliability of this addition is doubted. Several other third-century Christian writings allude to James, and the letter is quoted as scriptural in the pseudo-Clementine tractate *Ad Virgines.* In the early fourth century, the historian Eusebius both cites James and regards the letter as canonical. However, he also relegates it to the status of a "disputed book" in his survey of the state of the canon in his day (*History of the Church* 3.25.3; 2.23.25). This category encompasses books that were accepted by many Christians as scriptural but rejected by others. The doubts about James probably came from the Syrian church, where the general letters were often rejected. Theodore of Mopsuestia, one of the most influential Syrian theologians, for instance, refused to accept into the canon any of the general letters. Nevertheless, James was included in the fifth-century Syriac translation of the NT, and it is quoted with approval by two other giants of the eastern church: Chrysostom (d. 407) and Theodoret (d. 458).

While dissenting voices are found, therefore, the eastern church as a whole generally accepted James as a scriptural document. A similar pat-

1. See esp. pp. lxix-lxxi, lxxxviii-cix.

2. Johnson, 68-80.

3. B. F. Westcott speculated that "Jude" should be read in place of "James" in Cassiodorus's statement (*A General Survey of the History of the Canon of the New Testament* [6th ed.; London: Macmillan, 1889], 357-58).

tern emerges in the western church, although James was slower to gain acceptance there. Neither the Muratorian Canon (late 2d century) nor the Mommsen catalog (listing the African canon of c. 360) includes James.[4] In fact, the earliest undisputed reference to James in the western church comes only in the middle of the fourth century (Hilary of Poitiers and Ambrosiaster). Decisive, perhaps, for James's eventual place in the canon of the western church was the endorsement of the major figure Jerome. He included James in his Latin translation and cited it frequently. Moreover, he explicitly identified the author as the brother of the Lord. Augustine followed suit, and James landed a secure place in the canon of the Christian church.

How should we evaluate the rather slow and hesitant adoption of James into the early Christian canon? Some scholars think that the uncertainties expressed by some early Christians about James should raise doubts in our minds about the authenticity or authority of the letter for the church. But two factors suggest that this conclusion is unwarranted. First, the evidence we possess suggests that James was not so much *rejected* as *neglected.* While evidence for the use and authoritative status of James is not as early or widespread as we might wish, very few early Christians, knowing the letter, dismissed it. Second, the neglect that James experienced can be readily explained. Early Christians tended to accord special prominence to books written by apostles; and James was such a common name that many probably wondered whether the letter had an apostolic origin or not. Moreover, James is filled with rather traditional and quite practical admonitions: it is not the kind of book that would figure prominently in early Christian theological debates. At the same time some early Jewish-Christian groups misrepresented some of the teaching of James in support of their own heretical agendas. Knowledge of this use of James among orthodox theologians may well have led them to look askance at James.[5] Finally, the destination of the letter may also account for its relative neglect. The letter was probably written to Jewish Christians living in Palestine and Syria. These churches, partly as the result of the disastrous revolts against Rome in 66-70 and 132-35, disappeared at an early date; and letters written to them may similarly have disappeared for a time.[6]

The canonical status of James came under scrutiny again at the time

4. The absence of James in the Muratorian Canon may be accidental, since the text is mutilated (see Westcott, *History of the Canon,* 219-20; and, for a contrasting interpretation, Mussner, 41).

5. Martin, lxi.

6. It may be significant in this regard that Origen cites James only after his move from Alexandria to Palestine (see Laws, 24).

of the Reformation. The humanist scholar Erasmus raised doubts about the letter's apostolic origin, questioning whether a brother of Jesus could have written a letter composed in such good Greek. Luther also doubted the apostolic status of the letter, but his criticism of James went much further. His objections to James were primarily theological. Luther's quest for peace with God ended with his discovery of Paul's teaching about justification by faith alone. Justification by faith became for him and his followers, as later Lutheran theologians put it, "the doctrine on which the church stands or falls." It was because Luther gave to justification by faith central importance in defining NT theology that he had difficulties with letters like James that were silent about, or even appeared to be critical of, this doctrine. Hence Luther claimed that James "mangles the Scriptures and thereby opposes Paul and all Scripture" (*LW* 35:397). James was "an epistle of straw" (*LW* 35:362), to be relegated to the end of the NT, along with Jude, Hebrews, and Revelation. Clearly, then, Luther had doubts about whether James should be regarded with the same respect and authority as the more "central" NT documents. But we should be careful not to overemphasize the strength of his critique. He did not exclude James from the canon and quotes the letter rather frequently in his writings.[7] A balanced assessment of Luther's view of James is summed up well by Luther himself: "I cannot include him among the chief books, though I would not prevent anyone from including or extolling him as he pleases, for there are otherwise many good sayings in him" (*LW* 35:397).

The other reformers did not share Luther's negative view of James. Calvin, for instance, while admitting that James "seems more sparing in proclaiming the grace of Christ than it behooved an Apostle to be," also rightly noted that "it is not surely required for all to handle the same arguments."[8] He accepted the full apostolic authority of the letter and argued that Paul's and James's perspectives on justification could be harmonized so as to maintain the unity of Scripture. Calvin's approach to James is standard among the community of believers. And it is surely the right one. With a better appreciation of the Jewish background against which James is writing and the benefit of distance from the battles Luther was fighting, we can both value the distinctive message of James and see how that message can be harmonized with the message of Paul. James has his own contribution to make to our understanding of Christian theology and practice. That contribution, as we will argue later, provides an important counterweight to a potential imbalance from reading Paul (or

7. See D. Stoutenberg, "Martin Luther's Exegetical Use of the Epistle of St. James" (M.A. thesis, Trinity Evangelical Divinity School, Deerfield, IL, 1982).

8. Calvin, 277.

certain of Paul's letters) alone. The early Christians who, under the providential guidance of God, accorded to James canonical status recognized the inherent value of James in this regard. We can be grateful for the opportunity to read, appropriate, and live out the distinctive emphases of this important NT letter.

This is not to say that the acceptance of James as authoritative Scripture has been unquestioned since Calvin's time. Two challenges in particular need to be addressed. First, the academic community has raised several questions about the origin of James that have the real or potential effect of seriously undermining the letter's authority. We will deal with these matters in the sections that follow. Second, even when the letter is acknowledged to be fully canonical and authoritative for the church, Christians can effectively avoid the contribution of the letter to theology and practice by simply ignoring it or by failing to interpret the letter in its own terms. We can almost unconsciously operate with a "canon within the canon" that fails to do justice to the full scope of the revelation God has given us.

II. NATURE AND GENRE

Several facets of the book of James need to be considered as we think about the kind of book that we have before us.

First, the book's opening words identify what follows as a letter. The letter was a very broad literary category in the ancient world, encompassing everything from brief notes of information and request to long argumentative discourses. Identifying James as a letter is, therefore, both obvious and not very helpful. A closer examination of the nature of this particular letter takes us a bit further. Absent from James are the customary greetings, references to fellow workers, and travel plans that mark many ancient and NT (especially Pauline) letters. Also missing are references to specific people, places, or situations in the body of the letter. Where James does refer to a situation, he casts it in a vague, even hypothetical manner (e.g., 2:2-3, 15-17; 4:13-17).

As we noted above, it was for these reasons that early Christians classified James as a "general" letter: one written to the church at large rather than to a specific church or group of churches.[9] But while the letter does not single out individuals or places, it pretty clearly reflects a specific set of circumstances that would not be true of people living just any-

9. A few modern scholars agree; see, e.g., Klein, 185-87; Vouga, 24-25.

where. Most scholars agree, therefore, that James addresses a specific church or, more likely, group of churches. The letter is the form in which James has transmitted general admonitions concerning their situation. James is therefore more a "literary" than a personal letter; the closest parallel to it in the NT is perhaps 1 John.[10]

A second feature of James that would immediately impress the ancient reader is the degree to which James borrows from traditional teaching.[11] Two kinds of sources figure especially often in the letter. First, James depends more than any other NT author on the teaching of Jesus. It is not that James directly quotes Jesus — although Jas. 5:12 is virtually a quotation of Jesus' teaching about oaths in Matt. 5:33-37. It is, rather, that he weaves Jesus' teaching into the very fabric of his own instruction. Again and again, the closest parallels to James's wording will be found in the teaching of Jesus — especially as recorded in the Gospel of Matthew. And the topics he addresses as well as the particular slant that he takes on these topics mimics Jesus' own emphasis. The author of the letter seems to have been so soaked in the atmosphere and specifics of Jesus' teaching that he can reflect them almost unconsciously. Second, the letter also betrays a striking number of similarities to the words and emphases of a certain segment of Hellenistic Judaism, represented to some extent by the Alexandrian philosopher Philo, but especially by the apocryphal book Sirach and the pseudepigraphical book *Testaments of the Twelve Patriarchs.* The letter's dependence on such sources offers some help in identifying the author and place of writing; but we are concerned here with what this use of traditional material might suggest about the nature of the letter. But before we draw possible conclusions from this factor, another factor needs to be mentioned.

Striking to both the ancient and modern reader alike is the letter's lack of clear organization. The author moves quickly from topic to topic, and the logical relationship of the topics is often not at all clear. Recent scholarship, influenced by modern literary techniques and insights, has reopened the question of structure with a vengeance; and we will consider this matter more carefully later. But the very number of suggestions for the outline of the letter betrays the very point we are making here: the letter has no obvious structure, nor even a clearly defined theme. Moral exhortations follow closely upon one another without connections and without much logical relationship.

10. See esp. F. O. Francis, "The Form and Function of the Opening and Closing Paragraphs of James and 1 John," *ZNW* 61 (1970) 110-26; P. H. Davids, "The Epistle of James in Modern Discussion," *ANRW* 2.25.5 (1988) 3,628-29.

11. For a recent survey and sound conclusions, see Johnson, 34-46.

These three facets of the letter, combined with its hortatory focus, led Martin Dibelius to classify the letter as *paraenesis*.[12] And because Dibelius wrote one of the most influential modern commentaries on James, his view of the nature of the letter has found a good number of adherents. The ancient genre of *paraenesis*, according to Dibelius, was characterized by four factors that make it a perfect fit for James: (1) a focus on exhortation; (2) a general rather than specific situation; (3) the use of traditional material; and (4) loose organization. But the popularity of Dibelius's approach to the letter has waned considerably in recent years. Scholars have cast doubt on the whole idea that there was an identifiable *genre* such as *paraenesis* in the ancient world.[13] And where Dibelius saw nothing but isolated sayings, modern scholars are far more inclined to find important motifs and themes that bind the apparently diverse exhortations of James together.

Taking the place of *paraenesis* as probably the most popular genre identification for James is wisdom.[14] Indeed, many contemporary scholars insist that *paraenesis* should be seen as one component of wisdom literature.[15] The letter speaks directly about wisdom in a central passage (3:13-18; cf. also 1:5), and the brief, direct, and practical admonitions found at many places in the letter resemble the style of wisdom books from the OT (e.g., Proverbs) and the intertestamental period (e.g., Sirach, Wisdom of Solomon). Moreover, some of the concerns of James are also key concerns in these wisdom books (e.g., speech, dissension, wealth and poverty). But the issue of wisdom is not at all central to the book as a whole; and most of the letter, in fact, does not consist of the brief "proverbs" familiar from wisdom books. Much depends on how broadly we understand "wisdom"; contemporary scholarship has a tendency to subsume a great deal under that rubric. Suffice it to say here that only a very broad definition of "wisdom" would enable us to categorize James as a whole as wisdom; and we are not convinced that so broad a definition is justified.

Several other specific genre identifications have been suggested by scholars. But none has gained much acceptance. Perhaps the closest we can get to anything specific is to think of James as a sermon or homily.[16]

12. Dibelius, 1-11.

13. See the strictures of L. J. Perdue, "Paraenesis and the Epistle of James," *ZNW* 72 (1981) 241-56.

14. With varying emphases and in different degrees, see, e.g., Frankemölle, 80-88; Baker, 7-12; B. Witherington, *Jesus the Sage: The Pilgrimage of Wisdom* (Minneapolis: Fortress, 1994), 238-47.

15. J. G. Gammie, "Paraenetic Literature: Toward the Morphology of a Secondary Genre," *Semeia* 50 (1990) 43-51; Hartin, 21-80.

16. See esp. Wessel, 962 (reflecting the conclusions of his doctoral dissertation); also Rendall, 35; Davids, 23; Johnson, 17-24.

The author, separated from his readers by distance, cannot exhort them in person or at length. So he must put his preaching in written form, using a letter to cover briefly the main points that he wants them to understand.

III. AUTHOR

A. The Case for James the Brother of the Lord

The writer of the letter identifies himself simply as "James, a servant of God and of the Lord Jesus Christ" (1:1). The English name comes from the Latin *Jacomus* via old French *Gemmes.* The Greek name it translates, *Iakōbos,* occurs forty-two times in the NT and refers to at least four different men. Three of them are mentioned in one verse, Acts 1:13: "When they arrived, they went upstairs to the room where they were staying. Those present were Peter, John, James and Andrew; Philip and Thomas, Bartholomew and Matthew; James son of Alphaeus and Simon the Zealot, and Judas son of James." James the father of Judas is mentioned only here and in Luke 6:16 in the NT. His name occurs only because there is a need to distinguish this particular Judas from the better-known Judas Iscariot. James the son of Alphaeus is rather obscure, mentioned only in lists of apostles such as this one (cf. also Mark 3:18; Matt. 10:3; Luke 6:15) and perhaps in Mark 15:40 ("James the younger") and Matt. 27:56.[17] He was probably not well known enough to have written an authoritative letter to Christians under his own name alone. But James the son of Zebedee is one of the most prominent apostles in the gospel narratives. Along with Peter and John, he belonged to the "inner circle" of the Twelve and was therefore privileged to witness, for instance, the resurrection of Jairus's daughter (Mark 5:37 and par.) and the transfiguration (Mark 9:2 and par.; see also Mark 10:35, 41; 13:3). But this James was put to death by Herod Agrippa I (Acts 12:2), perhaps in about A.D. 44. And we probably should not date the letter of James quite this early. This leaves us with the other prominent James in the NT: James the brother of the Lord. He is mentioned in the Gospels (Matt. 13:55; Mark 6:3), but he became a follower of Jesus only after the resurrection (cf. 1 Cor. 15:7 and John 7:5). He attained a position of leadership in the early church (Acts 12:17), where we find him dialoging with Paul about the nature and

17. A few scholars (e.g., W. G. Kümmel, *Introduction to the New Testament* [rev. ed.; Nashville: Abingdon, 1976], 411) surmise that this James might be an entirely different person.

sphere of the gospel ministry (Acts 15:13; 21:18; Gal. 1:19; 2:9, 12). None of the other Jameses mentioned in the NT lived long enough or was prominent enough to write the letter we have before us without identifying himself any further than he does. Of course, it is always possible that a James not mentioned in the NT was the author of the letter. But we would have expected that so important a person would have left traces of himself in early Christian tradition. It is not surprising, then, that, with a few late exceptions,[18] Christians have traditionally identified the author of the letter with James the brother of the Lord.

The case for authorship to this point is inferential: a well-known James must have written the letter, and the brother of the Lord is the only James we know of who fits the profile. Proof is, in the nature of the case, unavailable. But several circumstances about the letter at least corroborate this conclusion.

First, the letter has a few suggestive similarities to the wording of the speech given by James of Jerusalem, the brother of the Lord, at the Apostolic Council (Acts 15:13-21) and to the letter subsequently sent out by him to Gentiles in northern Syria and southern Asia Minor (Acts 15:23-29). The epistolary "greeting" (Gk. *chairein*) occurs in Jas. 1:1 and Acts 15:23, but in only one other place in the NT; the use of "name" (*onoma*) as the subject of the passive form of the verb "call" (*kaleō*) is peculiar, yet is found in both Jas. 2:7 and Acts 15:17; the appeal "listen, my brothers" occurs in both Jas. 2:5 and Acts 15:13; and several other, less striking, similarities are also found.[19] None of the similarities proves common authorship, but they are suggestive.[20]

Second, the circumstances reflected in the letter fit the date and situation in which James of Jerusalem would be writing. We sketch some of these circumstances in the section that follows. Briefly, the readers seem to have been Jewish Christians who have left their homes in Palestine and are facing economic distress, including persecution at the hands of wealthy landowners. James, the NT makes clear, ministered mainly to Jewish Christians. The middle first century in the Middle East was marred by famine and general economic distress as well as by a tendency for wealthy people to buy up land and force farmers to work their land on their own terms (cf. Jas. 5:1-6). As leader of the Jerusalem church,

18. For example, some Spanish writers, from the seventh century on, claimed that their patron, James the son of Zebedee, was the author; and Calvin (p. 277) suggests that James the son of Alphaeus may have written the letter.

19. See esp. Mayor, iii-iv.

20. J. Painter (*Just James: The Brother of Jesus in History and Tradition* [Columbia, S.C.: University of South Carolina Press, 1997], 234-48) uses these similarities and several other factors to argue that Luke was the editor of the letter that we now have in the NT.

James would have been in a perfect position to address a letter to Jewish Christians who had been forced to flee from Jerusalem and its confines because of persecution. In fact, the situation Luke describes in Acts 11:19 fits very neatly with the scenario we are proposing: "Now those who had been scattered by the persecution in connection with Stephen traveled as far as Phoenicia, Cyprus, and Antioch, telling the message only to Jews." We can well imagine these early Jewish Christians leaving their homes, trying to establish new lives in new and often hostile environments, and, because of the sense of dislocation, losing some of their spiritual moorings. James, as their "pastor," would naturally want to encourage and admonish them.

Another aspect of the letter of James also fits well into the kind of early Jewish-Christian environment associated with James the brother of the Lord: its primitive Christian theology. James is far more theological than many scholars have given the letter credit for. But the theology rarely goes beyond accepted OT and Jewish perspectives, combined with some very basic, distinctly Christian conceptions: Jesus as Lord (1:1; 2:1) and coming judge (5:7, 9); the tension between the "already" of salvation accomplished (1:18) and "not yet" culminated (1:21; 2:14; 5:20); "elders" functioning as spiritual leaders in the local church (5:14). This is just the kind of theology we might associate with James as we know him from the NT.

B. The Challenge to the Traditional View

For seventeen centuries Christians, with only a few exceptions, accepted the view that the letter of James was written by the Lord's brother of that name known from the pages of the NT. But in the last two centuries a growing number of scholars have challenged this tradition. Before we investigate this challenge, it is worth asking why we should bother to debate the point. It is certainly not worth spending a lot of time to validate or overthrow the tradition as such. The point might be of interest to church historians but would have little import for those of us interested in reading and understanding the letter. But more than tradition is involved. The letter makes a claim about authorship: "James, a servant of God and of the Lord Jesus Christ, to. . . ." Identifying the James who wrote the letter may enable us to set the letter more accurately into its historical and canonical context. And by doing so, our interpretation of the letter and its contribution to the teaching of Scripture generally will be enhanced. An obvious case in point with respect to James is the teaching of chap. 2 on justification. But the matter of authorship is important for another reason. Precisely because the letter makes a claim about the author, the truthfulness of the letter as a whole is ultimately at stake. Of course, the letter makes no claim about *which* James wrote the letter; and so no question about the truthfulness of the letter is raised if we decide, with Calvin, for instance, that James the son of Alphaeus wrote the letter. But if, as many contemporary scholars maintain, the person who wrote the letter was not a person named James but someone writing in the name of the famous brother of the Lord, then new questions arise. Is the author trying to deceive us about the origin of the letter and thereby claim apostolic authority for a letter that does not deserve it? Or is the author simply utilizing a well-known ancient literary device whereby a famous person's teaching could be "reapplied" to a new situation? Our answer to these questions inevitably will effect the authority that we attribute to this letter. And so the issue needs careful investigation.

Three general theories of authorship need to be considered, although the first two can be quickly disposed of.[21] In what is now to be regarded as nothing more than a curiosity in the history of scholarship, a few scholars suggested that the letter, in its essence, is not a Christian book at all. They argued that an original Jewish document had been "Christianized" with a couple of superficial references to Jesus (1:1; 2:1).[22] The decisive blow to this extreme view is the degree to which the letter is permeated with references to the teaching of Jesus. A few others have suggested that the letter might have been written by another man named James: either the member of the Twelve by that name, James the son of Alphaeus (Calvin), or an unknown James (Erasmus, Luther).[23] But these views have none of the strengths and all of the weaknesses of the more usual identification with James the brother of the Lord.

By far the most usual alternative to the traditional view of authorship holds that the writer of the letter was an unknown Christian. The

21. We will not bother with some of the more imaginative (to put it kindly) theories, such as that the author was the Teacher of Righteousness known from the Qumran literature (R. Eisenman, "Eschatological 'Rain' Imagery in the War Scroll from Qumran and in the Letter of James," *JNES* 49 [1990] 173-84; for a brief response, see Painter, *Just James*, 230-34, 277-88).

22. L. Massebieau, "L'épître de Jacques — est-elle l'oeuvre d'un Chrétien?" *Revue de l'Histoire des Religions* 32 (1895) 249-83; F. Spitta, "Der Brief des Jakobus," *Zur Geschichte und Literatur des Urchristentums*, vol. 2 (Göttingen: Vandenhoeck & Ruprecht, 1896), 1-239. A. Meyer (*Der Rätsel des Jacobusbriefes* [Berlin: Töpelmann, 1930]) suggested that this original Jewish document was based on the "testament" of Jacob to his twelve sons (Genesis 49).

23. See also A. M. Hunter, *Introducing the New Testament* (Philadelphia: Westminster, 1957), 164-65 (although he is more cautious in the 3rd edition [1972], 168-69); Moffatt, 2.

name "James" in 1:1 may then have been added at a later date, in which case the letter in its original form would have been anonymous. Or it may have been added by the author himself to lend greater authority to the book and, perhaps, because the teaching of the letter had some relationship to James the brother of the Lord. In this case, the letter would be pseudepigraphical. This latter theory now dominates modern scholarship on James. Why is this so? Mainly because scholars are convinced that the letter contains features incompatible with authorship by James the brother of the Lord. Four such features are most often cited. We will examine each in turn.

1. If the letter had really been written by a brother of the Lord Jesus, the author would surely have mentioned that special relationship at some point in the letter. We might also have expected him to allude to the resurrection appearance that was perhaps instrumental in his conversion (cf. 1 Cor. 15:7).[24]

This is obviously an argument from silence and boils down to the question: How important was James's physical relationship to Jesus for his status in the early church? That his relationship to Jesus was known and could serve, if nothing more, as a mark of identification is clear from Gal. 1:19. But we have little reason to think that James's physical relationship to Jesus was important for the position he held in the early community.[25] In Acts, where James figures prominently as a leader of the Jerusalem church, his relationship to Jesus is never mentioned. Physical ties to Jesus became important only after the time of James's death. If anything, therefore, the author's failure to mention the relationship is an argument against the pseudepigraphical view. Moreover, James's physical relationship to Jesus never spilled over into a spiritual relationship. From what we can tell from the Gospels, James and the other brothers of Jesus remained estranged from him throughout the time of Jesus' earthly ministry (see Matt. 12:46; John 7:5). When Jesus' mother and brothers came to see him, he contrasted them with his "true family" — those who do the will of God (Mark 3:31-34 and par.). So the fact that James was Jesus' brother did not bring him spiritual insight; nor was it the basis for his position and authority in the early church. His failure to mention the relationship is not, therefore, surprising. Nor is it surprising that James, if he wrote the letter, makes no reference to the resurrection appearance. Paul, whose vision of the resurrected Christ led to his conversion and constituted his call to apostolic service, mentions the appearance in only two of

24. For example, Laws, 40.

25. See esp. R. Bauckham, *Jude and the Relatives of Jesus in the Early Church* (Edinburgh: T & T Clark, 1990), 125-30.

his thirteen letters. Tasker has pointed out the capriciousness of this sort of argument: James must be pseudepigraphical because the author does not mention his encounter with the resurrected Christ; 2 Peter must be pseudepigraphical because the author brings up his encounter with the transfigured Christ.[26] Indeed, the occasional nature of our NT letters renders any argument from what is included or not included in the letter quite tenuous. So many factors — the author's circumstances, his relationship to his readers, the purpose of the letter, the issues in the community — affect the content of the letter that it is precarious in the extreme to draw wide-ranging conclusions from the failure to mention a particular topic.

2. A second feature of the letter that leads many scholars to doubt that James of Jerusalem could have written it is the nature of its Greek and its cultural background. The Greek of the letter is idiomatic and even contains some literary flourishes (e.g., an incomplete hexameter in 1:17). The author frequently alludes to Jewish writings typical of the Hellenistic diaspora (Sirach, *Testaments of the Twelve Patriarchs,* Philo). Moreover, the author employs some words and phrases derived from Greek philosophy and religion (e.g., "the cycle of nature" [lit. trans.] in 3:6). Such Greek, critics argue, could not have been written by the son of a Galilean carpenter who, as far as we know, never left Palestine.

But this objection can be easily met.

First, we must not exaggerate the quality of James's Greek. While more polished and closer to the "higher *koinē*" than most NT Greek, the Greek of James is far from literary Greek. Absent are the elaborate sentences found, for instance, in Hebrews. As Ropes concludes, "there is nothing to suggest acquaintance with the higher styles of Gk. literature."[27]

Second, the alleged technical philosophical and religious terminology in the letter proves, on closer examination, to involve words and phrases that seem to have found a place in the mainstream of the language. They are the kinds of words that an ordinary educated person, familiar with the Hellenistic world, would have known. One does not need a college degree in philosophy, for instance, in our day to use words and phrases like "existentialist" or "language game." And Martin Hengel's classic study documented the degree to which Palestine had been penetrated by Hellenistic language and ideas.[28] James must have had some

26. Tasker, 20. Dibelius, who thinks that James is pseudepigraphical, also noted the subjectivity of this argument (p. 17).

27. Ropes, 25. T. Zahn, on the other hand, is probably too critical of the quality of James's Greek (*Introduction to the New Testament,* vol. 1 [reprint; Grand Rapids: Kregel, 1906], 112).

28. Hengel, *Judaism and Hellenism* (2 vols.; Philadelphia: Fortress, 1974).

education to have been elevated to the position in the church that he held. To claim that he could not have known and used these kinds of words is to assume far more about James's background than any of our sources reveals.

Essentially the same point can be made with respect to the general level of Greek in the letter. Hengel's work, which we mentioned in the last paragraph, was part of a larger reassessment of the alleged division between "Judaism" and "Hellenism" that dominated much early and mid-twentieth-century scholarship. Current scholarship recognizes that any such antithesis must at least be nuanced. Judaism was rather thoroughly penetrated by Hellenistic language and ideas; and there was undoubtedly a spectrum of acquaintance with Hellenism among Jews both in Palestine and in the Diaspora. Particularly relevant to the current issue is research that shows that many Palestinians, especially in Galilee and even from poor families, would have grown up with fluency in Greek.[29] So the question is: Could James have been exposed to the kind of influences that would have enabled him to write the semiliterary Greek we find in the letter? Without knowing the details of James's education, the extent of his travels, the books that he read, or the people he conversed with, this question is impossible to answer. We could guess that a person recognized as the leader of the Jerusalem church (containing, at least at some point, both "Hebraists" and "Hellenists" [Acts 6:1]) would have been capable of learning Greek quite well. J. N. Sevenster, who uses James as a test case for his investigation of the use of Greek in Palestine, concludes that James of Jerusalem could have written this letter.[30] This does not, of course, prove that James did write it. But it does mean that the Greek of the letter constitutes no obstacle to the ascription of the letter to James.

3. The letter's approach to torah is a third reason that scholars cite for concluding that James of Jerusalem could not have written it. Assumed in the letter is what might be called a rather "liberal" understanding of torah. Phrases like "the law of liberty" (1:25; lit. trans.) and "the royal law" (2:8) suggest the kind of perspective that arose among Jews who were seeking to accommodate the torah to the general Hellenistic world. Such an approach downplayed the ritual elements of the law in favor of its ethical demands. The failure of the letter ever to mention issues of the ritual law and its concentration exclusively on ethical issues con-

29. See esp. J. N. Sevenster, *Do You Know Greek? How Much Greek Could the First Jewish Christians Have Known?* (NovTSup; Leiden: Brill, 1968).

30. *Do You Know Greek?*, 191. See also N. Turner, *Style*, vol. 4 of *A Grammar of New Testament Greek*, by J. H. Moulton (Edinburgh: T & T Clark, 1976), 114.

firms that the author qualifies the law in the way that he does in order to match this "liberal" perspective. Yet such an approach to torah stands in stark contrast to the picture of James that we get from the NT and from early Christian tradition. It is "certain men . . . from James" who come to Antioch insisting that Jewish Christians observe kosher food laws and stop eating with Gentiles (Gal. 2:11-13). And it is James who requests that Paul demonstrate his loyalty to Judaism by undertaking to pay for and participate in purification rites in the Jerusalem temple (Acts 21:20-25). And in Christian tradition, James is famous for his loyalty to Judaism, being pictured an an example of "torah-piety."

However, while several scholars think this point is virtually conclusive,[31] it in fact rests on a serious overinterpretation of James, a questionable inference from the NT, and an uncritical acceptance of early Christian tradition. We begin with the Christian tradition.

James became a respected and beloved figure in the early church, especially among Jewish Christians. He was considered the first "bishop" of the Jerusalem church and was called the "righteous" or the "just" because of his faithfulness to the law and his devotion to prayer. Hegesippus, an early second-century Christian, describes James's death in his *Memoirs* (which have survived only in fragments quoted by other authors, mainly Eusebius). He claims that James was stoned to death by the scribes and Pharisees for refusing to renounce his commitment to Jesus (Eusebius, *History of the Church* 2.23). The Jewish historian Josephus confirms the essentials of this story, and he also enables us to date the incident to A.D. 62 (*Antiquities* 20.200-201). Hegesippus provides other information about James, most of it tending to portray him as a zealot for the law and as a Christian who generally championed a strong continuity with Judaism. Other early traditions take a similar tack in their portrayal of James, and these sources have given rise to the traditional view of James as a radical Jewish Christian.[32] However, scholars today recognize that most of these sources are quite tendentious, seeking to "capture" James for their own radically Jewish-Christian agenda.[33] Therefore, while

31. Dibelius (p. 18) claims that this is the decisive argument against the traditional view of authorship. See also Laws, 40-41.

32. The pseudo-Clementine *Epistle of Clement* 1:1 calls James "bishop of bishops"; the Gospel of the Hebrews (according to Jerome [*De viris illustribus* 2]) has the Lord appearing first to James after his resurrection; in *The Gospel of Thomas,* logion 12, the disciples ask Jesus, "'Who is to be our leader?'" and Jesus replies, "'Wherever you are you are to go to James the righteous, for whose sake heaven and earth came into being'" (cf. *The Nag Hammadi Library,* ed. J. M. Robinson [New York: Harper & Row, 1977], 119).

33. See, e.g., R. B. Ward, "James of Jerusalem in the First Two Centuries," *ANRW* 2.26.1 (1992) 799-810.

all our sources agree that James was a devout Jewish Christian, anxious to maintain good relationships with Judaism,[34] the picture of James as "an advocate of hidebound Jewish-Christian piety"[35] is a legend with no basis in fact.

The evidence from the NT is less clear-cut. James was certainly aligned with the Jewish-Christian wing of the early Christian community. And along with many Jewish Christians, he may well have assumed that Jews who recognized in Jesus of Nazareth their Messiah would continue to obey all the commandments of torah. In fact, the "incident" at Antioch may suggest that, at least at that date (around A.D. 46-47?), James was concerned to enforce torah-observance on Jewish Christians. But the whole episode that Paul describes in Galatians 2 is riddled with historical and theological issues. Among them is the question of the relationship between the "Judaizers" who came from Jerusalem and James himself. Did James himself send these people with his blessing? Or were they simply claiming to represent James without his authority?[36] Most interpreters think it is the former; and, if so, the text makes clear that James thought that Jewish Christians should continue to observe torah, even in the context of a mixed Christian community. He may have been especially concerned that news of Gentiles and Jews eating together would make the evangelism of Jews in Jerusalem all the more difficult.[37] James's request to Paul in Acts 21 reflects a similar concern. Situated in Jerusalem as he was, and with a growing radical Jewish movement (the Zealots) to contend with, James was anxious to show that Jews who recognized Jesus as their Messiah were not traitors to the Jewish tradition or to the Jewish people. Torah-observance and worship of Jesus the Messiah could exist together. To this extent, the NT confirms what seems to be the authentic element in the traditions about James: he was personally loyal to torah and sought in every way possible to maintain ties between the emerging early Christian movement and the Judaism in which he had been nurtured and in which he ministered.

But the key question is this: Could a person with this kind of torah-loyalty have written the letter we have before us? We think the clear answer to this question is yes. The letter, with its concern with the ethical dimensions of torah, stands squarely in a widespread tradition among Hel-

34. Painter (*Just James*, 102) argues that James was particularly worried that Paul's Gentile mission might lead to an abandonment of the mission to the Jews.

35. The phrase is Dibelius's (p. 17).

36. As, e.g., Lightfoot thought (J. B. Lightfoot, *The Epistle of St. Paul to the Galatians* [reprint; Grand Rapids: Kregel, 1957], 113).

37. See, e.g., F. F. Bruce, *The Epistle to the Galatians* (NIGTC; Grand Rapids: Eerdmans, 1982), 129-30.

lenistic-oriented Jews and reflected, in some ways, in the teaching of Jesus. But the critical point is this: neither the tradition nor Jesus emphasized the ethical aspects of torah so as to dismiss the ritual elements of torah. Jesus criticized the scribes and Pharisees for concentrating so much on tithing that they had neglected "justice, mercy and faithfulness" (Matt. 23:23). And so he calls them to practice these key ethical demands of torah. But he makes clear also that, in practicing these, they were not to "neglect" the other elements of the law. James also, following the lead of Jesus, focuses on the importance of obeying the royal law of love (2:8). And the fact that he illustrates the importance of every commandment of the law with reference to the prohibitions of adultery and murder (2:11) shows that he was concentrating at this point almost exclusively on the ethical aspect of the law. But nothing in James implies that he insisted on obedience to these ethical commands at the expense of observance of the ritual law. He is simply silent about the ritual law — presumably because it was not an issue in the communities he was addressing. So, in the end, we are faced with an argument from silence: the James who was so concerned about torah-observance in Galatians 2 and Acts 21 could not have written a letter in which this point was absent. But the argument is fallacious in that it ignores the occasional nature of the letter. James introduces only topics that were matters of concern for the people to whom he was writing. If they were, as we think, Jewish Christians who had fled Jerusalem but who had not yet mixed with Gentiles in worship, then observance of torah may not even have come up as an issue. What had come up was a failure to live out the basic ethical emphasis of torah: and James, much like Jesus in his day, focuses naturally on this matter.

4. The fourth reason for denying that James of Jerusalem could have written this letter involves the famous problem of the relationship between James and Paul, especially with respect to their teaching on justification. The letter insists that works are required for justification: "a person is justified by what he does and not by faith alone" (2:24). Paul, on the other hand, teaches that a person is justified by faith and not by "works of the law" (e.g., Rom. 3:28). The relationship of these two teachings is one of the biggest theological issues in the letter and, indeed, one of the most significant theological tensions within the NT. We will address the matter later in the Introduction (in the section on Theology) and in the commentary proper.

For now, however, we should note that, while the two seem to be in direct contradiction when statements of each are taken on their own, a careful study of the vocabulary of each and of the respective contexts in which they are speaking mitigates the tension significantly. In fact, most scholars now recognize that, like ships passing in the night, James's teaching does not really come to grips with what Paul was saying.[38] Either each is unaware of what the other is saying, or one of them is responding to a misunderstood form of the other's theology. Most scholars think the latter is the case and that James is reacting to a misunderstood Paulinism. They reach that conclusion because the slogan "justification by faith," to which James is responding, was so uniquely associated with Paul in the early church. For this reason, then, they argue that the letter could not have been written by James of Jerusalem, because this James had ample opportunity to learn the authentic Pauline view of justification. The two were key participants in the Jerusalem Council, where issues very much relating to Paul's teaching on justification were debated (Acts 15) and met later when Paul came to Jerusalem for a final time (Acts 21:18-25). And, in any case, the letter of James must have been written no earlier than the end of the first century, when Paul's theology was no longer understood in its proper context. W. G. Kümmel gives succinct expression to this argument: "The debate in 2:14ff. with a misunderstood secondary stage of Pauline theology not only presupposes a considerable chronological distance from Paul — whereas James died in the year 62 — but also betrays a complete ignorance of the polemical intent of Pauline theology, which lapse can scarcely be attributed to James, who as late as 55/56 met with Paul in Jerusalem (Acts 21:18ff.)."[39]

Adequate evaluation of this argument can come only after careful consideration of Jas. 2:14-26 as it relates to Paul's teaching on justification. For now, however, we can point out that the situation we have described in the last paragraph is capable of a very different explanation. If, indeed, James 2 fails to come to grips with the real point of Paul's teaching and the letter is written after A.D. 48 or so, when James and Paul met at the Jerusalem Council, then indeed it is difficult to attribute the letter to James of Jerusalem. But suppose the letter was written *before* A.D. 48. James would not yet have had direct contact with Paul. All he would know about Paul's "justification by faith alone" would come to him indirectly — and perhaps perverted by those who had heard Paul and misunderstood what he was saying. Paul probably began preaching almost immediately after his conversion (in A.D. 33?). How soon Paul came to understand and proclaim his distinctive justification message is impossible to know. But what might be the earliest Pauline letter, Galatians (perhaps A.D. 47-48), already presents a fully developed doctrine of justification. Christians living in the area possi-

38. See, e.g., Martin, xxxiii-xli; Johnson, 111-16; contra, e.g., Klein, 197-204; M. Hengel, "Der Jakobusbrief als antipaulinische Polemik," in *Tradition and Interpretation in the New Testament: Essays in Honor of E. Earle Ellis for His 60th Birthday,* ed. G. F. Hawthorne and O. Betz (Grand Rapids: Eerdmans, 1987), 253-63.

39. Kümmel, *Introduction to the New Testament,* 413.

bly addressed by James (Syria) would have had ample opportunity to hear Paul as he preached in Tarsus and, later, Antioch. On this scenario, James betrays a "complete ignorance of the polemical intent of Pauline theology" because James did not yet have direct knowledge of Paul's teaching.[40] Indeed, it is more likely that a "complete ignorance" of the thrust of Paul's teaching existed before his letters were written or widely circulated than long afterward. Many interpreters, for a number of reasons, reject almost out of hand an early date for the letter. But we hope to show below that a date as early as the scenario we have just sketched requires — the middle 40s — has much to be said for it.

C. Final Assessment

None of the four major objections to attributing the letter to James of Jerusalem is conclusive. But, to go on the offensive for a moment, a serious objection to the currently popular view of pseudepigraphical authorship needs to be mentioned. Proponents of the pseudepigraphical hypothesis often portray it in terms of a "transparent literary device." The person writing in the name of James would not have been seeking to deceive anyone. He would simply have utilized a popular literary convention of the time, according to which one could claim continuity with a particular religious figure by writing in that person's name.[41] Viewed in this light, the claim that James is pseudepigraphical would pose no challenge to the full truthfulness of the letter. The connection of the letter with James established in 1:1 is not intended to be, and would not have been understood to be, a claim about who wrote the letter. It is rather a claim about the theological tradition in which the letter stands. However, there is a decisive objection to this line of reasoning: we possess little evidence that pseudepigraphical epistles in the ancient world were accepted as authentic and truthful. In fact, one of the latest researchers on this matter claims, "No one ever seems to have accepted a document as religiously and philosophically prescriptive which was known to be forged. I do not know of a single example."[42]

40. See esp. G. Kittel, "Der geschichtliche Ort des Jacobusbriefes," *ZNW* 41 (1942) 96-97; Wessel, 965.

41. See esp. D. G. Meade, *Pseudonymity and Canon: An Investigation into the Relationship of Authorship and Authority in Jewish and Earliest Christian Tradition,* WUNT, vol. 39 (Tübingen: Mohr, 1986).

42. L. R. Donelson, *Pseudepigraphy and Ethical Argument in the Pastoral Epistles,* Hermeneutische Untersuchungen zur Theologie, vol. 22 (Tübingen: Mohr-Siebeck, 1986), 11. See also S. E. Porter, "Pauline Authorship and the Pastoral Epistles: Implications for Canon," *BBR* 5 (1995) 105-23.

The very fact that James was accepted as a canonical book, then, presumes that the early Christians who made this decision were sure that James wrote it. Those who did not think that James wrote it barred it from the canon for this reason. This means that we have to choose between (1) viewing James as a forgery, intended perhaps to claim an authority that the author did not really have — and therefore omit it from the canon; and (2) viewing James as an authentic letter from James. The "have-your-cake-and-eat-it-too" theory of canonical pseudepigraphon does not seem to be an alternative.

A few scholars, sensitive to this problem yet convinced by one or more of the objections to James's authorship examined above, have proposed compromise solutions, according to which James of Jerusalem, while not the final composer of the letter, had some connection with it. Those who have a problem thinking that James of Jerusalem could have written the Greek we find in the letter propose that he may have used an amanuensis.[43] We have solid evidence from extrabiblical literature and from the NT itself (cf. Rom. 16:21) that such amanuenses were regularly used. And James may well have done the same. Nevertheless, the hypothesis seems to be both unnecessary (since we think James could have written the Greek) and problematic. So much of the exact wording of the letter is bound inextricably to its content that it is difficult to separate the author from the final composer of the letter.[44] Another compromise view on authorship holds that the letter is a free translation of a discourse or series of homilies originally given by James in Aramaic.[45] Peter Davids has provided the clearest and best-worked-out defense of this kind of approach. Impressed with certain anomalies in the letter — good Greek alongside Semitisms, a curious unevenness in vocabulary, some disjointedness in flow — he suggests that a redactor has edited and expanded a series of Jewish-Christian homilies, given originally in Aramaic and Greek. James of Jerusalem may have been responsible for the first stage or even for both stages.[46] We have no way of proving or disproving this kind of proposal. But we question whether it is necessary. The Greek betrays no more inconsistencies than would be typical of a person writing in Greek whose native language was Aramaic; indeed, Dibelius claims that the Greek of the letter is "relatively homogenous."[47] The "disjointedness" of the letter

43. See, e.g., A. Robert and A. Feuillet, *Introduction to the New Testament* (Paris: Desclée, 1965), 364; cf. also Mussner, 8.

44. See Sevenster, *Do You Know Greek?*, 10-14.

45. F. C. Burkitt, *Christian Beginnings* (London: University of London, 1924), 65-71; see also F. F. Bruce, *Peter, Stephen, James and John: Studies in Non-Pauline Christianity* (Grand Rapids: Eerdmans, 1979), 113.

46. Davids, 12-13.

47. Dibelius, 34.

is a product of its genre and purpose; and would not an editor, as much as an author, seek to smooth out any rough spots? James may certainly have used some of his own sermons in writing the letter; but evidence for an earlier literary stage is not compelling.

When all the data are considered, the simplest solution is to accept the verdict of early Christians: the letter was written by James of Jerusalem, "the Lord's brother." Nothing in the letter is inconsistent with this conclusion, and several, albeit minor and indecisive, points favor it.[48]

EXCURSUS

A point of great controversy concerning James "the brother of the Lord" is his exact physical relationship to Jesus. As asceticism became a more dominant impulse in the church over the centuries, the view that Mary remained perpetually a virgin became ever more influential. The NT references to James as "the brother" of Jesus accordingly became controversial. Jerome argued that "brother" (Gk. *adelphos*) in these texts means "cousin." This view, usually called the "Hieronymian" (after a church father by that name), became very popular in Roman Catholic circles. A major difficulty for this interpretation, however, is the entire absence of evidence from the NT that the Greek word *adelphos* could mean "cousin." The use of this word requires that James and Jesus share at least one blood parent. The "Epiphanian" view holds that James was an older brother of Jesus, born to Joseph and a wife before Mary. Finally, advocates of the "Helvidian" view insist that James was born to Joseph and Mary after Jesus. The close association between Mary and the brothers of Jesus implied in the NT (e.g., Mark 3:32; 6:3) might favor the Helvidian interpretation.[49] Richard Bauckham, on the other hand, the latest scholar to investigate this matter, declines to decide between the Epiphanian and Helvidian views, inclining slightly perhaps to the Epiphanian.[50]

48. In the most recent critical commentary on James, Johnson concludes that the letter could well have been written by James of Jerusalem (see p. 121). See also Penner, 35-103; Hengel, "Jakobusbrief," 252; Bauckham, 11-25.

49. For a defense of this view, see esp. Mayor, vi-lv.

50. Bauckham, *Jude and the Relatives of Jesus*, 19-32. In favor of the Epiphanian view see also Lightfoot, "The Brethren of the Lord," in *Galatians*, 252-91.

IV. OCCASION AND DATE

We turn now from the question of the letter's literary features and form to the issue of its historical situation. What does the letter suggest about the situation of the readers? And what can we infer from that situation about the letter's place and time of origin?

A. The Readers and Their Situation

The letter reveals quite a lot about the people to whom it was written. First, they were almost certainly Jews. This conclusion, which is the scholarly consensus,[51] is suggested by references to distinctive Jewish institutions and beliefs. The believers James addresses meet in a "synagogue" (2:2); they share with the author the assumption that monotheism is a foundational belief (2:19) and that the law is central to God's dealings with his people (1:21, 24-25; 2:8-13; 4:11-12); they understand the OT imagery of the marriage relationship to indicate the nature of the relationship between God and his people (4:4). Many scholars would also cite the letter's address as evidence that the readers were Jewish. "The twelve tribes scattered among the nations" (1:1) certainly appears at first sight to be a reference to the Jewish people who live in the "diaspora" (a transliteration of the Greek word that the NIV translates "scattered among the nations"). But this initial conclusion is not so clear on closer examination. Intertestamental Judaism used the language of "the twelve tribes" to denote the true people of God in the last days — a usage that is also reflected in the NT (see the notes on 1:1). And since the early Christians came to understand that God's eschatological people included both Gentiles and Jews, James may have "transferred" the term from its original Jewish roots and applied it broadly to the church of his day. In a similar way, the word "diaspora," which originally denoted those places outside of Israel where Jews had been "scattered," could have here a spiritual sense: this world as the place where Christians must live, apart from their true heavenly homeland. However, while this interpretation is possible, the Jewish atmosphere of James, along with the probable early date of the letter, makes it more likely that the reference is more literal. The word suggests that the people to whom James writes are living out-

51. There are, however, exceptions: scholars who think that "twelve tribes" must stand for the entire people of God and, thus, all Christians (e.g., Klein, 185-90; cf. Vouga, 24-26; Baasland, 3,676-77). Adamson, on the other hand, suggests that James might have in view both Christian and non-Christian Jews (*James: The Man and His Message*, 11-12).

side the confines of Israel and also implies that they are Jews. Like other Jewish authors before him, James sends consolation and exhortation to the dispersed covenant people of God.[52]

The fact that the readers have been "dispersed," forced to live away from their home country, helps explain a second major characteristic of the readers of the letter: their poverty and oppressed condition.[53] Wealthy landowners take advantage of them (5:4-6); rich people haul them into court (2:6) and scorn their faith (2:7). One of the key purposes of the author is to encourage these suffering Christians in the midst of these difficulties, reminding them of the righteous judgment of God that is coming (5:7-11) and exhorting them to maintain their piety in the midst of their trials (1:2-4, 12). Some scholars find the key to the letter at just this point. Liberation theologians find in the letter a clear antithesis between wealth and unrighteousness on the one hand and poverty and righteousness on the other. The true people of God, James is suggesting, are the poor.[54] Ralph Martin, on the other hand, suggests a more historically based scenario. On his view, a major thrust of the letter is a call to Jews, influenced by the Zealot movement, to renounce violence in the face of oppression.[55] But, without denying the importance of the socioeconomic situation of the readers in understanding the letter's purpose, two considerations suggest that we should not give it a controlling role in understanding the letter. First, the most plausible interpretation of 1:10 yields the conclusion that some wealthy believers were also to be found in the community that James addresses (see the notes on that verse). This conclusion is reinforced by the admonitions to traveling merchants in 4:13-17. Careful reading of the letter prevents us from simply identifying the readers with the poor and their oppressors with the rich.

A second problem with the narrowly socioeconomic approach is the considerable amount of material in the letter that cannot be subsumed under this rubric. The situation of the church in the world provides one important context for the letter. But the letter ultimately has much more to say about the problem of the world getting into the church. In arguably the thematic center of the letter, the author warns his readers that "friendship with the world is hatred toward God" (4:4). One component of "pure and faultless" religion is "to keep oneself from being polluted by the world" (1:27). The worldliness of the church takes many forms: a

52. See D. J. Verseput, "Wisdom, 4Q185, and the Epistle of James," *JBL* 117 (1998) 700-703; Bauckham, 14-16.

53. Tamez, 23-24, and Vouga, 24-25 emphasize the sociological dimension of the address in 1:1.

54. See, e.g., Tamez.

55. Martin, lxvii-lxix.

fawning deference to the rich and callous indifference to the poor (2:1-4); uncontrolled, critical speech (3:9-12; 4:11-12; 5:9); wisdom that is "earthly, unspiritual, of the devil" (3:15), leading to violent quarrels (4:1-3); arrogance (4:13-17); and, most basically, "double-mindedness" (1:8; 4:8), a spiritual schizophrenia that interferes with prayer (1:5-8) and leads to a failure to put into practice what one professes to believe (1:21-27; 2:14-26). James's overall message is a call to repent from such compromising spirituality (4:4-10) and to intervene in the lives of those people who are straying down so dangerous a path (5:19-20).

Our point here, then, is simply this: while the social and historical situation of the readers may help us understand the problems they are dealing with, those problems are ultimately both more general and more basic than the immediate situation. The displaced status of these Jewish Christians has brought to the surface some basic spiritual issues; and it is to these spiritual issues that the author directs his exhortations.

B. Date

If we are right in identifying James the brother of the Lord as the author of the letter, then it must have been written before A.D. 62, when James suffered a martyr's death. Some scholars think that the letter was probably written very close to this date.[56] They note the many similarities between James and 1 Peter, and think that the problem of worldliness that surfaces repeatedly in the letter reflects a "settled" situation in the churches. But the letter contains parallels with many Jewish and Christian books, dated all the way from 100 B.C. to A.D. 150. As we noted earlier, these parallels usually involve traditional teaching that was common stock among early Christians. The parallels with 1 Peter are all of this nature. Nor is it clear that the Christians to whom James writes have been settled in their faith for a long time. None of the problems that arise in the letter is unusual among fairly young Christians. Temptations to compromise one's faith with the world afflict the believer almost immediately after conversion; and this is especially true when the convert has been taken out of his or her original nurturing context, as the readers of this letter had been.

Two indications favor a quite early date for this letter, sometime perhaps in the middle 40s. First, and most important, is the probable relationship between James's teaching on justification in chap. 2 and Paul's teaching on the same topic. As we have argued above in the section on

56. E.g., Tasker, 31-32; cf. also Hengel, "Jakobusbrief," 252.

Authorship, James shows awareness of Paul's distinctive emphasis on "justification by faith alone," but does not really come to grips with what Paul meant by this doctrine. Such a misunderstanding of Paul's teaching was unlikely after the two had met and hashed out a consensus on the requirements to be imposed on Gentiles for entry into the people of God at the Apostolic Council in A.D. 48 or 49 (Acts 15).[57] The historical scenario we suggest is that Paul's preaching in Tarsus from c. 36 (Acts 9:30; Gal. 1:21) and in Antioch from c. 45 (Acts 11:25-26) on had been misunderstood by some who heard him. They were apparently using the slogan "justification by faith alone" as an excuse for neglecting a commitment to discipleship and practical Christian living. It is this "perverted Paulinism" that James attacks in chap. 2. James probably did not even know that Paul's teaching was the jumping-off point for the view he is opposing. He would have attacked such a perversion, of course, at any date. But had he known what Paul truly preached (as he would have after A.D. 48), he would have put matters differently than he did.

A second indication of a relatively early date for the letter is the absence of any awareness of the conflict over torah that emerged in the early church as a result of the Gentile mission. Again, it was in about A.D. 47-48 that this issue first came to the forefront in the early church. "Some men came down from Judea to Antioch and were teaching the brothers: 'Unless you are circumcised, according to the custom taught by Moses, you cannot be saved'" (Acts 15:1). Gentiles, of course, had been admitted to the church before this time (Cornelius in Acts 10); and the Jerusalem apostles had discussed the matter (Acts 11:1-18). But it is clear from what transpires in Acts 15 that the crucial issue of the basis on which Gentiles should be admitted to the church had not been decided. The Apostolic Council sat to decide this matter, and James was the leader of that assembly. So from this time on James would have been well aware of the question of torah as it related to Gentiles. Again, of course, James is not writing to Gentiles, and so we might conclude that the absence of any reference to this issue is not surprising at any date. But James's casual references to torah in the letter (1:24-25; 2:8-13) make more sense if this issue had not yet arisen.

For these reasons, we think that James was probably written in the middle 40s, perhaps just before the Apostolic Council.[58] This period witnessed some severe economic crises (there was a famine in Judea in A.D.

57. According to Gal. 1:19, Paul had met James some years earlier; but the visit was probably brief and did not extend to theological discussion.

58. The nature of James's use of the Jesus tradition and his dependence on Jewish sources could also point to an early date; see Penner, 264-77; Hartin, 148-64.

46 [Acts 11:28]) and the beginning of the serious social-political-religious upheavals that would culminate in the Jewish war of rebellion in 66-70. Both circumstances fit the situation implied in the letter.

V. THEOLOGY

Some people claim that James has no theology. The validity of that claim depends entirely on what one means by "theology." To be sure, James says little about many basic Christian doctrines. The person and work of Christ, the ministry of the Holy Spirit, the theological significance of the church, the fulfillment of the OT in Christ — none is mentioned in James. But this kind of argument from silence (as we have noted elsewhere in this Introduction) does not carry much weight. James, like all the other letters of the NT, is occasional, written in a specific situation and addressing specific problems. Failure to mention even some basic Christian doctrines is therefore not only not surprising but expected — and paralleled by other NT letters. James, we have suggested, is writing to rebuke and exhort former parishioners about certain specific problems in their Christian practice. He knows that they are acquainted with the basic doctrines of the church and does not need to go over them again. More serious is the charge that James fails to ground his teaching in christology. Indeed, James mentions Jesus explicitly only twice (1:1; 2:1). So if by "theology" one means a system of beliefs explicitly built on the person of Christ, then, indeed, the letter of James lacks a "theology." But such a definition of theology is much too narrow. If we expand the definition to include teaching grounded in an understanding of God and his purposes in the world, then James is thoroughly "theological." Appeal to God's person, the values taught in his Word, and his purposes in history undergirds virtually everything in the letter. And while Jesus' person and work might be generally absent, his teaching is not. No NT document is more influenced by the teaching of Jesus than James. And so the judgment of Johnson, while perhaps an overreaction in the other direction, is worth noting: "It is not far wrong to consider James one of the most 'theological' writings in the NT."[59]

All this is not to deny that James is less theoretically oriented than, for instance, Paul. A practical pastor, James, we might surmise, does not have the theological genius and broad theological interests of Paul. In that sense, James is of course less "theological" than Paul. Yet even Paul,

59. Johnson, 85.

at certain points and for specific purposes, can write much like James does. Indeed, the closest parallel to the style of James in the NT is found in Rom. 12:9-21, where Paul quickly touches on key components of the "sincere love" that believers are to exhibit. For the purposes he has at that point, Paul does not need to allude directly to the great doctrines that are taught elsewhere in Romans. This is the style that pervades all of James.

Furthermore, we must not minimize the contributions that James does make to certain specific topics of Christian theology. In addition to the obvious importance of his teaching about faith and works in their relationship to the believer's final salvation, James also contributes significantly to our understanding of God, temptation, prayer, the law, wisdom, and eschatology. To be sure, all these arise in a practical context. But it will be a sad day for the church when such "practical divinity" is not considered "theology." Therefore, while the brevity and specific purposes of the letter prevent us from sketching a "theology of James," we are able to note briefly the contributions James makes to certain specific theological topics.

A. God

If we define "theology" in its strictest sense — the doctrine of God — then theology is very important in James. For he frequently grounds his exhortations about appropriate Christian conduct in the nature of God. H. Frankemölle is not far off when he claims that the overarching theme of the letter is the nature of God and that James closely ties all his key concepts back to his understanding of God.[60] Three characteristics of God are especially important in James: his oneness, his jealousy, and his grace.

James is, of course, a monotheist. The ancient Jewish confession "there is one God" is cited as an example of correct doctrine (2:19), and he reminds his readers that "there is only one Lawgiver and Judge" (4:11). But especially striking is James's emphasis on God's oneness. While the translation is debated, 1:5 probably refers to God as "single," that is, having one intent, in his giving. Christians can approach God confidently in prayer because he has a single and invariable purpose to give us what we need. The same point comes up again in 1:17, where God's constancy is cited as reason to conclude that he gives good gifts and would therefore never tempt human beings to sin. James's focus on this point may reflect the teaching of Jesus, who encouraged his disciples to ask God for whatever they needed because God, like a father, always gives good gifts to

60. H. Frankemölle, "Das semantische Netz des Jakobusbriefes: Zur Einheit eines unstrittenen Briefes," *BZ* 34 (1990) esp. 190-93.

his children (Matt. 7:7-11). James also cites the oneness of God as reason to conclude that all the commandments God has given must be obeyed (2:11). The undivided nature of God is especially important to James because it stands in direct contrast to the deepest problem of human beings: their tendency to be "divided" in their loyalties, wavering between God and the world (1:8; 4:4, 8). Christians, James implies, need to be like God to overcome this sinful tendency: firm, unchanging, constant in purpose and affection.

Because christology in James is insignificant and undeveloped, we have little evidence about how he might have related his affirmation of monotheism to the person of Christ. He normally uses the title "Lord" to refer to God (3:9; 4:10, 15; 5:4, 10, 11, 15) but also applies it to Jesus (2:1; 5:7, 8). And while James can insist that "there is one . . . Judge" (4:11), he also pretty clearly puts Jesus in the role of eschatological judge in 5:7 and 9. We find in the juxtaposition of these points an incipient trinitarianism. Without in any way modifying his inherited monotheistic profession, James attributes titles and functions to Jesus that are properly God's alone.

A second characteristic of God highlighted in James is also very traditional: God's jealousy. To be sure, this characteristic is mentioned in only one verse of James, 4:5, and the sense of the verse is hotly contested. But we think it very probable that James here cites the scriptural teaching about the jealousy of God for his people as substantiation for his call to them to abandon their flirtation with the world. And although James refers to this attribute of God in only this one verse, it is central to the argument of the letter.

Third, and in the same context, James refers to God's grace. In his holy jealousy, God demands the exclusive devotion of his people — a potentially fearsome and unattainable requirement. So James assures his readers that the same God who makes such stringent and all-encompassing demands also "gives us more grace" (4:6).

B. Eschatology

As we mentioned earlier, one of the chief characteristics of the Letter of James is its extensive borrowing from both Jewish and Greek moral teaching. But what sets James's admonitions apart is the eschatological context in which they are placed.[61] Future eschatology is clearly the dom-

61. For this theme, see esp. Penner and R. W. Wall, "James as Apocalyptic Paraenesis," *ResQ* 32 (1990) 11-22.

inant perspective in James. He frequently warns believers about the coming judgment in order to stimulate them to adopt the right attitudes and behavior (1:10-11; 2:12-13; 3:1; 5:1-6, 9, 12). And he reminds them of the reward they can look forward to if they live pleasingly for the Lord (1:12; 2:5; 4:10; 5:20). In keeping with early Christianity generally, James insists that the day of judgment and reward is imminent: "the Lord's coming is near"; "The Judge is standing at the door!" (5:8, 9). Some think that the early Christians held a view of imminence according to which they were certain that Jesus would return within a few years or decades at the most. But the language need not be taken so strictly. The sense of "nearness" that James and the other early Christians felt stemmed from two convictions: (1) now that the Messiah had come and the new age had dawned, the end of history was the next event in the divine timetable; and (2) that culmination of history could happen at any time. James, in other words, motivates his readers to godly living not by insisting that the Lord *would* come at any moment but by reminding them that he *could*.

Though future eschatology is the dominant perspective in James, the present eschatological nature of Christian existence is not ignored. The assertion that "God has chosen those who are poor in the eyes of the world to be rich in faith and to inherit the kingdom he promised those who love him" (2:5) leaves uncertain whether the kingdom is to be inherited in the future or is even now the possession of those who are chosen. But, in light of "the royal law," or "the law of the kingdom," in 2:8, the latter is likely. James also alludes to the "new birth" that ushers believers into the enjoyment of God's kingdom blessings (1:18). And the most likely interpretation of 5:3, reflected in the NIV translation "you have hoarded wealth in the last days," indicates that James believed that believers were already living in the age of eschatological consummation. All told, then, James provides sufficient indication that he holds to the typical NT pattern of "fulfillment without consummation" that we call "inaugurated eschatology." It is within the tension of this "already . . . not yet" that we must interpret and apply James's ethical teaching.

C. The Law

The law per se is not a topic of discussion in the Letter of James. References to it come in the context of exhortations about other issues. Calling for Christians to be "doers of the word," James refers to "the perfect law that gives freedom" (1:25). He rebukes partiality in the church by labeling it a clear violation of the "royal law," the demand that we love our neighbors as ourselves (2:8). In this same context, James goes on to stress the unity of the law (2:10-11) and to warn believers that they will be judged "by the law that gives freedom" (2:12). Finally, James condemns slander because it reveals an underlying criticism of the law itself (4:11). While not providing for us anything like a full theology of the law, these texts do suggest several conclusions about James's understanding of the law.

First, as we noted earlier, James reveals little concern about obedience of the ritual law. Noting this, scholars sometimes conclude that James of Jerusalem, famous in tradition for his allegiance to torah and concern to keep good relationships with Judaism, could never have written the letter we have before us. We noted in our response that (1) the picture of the torah-fanatic James in the tradition is tendentious and false; and (2) absence of concern for the ritual elements of the law in the letter does not mean the author was not concerned about it. The problems his readers face demand that James focus on certain key ethical issues. Naturally, therefore, it is to this element of the law that James makes frequent appeal.

Second, several of the issues James takes up in the letter appear also in Leviticus 19. The "love command," of course, comes in v. 18 of that chapter (see Jas. 2:8). But the chapter also rebukes false swearing (v. 12; cf. Jas. 5:12), the withholding of wages (v. 13; cf. Jas. 5:5), partiality (v. 15; cf. Jas. 2:1-7), and slander (v. 16; cf. Jas. 4:11-12). L. T. Johnson, noting these parallels, suggests that James read at least this section of Leviticus 19 as a summary of the basic intent of the law.[62] Though we cannot conclude that James would restrict the "Christian" law to these ethical emphases from Leviticus 19, the chapter is obviously of basic significance in the letter.

Third, at critical points James qualifies the law: it is "the *perfect* law of *liberty*" (1:25); "the *royal* law" (2:8); "the law of *liberty*" (2:12; lit. trans.). Labeling the law "perfect" was, as one might imagine, very common among Jews. And Jews could call the law "royal" (e.g., Philo, *Posterity and Exile of Cain* 102). But the context in which James uses these descriptions suggests that a distinctively Christian nuance is to be seen in the language. The adjective "royal" in 2:8 *(basilikos)* must be seen in relationship to James's reference to the "kingdom" *(basileia)* in 2:5. The love command cited in 2:8 is therefore "royal" because it was proclaimed by Jesus the King, or perhaps because it is the chief law of the kingdom he established. James's reference to the law here is not, then, a straightforward allusion to torah as understood by Jews but includes at least an element of Christian interpretation of that law. An even clearer indication along these same lines comes in James's reference to "the perfect law of liberty" in 1:25. Both pagans (especially the Stoics) and Jews could ascribe a liber-

62. Johnson, "Leviticus 19."

ating effect to law.[63] But James uses the phrase in a context where it replaces earlier use of the term "word" (1:22-23). This "word" is said to be "planted in" believers (1:21) and is identified in 1:18 as "the word of truth" through which Christians experience the miracle of the new birth.

James here makes clear that he sees a close relationship between what we often call, in a theological sense, "law" (God's will for the way we are to live) and "gospel" (God's gracious promises).[64] How close is this relationship? Some scholars think that James virtually merges law and gospel. "Law" for him is no longer the OT law, torah; it is the teaching of Jesus, the "law" of the kingdom, which includes both the invitation to salvation and the requirements for life in that kingdom.[65] But when we consider James's frequent allusions to Leviticus 19 and his situation early in the life of the Jewish-Christian church, elimination of reference to the OT law seems to be impossible. More helpful is the recognition that James's description of the law as "planted in" the believer almost certainly alludes to the famous "new covenant" prophecy of Jer. 31:31-34.[66] According to this prophecy, God would enter into a "new covenant" with his people and would, as part of that new covenant arrangement, write his law on the hearts of his people (v. 33). The law that God had first communicated to his people in written form will now be internalized, undergoing transformation and perhaps modification in the process. Ultimately, however, James provides us little concrete information about the exact identity and scope of "law." He is more concerned to make sure that his readers understand that they cannot experience the benefits of God's word in the gospel without at the same time committing themselves in obedience to God's word as law.

The continuing OT element in the law in James leads directly into the fourth important feature of the law in James: its status as a continuing guide to Christian living. This inference from James's allusions to the law creates, it is alleged, a theological contradiction with Paul. Indeed, A. T. Cadoux claims that the tension between James and Paul on this issue is more serious than their divergent views of justification.[67] Luther summarizes the objection like this: James "calls the law a 'law of liberty' though Paul calls it a law of slavery, of wrath, of death, and of sin." An adequate resolution of this alleged tension would require an entire monograph. But two quick observations may help at this stage. First, while the subject

63. For the Stoics, see, e.g., Epictetus, *Discourses* 4.1.158; Seneca, *De vita beata* 15.7; for the Jews, see, e.g, Philo, *Every Good Man Is Free* 45; *b. Abot* 62b.

64. Frankemölle, 202-12.

65. See, e.g., Mayor, 74; W. Gutbrod, *TDNT* 4:1,081-82.

66. See, e.g., Mitton, 72.

67. Cadoux, 81.

of a longtime and still unresolved debate, Paul's view of the use of the OT law in guiding Christian behavior is largely negative. Christians have "died to the law" (Rom. 7:4); they are no longer "under it" (Rom. 6:14, 15). The law, Paul suggests in Galatians 3, belongs to a past epoch in God's dealings with his people. However, without taking anything away from this salvation-historical judgment, we must also note that Paul can presume some kind of relationship between the Christian and the OT law (e.g., Rom. 8:7; 1 Cor. 7:19[?]; 9:9; Eph. 6:2). This is not the place to pursue the matter of Paul and the law further. Suffice it to say, however, that James's perspective is not so clearly incompatible with Paul's as some might suggest.

More important for our purposes is the possibility that James maintains the continuing authority of the OT law for Christians only insofar as it has been "fulfilled" by Jesus. James's appeal to the "love command" as *the* royal law forges a direct link with Jesus; and James, of course, alludes to the teaching of Jesus throughout his letter. What this suggests is that James does not explicitly separate the teaching of Jesus from the OT law because they have for him become intertwined. As Wessel puts it, "'law of freedom' is a Palestinian Jew's way of describing the Christian standard of conduct found in the *didache*."[68] This standard of conduct is still law because it continues into the new age of salvation the will of God expressed in torah, but it is now a law "of liberty" because it comes to us from the one whose "yoke is easy" and "burden is light" (Matt. 11:30).

D. Wisdom

In our discussion of the genre of James, we noted that James has often been classified as a wisdom document. This classification is based more on the letter's proverbial style and general moral tone than on actual references to the concept of "wisdom." But James does refer to wisdom specifically twice. In 1:5, James exhorts his readers to ask God for wisdom — perhaps so that they can understand and respond properly to the trials they are experiencing (see 1:2-4). As in the OT, wisdom here involves insight into God's purposes and ways, and possessing it leads to spiritual maturity (1:4). Wisdom plays a central role in 3:13-18, where James contrasts "earthly, unspiritual, demonic" wisdom (v. 15) with "the wisdom that comes from heaven" (v. 17). Again, as in the OT, wisdom in this passage is tied to behavior. People with the wrong kind of wisdom are selfish

68. Wessel, 960; see also Goppelt, 2.203-6; D. Guthrie, *New Testament Theology* (Downers Grove: Inter-Varsity, 1981), 699.

and contentious and become embroiled in "disorder and every evil practice" (v. 16). But those who possess divine wisdom are humble and anxious to perform good deeds (v. 13). This kind of wisdom, James says, is "first of all pure; then peace loving, considerate, submissive, full of mercy and good fruit, impartial and sincere" (v. 17).

What James says about wisdom in these passages is reminiscent of the OT teaching found in Proverbs and some of the Jewish books, such as Sirach, that continue the OT tradition. Other intertestamental Jewish books reveal significant development in the concept of wisdom. Some of them implicitly identify wisdom with torah (a development that can be seen already in Sirach). Others take up the personification of wisdom in Proverbs, exploiting especially the metaphysical associations of the concept in Prov. 8:22-36. Wisdom in these Jewish authors becomes a mediator between God and human beings and takes on semidivine characteristics. Certain NT writers may utilize some of these Jewish developments in their formulations of christology (e.g., Col. 1:15-20) and other doctrines. But none of these developments is evident in James. On the other hand, the OT (and some Jewish texts) suggest a close relationship between wisdom and the Spirit of God; for example, Isa. 11:2: "The Spirit of the Lord will rest on him — the Spirit of wisdom and of understanding, the Spirit of counsel and of power, the Spirit of knowledge and of the fear of the Lord." James makes only one possible reference to the Spirit (4:5); but his description of the "fruit" of wisdom (3:17, quoted above) is very similar to Paul's famous list of the "fruit of the Spirit" (Gal. 5:22-23). "Wisdom in James," Davids therefore concludes, "functions as the Spirit does in Paul."[69] We may grant Davids's point only if we compare James's wisdom and Paul's Spirit on one specific point. For Paul, of course, develops a wide-ranging theology of the Spirit, and none of that development is evident in James. And, while wisdom certainly has its place in James's theology, it cannot be given the central and integrating role that some scholars have wanted to give it.[70] As we have noted, James mentions wisdom only twice, and in neither text is wisdom his real topic. A larger role for wisdom in the letter can only be discovered by arguments from parallel language: what James says is similar to what some OT or Jewish texts say about wisdom; therefore, James must be thinking of wisdom. But rarely are these parallels so distinctive to wisdom contexts as to justify such a conclusion.[71]

69. Davids, 56; see also J. A. Kirk, "The Meaning of Wisdom in James: Examination of a Hypothesis," *NTS* 16 (1969-70) 24-38.

70. See, e.g., Hoppe, 51-71.

71. See Johnson, 33-34.

E. Poverty and Wealth

According to Mussner, "There is hardly a single element of the OT–late Jewish tradition about poverty and piety that is not also encountered in the letter of James."[72] This being so, we can best appreciate James's teaching on this matter if we first have a sense of the OT-Jewish tradition. The subject is broad and somewhat controversial, but three elements of the tradition especially relevant to James may be noted.

First, God has a particular concern for the poor, the downtrodden, the outcasts. God is "A father to the fatherless, a defender of widows" (Ps. 68:5); "he defends the cause of the fatherless and the widow, and loves the alien, giving him food and clothing" (Deut. 10:18). So also James claims that "God has chosen those who are poor in the eyes of the world to be rich in faith" (2:5). Second, God's people must imitate God by showing a similar concern for the poor and disadvantaged. The Deuteronomy passage, quoted above, continues, "And you are to love those who are aliens, for you yourselves were aliens in Egypt" (v. 19). The prophets regularly denounce Israel for failing to obey this aspect of God's law (see, e.g., Amos 2:6-7). James likewise makes the care of orphans and widows one of the key elements of pure and faultless religion (1:27).

A third strand in the OT tradition, particularly visible in the Psalms, is the association of the "poor" *('ani)* with the righteous (see, e.g., Psalm 10; 37:8-17; 72:2, 4; Isa. 29:19). The poor person, helpless and afflicted by the wealthy and powerful, calls out to God for deliverance. God, in turn, promises to rescue the poor from his or her distress and to judge the wicked oppressor. In these texts, and others like them, the OT writers appear to merge the economic category "poor" with the spiritual category "righteous." And, as the flip side, in a similar way the "rich" are sometimes associated with the wicked. These verses reflect a specific social-economic-theological context, in which the vast majority of the true people of God are poor and oppressed. James seems to have been written in the same kind of context. In a probable allusion to Jesus' beatitude "Blessed are the poor" (Luke 6:20), he notes how God has singled out for attention the poor (2:5). Jesus' corresponding word of judgment, "Woe to the rich" (Luke 6:24), is also taken up in James's strong condemnation of the rich in 5:1-6. The strength of James's language, along with his obvious dependence on Jesus' teaching and the OT tradition, has made James one of the favorite biblical books among liberation theologians. James, they assert, draws clear lines between the poor and the righteous on the one hand and the rich and the wicked on the

72. Mussner, 80 (my translation).

other. The poor are, in effect, God's people; while the rich and powerful are destined for destruction.

But the picture is not so simple. The OT tradition is not nearly as clear-cut as some interpreters have suggested it is. While the poor are often pictured as the objects of God's concern and deliverance, they are not often simply *identified* with the righteous. And rarely, similarly, is the word "rich" a synonym for the wicked. (See the notes on 1:10.) The situation in James is also complicated by 1:10-11. Commentators are evenly split over the identity of the "rich person" in this passage: Is the person a "brother" (cf. 1:9) or not? We argue that this person probably is a Christian; and, if so, it shows that James does not identify wealth with wickedness nor confine God's people only to the poor. Moving in the same direction is the way in which James justifies his condemnation of the rich in 5:1-6. Their doom comes because of specific sinful actions: hoarding money at the expense of the poor (vv. 2-3), senseless luxury (v. 5), defrauding workers (v. 4), persecuting the righteous (v. 6). So the use of James in support of liberation theology is not justified. Economic status and spiritual status do not exactly correlate.[73]

Nevertheless, in our appropriate concern to distance James from an extreme "liberation" perspective, we must be careful not to rob his denunciation of the rich of its power. The very possession of wealth, when others are going without the basic necessities of life, suggests James, is sinful (see our comments on 5:2-3). This is a word that the church in the developed countries in our day needs to hear and take seriously. If those suffering oppression are tempted to radicalize James's message about poverty and wealth, those of us enjoying a comfortable lifestyle are equally prone to trivialize that message.

F. The Christian Life

James's most important contribution to NT theology comes in the realm of ethics: "no other book of the New Testament concentrates so exclusively on ethical questions."[74] A full treatment of this topic would therefore demand virtually a repetition of the commentary. But a few general issues deserve mention here.

First, as we noted earlier, James's ethics must be set in the context of his eschatology. His exhortations, while sometimes having the appear-

73. See, e.g., Penner, 270-73.

74. W. Schrage, *Ethik des Neuen Testaments* (Göttingen: Vandenhoeck & Ruprecht, 1982), 226 (my translation); cf. also Laws, 27.

ance of the timeless, prudential focus of wisdom teaching, are always oriented, at least implicitly, to the "born again" (1:18) but not yet "saved" (1:21; cf. 2:14; 5:20) condition of his readers. He recognizes that his readers will not entirely be able to escape the influence of sin (3:2), but he calls on them to pursue the goal of being "perfect and complete" (1:4). Human "dividedness," the condition James calls *dipsychos,* "double-minded" or "double-souled," is the essence of the problem. People tend to be like waves of the sea, tossed and driven one way and another (1:6). This "divided" condition manifests itself in speech, when the same person utters both blessing and cursing (3:9-10), and, in a different way, when the Christian professes orthodox doctrine but does not live an orthodox life (2:14-26). In response to this tendency toward dividedness, James above all calls on his readers to progress toward Christian maturity, toward what Wesley called Christian perfection: "It is purity of intention, dedicating all the life to God. It is the giving God all our heart; it is one desire and design ruling all our tempers. It is the devoting, not a part, but all our soul, body, and substance to God."[75]

James's well-known insistence that believers not just hear, but *do* the word of God (1:22) and his demand for a "faith that works" (2:14-26) reflect the same concern. Obedience to the "law of liberty" must be heartfelt and consistent. And God's law focuses on love for the neighbor (2:8). Therefore, "pure and undefiled religion" will manifest itself in loving concern for the helpless in society (1:27), in a meek and unselfish attitude toward others (3:13-18). It will renounce discrimination (2:1-13) and not speak evil of others (4:11-12).

Prayer is another component of the Christian life that receives attention in James. He encourages us to approach God by reminding us that he is a Father who gives good gifts (1:17) and who delights to answer the requests of his people (1:5). But James is especially concerned that we understand the condition for receiving our requests from God: faith (1:6-8; 5:14). Selfish asking will not move God to respond to our requests (4:3). Still, God does not make impossible demands on us when we pray; Elijah, a person with all our human frailties, received spectacular answers to his prayers because he was a "righteous man" in relation with God (5:17-18).

G. Faith, Works, and Justification

The most important, and controversial, contribution of James to NT theology comes in his teaching about the importance of works for justification

75. J. Wesley, *A Plain Account of Christian Perfection* (1766; *Wesley's Works* 2.444).

(2:14-26). Indeed, many theologians mention James only because he seems to contradict the critical doctrine of "justification by faith alone" taught by Paul. But this is not fair to James. He has his own point to make; and it must be appreciated for what it is and not shunted aside in a wrongheaded or hasty insistence on theological integration. James condemns any form of Christianity that drifts into a sterile, actionless "orthodoxy." Faith, not what we do, is fundamental in establishing a relationship with God. But faith, James insists, must be given content. Genuine faith, he insists, always and inevitably produces evidence of its existence in a life of righteous living. *Biblical* faith cannot exist apart from acts of obedience to God. This is James's overriding concern in the passage in question, as he makes clear repeatedly: "faith by itself, if it is not accompanied by action, is dead" (2:17); "faith without deeds is useless" (2:20); "faith without deeds is dead" (2:26). As we have suggested, James makes such a point of this because he has come to realize that some Christians, misunderstanding Paul's teaching, were taking an extremely narrow view of faith, confining it to verbal profession (v. 19). Such "faith," James responds, is not really faith at all. It is an imposter, masquerading as true biblical faith. Therefore, it can neither justify the sinner (2:24) nor save him at the judgment (2:14). Because some scholars have given the wrong impression at just this point, we need to stress that this sterile, word-only, "faith" is not James's own understanding of faith. He presents faith as a firm, unswerving commitment to God and Christ (2:1) that is tested and refined in trials (1:2, 4) and grasps hold of the promises of God in prayer (1:5-8; 5:14-18). James by no means has a "sub-Christian" or "sub-Pauline" view of faith. In fact, on the meaning and significance of faith, James and Paul appear to be in complete agreement. For Paul also, in the famous words of Gal. 5:6, it is "faith working through love" that secures the inheritance of God.

On another point, however, resolution between James and Paul does not seem so easy. Paul insists that a person is "justified by faith apart from works of the law" (Rom. 3:28, lit. trans.), while James contends that a person "is justified by works and not by faith alone" (2:24, lit. trans.). They agree in making faith fundamental to justification, but they disagree on the place of "works." To be sure, Paul speaks of "works of the law" and James simply of "works." But, at bottom, they mean the same thing; and so harmonization of the two perspectives cannot be based on this distinction. We provide further rationale and details on this point in our exegesis of 2:21-26. And we also set in place a framework within which the apparent contradiction between Paul and James can be resolved. Here we want to put the matter is a larger, more theological perspective. But to do so, we must first situate James's teaching about salvation within the theology of second-temple Judaism.

The last twenty years have seen the establishment of a new paradigm in the interpretation of Jewish soteriology. The label given this new paradigm, "covenantal nomism," summarizes its main emphases. "Covenant" was basic to Jewish life. Jews viewed themselves as the chosen people, a nation selected by God to be his own and to carry out a mission to the world. Because God freely entered into this covenant with Israel, grace is at the heart of the Jewish view of salvation. Far from being a religion of "works" or "law," then (as it often has been portrayed), Judaism was a religion of grace. But what, then, do we do with the obvious emphasis among the Jews on doing the law? Here is where the second term in the label, "nomism," comes into play. As an obvious counter to the typical accusation that Judaism was "legalistic," "nomism" signifies that Jews obeyed the law as a grateful response to God's electing grace. They did not think that they needed to do the law to get saved — because they already were saved through the covenant. They did not do the law, then, to "get in" but to "stay in."[76]

In its main lines, covenantal nomism is an accurate and helpful picture of Jewish soteriology in the NT period. But it does require two important adjustments. First, as is the case with many such general "paradigms," covenantal nomism fails to recognize adequately the diversity of second-temple Judaism. It may accurately portray the viewpoint of certain Jews and perhaps even the most influential Jewish theologians of the time. But Jews in the NT period differed quite seriously over many rather basic theological issues. Study of the literature Jews wrote during this time shows many differences over the way in which covenant, grace, and the law were integrated together. We must therefore reckon with the strong possibility that many Jews, and perhaps even some major Jewish groups, were more "legalistic" than the generalized picture of covenantal nomism would suggest.

Second, we must adjust the usual way in which obedience to the law is related to salvation in covenantal nomism. While the distinction between "getting in" and "staying in" may be valid enough when applied to the covenant, we cannot necessarily apply the same distinction to the issue of salvation. For belonging to the covenant (in the sense of being born into the people of Israel) was not a guarantee of salvation. Jews viewed salvation as a decision made by God at the time of the judgment. God's grace in the covenant provided the sufficient means for salvation; but the individual Jew still had to commit himself or herself to obey the

76. The fountainhead of this new paradigm is the monograph by E. P. Sanders, *Paul and Palestinian Judaism: A Comparison of Patterns of Religion* (Philadelphia: Fortress, 1977).

law in order to be saved on the last day. To put it another way, second-temple Jewish soteriology was synergistic: it required human beings to cooperate with God's grace through obedience to the law for salvation.

Here, then, is the point of intersection between Jewish views and James 2. For the teaching of James 2, as we have presented it above, seems to match exactly this synergistic interpretation of salvation. James implies that the Christian life begins through an act of God's grace: as one of his greatest gifts, he "chose to give us birth through the word of truth" (1:18). Faith in Christ is the foundation for our relationship to God (2:1); like Abraham, Christians believe God and thereby find righteousness (2:22-23). But, James insists, final salvation, deliverance in the judgment of God — "justification" in James 2 — takes into account one's works. Here, we might conclude, we find the basic pattern of covenant nomism, reinterpreted in "new covenant" terms: one "gets into" relationship with God by faith in Christ, but "stays in" that relationship through obedience to the "royal law" (2:8).

Many interpreters are content to let matters rest with this conclusion. But anyone who takes seriously the place of James within the canon of the NT must ask further about the relationship of this apparent synergism in James to soteriological viewpoints elsewhere in the NT, especially Paul. To be sure, such an enterprise is frowned upon by many modern scholars, who seem to believe that any attempt at theological integration is a betrayal of history and sound exegesis. Everything depends, of course, on one's view of Scripture as a whole. Taken as a series of relatively independent historical attestations of the development of early Christianity, the NT letters can — indeed, must — be interpreted without reference to one another. Indeed, so resolutely opposed to any "dogmatic" interpretation of the Bible are some interpreters that they dismiss the kind of application of larger conceptual categories to various documents from the same movement that is typical in the study of other religions. Scholars who adopt this approach often push James and Paul to extremes in their views of soteriology. They conclude that Paul and James present contradictory viewpoints on this matter and that the NT does not therefore teach a single, unified viewpoint on salvation.[77]

But if the NT is, as it claims to be, a revelation from God; if the NT letters are not just independent writings but part of one larger book with one ultimate author, then the search for a unified view within Scripture is not only appropriate but necessary. This is not the place to outline, let alone defend, such a view of Scripture. But this is the perspective that we

77. See, e.g., J. D. G. Dunn, *Unity and Diversity in the New Testament* (Philadelphia: Westminster, 1977), 251-52.

adopt in this commentary. One must, of course, pursue integration of the diverse witness of the NT while maintaining the integrity of each of the passages under discussion. Forced harmonization of Scripture is both bad exegesis and bad theology. But it is not "forced harmonization" to seek underlying theological categories that might enable one to bring together conceptually texts that apparently go in different directions.

Nor do we want to suggest that resolution between Paul and James is necessarily easy — even with all the sympathy in the world. The history of Christian theology is littered with the debris left over from intense theological debates on precisely this point. One might point here, for example, to the controversy among Anglican theologians in the late seventeenth and early eighteenth centuries or to the 1980s debate between, among others, Zane Hodges and John MacArthur over the relationship between obedience and assurance.[78] The suggestions that follow, therefore, must be viewed as a very modest contribution to an ongoing theological agenda.

If, then, we seek such harmonization, what are our alternatives? They would seem to be two: to find in Paul the same kind of basic synergism that seems to be apparent in James; or to find in both Paul and James a basically "monergistic" view of salvation. The former alternative has been adopted by many Roman Catholic as well as Protestant theologians. They will often speak bluntly of two "justifications": the initial act of acceptance (Paul) and the final vindication (James).[79] The first justification is based on faith alone; the second, however, is based on works in addition to faith. But it is questionable whether such a conclusion is fair to Paul.

To be sure, theologians strenuously debate the apparent conflict in Paul himself between his teachings of "justification by faith" and "judgment by works." But while this is obviously not the place to delineate Paul's view of salvation, suffice it to say here that we are not convinced Paul teaches a synergistic view. "Justification by faith," as Paul expounds it in Romans 1–8, means two things: (1) a person is brought into relation-

78. See, e.g., Z. Hodges, *Dead Faith: What Is It?* (Dallas: Redención Viva, 1987); J. F. MacArthur, Jr., *The Gospel according to Jesus* (Grand Rapids: Zondervan, 1988); Hodges, *Absolutely Free!* (Grand Rapids: Zondervan, 1989); MacArthur, "Faith according to the Apostle James," *JETS* 33 (1990) 13-34. This modern version of an old debate could have profited from greater reliance on viewpoints and considerations hammered out in the course of the earlier controversies.

79. A view much like this was taught by the Reformation-era Roman Catholic theologian Robert Bellarmine, the reformer Martin Bucer, the seventeenth-century divine James Ussher (Sermon XV, XIII, p. 239) (for these, see A. E. McGrath, *Iustitia Dei: A History of the Christian Doctrine of Justification* [2 vols.; Cambridge: Cambridge University Press, 1986, 1987], 2.34-35, 109), and Wesley (see Minutes of 1744 [*Wesley's Works,* VIII, p. 277, Q. 14]).

ship with God by faith alone, with no basis whatsoever in "works"; and (2) the verdict of justification is final: it guarantees ultimate salvation. Paul, in other words, teaches a monergistic view of salvation: God himself provides it. To be sure, Christians must respond to God's work of grace: "works" are important in Paul also. But "works" are themselves the "work" of God (cf., e.g., Phil. 2:13), "fruit" that the Spirit produces within us. Without therefore diminishing the importance of human response in Paul, we cannot legitimately categorize his view as synergistic.

But can James then be interpreted in a similar monergistic way? The most popular evangelical approach to James 2 suggests just that. By viewing "justify" in James as a demonstration of righteousness, the text can, in effect, be removed from the soteriological level entirely. The synergism of James would apply to the way we show that we are righteous only. However, as we argue in the exegetical section of the commentary, this view cannot be sustained. "Justification" in James 2 is God's ultimate vindication of the Christian in the judgment — and it therefore has inescapable soteriological implications. To be sure, we should not therefore speak, at the theological level, of two "justifications." That term is best applied to Paul's teaching on this matter; what James talks about in chap. 2 should be categorized under the theological term "judgment."

The answer to the problem, we would suggest, lies in reading James's teaching about "works" in light of Paul's teaching that Christian works are themselves the product of God's work of grace through the indwelling Holy Spirit. What appears on the surface to be synergism in James can, without contradiction with anything James says, be read in light of the monergism of Paul. While not explicitly taught by James, a monergistic interpretation fits well into the emphasis in chap. 2 on true faith. James, it will be remembered, is not arguing that a Christian must "add" works to faith; he insists that true saving faith *will* "work." It is but a short step from this insight to attributing the motive power of faith to the work of God. And, as T. Laato has shown, James gives evidence of a monergistic view of salvation in his emphasis on the creative power of the new birth in 1:18.[80] At the theological level, then, we think that Paul and James are complementary rather than contradictory. Faith alone brings one into relationship with God in Christ — but true faith inevitably generates the works that God will take into account in his final decision about the fate of men and women.

What James says in these verses, we must remember, is dictated by the circumstances he is addressing. Unlike Paul, who was faced in

80. T. Laato, "Justification according to James: A Comparison with Paul," *TrinJ* 18 (1997) 47-61.

Galatians and, to a lesser extent, in Romans by "Judaizers" insisting on obedience to the law as a condition for salvation, James was facing professing Christians who were dismissing the importance of obedience in the Christian life. Works, claims Paul, have no role in getting us into relationship with God. Works, insists James, do have a role in securing God's vindication in the judgment. Paul strikes at legalism; James at quietism. Each message needs to be heard.[81] Luther, faced with forms of Roman Catholic medieval theology that placed great emphasis on works in salvation, naturally focused on Paul in his preaching. Wesley, on the other hand, confronting a church largely indifferent to the moral imperatives of the gospel, appropriated the perspective of James. So in our day as well. Christians need to continue to pay attention to the warning of James that true faith is to be tested by its works and that only a faith that issues in works is genuinely saving faith. James recognizes that Christians continue to sin (see 3:2), so he clearly does not expect 100 percent conformity to the will of God. But how high must the percentage be? How many works are necessary to validate true, saving faith? James, of course, gives no answer. But what we can say with confidence on the basis of James's teaching is that the claim of anyone who is totally unconcerned to lead a life of obedience to God to have saving faith must be questioned.

VI. STRUCTURE AND THEME

As we noted in our analysis of the letter's nature and genre, James consists of several substantial blocks of teaching on specific topics (2:1-13; 2:14-26; 3:1-12; 5:1-6) along with many briefer exhortations that appear to have little relationship to one another (1:2-4, 5-8, 9-11, 12, 13-18, 19, 20-21, 22-25, 26-27; 3:13-18; 4:1-3, 4-10, 11-12, 13-17; 5:7-11, 12, 13-18, 19-20). Many scholars have therefore endorsed Luther's judgment, who accused the author of "throwing things together . . . chaotically."[82] Dibelius modernizes this basic view in his form-critical approach, treating James as a collection of loosely strung-together paraenetic components. However, the last three decades have witnessed a serious reconsideration of this matter of James's structure. Adamson, in his 1976 commentary, claims that the letter displays a "sustained unity."[83] Davids, writing in 1982,

81. See D. O. Via, "The Right Strawy Epistle Reconsidered: A Study in Biblical Ethics and Hermeneutic," *JR* 49 (1969) 253-67.

82. Luther, "Preface to the New Testament" (1522), in *LW* 33.397.

83. Adamson, 20.

builds on the epistolary structure identified by F. O. Francis, suggesting that James displays a careful literary structure: a "double opening statement" (1:2-27); a body (2:1–5:6); and a conclusion (5:7-20). He further argues that each section repeats the three basic themes of the letter: testing, wisdom/pure speech, and poverty/wealth.[84] The insights of Francis and Davids have served as the starting point for more concerted and sophisticated literary analysis of the letter, typical of biblical studies over the last twenty years. The most thorough example of this approach is found in the work of H. Frankemölle. He identifies 1:2-18 as the opening (the *exordium*) and 5:7-20 as the closing (the *peroratio*). These texts display similar wording and themes, acting as the frame around the body of the letter. The opening section announces the key themes of the letter; structurally, therefore, each of the topics that James takes up can be attached to one of the brief exhortations found in 1:2-18. For instance, the call to be "mature and complete" (1:4) is taken up in 1:19-27; James's invitation to ask God for wisdom is followed up in 3:13-18; 2:14-26 elaborates the opening call to faith in 1:6-8, and so on.[85]

Several comments on these suggestions are in order. First, we should avoid the assumption, clearly evident in several commentaries and studies, that a lack of clear organization puts James in a bad light. Structure is tied to genre and purpose. Some kinds of writing, by their very nature, do not have a clear organizing principle or readily identifiable logical progress. This is not necessarily a bad thing; indeed, it may be integral to the writing's effectiveness. So, if we were to conclude that James did consist of a series of brief, relatively independent, exhortations, nothing negative about the letter could be inferred.[86]

Nevertheless, second, a closer look at the letter reveals far more organization than Dibelius recognized; although less, we think, than Frankemölle and others have thought they discovered. Several themes are persistent in the letter. Testing figures prominently in both the opening (1:2-4, 12) and closing (5:7-11) sections of the letter, where James uses some similar vocabulary to make the link fairly obvious. Testing, then, while perhaps not the topic of the letter, is nevertheless, James suggests, the context in which it must be read. This testing, while taking many forms (1:2), is particularly manifest in the poverty and oppression that so

84. Davids, 22-29.

85. See esp. Frankemölle, "Semantische Netz," with a useful chart on p. 193. An approach to the structure of James that takes a similar methodological tack and that shares some similar basic conclusions is that of Wuellner (Wuellner is largely followed by J. H. Elliott, "The Epistle of James in Rhetorical and Social Scientific Perspective: Holiness-Wholeness and Patterns of Replication," *BTB* 23 [1993] 71-81).

86. See esp. Bauckham, 62-63.

many of the readers of the letter are suffering; this, then, becomes a second general motif (1:9-11; 2:1-13; 5:1-6). Thus far we follow Davids. But we are not sure his third major theme, wisdom/pure speech, is so clear. Wisdom, as we have seen, is mentioned in both 1:5 and 3:13-18; but it does not rise to the level of a topic in its own right. Godly speech also comes up several times (1:20, 26; 3:1-12; 4:11-12; 5:12), but it is not clearly connected to wisdom. And other topics appear to be of almost equal importance: faith (1:6-8; 2:14-26; 5:14), humility (3:13-18; 4:13-17), the law (1:25; 2:8-13; 4:11-12). To go further than this — identifying particular parts of the letter with the conventional elements of Greco-Roman rhetoric, linking sections via similar vocabulary, imposing on the letter a structure derived from other biblical passages — is to force the letter into a mold that does not naturally fit.

Third, then, our own proposal is to recognize several key motifs that are central to James's concern (see the paragraph above) but to acknowledge that they are often mixed together with other themes in paragraphs that cannot be labeled as neatly as we might like. Specifically, we think the body of the letter (1:2–5:11) can be divided into five general sections. The first, 1:2-18, while having trials as the unifying motif, touches on several other subjects. The second section, 1:19–2:26, is marked especially by a concern for obedience to the word. The rebuke of partiality, while clearly an important subject in its own right, can at least be loosely tied to this theme through its concluding warning about judgment (vv. 12-13). At first sight, 3:1–4:12 does not display any thematic coherence at all. But closer inspection reveals that the section begins (3:1-12) and ends (4:11-12) with exhortations about proper speech and that 3:13–4:3 borrows from a popular ancient *topos* about envy and violence. And sinful speech is sometimes linked to this *topos* as well. The paragraph 4:4-10 stands apart; indeed, as we will suggest below, James bursts out here with an expression of his deepest concern about the readers of the letter. Far more loosely connected is the fourth section, 4:13–5:11. However, as we argue in the commentary, James's exhortation to patience in 5:7-11 is tied to the rebuke of the rich in 5:1-6 via a widespread biblical theme. The two paragraphs 4:13-17 and 5:1-6, on the other hand, share similar opening statements. Both paragraphs denounce arrogance and can be generally connected by means of that topic.

What, finally, emerges as the central theme or purpose from these various exhortations? Or is there no overarching theme? Clearly any theme that can encompass the varied material of the letter must be quite broad. Perhaps we would do better not to speak of a "theme" but of a central concern. This, we think, can be discovered in the emotional climax of the letter, 4:4-10.[87] Here James abandons his customary address "brothers" or "dear brothers" to castigate his readers as "adulteresses." The feminine form reflects the biblical tradition according to which the covenant between God and his people is portrayed as a marriage, with God's people in the role of bride. James is labeling his readers spiritual adulterers. They are seeking to be "friends with the world" and in the process are turning the Lord, who in his holy jealousy demands complete allegiance from his people, into their enemy (4:4-5; for substantiation of this interpretation, see the commentary). James makes the same point by warning the readers about being "double-minded" (*dipsychos;* cf. 1:8 and 4:8). As other interpreters have pointed out, James uses oppositions throughout his letter to set before his readers a stark choice: they can decide to remain entirely loyal to the Lord by obeying his word (1:21-25; 2:14-26), following the "wisdom from above" (3:16), displaying "pure and undefiled religion" (1:27); or they can compromise their loyalty by an inconsistent lifestyle, manifesting the influence of "worldly" wisdom (3:15) and thereby "deceiving" themselves about their spiritual status (1:22).[88] Basic to all that James says in his letter is his concern that his readers stop compromising with worldly values and behavior and give themselves wholly to the Lord.[89] Spiritual "wholeness," then, we suggest, is the central concern of the letter.

87. Johnson (84) agrees: "the thematic center for the composition as a whole."
88. See esp. Frankemölle, "Semantische Netz," 184-87; Johnson, 14.
89. See also Baker, 20; Bauckham, 100-101, 177-85.

James 1

I. ADDRESS AND GREETING (1:1)

Many readers skip the opening verses of NT letters, treating them as unimportant formal details. But this is a mistake. For the letter introductions usually contain more than bare names. They also describe the writer and the recipients in ways that provide us with important clues about the nature and purposes of the letter that follows. The introduction of James is no exception.

First, James makes clear that he is writing a letter — not a short story or a theological treatise. Knowing this, we are in a better position to evaluate what he writes. We will expect, for instance, that James writes for a specific audience — the addressees of the letter — and that what he says will be largely determined by their situation and needs. This being the case, we will not be surprised if James moves rapidly from topic to topic as he takes up these various needs and issues. Further, we will want to listen carefully to what James says in the hope of understanding better what the needs and issues of the readers might be. We would not expect James to say much about the readers' situation, since this is information they all share. But we do not know these circumstances, and the more we can learn about that situation the more accurately we can interpret what James is saying to them. For it is only by accurately understanding what James says to these original readers that we will be able to apply his teaching to twenty-first-century readers.

Ancient letters typically began with an identification of the sender, a reference to the recipients, and a greeting: for example, "Antiochus to Julius, greetings." New Testament letters expand this simple opening by elaborating each of these elements, sometimes at considerable length. In his letter to the Romans, for instance, Paul takes six verses to explain who he is before getting around to acknowledging his readers and greeting them. James's expansions are much briefer. He adds only a brief title to his own name. Instead of identifying the recipients of his letter by name or place of residence, he describes them with a loaded, though ambiguous, theological phrase. And he retains the simple "greetings" of most ancient letters.

> 1 *James, a servant of God and of the Lord Jesus Christ, To the twelve tribes scattered among the nations: Greetings.*

"James," as we argued in the Introduction, is the "brother of the Lord" mentioned by Paul in Gal. 1:19 (cf. also Gal. 2:9, 12; 1 Cor. 15:7), the James who was leader of the early church in Jerusalem (Acts 12:17; 15:13; 21:18). We have also noted that many contemporary scholars doubt that James himself is the author of the letter. They argue that someone else, perhaps in the latter years of the first century, wrote in his name. But this theory faces serious difficulties (see the Introduction for details). We should accept the straightforward claim of this verse: the best-known James in the early church, the Lord's brother, wrote this letter.

But if James the Lord's brother wrote this letter, why does he not mention his special relationship to Jesus? Probably because being a brother of Jesus gave James no authority to admonish other Christians as he does in this letter. What qualified James to write such a letter was not his physical relationship to Jesus but his spiritual relationship. James was not, of course, one of the original twelve apostles. But, like Paul, James might have been added to the ranks of the apostles after the resurrection. And Gal. 1:19 suggests that Paul, at least, viewed James as an apostle: "I saw none of the other apostles — only James, the Lord's brother."[1]

Nevertheless, James does not claim this status for himself. He identifies himself simply as "a servant of God and of the Lord Jesus Christ." By calling himself a "servant," James of course acknowledges his subservient status. Indeed, the Greek word translated "servant" in the NIV also means "slave" (see NLT). But being a "servant of God" — because it is God, the sovereign of the universe whom one serves — also carries great honor. For in the OT, this title is applied to the great leaders of the people of Israel, such as Moses (Deut. 34:5; Dan. 9:11) and David (Jer. 33:21; Ezek. 37:25). As do Paul (cf. Rom. 1:1; Gal. 1:10; Phil. 1:1; Tit. 1:1) and Peter

1. The Greek for "only" is *ei mē,* "except," and probably refers to the entire previous statement: "[Besides Peter] I saw none of the other apostles except James." See, e.g., R. N. Longenecker, *Galatians* (Waco, Tex.: Word, 1990), 38.

(2 Pet. 1:1), James therefore identifies himself in the letter opening with a title that suggests his authority to address — and admonish — the readers.

If the title "servant of God" is common, the full description "servant of God and of the Lord Jesus Christ" is not. Only here in the NT does this language occur. James could intend both titles, "God" and "Lord," to apply to Jesus — "Jesus Christ, both God and Lord."[2] But we would have expected the titles to occur in the opposite order had this been James's intention. His point rather is that he serves both God and "the Lord Jesus Christ." We are so used to the combination "Jesus Christ" that we forget that "Christ" is a title, equivalent to the OT/Jewish "Messiah." While rarely used in the OT, this title was beginning to be used in the NT period to denote the deliverer/king expected by Jews in the last days. James's addition of the title "Lord" reflects a very early Christian understanding of Jesus, as seen in Peter's claim in his Day-of-Pentecost sermon: "God has made this Jesus, whom you crucified, both Lord and Christ" (Acts 2:36). James's view of his half-brother Jesus had undergone quite a transformation since the days they grew up in the same household together!

Following the pattern of most NT letter writers, James addresses his readers in terms both of their status and location; they are "the twelve tribes" "scattered among the nations." "The twelve tribes," of course, reflects the historical origins of Israel, made up originally of the people descended from the twelve patriarchs. As a result of the Assyrian and Babylonian victories, most of the "tribes" were exiled and scattered. Yet the Lord, through the prophets, promised that he would regather the exiled people of Israel and so reconstitute the twelve tribes once again (Isa. 11:11-12; Jer. 31:8-14; Ezek. 37:21-22; Zech. 10:6-12; cf. also *Pss. Sol.* 17:26-28). This was common expectation; see especially *T. Benjamin* 9:2: "But in your allotted place will be the temple of God, and the latter temple will exceed the former in glory. The twelve tribes shall be gathered there and all the nations, until such time as the Most High shall send forth his salvation through the ministration of the unique prophet." Jesus' choice of twelve apostles suggests that his mission was to bring into being this eschatological Israel. See especially Matt. 19:28 (par. Luke 22:30): "Jesus said to them, 'I tell you the truth, at the renewal of all things, when the Son of Man sits on his glorious throne, you who have followed me will also sit on twelve thrones, judging the twelve tribes of Israel.'" The book of Revelation similarly pictures the people of God of the last days in terms of 12,000 people drawn from each of the twelve tribes (Rev. 7:5-8)

2. Vouga, 31, 36; see also M. Karrer, "Christus der Herr und die Welt als Stätte der Prüfung: Zur Theologie des Jakobusbriefes," *KuD* 35 (1989) 168-73.

and of the heavenly Jerusalem, with twelve gates on which "were written the names of the twelve tribes of Israel" (Rev. 21:12). By calling his readers "the twelve tribes," then, James claims that they constitute the true people of God of the "last days."

The phrase "scattered among the nations" translates a Greek phrase meaning, literally, "in the diaspora." "Diaspora," or "Dispersion" (NRSV), became a technical name for all the nations outside of Palestine where Jewish people had come to live (2 Macc. 1:27; John 7:35). In his first letter, Peter uses this term to address his readers, who are almost certainly Gentiles (1:1). Here the word probably has a figurative meaning, characterizing Christians as people who live in this world, apart from their true, heavenly, "homeland." But the early date and Jewish audience of James suggest a more literal meaning for the term here. As we argued in the Introduction, James writes to Jewish Christians who have been "dispersed" as a result of persecution (Acts 11:19).

II. THE PURSUIT OF SPIRITUAL WHOLENESS: THE OPPORTUNITY AFFORDED BY TRIALS (1:2-18)

As we noted in the Introduction, finding structure in the Letter of James is not easy. He obviously has many different issues that he wants to raise with his former parishioners and moves rather quickly from one to another. What relationship, if any, these topics bear to one another is not clear. Nowhere in the letter is this question of structure more difficult than in chap. 1. In rapid-fire sequence, James:

- encourages his readers to respond positively to their trials (1:2-4);
- exhorts them to ask in faith for wisdom (1:5-8);
- comforts the poor and warns the rich (1:9-11);
- pronounces a blessing on Christians who endure trials (1:12);
- warns believers not to blame God for temptations (1:13-15);
- reminds his readers that all good gifts, including the new birth, come from God (1:16-18);
- warns his readers about sins of speech (1:19-20);
- exhorts believers to be obedient to the word they have received (1:21-25);
- and reminds them of the essence of "true religion" (1:26-27).

Wordplays, evident in the Greek text but usually not in the English, forge literary links between many of these sections:

- *chairein* ("greetings") in v. 1 is picked up by *charan* ("joy") in v. 2
- *leipomenoi* ("lacking") in v. 4b is picked up by *leipetai* ("lacks") in v. 5
- *peirasmon* ("trial") in v. 12 is picked up by *peirazomenos* ("when tempted") in v. 13
- Note also that *teleios* ("perfect," "complete") occurs in vv. 4, 17, and 25

But, beyond these wordlinks, James does little to suggest relationships among these sections. So it is left to the reader to discern any common themes or connections among them. One obvious connection is the similarity of vv. 2 and 12, which both encourage endurance of trials. Many scholars, therefore, think that this is the opening paragraph of the letter and that it may even introduce the key theme of the letter: enduring trials (vv. 2-4 and 12)[3] or spiritual completeness (vv. 4, 5-8).[4] But vv. 13-15 have a close linguistic connection with vv. 2 and 12: the word "temptation" that is at the heart of vv. 13-15 translates the same Greek word that is translated "trial" *(peirasmos).* So these verses continue the topic of vv. 2-12 in a slightly different direction. Verses 16-18 are more difficult to place. Since v. 18 introduces the "word" of God, the theme that dominates vv. 21-25, we might want to put a major break between v. 15 and v. 16.[5] But vv. 19-20, with their warning about hasty speech, change the subject yet again, making any connection between v. 18 and vv. 21-25 more difficult. So, while vv. 16-18 are definitely transitional, they probably look back more to vv. 2-15 than ahead to vv. 21-25.[6] Verses 19-20, on the other hand, also stand alone, but they are connected with vv. 21-25 via the inferential conjunction "therefore."

Verses 2-18, then, comprise the opening section of the letter. But, as the diversity of opinions about the structure of the chapter reveals, it is hardly a clearly defined section. Nor does it have a unifying theme. Only by reading into the text considerably more than James says can a single

3. See, e.g., Davids, 35: ". . . the problem of testing forms the thread which ties the epistle together."

4. Wuellner; H. von Lips, *Weisheitliche Traditionen im Neuen Testament* (Neukirchen/Vluyn: Neukirchener, 1990), 412-14; Penner, 144-49; Elliott, "The Epistle of James," 71-72 (who sees spiritual completeness as the theme). Francis ("Form and Function," 118), Klein (37-38), Davids (65), and Johnson (174-75) view 1:12(13)-27 as a second "opening," introducing still another of the letter's central themes: doing the word of God.

5. See Crotty, 47-48; Baasland, 3,655-56.

6. Those who take vv. 2-18 as the basic unit here include Dibelius (69-71), Ropes (128-29), Mussner (62-63), Vouga (19-20), Hartin (28), and, especially forcefully and in great detail, Frankemölle (137; see also idem, "Semantische Netz," 175-84; "Zum Thema des Jakobusbriefes: im Kontext der Rezeption von Sir 21,1-18 und 15,11-20," *BN* 48 [1989] 24-33). Cf. also Martin (30-32), who extends the paragraph through v. 19a.

topic be imposed on the section as a whole. But we can, perhaps, identify key motifs that recur in a way that suggests that they are basic to James's concern at this point. The first of these is the endurance of trials. This theme occurs at the beginning of the passage (vv. 2-4) and again in v. 12. And much of the material in these verses can be tied to this theme more or less directly. But perhaps even more important is the second motif: spiritual wholeness, or integrity. Perseverance in trials has as its ultimate outcome believers who are "mature and complete, not lacking anything" (v. 4). The opposite of this whole and consistent Christian is the doubter, the "double-minded man," who will not find his prayers for wisdom answered (vv. 5-8). These texts portray the positive and negative side of a concern that is central to the entire letter: a consistent and undivided commitment to God in Christ. So broad is this motif that the other issues James raises in vv. 2-18 can also be related to it. By recognizing one's status before God, both poor and rich Christians will preserve their integrity before the Lord (vv. 9-11). Enduring trials of various kinds (v. 12) is naturally essential to maintain spiritual wholeness. And trials can be successfully resisted only by remembering that God, while sending them, never seeks our downfall (vv. 13-15). Indeed, James concludes, God is the source of every good gift we enjoy — including the new birth that Christians enjoy and that makes up the first step in God's plan to bring "wholeness" to all of creation (vv. 16-18).

A. Enduring Trials Brings Spiritual Maturity (1:2-4)

> 2 *Consider it pure joy, my brothers, whenever you face trials of many kinds,* 3 *because you know that the testing of your faith develops perseverance.* 4 *Perseverance must finish its work so that you may be mature and complete, not lacking anything.*

After the initial epistolary opening, most NT letter writers express appreciation for their readers in the form of a thanksgiving or offer a blessing to God for his abundant spiritual provision. Not so James. He launches directly into exhortation. By placing trials in this position of prominence in the letter, James suggests that the tough times the believers were facing were a key reason for his writing to them.[7] As do Paul (Rom. 5:2-4) and Peter (1 Pet. 1:5-7) in similar passages, James reminds his readers that God brings difficulties into believers' lives for a purpose, and that this purpose can be accomplished only if they respond in the

7. See Davids, 35-37.

right way to their problems. Feeding into James's teaching on trials, we should note, is the intense wrestling with the problem of undeserved suffering occasioned by the persecutions endured by Jews during the intertestamental period. Why does God allow the righteous to suffer? is, indeed, one of the most perplexing and difficult questions that God's people can ask. James gives no complete answer. But implicit in what James says is a conviction that the suffering of believers is always under the providential control of a God who wants only the best for his people.

2 James's favorite address of his readers is "my brothers" (see also 2:1, 14; 3:1, 10, 12; 4:11; 5:7, 9-10, 12, 19) or the variant "my dear brothers" (1:16, 19; 2:5). Both Jews and pagans broadened the word "brother" to describe fellow members of the same religion (in the NT, see, e.g., Matt. 5:22; Acts 3:22; 13:15). When used in this spiritual sense, the word included both men and women; hence the rendering "brothers and sisters" (NRSV; NLT) in modern English is justified. *Consider it pure joy,* James commands his brothers and sisters, *whenever you face trials of many kinds.* "Pure joy" is a good rendering of the Greek phrase *pasan charan* (lit., "all joy") since the word *pas* here probably suggests intensity (complete and unalloyed joy) rather than exclusivity (nothing but joy). A parallel to this use of "all" is found in 1 Pet. 2:18, where Peter exhorts slaves to be submissive to their masters "in all fear" (e.g., wholehearted and sincere fear). James does not, then, suggest that Christians facing trials will have no response other than joy, as if we were commanded never to be saddened by difficulties. His point, rather, is that trials should be an occasion for genuine rejoicing. Why this is so, he will explain in vv. 3-4.

The word that is translated "trial" — *peirasmos* — and its verbal cognate — *peirazō* — are important words in this section: we find *peirasmos* in vv. 2 and 12 and *peirazō* in vv. 13 and 14. These words have two distinct meanings in the NT. They can denote either an outward trial or process of "testing" or they can denote the inner enticement to sin: "temptation" or "tempt." The latter meaning is seen in verses such as 1 Tim. 6:9: "People who want to get rich fall into *temptation* and a trap and into many foolish and harmful desires that plunge men into ruin and destruction" (see also Luke 22:40, 46). 1 Pet. 4:12, on the other hand, is a good example of the other meaning: "Dear friends, do not be surprised at the painful *trial* you are suffering, as though something strange were happening to you" (see also 1 Pet. 1:6; Matt. 26:41; Luke 22:28; Acts 20:19; Rev. 3:10). In several verses, the meaning of the word is not clear. The Lord's Prayer is a good example: most English translations have rendered "Do not lead us into temptation," but many contemporary scholars argue for "Do not bring us to the time of trial" (NRSV). In other verses, the meaning of *peirasmos/peirazō* may even combine these ideas, in the sense that the external trial is at the same time a point of temptation (see, e.g., Luke 4:13; 1 Cor. 10:13; Heb. 3:8). A combination of meanings of this kind may well be present in vv. 13-15. In v. 2, however, *peirasmos* means "trial." The surrounding language makes this clear: believers run the risk of "falling into" (*peripiptō;* translated "face" in NIV) these trials, which have as their purpose the "testing" of faith and need to be "endured." These same terms are used elsewhere in the NT when *peirasmos* has the meaning "trial" (see esp. 1 Pet. 1:6; and cf. v. 12).

What were the "trials" that James's readers were enduring? Poverty must certainly have been prominent among them. James's letter is filled with references to poverty and wealth (1:9-11; 2:1-7; 2:15-17; 4:13–5:11), and he makes clear that at least the majority of his readers are poor. James 2:6-7 makes pretty clear that religious persecution was one of the causes of the poverty the believers were experiencing. Rich people, who were "slandering" the name of Christ, were "exploiting" the Christians and "dragging them into court." See also 5:1-6, where James accuses rich people of "killing" the righteous by withholding wages from them. We can imagine a situation in which wealthy Jews found the readers' commitment to Jesus as Messiah perverse and therefore harassed them in various ways. But contributing to the readers' poverty as well was their situation as exiles, forcing them to establish themselves in a new and strange situation. And this in turn suggests that the "trials" James mentions include more than religious persecution. By stressing that the trials were "of many kinds," James deliberately casts his net widely, including the many kinds of suffering that Christians undergo in this fallen world: sickness, loneliness, bereavement, disappointment.

3 Why can believers react to trials with so strange and unexpected a response as joy? Because we know that God uses trials to perfect our faith and make us stronger Christians. So runs James's answer in vv. 3-4. He touches here on what must have been a standard early Christian encouragement to suffering believers, because both Paul (Rom. 5:3-4) and Peter (1 Pet. 1:6-7) say much the same thing that James says here. Trials, James explains, involve a *testing* of faith. "Testing" translates a rare Greek word *(dokimion),* which is found elsewhere in the NT only in 1 Pet. 1:7 and in the Septuagint only in Ps. 11:7 (ET 12:6) and Prov. 27:21. Peter apparently uses the word to denote the result of testing; the NIV translates "genuine." But the two OT occurrences both denote the process of refining silver or gold, and this is the way James uses the word. The difficulties of life are intended by God to refine our faith: heating it in the crucible of suffering so that impurities might be refined away and so that it might become pure and valuable before the Lord. The "testing of faith" here, then, is not intended to determine whether a person has faith or not; it is intended to purify faith that already exists.

Testing produces, first of all, *perseverance.* The etymology of the Greek word points to the idea of "remaining under," and, in this case, etymology steers us in the right direction. The picture is of a person successfully carrying a heavy load for a long time. The NT repeatedly emphasizes the need for Christians to cultivate this quality of perseverance or steadfastness when facing difficulty (see, e.g., Luke 8:15; 2 Thess. 1:4; Rev. 2:2; 13:10). But James suggests that trials can also produce this quality of endurance. Like a muscle that becomes strong when it faces resistance, so Christians learn to remain faithful to God over the long haul only when they face difficulty. Trench, in his famous book on synonyms,[8] distinguishes between the word *makrothymia* and the word *hypomonē.* The former, usually translated "patience," requires Christians to put up lovingly with other people; the latter, used here, requires Christians to bear up under their trials. Such a distinction may be valid and helpful in explaining the word here, but it does not always hold up. Later in the letter, James will exhort the readers to "be patient" (Gk. *makrothymeō*) until the coming of the Lord; and both endurance of trial and patience with others seem to be denoted there.

4 When faith is tested, then, the immediate result is, or should be, *perseverance.* But valuable as it is, perseverance is not itself the final goal of testing. Rather, James says, believers should "let endurance have its perfect [or complete] work." This translation is a fairly literal rendering of the Greek, which we need as the basis for a solid understanding of what James intends here. The translation reveals, first, that the benefits of testing come only to believers who respond to them in the right way: Christians must *allow* endurance to do its intended work. It is quite typical of James's hortatory style to so emphasize the need for Christian response; contrast the parallel texts we have noted in Paul and Peter, where no such imperative disrupts the sequence of virtues. But, second, what is this "perfect work" that perseverance is intended to achieve? The phrase could denote the full extent of the perseverance itself; the NLT translates "So let it grow, for when your endurance is fully developed. . . ."[9] But James's deep concern throughout the letter that believers respond to God's grace with sincere obedience suggests rather that the word "work" here summarizes the many dimensions of the ideal Christian character.[10] The REB captures this idea fairly well: "Let endurance perfect its work in

8. R. C. Trench, *Synonyms of the New Testament* (reprint; Grand Rapids: Eerdmans, 1973), 195-98.

9. See, e.g., Mayor, 36.

10. See esp. Klein, 55-56.

you that you may become perfected." This translation, with its use of the English word "perfect," brings to our attention the third question that this exhortation of James's raises. The Greek word here is *teleios,* and its meaning can go in two slightly different directions. In Greek moral philosophy, this word usually had the meaning "perfect." But in the OT and in Jewish literature, *teleios* is colored by its Hebrew background and comes to mean "complete" or "mature." Noah, for instance, is the "complete" man par excellence (Gen. 6:9; Sir. 44:17; *Jub.* 23:10). Most scholars think that Jesus uses the word in this sense when he calls on his disciples to be *teleios* (Matt. 5:48). However, we recall that Jesus compared the *teleios* disciples were to aim for with the *teleios* of God himself. This suggests that the rendering "mature" does not quite capture the idea. And the difference between "perfect" and "complete" is not very large. For the Christian who has attained "completeness" will also be "perfect" in character. James, we must remember, is presenting this as the ultimate goal of faith's testing; he is not claiming that believers will attain the goal. But we should not "lower the bar" on the expectation James sets for us. Nothing less than complete moral integrity will ultimately satisfy the God who is himself holy and righteous, completely set apart from sin.

The last words in the verse underscore this point: when endurance is allowed to run its course and attain its goal, believers will be *mature and complete, not lacking anything.* "Mature" translates *teleios,* and we would argue again for a stronger rendering. The word "complete" suggests the idea of wholeness and soundness, in contrast, for instance, to ill health (see Acts 3:16).[11] Testing, James suggests, is intended to produce, when believers respond with confidence in God and determination to endure, a wholeness of Christian character that lacks nothing in the panoply of virtues that define Godly character. This concern for spiritual integrity and wholeness lies at the heart of James's concern, and he will come back to the matter again and again (see esp. 1:7-8 and 4:4-5).

B. Wholeness Requires Wisdom, Which God Gives to All Who Ask in Faith (1:5-8)

> 5 *If any of you lacks wisdom, he should ask God, who gives generously to all without finding fault, and it will be given to him.* 6 *But when he asks, he must believe and not doubt, because he who doubts is like a wave of the sea, blown and tossed by the wind.* 7 *That man should not think he will receive anything from the Lord;* 8 *he is a double-minded man, unstable in all he does.*

11. See esp. Johnson, 178.

After encouraging his readers to embrace trials for the potential they have to spur spiritual growth (vv. 2-4), James exhorts them to pray in undivided faith for the wisdom that a gracious God is anxious to give to those who ask (vv. 5-8). James uses a verbal link to connect these two brief paragraphs, with the word *lack* ending the former (v. 4b) and introducing the latter (v. 5a). But a sequence in content is more difficult to find. James gives us little help, using the vague Greek conjunction *de* (a weak "but" or "and") to introduce v. 5. We find more potential help in Jewish wisdom sources, which sometimes bring together some of the topics that James addresses in vv. 2-8. Several texts, for instance, suggest that wisdom is that quality needed if God's people are going to endure trials with fortitude and godliness (see, e.g., Sir. 4:17).[12] Other passages connect wisdom with perfection; see, for example, Wis. 9:6: "even if one is perfect among the sons of men, yet without the wisdom that comes from you he will be regarded as nothing." And a few passages even bring together the themes of testing, wisdom, and spiritual integrity. Wisdom 10:5 claims that it was wisdom that preserved Abraham "blameless before God" when God tested him by requiring him to sacrifice his son Isaac. Throughout his letter, James indicates an awareness of these kinds of Jewish traditions, so we are probably justified in thinking that this material influenced James's sequence of writing here.[13] The spiritual perfection that is the goal of trials (vv. 2-4) will be achieved only when divine wisdom is present. And wisdom can be had for the asking — albeit, an asking that is sincere and uncorrupted (vv. 6-8).

5 James's exhortation to his readers to ask for *wisdom* echoes widespread OT and Jewish teaching. "The Lord gives wisdom," claims Prov. 2:6, and the importance of wisdom is the central theme of this OT book. Wisdom is the means by which the godly can both discern and carry out the will of God (e.g., 2:10-19; 3:13-14; 9:1-6). Wisdom will therefore keep a person from immorality and enable him or her to be acceptable to the Lord. Finding wisdom, claims Proverbs, means finding life and receiving favor from the Lord (8:35). Intertestamental Jewish books like Sirach and the Wisdom of Solomon continue these wisdom themes and develop others in new directions. Already in Proverbs, for instance, wisdom is personified, given an active role in guiding the lives of God's people, and, in the most famous of such passages, said to have been the instrument through which God created the world (8:22-31). Certain Jewish authors (e.g., Philo) come close to transforming this literary device into an assertion of reality, portraying wisdom as some kind of personal being.

12. See the discussion in Martin, 17-18.
13. See, e.g., Davids, 55; Martin, 17-18; Johnson, 179; Hartin, 86.

Scholars have given considerable attention to this stream of Jewish teaching in recent years both because of its possible influence on NT christology and because feminist approaches to the Bible find in "lady wisdom" a counterweight to the dominantly male biblical images of God. But James betrays no interest in these more metaphysical speculations. His view of wisdom remains solidly in the practical tradition of Proverbs, the Wisdom of Solomon, and Sirach.

In addition to OT and Jewish wisdom teachings, James is undoubtedly also influenced in this verse by another tradition, closer to hand: the teaching of Jesus. James betrays close acquaintance with Jesus' teaching throughout his letter (see the Introduction). It is therefore more than likely that the combination of exhortation and promise in the second part of v. 5 — *he should ask God, who gives generously to all without finding fault, and it will be given to him* — is an intentional echo of Jesus' pithier "Ask and it will be given to you" (Matt. 7:7a). Jesus goes on in this section of the Sermon on the Mount to ground God's response to our prayer in his character. Human fathers give good things to their children; how much more, Jesus reasons, will "your Father in heaven give good gifts to those who ask him!" James follows the same pattern. God gives us wisdom when we ask because he is a God who *gives generously.* The NIV translation "generously" reflects the dominant tradition in English versions.[14] This certainly seems to be the meaning of the cognate word that Paul uses in his discussion of giving in 2 Cor. 8:2; 9:11, 13 (cf. also Rom. 12:8).

Yet another possibility should be considered. The Greek word involved is found only here in the NT. It comes from a root whose basic meaning is "single," "simple," an idea retained in Paul's use of a word cognate to this one in Eph. 6:5 (cf. Col. 3:22): "Slaves, obey your earthly masters . . . with *sincerity* of heart." 1 Corinthians 11:3 displays a similar usage of this word, Paul expressing his fear that the Corinthians' minds might be led astray from their "*sincere* and pure devotion to Christ."[15]

Another cognate word may have this sense of "single," "undivided," in Luke 11:34, as the famous KJV rendering puts it: "The light of the body is the eye: therefore when thine eye is *single,* thy whole body also is full of light."[16] This occurrence is particularly important, since we know that James is dependent on Jesus' teaching in this verse. When we turn to the usage of this word group in the LXX, we find an even more

14. The Greek word is *haplōs;* important cognates are *haplotēs, haploō,* and *haplous.* See esp. Hort, 7-9, for a good defense of the translation "generosity" here.

15. The word also occurs in a textual variant in 1 Cor. 1:12, where the idea would again have to do with "sincerity" or "integrity."

16. See the discussion in I. H. Marshall, *The Gospel of Luke* (NIGTC; Grand Rapids: Eerdmans, 1978), 489.

striking pattern. Only once does any of the words refer to generosity (3 Macc. 3:21), while all of the eleven other occurrences denote "sincerity" or "integrity" or "blamelessness." Proverbs 10:9 is a good example: "The man of *integrity* walks securely, but he who takes crooked paths will be found out." Wisdom 1:1(-2), because of the way James echoes several of its themes, is also quite significant: "Love righteousness, you rulers of the earth, think of the LORD with uprightness, and seek him with *sincerity* of heart; because he is found by those who do not put him to the test, and manifests himself to those who do not distrust him."[17] These texts come from OT and Jewish wisdom contexts that we know exercised great influence on James. They suggest that he has taken an OT term denoting "integrity" and applied it to God. Such a linguistic move would make sense in light of James's tendency to portray Christian character as a reflection and outgrowth of God's.[18] And arguably the most important theme in James is his concern that Christians display spiritual integrity: singleness of intent combined with blamelessness in actions. Furthermore, this very point surfaces explicitly in vv. 7-8. Taken together, then, the evidence suggests that James is not so much highlighting God's generosity in giving as his single, undivided intent to give us those gifts we need to please him.[19]

The negative qualification to God's giving, "without finding fault," also fits this interpretation. According to Sirach, "a fool's gift will profit you nothing, for he has many eyes instead of one. He gives little and upbraids *(oneidizei)* much" (20:14-15a). In contrast, James portrays God as one who gives "simply," "with one eye," and without *finding fault (oneidizontos).* So, James makes clear, the believer should have no hesitation in asking God for wisdom, as if God would scold us for not already having all the wisdom we need. Calvin comments,

> Since we see that the Lord does not so require from us what is above our strength, but that he is ready to help us, provided we ask, let us, therefore, learn whenever he commands anything, to ask of him the power to perform it.[20]

6 In v. 5, James called on us to ask God in prayer for the wisdom we might lack. But he now makes clear in vv. 6-8 that we must ask with

17. See also 2 Sam. 15:11; 1 Chron. 29:17; Job 21:23; 22:3; Prov. 11:25; 1 Macc. 2:37; 2:60; 2 Macc. 6:6; Wis. 16:27. The Hebrew word in all but one of these texts where there is a Hebrew original is *tam,* "to be complete, finished," "to have integrity."

18. See especially the work of Frankemölle (esp. "Zum Thema des Jakobusbriefes," 21-49).

19. See esp. Dibelius, 77-79; Martin, 18.

20. Calvin, 282.

the right attitude. Indeed, our asking must coincide with the way in which God gives: he gives with singleness of intent; we must ask with singleness of intent. Specifically, James calls on us to *believe and not doubt* as we come to God in prayer. James, of course, has been speaking explicitly about asking God for wisdom. But James does not return to the topic of wisdom in vv. 6-8, and his teaching here finds parallels in other NT texts about prayer in general. So we are probably justified in taking his teaching in these verses to apply to any prayer. James refers to faith, or to believing, fourteen times in his letter. Nine of the references come in his famous section on "faith and works" (2:14-26), where he emphasizes that true Christian faith is an active quality, producing fruit that ultimately counts before God in the judgment. But the active nature of faith in James is not confined to this paragraph. In 2:1 (cf. also 2:5), James insists that faith in Christ is inconsistent with favoritism toward Christ's people. And in both this verse and in 5:15, he makes God's answering of prayer contingent on faith. James is again reflecting the teaching of Jesus, who, in response to the disciples' amazement at the withering of the fig tree, said, "I tell you the truth, if you have faith and do not doubt, not only can you do what was done to the fig tree, but also you can say to this mountain, 'Go, throw yourself into the sea,' and it will be done. If you believe, you will receive whatever you ask for in prayer" (Matt. 21:21-22). This text is a favorite with those false prophets who claim that God has promised "health and wealth" to every Christian — if only his or her faith is strong enough. But neither Jesus nor James intends to give to Christians a blank check on which they can write whatever they want and expect God to back it up. The "whatever you ask" is clearly qualified by Scripture elsewhere to include only what God has promised to give his people (see, further, our comments on 5:14). In James this point is clear from the connection with v. 5, where he speaks first of God's desire to give wisdom to his people.

In both Matthew and James, the opposite of *believing* is *doubting.* This word means basically "differentiate," and is often used in the NT in the sense of "create distinctions" (Jas. 2:4), "judge" (1 Cor. 14:29), or "dispute" (Acts 11:2). But in the middle voice a reflexive idea is sometimes introduced: "dispute with oneself." Hence the idea of "doubt." But as the word's basic meaning suggests, James is probably thinking of a strong kind of doubting: a basic division within the believer that brings about wavering and inconsistency of attitude toward God. Paul uses the same word in his description of Abraham's faith. Abraham, Paul says, "did not *waver* through unbelief regarding the promise of God" (Rom. 4:20). Paul, of course, is well aware that Abraham did, in fact, doubt God's promise on at least one occasion, greeting God's promise about his son with laughter (Gen. 17:15-18). Paul's point is not that Abraham never entertained any doubt about God's promise but that Abraham, over many years, displayed a consistency in his faith in God. James is not, then, here claiming that prayers will never be answered where any degree of doubt exists — for some degree of doubt on at least some occasions is probably inevitable in our present state of weakness. Rather, he wants us to understand that God responds to us only when our lives reflect a basic consistency of purpose and intent: a spiritual integrity.

Verses 6b-8 expand on this very point, painting a picture of the inconsistent person who cannot expect to receive anything from God. As the *because* in the middle of v. 6 indicates, James uses this description to explain why believers need to have a consistent faith as they pray to God. At the end of v. 6, James compares the person who *doubts* to *a wave of the sea, blown and tossed by the wind.* The picture here is not of a wave mounting in height and crashing to shore, but of the swell of the sea, never having the same texture and shape from moment to moment, but always changing with the variations in wind direction and strength.[21] James probably takes the imagery from Jewish tradition. The philosopher Philo, for instance, uses the same imagery to describe God's purpose in bringing the people of Israel into the promised land:

> He brought thee there in no random manner, but according to his own oath. And he brought thee there not to be carried hither and thither, ever passive amid the surge and eddy and swirl *(klydōna),* but that quit of the wild sea thou shouldst spend thy days under clear sky and in calm water, and reaching virtue as an anchorage or roadstead, or haven of most pure shelter, mightest there find a stable resting-place.[22]

So the *doubter,* not possessing an "anchor for the soul" (Heb. 6:19), does not pray to God with a consistency and sincerity of purpose. Prey to the shifting winds of motive and desire, he wants wisdom from God one day and the wisdom of the world the next.

7-8 The correct punctuation of these verses is a matter of contention. The three main alternatives are well exhibited in the translations of the NIV, the NRSV, and the RSV:

- NIV: That man should not think he will receive anything from the Lord; he is a double-minded man, unstable in all he does. (See also NASB; REB; NLT; TEV.)

21. See particularly Hort, 10-11, on the meaning of the word *klydōn* here.
22. *On the Sacrifice of Cain and Abel* 90.

- NRSV: For the doubter, being double-minded and unstable in every way, must not expect to receive anything from the Lord. (See also NJB.)
- RSV: For that person must not suppose that a double-minded man, unstable in all his ways, will receive anything from the Lord.

The RSV rendering differs from both the others in taking "the double-minded man" of v. 8 to be the subject of the verb "receive" rather than a simple appositive description of "that man" at the beginning of v. 7. But this reading of the verses has been abandoned by the revisers of the RSV (note the NRSV quoted above), and probably rightly so. "That person" is derogatory language, and we would expect the negative characterizations of v. 8 to describe the same person. The difference between the NIV and NRSV, on the other hand, is minor, involving nothing more than a different way of indicating that v. 8 is a further description of "that man"/"the doubter" in v. 7.

The NIV *that man* is better rendered in modern English with "that person," since the underlying Greek *(anthrōpos)* almost certainly includes reference to both men and women.[23] James, of course, alludes back here to the doubting person that he has described at the end of v. 6. A person like that should know better than to expect his or her prayers to be answered. And in case we have missed the point, James goes on in v. 8 to show why this is the case. *He* [i.e., "that man"] *is a double-minded man, unstable in all he does.* The Greek word behind *man* is not now *anthrōpos,* as it was in v. 7, but *anēr.* This latter word normally denotes a man or a husband (as opposed to a woman or a wife), but this seems to be one of the few places where it has a generic reference.[24] The Greek word for *double-minded* is *dipsychos,* which is literally translated "double-souled." This is the first time in Greek literature that this particular word occurs.[25] James, who uses this same word again in 4:8, has probably coined the term in order to accentuate his concern that believers display a wholehearted, consistent, and integral faith commitment to God. However, while he may be the first to use this particular word, he is certainly not the first to enunci-

23. Note that the NRSV avoids the problem by identifying the person as "the doubter" (see v. 6).

24. The lexica (BAGD, LSJ) allow for this occasional broader reference for *anēr.* And note the comment of D. A. Carson: ". . . I am almost prepared to say that in the peculiar idiolect of James, *anēr* in his usage functions the way *anthrōpos* does among other writers" (*The Inclusive Language Debate: A Plea for Realism* [Grand Rapids: Baker, 1998], 162).

25. See S. E. Porter, "Is *dipsuchos* (James 1, 8; 4, 8) a 'Christian' Word?" *Bib* 71 (1990) 469-98.

ate the concept. The OT blesses those who pursue God with "a whole heart" (Ps. 119:2) and condemns the person who exhibits a "divided heart" (Ps. 12:2; Hos. 10:2). Jesus singled out Deut. 6:5, with its demand for total allegiance, as one of the greatest commandments in the OT: "Love the Lord your God with *all* your heart and with *all* your soul and with *all* your strength." Other OT and Jewish texts utilize the "two ways" tradition, according to which human beings are presented with the choice of two different life-directions, a choice that will ultimately affect their eternal destiny. See, for example, Sir. 2:12: "Woe to timid hearts and to slack hands, and to the sinner who walks along two ways!" Pinning James's background down to one of these texts or traditions is impossible; for, indeed, consistency and integrity in one's walk before God are demanded throughout Scripture.

James concludes with a final negative characterization of this "doubter" who will not find his prayers answered: he is *unstable in all his ways. Unstable* translates a word that occurs only in James in the NT (cf. 3:8) and only in Isa. 54:11 in the LXX, where it refers to the effects of a violent storm. James may therefore be carrying on the imagery of the raging sea from v. 6,[26] although evidence falls far short of proof. The "all he does" reflects again James's concern to portray a basic inconsistency in attitude and spirit rather than an occasional doubt or lapse. It is what we might call "spiritual schizophrenia" that James criticizes in these verses explicitly and implicitly throughout his letter: a basic division in the soul that leads to thinking, speaking, and acting that contradicts one's claim to belong to God.

C. Both Poor and Rich Christians Need to View Themselves as God Does (1:9-11)

> 9 *The brother in humble circumstances ought to take pride in his high position.* 10 *But the one who is rich should take pride in his low position, because he will pass away like a wild flower.* 11 *For the sun rises with scorching heat and withers the plant; its blossom falls and its beauty is destroyed. In the same way, the rich man will fade away even while he goes about his business.*

This short paragraph presents two major, interrelated, interpretive issues. The first is, once again, the relation of the issue James deals with here to the context. James provides no explicit indication of what that re-

26. Mussner, 72.

lation might be, so the connection can only be determined by analyzing the meaning of these verses in light of the surrounding ones. But it is the meaning of the verses that is the second major issue. The heart of the paragraph is a contrast between a "brother in humble circumstances" and "one who is rich." Each is exhorted by James to "take pride" or "boast": the humble brother in his "high position" and the rich person in his "low position." What makes the interpretation difficult and contentious is the problem of identifying the "one who is rich."[27] About half the commentators on James think that this rich person is a Christian.[28] They think that James is encouraging this brother not to take pride in his wealth, but in his identification with Christ — what would appear in the eyes of the world to be a "low position." Verses 10b-11, then, ground that command by reminding the brother that wealth and social status are transitory. The other view, equally supported in the literature, is that the rich person is a non-Christian.[29] James would then be using scornful irony in v. 10, as he exhorts the rich person to "take pride in" the only thing that will be left to him in the judgment: his condemnation, described in vv. 10b-11. A decision between these two very different interpretive options is so difficult that we will keep the option open as we comment on the verses, assessing each view against the specifics of the text. Once we have analyzed the details of the text, we will be in a position to adopt — very hesitantly — one view or the other. Only then will we be able to assess the function of the verses within James's argument.

9 The *brother* describes a person (man or woman) who belongs to the family of God through faith in Christ (see the comments on v. 2). James's description of this brother conjures up a rich biblical tradition. The word he uses could be translated "lowly," "poor," or "humble" (NIV paraphrases with "humble circumstances"). The LXX, especially in the Psalms, uses the word to depict a person who is of little significance in the world's evaluation, even one who is oppressed by the world (see, e.g., Ps. 10:18; 18:27; 34:18; 81:3; 102:17; 138:6). Used in this sense, the word is sometimes paired with "orphan" or "widow." The word occurs in this

27. For a survey of options against the background of James's first-century context, see Baasland, 3,673-76.

28. For example, Mayor, 45-46, 189; Ropes, 145-46; Moffatt, 15; Hort, 14; Knowling, 13-14; Mitton, 36-41; Adamson, 76-77; Mussner, 74; Hiebert, 78; Frankemölle, 241. See also Blomberg, 149-50. Translations that explicitly adopt this view are REB, NLT, and TEV.

29. For example, Huther, 44-46; Windisch, 7; Dibelius, 85-87; Davids, 76-77; Laws, 62-64; Martin, 25-26; Penner, 204-10; G. M. Stulac, "Who Are 'the Rich' in James?" *Presbyterion* 16 (1990) 89-102. Davids (77) and Johnson (190-91) suggest that James addresses the person as ostensibly a Christian, but effectively denies the reality of that status by what he says about him.

sense in Mary's song of praise to the Lord, where she reflects a widespread belief about the reversal of fortunes that the Lord would one day bring about: "He has brought down rulers from their thrones but has lifted up the humble" (Luke 1:52). Usually included in these lowly circumstances is poverty, and so the word can at times virtually be equivalent to "poor" (e.g., Amos 2:7; 8:6; and note that several versions [NLT; TEV; CEV] translate with "poor" here). But the word can also focus less on status or outward circumstances and more on attitude, in which case the opposite of the word is "haughty" or "proud"; see especially Prov. 3:34, quoted in both Jas. 4:6 and 1 Pet. 5:5: "He [the Lord] mocks proud mockers but gives grace to the humble" (see also Matt. 11:29; 2 Cor. 7:6; 10:1). Since the contrast in this context is between "humble" and "rich" (v. 10), James is clearly using the word to describe the believer's socio-economic situation. If, as we think, the Christians to whom James writes have been forced to leave Jerusalem and establish new homes in Syria and northern Palestine, most of them would be facing tough financial situations as well as social dislocation and even ostracism.

But James wants them to look beyond their "worldly" situation and *take pride* in their *high position.* "Take pride" translates a single Greek verb that is used widely by Paul but by no one else in the NT except James (here and in 4:16). The trajectory of the term is set decisively by the famous exhortation in Jer. 9:23-24:

> "Let not the wise man boast of his wisdom or the strong man boast of his strength or the rich man boast of his riches, but let him who boasts boast about this: that he understands and knows me, that I am the LORD, who exercises kindness, justice and righteousness on earth, for in these I delight," declares the LORD.

From this text it becomes clear that "boasting" is not in itself always wrong; it is a matter of what it is that one is boasting in, or taking pride in. Christians, however difficult their circumstances in this world, can always take pride in their "high position," or "exaltation." The Greek word James uses depicts the realm from which the Spirit descended (Luke 24:49) and to which Christ has ascended (Eph. 4:9). By faith believers even now belong to that heavenly realm, though we still await the day when our "bodies of humility" will be transformed into "bodies of glory" (Phil. 3:20-21). James's point, then, is that believers must look beyond the world's evaluation to understand who they are and look to God's view of them. And he has "chosen those who are poor in the eyes of the world to be rich in faith and to inherit the kingdom he promised to those who love him" (Jas. 2:5).

10a The syntactical structure of vv. 9-10 would lead us at first sight to think that the *one who is rich* is also a "brother." For "rich" in v. 10 is most naturally taken as a modifier of "brother" in v. 9, parallel to "humble": "Let the brother who is lowly . . . but let [the brother] who is rich. . . ." But this does not settle the matter. For we have seen that James is influenced in v. 9 by a biblical tradition that associates the godly person with humble circumstances and poverty. As we might expect, then, opposing terms such as "rich" frequently take on negative connotations. The antithesis is particularly evident in the teaching of Jesus in Luke's gospel. According to Luke, Jesus pronounces a blessing on the "poor" but utters a woe upon the "rich" (Luke 6:23-24); note also the contrast between the "rich man" who suffers condemnation and "poor" Lazarus who finds blessing in the afterlife (Luke 16:19-31). James, perhaps because of the environment in which he writes, seems to echo this tradition. He mentions "rich" people in two other paragraphs (2:1-6; 5:1-6), and in each place they are presented as wicked oppressors of the people of God. This being the case, we can understand why so many interpreters think that *the one who is rich* must be a non-Christian.

However, this conclusion is not certain. The word "rich" in fact occurs quite rarely in the OT as a synonym for the wicked.[30] And in some of the intertestamental Jewish writings to which James is indebted, rich people are presented in a carefully nuanced way: prone to pride, selfishness, and exploitation of the poor, but able to be redeemed and encouraged to honor God with their wealth (see esp. Sir. 31:5-11). And, of course, beside the rich man condemned for his luxurious lifestyle, we also find in Luke a rich tax-collector, Zacchaeus, who finds salvation. James also implies that the community to which he writes might at least have within it some who are fairly well-off, for they are able to travel on business and brag about their hopes to make money (4:13-17). While James's negative use of the word elsewhere must be given weight, then, the word "rich" in itself does not settle the matter of the spiritual status of the person James here addresses.

If the *one who is rich* is a Christian, then James's encouragement to that person to *take pride in his low position* will mean that the rich believer is to boast not in his wealth or his elevated social position, but in his identification with Christ and his people, a matter of "humiliation" in the eyes of the world. James would then be reflecting the Jeremiah "boasting" passage we quoted earlier, echoed in Sir. 10:22: "The rich, and the eminent, and the poor — their glory is the fear of the Lord." If, however, *the one who is rich* is an unbeliever, then James will be using irony to de-

30. The only fairly clear reference is Isa. 5:14.

pict his condemnation. Go ahead and boast, James is saying to the rich; all you really have to "boast" about is the eschatological humiliation that is coming to you in the judgment. Jesus seems to use the verb cognate to this noun with this kind of meaning in Matt. 23:12: "Whoever exalts himself will be humbled, and whoever humbles himself will be exalted" (cf. also Luke 14:11; 18:14). Judging between these two options here is difficult. We do find lexical evidence that the word James uses here can refer to judgment. But the irony needed to make this interpretation work is not as evident as it might be.

10b-11 James backs up his warning to the rich person with a reminder of the transitoriness of all human wealth and status. The annual death of vegetation provides a natural metaphor for this purpose, and James draws on a rich biblical tradition when he uses it here. The most famous example is Isa. 40:6b-8: "All men are like grass, and all their glory is like the flowers of the field. The grass withers and the flowers fall, because the breath of the LORD blows on them. Surely the people are grass. The grass withers and the flowers fall, but the word of our God stands forever." But see also Ps. 103:15-16: "As for man, his days are like grass, he flourishes like a flower of the field; the wind blows over it and it is gone, and its place remembers it no more." Ps. 49:16-17 abandons the metaphor and goes straight to the heart of the matter: "Do not be overawed when a man grows rich, when the splendor of his house increases; for he will take nothing with him when he dies, his splendor will not descend with him." And so, James asserts, the rich person *will pass away like a wild flower.* Those who think that this "rich person" is a non-Christian whom James is condemning usually take the imagery of "passing away" to refer to judgment.[31] But the verb "pass away" is never used in the NT to denote judgment. Rather, it typically has the idea "cease to exist," as, for example, in Matt. 24:35: "Heaven and earth will pass away, but my words will never pass away" (cf. also Matt. 5:18; 1 Pet. 3:10). However, the lexical point cannot be pressed too far, since James is using the verb here as part of an image. The question is properly what the image of the fading flower refers to: eschatological judgment or simple transitoriness?

The imagery continues in v. 11. *Scorching heat* or some such translation is found in most English versions, presumably because of the connection with the rising of the sun and because this is the meaning of word in both its other NT occurrences (Matt. 20:12; Luke 12:55). But "scorching wind" (NASB) is also a viable translation, since the word James uses here usually occurs in the LXX as a reference to the hot desert wind from the east (Hos. 12:2; 13:15; Jon. 4:8; Isa. 49:10; Jer. 18:17; 51:1 [LXX 28:1]; Ezek.

31. See, e.g., Martin, 26.

17:10; 19:12). In any case, the emphasis is on the dryness that the sun and/or wind brings, causing the plant to wither and the beauty of the blossom to be destroyed.[32] *In the same way,* James asserts, *the rich man will fade away even while he goes about his business.* "Business" is a good translation for a Greek word that can mean either "journeys" (the word is plural) or "way of life." "Fade away" continues the vegetation imagery of the verses, since the word was used to depict the dying of grass and flowers (Job 15:30; 24:24; it does not occur in the NT). But it can also refer to the death of human beings.[33] Here James depicts the rich person suddenly dying even in the midst of his or her business undertakings. This language might support the view that the rich person whom James addresses in these verses is a non-Christian. For the phrase *in the same way* makes clear that James is now introducing the point of the imagery he has used; and the point seems to be the utter destruction of the rich person. Again, however, the point is not decisive. Destruction of some kind is plainly intended, but James may just as well be thinking of the death of the rich man as of his condemnation.

We must now draw the threads of our exegetical analysis together and come to a conclusion. While the evidence does not all point in the same direction, we think that the balance shifts toward the view that James in these verses addresses two Christians, a poor one and a rich one. He exhorts each of them to look toward their spiritual identity as the measure of their ultimate significance. To the poor believer, tempted to feel insignificant and powerless because the world judges a person on the basis of money and status, James says: take pride in your exalted status in the spiritual realm as one seated in the heavenlies with Jesus Christ himself. To the rich believer, tempted to think too much of himself because the world holds him in high esteem, James says: take pride not in your money or in your social position — things that are doomed all too soon to fade away forever — but, paradoxically, in your humble status as a person who identifies with one who was "despised and rejected" by the world. The point of the passage is, then, that Christians must always

32. The NIV, along with most English versions, renders the four verbs in v. 11a in the present tense: "rises," "withers," "falls," "is destroyed." Yet the Greek verbs in each case are in the aorist. Traditional grammars saw this use of the aorist as anomalous since the aorist, they taught, was, at least in the indicative, a "past" tense. Some contemporary grammarians, however, argue that the aorist is not basically a past-referring tense and that the use of the aorists in this verse reflects its usual complexive aspect in an "omnitemporal" application of the tense (see esp. S. E. Porter, *Verbal Aspect in the Greek of the New Testament, with Reference to Tense and Mood* [Studies in Biblical Greek 1; Frankfurt: Peter Lang, 1989], 223).

33. See BAGD, who refer to a grave inscription and Josephus, *War* 6.274; *T. Simeon* 3.3.

evaluate themselves by spiritual and not material standards. Maintaining such a perspective in a world that so insistently confronts us with a very different standard of measurement is not easy. But if the church is to be the kind of "countercultural" society that Jesus intended it to be, establishing and propagating such a perspective is essential.

We are now, finally, in a position to evaluate the place of these verses in their context. "Trials" introduced the larger section to which these verses belong (vv. 2-4); and James will return to this topic in the very next verse. So James may intend us to see poverty and wealth as a, or perhaps even *the,* greatest "test" for Christians.[34] But these verses might also be tied to James's overriding concern throughout this section: that Christians display a consistent and integral spirituality that avoids the "double-souled" attitude typical of too many who claim to be followers of Christ. Money and the things that money can buy, James well knows, are a tremendously powerful lure to compromise one's wholehearted commitment to the Lord. And so his thoughts move naturally from the need to approach God with a consistent and unwavering faith (vv. 6-8) to one of the chief threats to that kind of faith. As Jesus warned us, "No one can serve two masters. Either he will hate the one and love the other, or he will be devoted to one and despise the other. You cannot serve both God and Money" (Matt. 6:24).

D. God Rewards the Person Who Endures Trials (1:12)

> 12 *Blessed is the man who perseveres under trial, because when he has stood the test, he will receive the crown of life that God has promised to those who love him.*

With this verse, James returns to the opening topic of the paragraph: trials. Verbal similarities reveal the connection. "Trial" occurs in both vv. 2 and 12; the verb "persevere" in v. 12 picks up "perseverance" in vv. 3-4; and "test" in v. 12 matches the "testing" of v. 3. In the earlier passage, James exhorted believers to respond to trials with joy because such testing of their faith would produce perseverance. Now he promises a reward for those who successfully endure trials by remaining firm in the midst of the testing. The "blessing" formula is well known in both the OT (e.g., Ps. 1:1) and the NT (e.g., Matt. 5:3-12). The tendency to translate with the word "happy" (e.g., TEV, REB) is a misguided effort to avoid unclear "religious" language and should be resisted. A person who is

34. See, e.g., Ropes, 145; Mussner, 72; Martin, 22-24.

"blessed" may not be "happy" at all. For our emotional state may and will vary with the circumstances of life. But we can be assured that, whatever those circumstances, if we endure them with faith and commitment to God, we will be the recipients of God's favor. According to the NIV, this blessing comes to the *man* who endures trial (see also REB; TEV). The Greek word is the same one that James used in v. 8: *anēr,* which is usually gender specific: a "man" in distinction from a woman; or a "husband" in distinction from a wife. But this is almost surely another instance in which James uses this word as equivalent to *anthrōpos,* "person."

As in v. 2, "trial" refers to any difficulty in life that may threaten our faithfulness to Christ: physical illness, financial reversal, the death of a loved one. James's wording suggests that he is not thinking of any particular trial, but of the nature or essence of "trial."[35] In v. 4, perseverance was said to produce a settled and complete Christian character. Here also it is perseverance that brings God's blessing. This blessing, of course, is something that Christians can enjoy in this life, as they experience the goodness of God and the spiritual joy that he brings to us. But James's attention here is on the future culmination of that blessing, as the final part of v. 12 indicates. Christians who stand up under the test *will receive the crown of life that God has promised to those who love him.* The word *crown* conveys to most of us a gem-studded headpiece worn by kings and queens. But people in the Greco-Roman world would probably have thought more often of the laurel wreath given to the victors in athletic contests. Paul uses the word in this way in 1 Cor. 9:25: "Everyone who competes in the games goes into strict training. They do it to gain a crown that will not last; but we do it to get a crown that will last forever." James probably also has the imagery in view, since the victory of a trained and disciplined athlete in a race is a fitting image for the reward that God bestows on those who remain faithful to him over the often long and difficult race of life. If James, then, uses the *crown* to refer to the idea of reward, then the word *life* following *crown* will indicate what the reward is.[36] Revelation 2:10, a word of Jesus to suffering Christians, is similar: "Be faithful, even to the point of death, and I will give you the crown of life." James indicates that God has *promised* the reward to *those who love him.* It is fruitless to try to pin down a specific promise that James might have in mind, for promised reward for obedience and faithfulness is found throughout the Scriptures.

Clearly James's overall purpose in this verse is to encourage believ-

35. The lack of an article in Greek can have this effect.

36. We are then assuming that *tēs zōēs* is an epexegetic genitive: "the crown which is life."

ers to endure trials faithfully so that we might receive the reward that God has promised. Some Christians have a difficulty with rewards, objecting that our obedience to Christ should be pure and disinterested, unmotivated by any such crass consideration as future reward. This objection is understandable, and it is certainly the case that far too many Christians bring a selfish and calculating "bottom line" mentality into their service of the Lord, asking "What's in it for me?" at every step. But the contemplation of heaven's rewards is found throughout the NT as a spur to our faithfulness in difficult circumstances here on earth. Keeping our eyes on the prize can help motivate us to maintain spiritual integrity when faced with the temptations and sufferings of earthly life. Moreover, as Mitton aptly observes, "the rewards are of a kind that only a true Christian would be able to appreciate."[37]

E. While God Tests His People, He Never Tempts Them to Sin (1:13-18)

13 *When tempted, no one should say, "God is tempting me." For God cannot be tempted by evil, nor does he tempt anyone;* 14 *but each one is tempted when, by his own evil desire, he is dragged away and enticed.* 15 *Then, after desire has conceived, it gives birth to sin; and sin, when it is full-grown, gives birth to death.* 16 *Don't be deceived, my dear brothers.* 17 *Every good and perfect gift is from above, coming down from the Father of the heavenly lights, who does not change like shifting shadows.* 18 *He chose to give us birth through the word of truth, that we might be a kind of first fruits of all he created.*

Verse 12 is the hinge between vv. 2-11 and vv. 13-18. Older commentators (and most English versions), noting the shift in subject that occurs between vv. 11 and 12 and the introduction in v. 12 of the "test"/"tempt" language that dominates the next several verses, attach the verse to vv. 13-15. But the trend in recent years is to attach v. 12 to vv. 2-11.[38] This trend reflects the current literary approach to the Bible, with its interest in the various devices that ancient authors used to organize their material. One of these devices, *inclusio,* uses common words or ideas at both the beginning and the end of a discrete section of material. As the verbal resemblances we pointed out above reveal, vv. 2-4 and v. 12 appear to form just such an *inclusio.* But v. 12 has obvious connections with vv. 13-15 as

37. Mitton, 44.
38. See, e.g., Johnson, 174-76; Klein, 44-45.

well. The Greek word for "test" in v. 12, *peirazō,* is the same word that is translated "tempt" in vv. 13-14. Using this term as a link-word, therefore, James makes the transition from testing to temptation. God, James has said, promises a blessing to those who endure trials. Every trial, every external difficulty, carries with it a temptation, an inner enticement to sin. God may bring, or allow, trials; but he is not, James insists, the author of temptation (v. 13). Enticement to sin comes from our own sinful natures, not from God (vv. 14-15).

Verses 16-18 are not easy to locate within the logic of James's argument. The presence of the word "father" in both vv. 17 and 27 might form another *inclusio.*[39] But the connection seems to be incidental, not material. And more important connections link vv. 16-18 to what precedes: the verb "bring forth" *(apokyō)* (vv. 15 and 18) and the motif of God as a sincere and beneficial giver (vv. 5 and 17).[40] Probably, then, after the transitional v. 16, vv. 17-18 state the positive side of the case that James has made in vv. 13-15. God is not the author of temptation, or of anything evil. He is, rather, one who gives good gifts to his people — and, preeminently, the gift of the new birth.

13 The NIV translation suggests that all of v. 13 is about temptation: *When tempted, no one should say, 'God is tempting me.' For God cannot be tempted by evil, nor does he tempt anyone.* Most English versions agree; but note the rendering in the NJB: "Never, when you are being put to the test, say, 'God is tempting me'; God cannot be tempted by evil, and he does not put anybody to the test." According to the interpretation reflected in this translation, James makes the transition from testing to temptation within v. 13.[41] This is the best way to handle the movement of the text. No solid line should be drawn between v. 12 and v. 13, as if James drops the topic of testing to take up the issue of temptation. His concern, rather, is to help his readers resist the temptation that comes along with the trial. For every trial brings temptation. Financial difficulty can tempt us to question God's providence in our lives. The death of a loved one can tempt us to question God's love for us. The suffering of the righteous poor and the ease of the wicked rich can tempt us to question God's justice, or even his existence. Thus testing almost always includes temptation, and temptation is itself a test. "Preserving under the trial" (v. 12) demands that we overcome these kinds of temptations. But James is specifically concerned with a particular facet of the biblical worldview that might make such resistance to temptation difficult. The OT often

39. Wuellner, 47.

40. Klein, 44; Frankemölle, 276-82.

41. Among the commentators, see esp. Laws, 69.

makes clear that God himself brings trials into the lives of his people. "God tested Abraham" when he ordered him to sacrifice his son Isaac (Gen. 22:1). He tested Israel by leaving the people surrounded by pagan nations (Judg. 2:22). And he tested King Hezekiah by leaving him to his own devices in his reception of the Babylonian envoys (2 Chron. 32:31; cf. 2 Kings 20:12-19). But while God may test or prove his servants in order to strengthen their faith, he never seeks to induce sin and destroy their faith. Thus, despite the fact that the same Greek root *(peira-)* is used for both the outer trial and the inner temptation, it is crucial to distinguish them. That other Jews felt the need to make the same point is clear from the intertestamental book Sirach, which warns:

> Do not say, "It was he who led me astray"; for he has no need of the sinful. The LORD hates all abominations; such things are not loved by those who fear him. It was he who created humankind in the beginning, and he left them in the power of their own free choice. If you choose, you can keep the commandments, and to act faithfully is a matter of your own choice. He has placed before you fire and water; stretch out your hand for whichever you choose. Before each person are life and death, and whichever one chooses will be given. For great is the wisdom of the LORD; he is mighty in power and sees everything; his eyes are on those who fear him, and he knows every human action. He has not commanded anyone to be wicked, and he has not given anyone permission to sin. Do not desire a multitude of worthless children, and do not rejoice in ungodly offspring. (Sir. 15:11-20)

Thus James insists that *God cannot be tempted by evil.* This rendering, which is paralleled in most English translations, understands the rare word *apeirastos* as a passive verbal adjective with the meaning "unable to be tempted." But two other possibilities should be mentioned. Hort compared the word to the similar, and more frequent, word *apeiratos,* which has the meaning "inexperienced." Davids, on the other hand, argues for the meaning "ought not to be tested." This, he suggests, makes better sense than the traditional interpretation — for how can God's inability to be tempted be an argument against thinking that God tempts others? And this interpretation would also tie in nicely with the OT condemnation of Israel for testing God in the wilderness.[42] Neither alternative is preferable to the traditional interpretation. Hort's suggestion ignores the probable play on the word *peirazō:* God does not "tempt" because he cannot be "tempted." (And it is worth noting that the REB ["God cannot be

42. Davids, 82-83, and, in greater depth, "The Meaning of APEIRASTOS in James I.13," *NTS* 24 (1977-78) 386-92.

tempted by evil"] has moved away from the NEB endorsement of this view ["God is untouched by evil"].) Davids has a point when he questions the logic involved in the traditional view, but his own interpretation gives to *apeiratos* a very poorly attested meaning.[43] If we adopt the NIV rendering, then, how does the clause contribute to James's argument? Presumably, it is to be seen as a preliminary observation leading on to the main point: *he himself tempts no one.* "What must be understood is that temptation is an impulse to sin, and since God is not susceptible to any such desire for evil he cannot be seen as desiring that it be brought about in man."[44]

14 In keeping with the movement of the passage from Sirach quoted above, James now attributes temptation to each person's *evil desire.* No Greek word corresponding to "evil" is found in the text, but the NIV rendering is nevertheless justified. "Desire" *(epithymia)* can have a neutral meaning in the NT (cf. Luke 22:15; Phil. 1:23), but the context here makes it clear that James uses it with its more typical NT sense: fleshly, illicit desire. The word often carries for us a sexual connotation (and it has this sense in the NT), but it usually has a broader meaning, including any human longing for what God has prohibited. Similar occurrences of the word are found in 1 Pet. 2:11 — "Dear friends, I urge you, as aliens and strangers in the world, to abstain from sinful desires, which war against your soul" — and 1 John 2:17 — "The world and its desires pass away, but the man who does the will of God lives forever." Other Jewish writers used the word in a similar way; cf. Philo, in his tractate on the *Decalogue* (par. 153): "For all the wars of Greeks and barbarians between themselves or against each other . . . are sprung from one source, desire, the desire for money or glory or pleasure. These it is that bring disaster to the human race." James's use of the singular word to denote an innate tendency toward sin also reminds us of the later rabbis' use of the Hebrew word *yetzer.* They portray the battle between good and evil essentially as a conflict between the "good desire" and the "evil desire."[45] Jewish writers often emphasized this point in order to establish a firm ground for moral exhortation. Obedience to God's laws was possible because God had given people, in the form of the "good desire," the ability to obey. James, however, makes no mention of any such innate positive tendency; and

43. Davids argues that *apeirastos* means "ought not to be tempted" in the NT apocryphal books *Acts of John* 57 and *Pseudo-Ignatius* 11, but the definition "unable to be tempted" is preferable in both. Furthermore, his view has difficulty explaining *estin* ("is") and must give an unusual force to the genitive *kakōn.*

44. Laws, 71.

45. On this theme in James, see esp. J. Marcus, "The Evil Inclination in the Epistle of James," *CBQ* 44 (1982) 607-21.

his silence on this point might tempt us to align him with Paul's more pessimistic (in comparison with Jewish notions) perspective on human ability. But this would be to engage in an argument from silence. The most we can say is that James, like other Jewish and Christian authors, wants to place the responsibility for temptation and sin squarely on the shoulders of each human being. Nor should we make anything of James's omission of Satan as a source of temptation. James refers to Satan elsewhere (4:7). But his purpose here is to highlight individual responsibility for sin. And, as Bengel remarks, "Even the suggestions of the devil do not occasion danger, before they are made 'our own'."[46]

James uses metaphorical language to convey the mode of operation of the *evil desire:* temptation arises when a person is *dragged away and enticed* by *his own evil desire.* The metaphor comes from fishing. The bait on the fisherman's hook would *entice* the fish; and, once hooked, the fish would be *dragged away.* James, who if not a fisherman himself was certainly well acquainted with the profession from his upbringing near the Sea of Galilee, may be thinking of fishing as he uses the words here. And the analogy is certainly apt. The picture of Satan casting the enticements of sin before us and then hooking us and dragging us away when we "bite" is both vivid and terrifying. However, we must note that the two verbs involved here had been used by Jewish authors before James to refer to the operation of sin.[47] The philosopher Philo provides a striking example: "There is no single thing that does not yield to the enticement of pleasure, and get caught and dragged along in her entangling nets" (*Husbandry* 103). And Peter uses one of the verbs to characterize the enticements offered by false teachers (2 Pet. 2:14, 18). The fact that these verbs were already being used with this kind of spiritual application creates the suspicion that, by James's day, the metaphor may have been a "dead" one. In other words, while originally taken from the context of fishing, the words had been used in a spiritual sense often enough to have lost any notion of that original context (much like "I took the bait"). And the order in which James puts the verbs — "drag away" and then "entice," contrary to what happens when fishing — might confirm this suspicion.

15 James shifts metaphors to describe the havoc that *desire* can wreak in the spiritual life. Aided by the fact that the underlying Greek word is feminine, James pictures *desire* as *conceiving* and *giving birth to* sin. And sin, once in existence, if it becomes *full-grown,* produces death. James

46. Bengel, 7.

47. The verbs James uses are *deleazō* and *exelkō.* Most commentators (e.g., Hort, 25-26) assume that James uses the latter verb as equivalent to its uncompounded form (*helkō*). It is this uncompounded form that occurs in the Philo passage.

does not tell us how it is that *desire* might conceive and give birth. But he undoubtedly has in mind the active response of a person who is tempted. Temptation, James has said, involves the innate desire toward evil as it is enticed by the superficial attractiveness of sin. If a person should welcome rather than resist that temptation, desire conceives; and if not turned away immediately, it produces sin. James implies that temptation, in and of itself, is not sinful. Only when *desire* "conceives" — is allowed to produce offspring — does sin come into being. The point is an important one, for some extremely sensitive Christians may feel that the fact of their continuing to experience temptation demonstrates that they are out of fellowship with the Lord. To be sure, as one develops more and more of a Christian "mind," the frequency and power of temptation should grow less. But temptation will be part of our experience, as it was the experience of the Lord himself (Heb. 2:18), throughout our time on earth. Christian maturity is not indicated by the infrequency of temptation but by the infrequency of succumbing to temptation.

The underlying imagery of this verse taps into some very well-known OT wisdom texts. For the image of "desire" as a seductress luring the believer into an adulterous union that brings death is reminiscent of the role played by the "loose woman" in Proverbs 5–9. This figure, who leads her guests into the depths of Sheol (Prov. 9:18), is contrasted with wisdom, who gives life to those who embrace her (Prov. 8:35). Since James has mentioned wisdom in v. 5, it may be that he has this OT imagery in mind as he contrasts the life given to those who endure trials (v. 12) with the death produced in those who allow desire to run its course (v. 15). Solomon's vivid metaphor is designed to paint temptation in its true colors. So also James wants to warn believers of the danger of giving in to temptation in the midst of trials.

16 The NIV, along with most English versions (the NASB is an exception), attaches James's plea *Don't be deceived, my dear brothers* to the verses that follow. This arrangement is probably justified, since James usually uses the vocative "brothers" to open new sections (1:2, 9, 19; 2:1, 5, 14; 3:1, 11; 4:11; 5:7, 12, 19; exceptions are 2:15; 3:10, 12; 5:9, 10). James therefore does not want his readers to make any mistake about what he is about to say about God as the source of all good gifts. But the warning also refers back to the reminder about the source of temptation in vv. 13-15. It therefore serves as a transition between vv. 13-15 and vv. 17-18.[48] Believers, James is saying, must not be led astray into thinking that God himself is tempting them to evil; on the contrary, he is the invariable giver of good gifts to his children.

48. See, e.g., Frankemölle, 288-89.

17 Verses 17-18 form another of those small units that are so common in the first chapter of James. Commentators who tend to view the letter as a series of brief sayings drawn from Christian and Jewish tradition (e.g., Dibelius) are content to let the verses stand on their own. But most modern commentators rightly recognize that James uses these brief sections to pursue a broader purpose. As we noted in the Introduction, vv. 2-18 are bound into a loose unity by the theme of trials and the mature Christian response that is appropriate to them. As the conclusion to this unit, vv. 17-18 serve several purposes. First, they bring us back to the theme of the singleness and integrity of God, especially in his giving (see v. 5). Second, as we have noted, this theme in turn provides a contrast with vv. 13-15: God does not tempt to evil; he gives good gifts. And, third, the mention of the "word" (of God) in v. 18 introduces the theme that will dominate vv. 19-27.

The NIV *every good and perfect gift* abbreviates the Greek text, which, literally translated, has "every good giving and every perfect gift." Why James repeats substantially the same idea twice is debated. A few commentators think that the word "good" might be a predicate adjective: "every giving is good." James may then intend this statement to stand in contrast to the following one: "every giving is good, *but* every perfect gift comes from God."[49] But if this had been James's intention, we would have expected him to use an adversative conjunction in Greek (corresponding to "but" in my rendering). A better explanation for the repetition focuses on the style rather than on the content of the words. A popular poetic device among the Greeks was the hexameter, a series of words whose syllables formed six rhythmical sections. The words of the Greek text here form an imperfect hexameter. The repetition of the "giving" idea, then, is necessary in order to create this literary form, and no difference in meaning between the two Greek words should be seen.[50] The same is probably true of the adjectives "good" and "perfect," although the latter word (Gk. *teleios*) touches on a key motif in James and creates something of an *inclusio* with the same word in v. 4.

Recognizing the literary device present here also helps explain the somewhat unusual way James puts his point. In order to create the appropriate contrast with vv. 13-15 — God does not tempt to evil — we would have expected James to say something like "God gives only good and perfect gifts." Yet, instead of an assertion about God, we have an as-

49. Hort, 27; Tasker, 47-48.

50. James uses *dosis* and *dōrēma*. NT usage is not common enough to judge their relationship (each is used only twice; *dosis* occurs also in Phil. 4:15, and *dōrēma* in Rom. 5:16). Philo distinguishes *dosis* and *dōrea* (a word similar to the one James uses) at least once (*Cherubim* 84), but elsewhere he uses these two words interchangeably.

sertion about the origin of good gifts. This way of phrasing the matter may arise because James is quoting a saying already current in the early church.[51] Its literary form would make it easy to remember, and quoting it here would be an effective way of reminding the readers of a truth they already know.

The REB attaches the words "from above" to the verb "coming": "Every good and generous action and every perfect gift come from above." But most translations are similar to the NIV, taking "from above" as the predicate of the first clause: *every good and perfect gift is from above, coming down from the Father of the heavenly lights.* "Heavenly lights" is a good interpretive paraphrase of the Greek, which has simply "lights." For the word often refers to the "lights" that appear in the sky: the sun, moon, and stars (see Ps. 136:7-9; Jer. 31:35). While Scripture nowhere else calls God "the Father of lights," the idea is clear enough. When God is presented as "father," his creative power is often intended; see, for example, Job 38:28: "Does the rain have a father? Who fathers the drops of dew?" James, therefore, cites God's creation of the heavenly bodies as evidence of his power and continuing care for the world. The OT frequently makes a similar point (cf. Job 38:4-15, 19-21, 31-33; Ps. 136:4-9; Isa. 40:22, 26; and note also Sir. 43:1-12).

James's final description of God in this verse is less clear in its wording and in its meaning. The interpreter first has to choose among at least six different forms of the Greek text. However, of these, only two deserve serious consideration. One of these, found in two of the best Greek manuscripts we possess, yields the translation "variation due to a shadow of turning" (see the NRSV margin).[52] But the text does not make good sense, and the standard Greek text as well as almost all English translations has rightly adopted an alternate reading that is literally translated "variation or shadow of turning."[53] The Greek words translated "variation" and "turning" often refer to astronomical phenomena in the ancient world, and the earlier reference to God as "the Father of lights" makes it almost certain that this is James's intention here. "Variation" connotes the orderly and periodic movements of sun, moon, planets, and stars. "Shadow of turning" should probably be taken to mean, as NRSV renders, "shadow due to change" (taking *tropēs* as a genitive of source). This phrase could refer to the phases of the moon or to the con-

51. For example, Mayor, 57; Ropes, 159; Dibelius, 99; Davids, 86.

52. The Greek is *parallagē [h]ē tropēs aposkiasmatos.* It is the reading of the original hand of Codex Sinaiticus (A) and Codex Vaticanus (B) and is supported by Ropes, 162-64.

53. The Greek of this reading is *parallagē ē tropēs aposkiasma,* found in the corrrector of Sinaiticus, Codex Alexandrinus, and several other manuscripts.

stant variation of night and day. But we should probably not press for any exact correspondence. James is not writing a scientific treatise but is using general language about the constant motion of the heavenly bodies to make a point about God: he does not change like the heavens do. Philo, the first-century Jewish philosopher, made a similar point by contrasting God with his creation: "Every created thing must necessarily undergo change, for this is its property, even as unchangeableness is the property of God" (*Allegorical Interpretation* 2.33). James has made a similar point about God earlier in the same section, claiming that God gives to all who ask him with a single, undivided, intent (v. 5). Indeed, the integrity and undividedness of God — in contrast to the duality and instability of man (cf. vv. 7-8) — is a key motif of the letter as a whole.

18 James again gives no direct indication of a relationship between the verses. But the logic of the argument suggests that we view birth through the word of truth as an outstanding example of our faithful God's gifts to his creatures. The imagery of birth, especially following reference to God as "father," may refer to God's creation of human beings.[54] Philo uses the Greek verb behind "give birth" *(apokyeō)* in just this sense, and the last words of the verse, *all he created,* clearly brings in the creation motif. And since those to whom God gives birth are called the "firstfruits," what they have experienced must be a foretaste of what all of creation has experienced. But James could also be referring to God's redemptive work rather than his creative work. Donald Verseput has pointed out that v. 17, with its language of God as "the Father of lights," may echo the Jewish morning prayer, a prayer that moves directly from acknowledging God as creator of the heavenly lights to God as redeemer of his people.[55] Moreover, the language James uses in the verse, while capable of a general "cosmological" application, is more likely to be read in a soteriological light. The verb "give birth to," in its only other occurrence in the NT, has been used in v. 15 metaphorically with reference to spiritual birth. "Firstfruits" is a customary way of denoting Christians in the NT (see especially 2 Thess. 2:13; Rev. 14:4; and also Rom. 16:5; 1 Cor. 16:15). But the most important piece of evidence in favor of a redemptive "birth" here is the phrase "the word of truth." The syntax suggests that this "word" is the instrument through which God brings people to life. All four of the other occurrences of the phrase in the NT refer to the gospel as the agent of salvation (2 Cor. 6:7; Eph. 1:13; Col. 1:5; 2 Tim. 2:15). And this reference to "word" must also be seen in relation to the other

54. Hort, 32; Laws, 75-78 (hesitantly); L. E. Elliott-Binns, "James I.18: Creation or Redemption?" *NTS* 3 (1956-57) 148-61; Klein, 129-34; cf. Frankemölle, 298-302.

55. "James 1:17 and the Jewish Morning Prayers," *NovT* 38 (1996) 1-15.

important uses of the same term (Gk. *logos*) in this context (vv. 21, 22, 23). The "implanted word" of v. 21 is sometimes thought to be a consciousness of God resident by nature in every human being. Yet this word, James says, can "save your souls": indication, again, that the gospel is in view. In the final analysis, a decision between the creative and the redemptive "birth" in v. 18 depends on the context in which we view James's language. Reference to creation is probable if we insist that James's terms come from the milieu of the OT and late Judaism. Reference to redemption, however, is likely if the language reflects early Christian teaching. Writing as early as James does and with so obvious a Jewish context makes it difficult to know just where to situate James in relationship to the developing Christian tradition. But we think the phrase "word of truth," coupled with the allusion to this same word as able to "save your souls" in v. 21, tips the scales in favor of the redemptive interpretation.

James, therefore, appeals to the "new birth" of Christians as a striking example of God's good and faithful giving. James stresses the free and unconstrained nature of this giving by beginning the verses with the participle "willing" *(boulētheis),* variously translated "in the exercise of his will" (NASB); "in fulfillment of his own purpose" (NRSV); "he chose" (NIV). God's grace has been extended through the gospel to people so as to bring into existence a foretaste, or down payment ("firstfruits"), of a redemptive plan that will eventually encompass all of creation.

III. THE EVIDENCE OF SPIRITUAL WHOLENESS: OBEDIENCE TO THE WORD (1:19–2:26)

Obedience to the word of God binds these verses together in a loose unity. Key words in the section are "word" *(logos)* (of God) (1:21, 22, 23), "law" *(nomos)* (1:25; 2:8, 9, 10, 11, 12), and "works" *(erga)* (2:14, 17, 18, 20, 21, 22, 24, 25, 26; cf. 1:25). As the list of verses reveals, James focuses on each of these in turn. First, picking up the language of v. 18, James calls on his readers to "humbly accept" the word (v. 21). This idea he unfolds in vv. 22-27, where he shows that accepting the word requires doing it (vv. 22-24). He then shifts from "word" to "law" in order to underscore the demand that God's word makes upon his people (v. 25) and lists three specific ways in which God's word/law needs to be practiced (vv. 26-27). A shift of topic seems to greet us at the beginning of chap. 2, but as we read on, we realize that James wants us to see that treating poor people the same as rich people (2:1-7) is another form of obedience to the law

(2:8-13). James's preoccupation with obedience and its importance for the judgment (vv. 12-13) might seem to minimize the centrality of faith for Christian life and salvation. And so he seeks to show how faith and works, though distinct, are nevertheless inseparable in any true relationship to God (2:14-26).

Little relationship between this larger section and the first major part of the letter (vv. 2-18), beyond some verbal connections, is evident at first sight. But at least a general relationship can be discerned. James's main concern in this first section has been to encourage Christians under the pressure of trials to respond with a steadfast endurance (vv. 3-4, 12) that is rooted in unwavering faith (vv. 6-8). Constancy, consistency, and singleness of purpose stand out as key Christian virtues. Such unflinching loyalty to God comes to expression, James may be suggesting, in obedience to God's word.

A. Hasty Speech and Anger Do Not Please God (1:19-20)

> 19 *My dear brothers, take note of this: Everyone should be quick to listen, slow to speak and slow to become angry,* 20 *for man's anger does not bring about the righteous life that God desires.*

James has wrapped up his first general exhortation with an allusion to the word of God (v. 18). That "word" will be the focus of vv. 21-27, where James calls believers to recognize in God's word the demand of obedience that comes to all who claim the blessing of the new birth. But before he turns to this topic, James interjects a brief exhortation about speech and anger. This concern with improper speech and the anger that can often cause such speech is a traditional theme of Jewish wisdom literature. But James appropriates the tradition because he recognizes that his readers are struggling in just this area — as his repeated attention to "the tongue" and unbridled passions makes clear (see 1:26; 3:1-12; 4:1-3, 11-12; 5:12). Verses 19-20 may then be viewed as James's brief announcement of a motif that is woven like a thread through the fabric of the letter.

The basically independent character of the verses might suggest that they should be given a place in the outline of the letter equal to vv. 2-18 and 1:21–2:26. But it is better to view them as a transitional introduction to the major unit that follows. The address "my dear brothers" usually introduces a new topic in the letter of James (see the comments on v. 16). And the "therefore" of v. 21 shows that the negative warnings of vv. 19-20 act as the basis for the positive exhortation to "accept the word."

19 In place of the NIV's *take note of this,* the NASB has "this you know" (NASB), and the KJV "wherefore" (KJV). The KJV translation is based on a variant in the Greek text that should not be accepted.[56] The NASB, on the other hand, reads the same Greek word as the NIV — *iste,* "you see" — but takes it to be an indicative rather than an imperative.[57] But the imperative is more likely here since this is the kind of verb that James usually pairs with his address "my beloved brothers." This general call to pay attention signals a pause in James's argument as he switches from one topic to another.

The abrupt introduction of a new topic in vv. 19-20 has naturally led commentators to seek to integrate them more fully into the context. The most popular option is to assume that the object of the command "be quick to listen" is the word of God, mentioned in v. 18 and prominent in vv. 21-25.[58] We would then have to infer the same object of the next, coordinate command. If this were so, the command to be "slow to speak" the word of God would have to have a sense similar to Jas. 3:1: "Not many of you should presume to be teachers." But this idea would be difficult to discover without 3:1 — which comes later in the letter. Moreover, the third, grammatically parallel command, "be slow to anger," is difficult to explain on this reading of the verse.

But an even better reason for rejecting the "word of God" interpretation is James's obvious dependence on a widespread Jewish wisdom teaching about speech and anger. The admonition to display wisdom by listening much and talking little is found quite often. Indeed, one of the best known of all the proverbs is the one found in Prov. 17:28: "Even a fool is thought wise if he keeps silent, and discerning if he holds his tongue" (see also 10:19; 11:12, 13; 13:3). The theme is echoed in Jewish intertestamental literature, a good example being Sir. 5:11-13: "Be quick to hear, and be deliberate in answering. If you have understanding, answer your neighbor; but if not, put your hand on your mouth. Glory and dishonor come from speaking, and a man's tongue is his downfall." Moreover, these same wisdom books sometimes link hasty speech and unrighteous anger; see, for example, Prov. 17:27: "A man of knowledge uses words with restraint, and a man of understanding is even-tempered." The "quick-tempered" person, this proverb suggests, is the person who is likely to speak without careful consideration. Uncontrolled anger leads to uncontrolled speech. How often do we find ourselves regretting words spoken "in the heat of the moment"! The wise

56. Although Adamson, 78, n. 132, argues for it. The Greek variants are *iste,* "you see," and *hōste,* "therefore."

57. For support of this interpretation, see Mayor, 65; Perdue, "Paraenesis," 244-45.

58. Ropes, 168-69; Adamson, 78; Hort, 35-36; C. E. B. Cranfield, "The Message of James," *SJT* 18 (1965) 186.

person, James reminds us, will therefore learn to control the emotion of anger and so eliminate one of the most common sources of hasty and unwise speech. Psychologists will sometimes claim that emotions, since they are a natural product of the personality, cannot truly be controlled — only suppressed or ignored. But James's exhortation here (and many similar biblical exhortations) presume differently. Emotions are the product of the entire person; and, by God's grace and the work of the Spirit, the person can be transformed so as to bring emotions in line with God's word and will.

20 James now explains (note the *for*) why Christians should be *slow to become angry: man's anger does not bring about the righteous life that God desires.* The NIV's "righteous life that God desires" is a paraphrase of the Greek, which, literally translated, says "the righteousness of God" (cf. KJV; NASB; NRSV). God's righteousness is one of the great theological themes of the OT. The starting point for the theme is the use of the language to describe an attribute of God: his moral purity and especially his reliability and faithfulness in carrying out all that he has promised. An example of this meaning is David's prayer in Ps. 35:24: "Vindicate me in your righteousness, O LORD my God; do not let them [his enemies] gloat over me." Confident of his own right standing with God, David seeks deliverance on the basis of God's promised word to support his people and destroy his enemies. In other OT verses, "God's righteousness" expresses more of a relational and dynamic concept, focusing on the actual act of vindication. Note, for example, that Isaiah prophesies, in the name of the Lord, "I am bringing my righteousness near; it is not far away; and my salvation will not be delayed. I will grant salvation to Zion, my splendor to Israel" (46:13). Prophecies like this provide the basis for Paul's well-known use of the phrase "righteousness of God" to summarize the gospel (see, e.g., Rom. 1:17; 3:21-22). Paul refers to an activity of God by which he puts people in right relationship with himself; and this use of the OT language is the most important and distinctive we find in the NT.

But we would be wrong to think that James must be using the phrase in the same way that Paul does. Indeed, perhaps no greater mistake can be made in interpreting James than to read his letter in the light of Paul. James, we must remember, is writing (we have argued) before Paul had written any of his letters and probably has no direct knowledge of Paul's teaching. James must be read against the background of the OT, Judaism, and the teaching of Jesus — not the apostle Paul. To be sure, James shares with Paul the use of Gen. 15:6, with its reference to "righteousness" (2:23). And we would certainly make an equally significant mistake to assume that James could not have applied OT language in ways very similar to those of Paul. But the word "righteousness" in Jas.

1:20 must be understood in light of the verb that governs it. And the combination "do" or "produce" righteousness makes it very difficult to think that James could be referring to God's act or gift of righteousness. For how could anyone think that human anger could lead to such righteousness? "Do righteousness" can mean "exact justice" (see perhaps Heb. 11:33). The REB translates in this way, and the idea would seem then to be that James wants to dismiss any idea that people could justify their anger because it is accomplishing God's own ends of retribution. But this meaning of "righteousness" is unusual. We are on firmer ground in thinking that James uses the phrase "produce righteousness" with the meaning it normally has in the Bible: do what God requires of his people. Jesus used the word "righteousness" in just this sense when he called on his followers to exhibit a "righteousness" exceeding that of the Pharisees and teachers of the law (Matt. 5:20; see also 5:6, 10; 6:33).[59] This meaning makes excellent sense in this verse. James's very simple point is that human anger does not produce behavior that is pleasing to God. Presumably, he is thinking especially of different sinful acts, such as violence, murder (see Matt. 5:21-26 and Jas. 4:2-3), and especially, in this context, unwise speech, that stem from anger.

Does James intend to prohibit all anger of any kind — even what we sometimes called "righteous anger"? Probably not. James falls into the wisdom genre at this point. And wisdom sayings are notorious for the use of apparently absolute assertions in order to make a general, "proverbial" point. Qualification of that general truth is often found in other biblical contexts. So we can assume that James intends us to read his warning as a general truth that applies in most cases: human anger is not usually pleasing to God, leading as it does to all kinds of sins. That it can never be pleasing to God would be an interpretation that is insensitive to the style in which James writes at this point.

B. Obedience to the Word Is the Mark of Genuine Christianity (1:21-27)

21 *Therefore, get rid of all moral filth and the evil that is so prevalent and humbly accept the word planted in you, which can save you.* 22 *Do not merely listen to the word, and so deceive yourselves. Do what it says.* 23 *Anyone who listens to the word but does not do what it says is like a man*

59. A few scholars insist that "righteousness" in Matthew be given a forensic, Pauline sense. But they are in a minority, and most agree that the word refers to human behavior in Matthew.

who looks at his face in a mirror 24 *and, after looking at himself, goes away and immediately forgets what he looks like.* 25 *But the man who looks intently into the perfect law that gives freedom, and continues to do this, not forgetting what he has heard, but doing it — he will be blessed in what he does.* 26 *If anyone considers himself religious and yet does not keep a tight rein on his tongue, he deceives himself and his religion is worthless.* 27 *Religion that God our Father accepts as pure and faultless is this: to look after orphans and widows in their distress and to keep oneself from being polluted by the world.*

The theme of this paragraph is obvious: those who have experienced the new birth by means of God's word (v. 18) must "accept" that word (v. 21) by doing it (vv. 22-27). James's concern with practical obedience is signaled by his shift from the term "word" (of God) (vv. 21-23) to "law" (v. 25) and by the frequency of the term "doer" (vv. 22, 23, 25). The "religion" that counts before God (v. 27) and that is able to save the soul (v. 21) must come to expression in a lifestyle of obedience to the word of God, "implanted" within each believer (v. 21).

The point of transition in James's argument is not immediately clear. Most English translations and commentators put the transition between vv. 21 and 22. But the introduction of the topic of the "word" in v. 21 suggests that it belongs with the material following it. The *therefore* at the beginning of v. 21, on this reading of the sequence of thought, may connect the discussion in vv. 21-27 with v. 18 rather than with vv. 19-20. And a close connection between v. 18 and vv. 21-27 is suggested by a similar sequence of ideas in 1 Pet. 1:23–2:2. In both passages, new birth through the word of God is followed by the command (introduced with "therefore" [*dio*]) to "get rid of" evil behavior and to embrace the word of God.[60] Peter, of course, is writing after James; so there is no question of direct borrowing. But what the two passages suggest is that James and Peter may each, independently, be appropriating a familiar teaching from the early church in which a reminder of the spiritual birth God had graciously given his people through his word was followed by exhortation to shun the kind of behavior associated with the old life and to begin living by the standard of the word that had saved them.[61] Corroborating this possibility is the similarity between James and 1 Peter at a number of other points (see the Introduction).

60. This assumes that *to logikon adolon gala* in 1 Pet. 2:2 refers to the Word of God (cf. the AV "sincere milk of the word" and the arguments of J. N. D. Kelly, *A Commentary of the Epistles of Peter and Jude* [New York: Harper & Row, 1969], 85).

61. Many scholars would locate the origin of this tradition in the baptismal ceremony.

21 The NIV *rid yourselves of* translates a Gk. verb *(apotithemai)* that means to "take off." The word connotes the idea of removing clothes (cf. Acts 7:58), and the imagery is applied metaphorically in the NT to the "stripping off" of the pre-Christian lifestyle from the believer (see Rom. 13:12; Eph. 4:22, 25; Col. 3:8; Heb. 12:1; 1 Pet. 2:1). James's use of this term is another indication that he is probably citing common early Christian teaching here. The Greek verb is a participle, which could justify viewing the action as more of an assumption or subordinate idea than a command; see NASB: "putting aside all filthiness and all that remains of wickedness, in humility receive. . . ." But Greek participles in these situations often become virtually equivalent to the imperative verbs they depend on. So the independent command that we find in most English translations is probably justified here.

What James calls on the believer to "take off" is *moral filth and the evil that is so prevalent.* "Moral filth" continues the clothing imagery suggested by the verb "take off." The Greek word lying behind the NIV phrase occurs only here in the Bible *(rhyparia),* but James uses the adjective from the same root in 2:2 to characterize the clothes of a poor person. And we find the same term used to describe the garments that the high priest Joshua must discard before being given a new, splendid set of clothes in Zech. 3:3-4. The NIV "moral," therefore, is an attempt to capture the ethical nuance of a word that basically means "filth" (NLT) or "sordidness" (NRSV). James chooses a word that reminds us just how offensive and detestable sin really is. Coupled with "moral filth" is *the evil that is so prevalent.* This somewhat stiff NIV rendering seeks to capture the idea of "abundant" or "surplus" of evil that the Greek suggests. Another option is to take the Greek to refer not to an abundance of evil but to a "remainder" of evil; see, for instance, NASB: "all that remains of wickedness" (cf. also NJB: "remains of evil"). This meaning is possible, but unlikely. The Greek word involved *(perisseia)* is used three other times in the NT (Rom. 5:17; 2 Cor. 8:2; 10:15), each time with the meaning "abundance." James warns believers that putting off sin involves a fight against a foe that takes many different forms. Like an army with many soldiers, sin attacks us persistently and in many guises. Knock down one sin, and another quickly arises to takes its place in the spiritual conflict in which we are engaged.

NT authors who use the imagery of "putting off" to refer to sin often complete the metaphor by calling on believers to "put on" a new suit of clothes — the righteous living to which Christ calls us. James, significantly, abandons the imagery at this point, using as his positive command the verb *accept* or "receive." He does so because he wants to focus attention on a more basic issue than the adopting of a new code of behavior: the influence of God's word in producing that new kind of behavior. James's description of the word here as *planted in you* has caused considerable controversy. Arguing that the Greek word *(emphytos)* must mean "inborn," some scholars insist that James must be referring to a natural human capacity to respond to God's revelation: "the original capacity involved in the Creation in God's image which makes it possible for man to apprehend a revelation at all."[62] But this conception, besides having rather dubious biblical support, is too general for the context, where "the word" is described as having the power to save (v. 21) and to regenerate (v. 18) and is eventually equated with the "law of liberty" (v. 25). James must be referring to the word of the gospel and not to an innate quality within human beings.[63]

If this is James's meaning, then *emphytos* will have the sense "implanted" rather than "innate."[64] The word is not something that all people have within them from birth onward, but an entity that has taken up residence within believers. James likely draws this striking conception of the implanted word from the famous new covenant prophecy of Jeremiah 31.[65] The prophet, noting the failure of Israel to live up to the terms of the Mosaic covenant, announces on behalf of God a new covenant that God would enter into with his people. As a prominent component of that new covenant arrangement, God promises to put his law within his people, to write it on their hearts (Jer. 31:33). The repeated failures of Israel to obey the law that God gave to them had made it clear that the human heart was not capable of submitting to external rules. A new, interior work would have to be done, giving people a "new heart" (see the somewhat parallel passage in Ezek. 36:24-32) so that they could respond truly and obediently to God's word. James's language reminds his readers that they have experienced the fulfillment of that wonderful promise. But it also reminds them that the word that has saved them cannot be dispensed with after conversion. God plants it within his people, making it a permanent, inseparable part of the believer, a guiding and commanding presence within.

If this interpretation is on the right lines, then the command to *accept the word implanted in you* is not a command to unbelievers to be con-

62. Hort, 37-38. He cites Wis. 2:10, where the only other occurrence of the word in "biblical" Greek is found.

63. See, e.g., Klein, 135-37.

64. For this meaning of *emphytos,* see Herodotus 9:94, *Epistle of Barnabas* 1:2; 9:9 (where the reference is to the gospel), and the note in Adamson, 98-100.

65. Klein, on the other hand, thinks that James may draw his ideas from Deuteronomy 30, where Moses reminds the people that God has put the "word" (= the torah) in their mouths and in their hearts (v. 14; cf. Rom. 10:6-8) (136-37).

verted ("accept the word" means this elsewhere in the New Testament),[66] but to believers to allow the word to influence them in all parts of their lives. By adding the word *humbly* to the command, James reminds us that we need to be open and receptive to the work of the word in the heart. Christians who have truly been "born again" (v. 18) demonstrate that the word has transformed them by their humble acceptance of that word as their authority and guide for life. Jesus made a similar point with different imagery: the believer is to prepare "good soil" in his or her heart in order that the "seed" of the word that has been planted there might produce much fruit (Mark 4:3-20). In place of "fruit," James refers to "the salvation of your souls" (a literal translation). As so often in the OT, "soul" (Gk. *psychē;* Heb. *nephesh*) probably does not here refer to a "part" of the human being, but to the human being as a whole; the NIV rendering, *which can save you,* is therefore probably on target. We should especially note that James here portrays salvation as future from the standpoint of the believer. Some Christians, accustomed to equating salvation with conversion or regeneration, might be troubled by this future orientation. But, in fact, such a focus is quite customary in the NT, where the verb "save" and the noun "salvation" often refer to the believer's ultimate deliverance from sin and death that takes place at the time of Christ's return in glory (see, e.g., Rom. 5:9, 10; 13:11; 1 Thess. 5:9; Phil. 2:12; 1 Tim. 4:16; 2 Tim. 4:18; Heb. 9:28; 1 Pet. 1:5, 9; 2:2; 4:18). James's other uses of the terminology share this future orientation (2:14; 4:12; 5:20; in 5:15, "save" applies to physical, not spiritual, deliverance). This perspective on salvation is important to keep in mind if we are to understand James's theology correctly.

22 James's exhortation to Christians to "accept" the implanted word (v. 21) is the main point of vv. 21-27. But, typical of his concern that believers demonstrate the reality of faith in obedient lives, James goes on to specify just what it means to "accept" the word. Essentially, James argues in vv. 22-25, to "accept" the word means to "do" it. "Doing" frames vv. 22-25: "Be *doers* of the word" (the Greek equivalent of these words comes at the beginning of the verse) opens the paragraph, "blessed in what he *does*" concludes it. Before exploring this main idea further, we should note that James's concern with doing does not mean that he thinks hearing the word is unnecessary. It is not listening to the word that James opposes or diminishes, but *merely* listening. While apparently not a matter of concern in the letter, James would certainly endorse the need to pay careful attention to what the word says, studying it, meditating on it, and pondering its meaning and application. How else could one know

66. Luke 8:13; Acts 8:14; 11:1; 17:11; 1 Thess. 1:6; 2:13.

what it commands us to do? Indeed, James's imagery of the "implanted" word might suggest that careful scrutiny of God's word is no longer needed. But, against its OT background, this concept of the word "written on the heart" does not mean that we possess automatic knowledge of God's will. Rather, the idea is that we have access to God's word and, especially, that we have new hearts, moved by the Spirit to enable us to obey that word. Some Christians have made the mistake of pushing the metaphor of the "implanted" word — and others like it in the NT — too far and concluded that believers are almost totally passive with respect to the revealing and doing of God's will. The very clear commands in this passage and in many others for Christians to take an active role in both hearing and doing should show how imbalanced such a view really is.

And so, James insists, listening to God's word must lead to "doing" it. Only then are we truly "accepting" the word. With this exhortation we find ourselves right at the heart of James's pastoral concern; and v. 22 is rightly the best-known verse in the letter. However, James's concern is certainly not a new idea in the history of religion. The Greek and Roman philosophers and moralists emphasized the need for teachers and adherents of particular viewpoints to show their sincerity by "practicing what they preached." And the absolute bottom-line importance of doing God's word in practice was also widespread among the Jews. "Not the expounding [of the law] is the chief thing, but the doing [of it]" is a representative comment, from a second-century rabbi.[67] Paul reflects this Jewish perspective at one stage of his argument in Romans: "it is not those who hear the law who are righteous in God's sight, but it is those who obey the law who will be declared righteous" (Rom. 2:13). And, last but not least, James shows again here his dependence on the teaching of Jesus: "Blessed rather are those who hear the word of God and obey it" (Luke 11:28). In his message of the kingdom, Jesus announced the overwhelming, amazing wonder of God's sovereign grace reaching down to reclaim sinful people for himself. But no one emphasized as strongly as Jesus the need for people touched by God's grace to respond with a radical, world-renouncing obedience. Both the gracious initiative of God and the grateful response of human beings are necessary aspects of the gospel. The word, through which we are born into new life (v. 18) and which becomes implanted in us (v. 21), is a word that must be put into practice.

People who *merely listen to the word,* James says, are on dangerous ground: they *deceive* themselves. Paul uses this same verb in Col. 2:4 (its only other occurrence in the NT), where he warns the Colossian Christians about false teachers who "deceive" people "by fine-sounding argu-

67. Simeon b. Gamaliel in *m. Abot* 1:17.

ments." The idea of "deceive" in these contexts is clear: to be "deceived" is to be blinded to the reality of one's true religious state. People can think that they are right with God when they really are not. And so it is for those people who "hear" the word — regular church attenders, seminary students, and even seminary professors — but do not "do" it. They are mistaken in thinking that they are truly right with God. For God's word cannot be divided into parts. If one wants the benefits of its saving power, one must also embrace it as a guide for life. The person who fails to do the word, James therefore suggests (in an anticipation of his argument in 2:14-26), is a person who has not truly accepted God's word at all.

23 In vv. 23-25, James uses an imperfect double simile to illustrate the importance of doing and not merely hearing the word of God. James first compares the person who *listens to the word but does not do what it says* to one who looks at his face in the mirror but immediately *forgets what he looks like* (vv. 23-24). But in v. 25 he abandons the simile to make a straightforward assertion about the person *who looks intently into the perfect law that gives freedom.* James's shift from simile to assertion midway through the illustration, combined with the use of different Greek words for similar ideas in the two parts of the illustration, makes the precise point of these verses difficult to pin down. Is James contrasting (1) *what* the two people look at; (2) *how* they look at it; or (3) what the *result* of their looking is?

In v. 23, the "hearer only" looks at "his face"; in v. 25, the "doer" looks at "the perfect law that gives freedom." Is this contrast the point of the comparison? Much depends on the apparently straightforward word "face" in v. 23. The NIV translation here conceals a difficulty in the Greek text, which adds a qualifying word to "face": *genesis.* This word, which of course exists in English as a transliteration, can have two different meanings here: "existence" or "beginning." We use the word in the latter sense in English; hence the title of the first book of the Bible. Of its five NT occurrences, the word has this meaning at least twice, referring to the "births" of Jesus and John (Matt. 1:18; Luke 1:14); and several OT verses use it with this meaning also (e.g., Hos. 2:5; Ezek. 4:14; 16:3, 4). If James intends the word to have this general meaning, then "the face of his origin" might refer to what God intended human beings to look like from the beginning. The person who sees that "ideal" nature of humankind reflected in the word of God is then faulted for failing to do anything to bring his or her life into conformity with that ideal. Some evidence for this view can be found in passages that connect "mirror" with "image" (e.g., Wis. 7:26), suggesting that what one sees in the mirror might be the original image of God.[68] However, while the word "genesis" naturally

68. Hort, 39; Martin, 50.

brings to mind the account of the world's origins, the word is never actually applied in the Bible to the "original" state of human beings. Moreover, the idea that a person might "see" his *invisible* nature in a mirror puts considerable strain on the simile that James uses.

The second meaning of the word, "existence," is then the more likely in this context. This appears to be the sense that James gives the word in his only other use of it (3:6; though the verse is difficult), and it has this meaning several places in intertestamental books (e.g., Jdt. 12:8; Wis. 7:5). Two interpretations are possible if the word has this meaning, a negative one and a relatively neutral one. In the former case, James would intend to connote the sinfulness of a human being's natural existence. A person who looks at himself in a mirror sees what he is really like, with all the "warts," but does nothing about it.[69] A neutral interpretation of the phrase, on the other hand, reads little into the addition of the word "existence." James adds it simply to connote the actual face that a person sees in the mirror: his "natural" face (NASB; NIV and NRSV support this interpretation by not even translating the word).[70] Some evidence for a relatively negative sense of the word *genesis* comes from Philo, who attributes to the world that "exists" transitoriness and uncertainty, in contrast to the stable and eternal nature of God (see, e.g., *Posterity and Exile of Cain* 23). But the evidence for this negative nuance is slight. All things considered, then, we should probably not read very much into James's addition of this phrase. Confirmation that we are on the right track with this conclusion comes from v. 24, where "his natural face" is replaced with the simply reflexive pronoun: "himself." At the most, it might add a slightly negative note to the sense, as if James wants to suggest that the face we see in a mirror is one that belongs to this world and that there is more to us than what we see reflected there.[71]

We doubt, then, that James intends us to find significance in the contrast between "natural face" and "perfect law" (v. 25). But before we conclude that James is therefore not putting emphasis on any contrast between *what* the "hearer only" and the "doer" see, we must look at another part of the "seeing" process in v. 23: the mirror. Mirrors, usually polished pieces of metal, were widely used in the ancient world. And, as in many of Jesus' parables, the mirror may have no real interpretive function in the analogy.[72] James would use it simply because it provides the basis for a convenient and well-known situation with which to compare the hear-

69. Mitton, 68-70.
70. So BAGD and most commentators (e.g., Dibelius, 115-16; Davids, 98).
71. Laws, 86.
72. Davids, 98.

ing of God's word. But ancient philosophers also pressed the idea of the mirror into service to illustrate certain concepts. Some contrasted the imperfect reflection seen in a mirror with actual observance of the object itself as a way of contrasting image with reality. The only other reference to a mirror in the NT has this general function: "Now we see but a poor reflection as in a mirror; then we shall see face to face" (1 Cor. 13:12a). If James uses the mirror imagery with this idea in mind, then he might be implying a contrast between what a mirror can reveal — truth about this world (the "natural face") — and what God's word can reveal — truth about ultimate reality. But this idea may be over-subtle in this context; and we should probably look in a different direction for James's choice of the mirror imagery. By far the most common metaphorical application of looking into a mirror, in a natural extension from its normal use, was to the process of moral self-reflection. If the mirror has any particular metaphorical meaning, therefore, it is probably that it serves as a natural comparison to any book in which one looks to find teaching about the moral life.

Having minimized the importance of any contrast in James's analogy between "what" is seen, we can now turn to the second question: Does he intend a contrast in *how* the seeing takes place? A superficial glance at the Greek text suggests that the answer to this question should be "yes," because James uses two different Greek verbs for "seeing" in this context. The verb *katanoeō* is used to depict the action of the "hearer only" looking at his reflection in the mirror; while the verb *parakyptō* occurs in v. 25 to describe the "doer" who looks at the perfect law. Noting this shift, many interpreters think that James intends to contrast the hasty glance that one gives to oneself in a mirror with the careful, intent observation that one gives to the law of God. It is, then, precisely because a person does not look carefully at the mirror that he immediately forgets what he has seen; whereas the person who really contemplates God's law naturally finds his life being changed by the experience. However attractive this view might be, it finds little support in the words that James uses here. The verb for "look" in vv. 23-24 simply does not have the connotation of a hasty or superficial glance. While some of its occurrences in the NT refer to a look without any particular nuance (Matt. 7:3; Luke 6:41; Acts 7:31, 32; 27:39), this verb usually means "consider carefully," "contemplate" (Luke 11:24, 27; 20:23; 11:6; Rom. 4:19; Heb. 3:1; 10:24). Noting this lexical evidence, Laws even suggests that we reverse the usual interpretation of these verses. James's point, she suggests, is that even a casual glance at God's law, being what it is, has the power to transform, in contrast to a careful contemplation of one's face in a mirror. But this interpretation, as we will see, puts a strain on the meaning of the verb *parakyptō* in

v. 25. We should probably, then, not find any great significance in James's shift from one verb for "seeing" to another in these verses. The point of his analogy lies elsewhere.

24 This point becomes clear in v. 24. Here James notes the *results* of the look into the mirror he has described in v. 23: *after looking at himself, [he] goes away and immediately forgets what he looks like.* These results are clearly contrasted with what James says of the person who looks into the perfect law in v. 25: *[he] continues to do this, not forgetting what he has heard, but doing it.* The more we try to find subtle allusions in some of the specific terms of the simile in v. 23, the more we are in danger of blunting this overriding emphasis. Indeed, the success of James's analogy presumes that both the person who looks in the mirror and the person who looks into God's word are capable of two different responses. The "hearer only" is faulted for not acting on what he sees in the mirror (implying that he could act on it if he chose), while the "doer" of v. 25 is commended for putting into effect what he has seen in God's law (implying that he could ignore it if he chose). The key failure of the "hearer only," then, is forgetting. We touch here on a pervasive and important biblical theme. The Lord constantly warned the people of Israel not to "forget" his mighty acts on their behalf but to "remember" his mercies and his law (Exod. 13:3; Num. 15:39; Deut. 6:12; 8:2; Mal. 4:4). In the NT, Peter, for instance, structures the exhortation in his second letter around the theme of memory (2 Pet. 1:12-13; 3:1, 8; cf. the contrast with the false teachers who "forget" in 3:5). To "remember" God, his acts and his teachings, is to contemplate them in such a way that they make a lasting impression on the heart and the mind. The person who "forgets" what he has seen in God's word is one who reads or listens superficially, not imprinting the message on the soul.

25 As James completes his contrast between the "hearer only" and the "doer," he abandons the simile of vv. 23-24. Rather than comparing the "doer" to one who looks in a mirror and remembers, in other words, James straightforwardly describes that doer. This person is one who *looks intently into the perfect law that gives freedom.* The NIV's "looks intently" is a fair equivalent for the verb James uses here (NASB also has "look intently"; NJB and NLT "look steadily"; TEV "look closely"). The verb has the basic meaning of "stoop down" but comes to be applied especially to the action of "looking by bending over." This sense is preserved in John 20:11, where Mary is said to have "bent over to look into the tomb" (cf. also John 20:5 and Luke 24:12, although a separate verb for "look" occurs in both these texts). The word loses any sense of physical movement at times, connoting simply "look carefully at," "investigate" (see the only other NT occurrence, 1 Pet. 1:12). As we noted in our comments on v. 23, any contrast between this verb and the one James uses in vv. 23 and 24 is difficult to support.

One of the most striking, yet easily overlooked, aspects of this passage is the introduction of the word "law" in this verse. Up to this point, James has spoken about the "word" of God (vv. 18, 21, 22, 23). Yet here, in a verse that carries on the same theme as he has established in these earlier verses, we find the word "law." Why has he shifted to this different word here? And what is the content of this "law" that James commends to his readers? Granted James's background and context, a reference to the law of Moses seems certain. The law God gave to Israel through Moses at Sinai was a center point in OT revelation and absolutely basic to the life of Jews at the time of Christ. For Jews, "law" meant torah, the rules and regulations that God had given his special people to govern their nation, their religion, and their day-to-day conduct. Like James, Jews often described the law of Moses as "perfect" (cf. Ps. 19:7) and even as liberating (e.g., *m. Abot* 6:2). Moreover, James quotes an OT command to exemplify the law in 2:8. But we must hesitate before simply equating "law" for James with the law of Moses. First, in chap. 2, James's description of the law suggests that he has at least one eye on the "fulfillment" of that law in the teaching of Jesus (see our comments on those verses). Second, James often bases his own commands to his readers on the teaching of Jesus, quoting the OT only rarely. Third, James nowhere makes clear that he expects his readers to continue to obey the Mosaic laws pertaining to sacrifice and ritual. Fourth, the flow of thought in these verses appears to demand a broader reference. The "law" of v. 25 must be substantially equivalent to the "word" of vv. 22-23. Yet that "word" must also be closely related to, if not identical to, the "word of truth" through which men and women are regenerated to salvation (v. 18). Taken together, these points suggest that James's "law" does not refer to the law of Moses as such, but to the law of Moses as interpreted and supplemented by Christ.[73] Perhaps, then, the addition of the word "perfect" connotes the law in its eschatological, "perfected" form, while the qualification "that gives freedom" refers to the new covenant promise of the law written on the heart (Jer. 31:31-34; see the comments on v. 21), accompanied by a work of the Spirit enabling obedience to that law for the first time.[74]

The NIV, with many other versions and commentators, takes the second of James's descriptions in this verse — after "the man who looks in-

73. See esp. Mussner, 241-42; Davids, 99-100; Goppelt, 2:203-6; Frankemölle, 203-5. It is less likely that James thinks of the moral examples found in the law (cf. L. T. Johnson, "The Mirror of Remembrance (James 1:22-25)," *CBQ* 50 [1988] 632-45).

74. Hoppe (95-97) suggests that the law brings freedom because the believer is enabled by Christ to fulfill its essence, the love command (see 2:8).

tently" — to be closely tied to that first verb: *continues to do this* (e.g., look intently).[75] This may be right, but it is also possible, with some earlier commentators, to think that the "continuing" has a broader reference, referring to one who, having heard the law, sticks to it by internalizing its message and using it to transform one's life. On this view, all of the next phrase, *not forgetting what he has heard, but doing it,* explains the idea of "continuing." James's Greek has a stronger rhetorical contrast than the smoothed out NIV rendering: "not a hearer of forgetfulness but a doer of work." "Of forgetfulness" is a typical Semitic construction that means "forgetful hearer" (cf. NASB), while "doer of work," a very awkward phrase in Greek or English, is apparently chosen as a rhetorical counterpart to the first phrase. It could mean "active doer,"[76] but more likely it means "one who does work," for example, one who puts into practice the deeds that the law demands.[77] The whole description contrasts with the person described in vv. 23-24, who immediately forgets what he sees in the mirror, neither taking what he has seen to heart nor doing anything about it.

James's addition of qualifying language after "continues" has led him astray from the original syntax of the sentence, so he starts over with "he" (Gk. *houtos,* "this one"). It is the one who looks intently into the law and perseveres in it who is blessed *in what he does.* This last phrase could mean that the person finds blessing as he puts the law into practice. The blessing would then refer to God's goodness and mercy upon people as they live obediently before him in this life. But the blessing is more likely to refer to future blessing — the salvation that comes when one "accepts" the word (v. 21).[78] "In his doing" may, then, have something of a causal flavor: he will be blessed "because he has been a doer."

26 James has grown progressively more practical and specific in his call to respond appropriately to the word of God. "Accept the word" (v. 21) becomes "do the word" (v. 22), which becomes "do the law." Verses 26-27 culminate this progression, as James suggests three ways in which believers can do the word/law. These three manifestations of obedience to the word introduce or touch on key ideas that James will return to again in the letter:

- controlling the tongue — (1:19-20); 3:1-12; 4:11-12
- concern for the "helpless" — 2:1-13, 15-16; cf. 5:1-6
- avoidance of "worldliness" — 4:4-10

75. See Johnson, 209.
76. Moule, 175, taking the genitive *ergou* as descriptive.
77. The genitive would then be objective; see Mayor, 74; Dibelius, 120.
78. Mussner, 110; Davids, 100.

And the idea of these verses — that true religion is manifested in a lifestyle of obedience to God — becomes the leitmotif of the next four chapters. To some extent, then, these verses set the agenda for the rest of the letter.

The words "religious" (v. 26) and "religion" (v. 27) are rare in the NT (Acts 26:5; Col. 2:18); and for much the same reason that many Christians avoid them. For they are very general in meaning, referring to worship in general, and especially often to the outward practice of ceremonies in honor of a god. Among Jewish writers, the words often referred to the cultic worship of the temple. Perhaps James deliberately chooses such broad terms in order to sharpen his point: *anyone* who has a claim to genuine religious experience must submit those claims to these tests.

The first "test," as we have seen, touches on an important theme in OT and Jewish wisdom literature (see 1:19-20): keeping *a tight rein* on the tongue. James is the only biblical author to use the imagery of the reins, or the bridle, in relationship to the tongue (see also 3:2), but the idea is clear enough. The bridle, along with the bit, was the instrument by which the rider controlled his horse, and it is a natural image of both control and direction (see 2 Kings 19:28; Isa. 30:28; 37:29). So a person whose religion is the "genuine article" will manifest that fact by being careful in what he or she says. Failure to control one's speech, James asserts, means that one is "deceiving" oneself about having true religion (see v. 22); that kind of religion is *worthless.* This word translates a Greek word *(mataios)* that is often used in Scripture to characterize idolatry as "vain" or "meaningless" (in the NT, see Acts 14:15; Rom. 1:21; Eph. 4:17; perhaps 1 Pet. 1:18). The "religion" that people who do not control their speech have is no better, James suggests, than idolatry.

27 We would badly misunderstand these verses were we to think that James is intending to summarize here all that true worship of God should involve. As Calvin says, "[James] does not define generally what religion is, but reminds us that religion without the things he mentions is nothing."[79] James is not polemicizing against religious ritual per se but against a ritual that goes no further than outward show and mere words. He is probably somewhat dependent on a widespread pagan and Jewish tradition that emphasized that proper cultic worship must be accompanied by ethical conduct.[80] Specific and concrete actions are needed to demonstrate the reality of one's claim to "have religion." The matters that James mentions in these verses were undoubtedly problems among the

79. Calvin, 299.

80. See D. J. Verseput, "Reworking the Puzzle of Faith and Deeds in James 2.14-26," *NTS* 43 (1997) 101-4.

Christians to whom he is writing. But they are also frequently mentioned in Scripture as key components of a biblical lifestyle. "Looking after widows and orphans" picks up a frequent OT refrain. In the ancient world, with an absence of money-making possibilities for women and any kind of social welfare, widows and orphans were helpless to provide for themselves. A mark of Israel's obedience, therefore, was to be a special concern for these helpless people. The Lord commanded the people: "Do not take advantage of a widow or an orphan" (Exod. 22:22), and the law specified that the people were to go out of their way to provide for the widow and the orphan (Deut. 14:29, passim). Isaiah, in a passage similar in many ways to these verses in James, announces that God will no longer recognize the worship his people offer him; they must repent and "seek justice, encourage the oppressed. Defend the cause of the fatherless, plead the cause of the widow" (Isa. 1:10-17). In these actions, the people of Israel were to imitate God himself, "a Father to the fatherless and defender of widows" (Ps. 68:5). It is probably for this reason that James describes God here as the "Father." One test of pure religion, therefore, is the degree to which we extend aid to the "helpless" in our world — whether they be widows and orphans, immigrants trying to adjust to a new life, impoverished third-world dwellers, the handicapped, or the homeless.

The third mark of true religion is more general than the other two and also less concrete: *to keep oneself from being polluted by the world.* James is careful not to give the impression that religion pleasing to God consists simply in outward acts or in social action. The "world" is a common biblical way of referring to the ungodly worldview and lifestyle that characterize human life in its estrangement from the creator. Christians who have ended that estrangement by accepting the reconciling work of God in Christ must constantly work to distance themselves from the way of life that surrounds us on every side — to keep themselves "spotless" (a literal rendering of the Greek word here) from the world's contaminating influence.

James 2

C. Discrimination against the Poor Violates Kingdom Law (2:1-13)

In this section, James applies many of the key ideas from 1:19-27 to a specific situation: discrimination against poor people within the Christian community. Doing the word (v. 22), "the perfect law" (v. 25), James has argued, includes showing compassion to the helpless (v. 27). By showing favor to the rich and treating the poor with contempt, the believers to whom James writes are acting in direct contradiction to this central demand of God's law. That law, especially as interpreted and applied by Jesus, their Lord and King, has at its heart love for the neighbor (v. 8; cf. 1:25). By discriminating against the poor, these Christians violate that law and thus put themselves in danger of being judged by it (vv. 9-13). In effect, James suggests, their actions suggest that they are among those people who may be "deceived" about the reality of their relationship to God (cf. 1:22, 26).

The command not to discriminate in v. 1 is therefore the main point of the section. In vv. 2-4, a specific example of such discrimination is offered and the conclusion that such action is, indeed, evil is drawn. James then gives three specific reasons why favoritism toward the rich and discrimination against the poor are evil. First, such an attitude stands in contradiction to God's own evaluation, who honors the poor (vv. 5-6a). Second, favoritism toward the rich betrays a fawning, servile mentality — for rich people are the very ones who are persecuting the Christian community (vv. 6b-7). And, third, discrimination against the poor violates the demand of love for the neighbor, the centerpiece of Jesus' reinterpretation of the law of God (vv. 8-13). This last section, besides being the most developed of the three, also begins moving the argument to a new issue. It therefore deserves its own separate section in the outline of the letter.

1. Discrimination in the Community Is Wrong (2:1-7)

1 My brothers, as believers in our glorious Lord Jesus Christ, don't show
favoritism. 2 Suppose a man comes into your meeting wearing a gold ring
and fine clothes, and a poor man in shabby clothes also comes in. 3 If you
show special attention to the man wearing fine clothes and say, "Here's a good seat for you," but say to the poor man, "You stand there" or "Sit on
the floor by my feet," 4 have you not discriminated among yourselves and
become judges with evil thoughts?

5 Listen, my dear brothers: Has not God chosen those who are poor in the eyes of the world to be rich in faith and to inherit the kingdom he promised those who love him?
6 But you have insulted the poor. Is it not the rich who are exploiting you? Are they not the ones who are dragging you into
court? 7 Are they not the ones who are slandering the noble name of him to whom you belong?

The space that James devotes to this matter in his letter suggests that discrimination was a problem among his readers. Yet James leaves us a bit uncertain about just what the problem was and how true to life the situation he describes might have been. The first issue arises because the account of the specific problem in vv. 2-3 could fit at least two different situations. With most commentators in the past, we could assume that he is depicting a typical weekly worship gathering of the Christian community. The "ushers," perhaps with tacit approval from the leaders of the assembly, conduct the splendidly dressed person to a fine seat, while contemptuously ordering a poorly dressed person to sit on the floor. But an alternative suggestion about the scenario James describes has been gaining ground: that the situation is a meeting of the Christian assembly to sit in judgment over a dispute between two of its members.[1] Advocates of this alternative note that James does not describe the situation with the typical language applied to early Christian worship gatherings ("church," *ekklēsia*) and that James specifically accuses his readers of being "judges with evil thoughts" (v. 4). The details of the situation in vv. 2-3 are similar to community judicial settings that the rabbis describe. See, for instance, *b. Shebuot* 31a: "How do we know that, if two come to court, one clothed in rags and the other in fine raiment worth a hundred

1. See esp. R. B. Ward, "Partiality in the Assembly: James 2:2-4," *HTR* 62 (1969) 87-97; Davids, 109; Martin, 57-58; Johnson, 223.

manehs, they should say to him, 'Either dress like him, or dress him like you'"; and *Sifre* 4.4 (on Lev. 19:15): "You must not let one litigant speak as much as he wants, and then say to the other, 'Shorten thy speech.' You must not let one stand and the other sit.'" If this was the situation, the scenario James has in view would correspond to the kind of informal Christian legal proceeding Paul recommends to the Corinthians in 1 Cor. 6:1-8.

The lack of specifics in this text makes a decision between these alternatives difficult; and, fortunately, James's main point is not affected by our decision. On the whole, however, the possessive "your meeting" in v. 2 seems to point to a definite, well-known gathering that better fits the worship service than a judicial assembly.

Whether James suggests that the scenario he describes had actually occurred or whether it is simply an illustration of the kind of problem he is addressing is also unclear. He does use language suggesting a hypothetical situation in vv. 2-3; but v. 6 — "You have insulted the poor" — implies that something like what James describes here had actually taken place.[2]

1 *My brothers* (fellow members of the family of God; see 1:2) again signifies a topic switch (see also 1:2, 16, 19). The Greek of v. 1 is difficult to render straightforwardly into English, and different translations must therefore make certain decisions in order to make sense of the verse at all. The NIV represents the sense of the Greek quite well, but we need to look at some of the decisions that its rendering reflects. "As believers . . . don't show favoritism" would be literally translated "Don't have faith . . . with [or in] favoritism" (NASB, as usual, is the most literal: "do not hold your faith . . . with an attitude of favoritism"). James's way of putting the matter makes clear that discriminating against people is inconsistent with true faith in Christ.

James refers directly to Jesus Christ only twice in his letter (cf. also 1:1); and a few scholars have thought that both are interpolations into an originally purely Jewish document. But no textual basis exists for the removal of the title, and this view is rightly treated by modern scholars as a curiosity of interpretive history. "Lord Jesus Christ" is, of course, a common combination of titles in the NT; but nowhere else is the word "glory" added to the series. This word is in the genitive case in Greek and follows the title "Our Lord Jesus Christ." Commentators attach it to these titles in at least seven different ways, but the most important options are: (1) "Our Lord Jesus Christ, the glorious one"; (2) "Our glorious Lord Jesus Christ" (NRSV; NIV; NLT); or (3) "Our Lord Jesus Christ, the Lord of

2. Martin, 60-61.

glory" (KJV; NASB; TEV). With the first rendering, "glory" is understood as an independent title that further qualifies "Lord Jesus Christ" (an epexegetic genitive). The basis for this interpretation is the common association of "glory" with God in the OT and with both God and Christ in the NT. "The Lord of glory" is a common title in the OT, and is transferred to Jesus in the NT (1 Cor. 2:8). And the word "glory" (translating the Heb. *kabōd*) can signify God's presence (see, e.g., 1 Sam. 4:22). In the NT, Peter uses the word "glory" to refer to God in describing the transfiguration: "[Jesus] received honor and glory from God the Father when the voice came from the Majestic Glory, saying . . ." (2 Pet. 1:17; see also Heb. 1:3; Rom. 9:4). And the NT authors ascribe the same glory to Christ (e.g., John 1:14). James, then, might be following a common NT pattern, in which attributes and titles given to God in the OT are applied also to Jesus Christ. As the manifestation of God's presence, he is "the glorious one."[3]

However, this interpretation, while theologically unobjectionable, suffers from a key difficulty: never in the OT or in the NT is the word "glory" used by itself as a title of God or of Christ.[4] This makes it unlikely that it has this significance here. On the other hand, the grammatical basis for the second alternative — "glorious Lord" — is very solid, the descriptive genitive being a favorite construction in James. On this view, James is attributing to the Lord Jesus the quality of splendor that is peculiar to God himself.[5] The third translation is the most ambiguous of the three, leaving it unclear just how the word "glory" relates to Lord. And for this reason, it is probably the best alternative. "Glory" has enough theological significance in its own right in the NT that turning it into a simple adjective — "glorious" — might weaken the sense James intends here. "Glory" is that state of "being-like-God" to which Christians are destined (e.g., Rom. 5:2; 8:18; 2 Cor. 4:17) and in which Jesus even now exists (Phil. 3:21; Col. 3:4; 2 Thess. 2:14; 1 Tim. 3:16; Tit. 2:13; Heb. 2:7, 9). Describing Jesus as *the Lord of glory* suggests particularly the heavenly sphere to which he has been exalted and from which he will come at the end of history to save and to judge (cf. Jas. 5:9). This reminder is particularly appropriate in a situation where Christians are giving too much "glory" to human beings.

A person who has faith in this Lord of glory, James insists, should not *show favoritism*. The NIV's "favoritism" comes from a Greek word

3. Mayor, 80-81; Hort, 47-48; Laws, 94-97; Tasker, 56-57; Adamson, 103-4.

4. Ps. 29:9 and Acts 7:55 are possible, but unlikely, exceptions.

5. Ropes, 187-88; Cantinat, 120-21; Dibelius, 127-28; Davids, 106-7; Mussner, 116; Martin, 60.

that means, literally, "receiving the face." The word was apparently invented by NT writers (see also Rom. 2:11; Eph. 6:9; Col. 3:25; related words are found in Jas. 2:9; Acts 10:34; 1 Pet. 1:17) as a literal rendering of a Hebrew word for partiality. To "receive the face" means to make judgments about people based on external appearance. James applies this principle to differences in dress that reflect contrasting social/economic situations. But the Greek word here is plural — "acts of favoritism" (NRSV) — and this makes clear that the prohibition has wide-ranging application. We are not to make decisions about people based on any external factor — whether it be dress, color of skin, or general physical appearance. The OT repeatedly stresses that God himself is impartial, looking at the heart rather than at the outside of a person, and God's people are to imitate him in this respect. In a passage that is echoed many times in the OT and which touches on many of the same issues James is concerned about in 1:21–2:26, Moses reminds the Israelites that "the LORD your God is God of gods and Lord of lords, the great God, mighty and awesome, who shows no partiality and accepts no bribes. He defends the cause of the fatherless and the widow, and loves the alien, giving him food and clothing" (Deut. 10:17-18). Even more pertinent may be Lev. 19:15: "Do not pervert justice; do not show partiality to the poor or favoritism to the great, but judge your neighbor fairly." For this text occurs in the same context from which James cites the famous "love command" in v. 8 (Lev. 19:18).[6]

2 James now gives an example of the favoritism that he has condemned in v. 1. Verses 2-4 is one conditional sentence in Greek, vv. 2-3 forming the protasis (the "if" clause) and v. 4 the apodosis (the "then" clause). The form of the condition suggests that James is giving a hypothetical example of the kind of behavior that he warns against. But the sequel to the example (vv. 6-7) makes clear that the readers were engaging in discrimination very much like this.

The scenario is a "meeting." The Greek word is *synagōgē,* used widely by the Jews to denote the place where they met for worship, instruction, and encouragement in their faith. Some think James's use of the word here indicates that he was writing to Jewish Christians who were still attending Jewish synagogue meetings.[7] Good evidence for this interpretation comes from the NT use of the word *synagōgē,* which everywhere else refers to the Jewish house of worship (fifty-five other occurrences, all but two in historical narratives in the Gospels and Acts). But James's qualification of this "synagogue" as "your synagogue" implies

6. See esp. Johnson, "Leviticus 19," 391-401.

7. Adamson, 105.

that Christians had control over the meetings. Another possibility, then, is to think that James uses the word in its more general sense, a "gathering" or an "assembly" (so most English translations). This assembly might be a gathering of the community to adjudicate a dispute between two of its members or, more likely, the weekly meeting for worship and instruction (see the introduction to this section). Jewish Christians who had recently embraced Jesus as their Messiah would naturally carry over into their new covenant worship the terms and conventions familiar to them from their past experience — even as they began using more technical "Christian" terms as well (cf. "church" in 5:14). *Synagōgē* is used of an "assembly" of Christians ("righteous men") in Hermas, *Mandates* 11.9.

Into this meeting come two people, distinguished from each other by their dress. One is *wearing a gold ring and fine clothes.* The "gold ring" was an emblem of the upper-level Roman "equestrian" class, although James may not intend quite so specific an identification. "Fine" translates a Greek word that means "bright, shining" and is applied, for instance, to the clothing of heavenly beings (Acts 10:30; Rev. 15:6). In stark contrast is a *poor man in shabby clothes.* "Shabby" translates a word from the same root as the word James used in 1:21 to characterize the sinful "filth" that Christians must put off. The image James conjures up is of the typical homeless person in our day, dressed in mismatched, stained, and smelly rags.

3 Since both these people have to be told where to go after entering the meeting, they may be visitors.[8] That visitors sometimes attended early Christian worship services is implied by 1 Cor. 14:23. But it may be more likely that we are to think of these two people as new converts.[9] Those greeting the well-dressed person show "special attention" to him by conducting him to a good seat. The verb translated "show attention" can mean simply "look at" but often has the connotation of "look at with favor," "have regard for" (as in both other occurrences of the word in the NT: Luke 1:48; 9:38). The poor person, on the other hand, is treated with disdain and even contempt, and told to *stand there* or *sit on the floor by my feet.* The exact Greek text is unclear at this point, many good manuscripts adding the equivalent of the word "here" in the second command (see REB: "you stand over there, or sit here on the floor by my footstool").[10] But a greater difficulty is that the Greek for the second command is "sit under my footstool" (see KJV). Since footstools were very low to the ground, it is impossible to imagine a person getting under one of them.

8. Ropes, 191; Tasker, 57.
9. Martin, 62; Frankemölle, 387-88.
10. This reading is preferred by Metzger, 680; cf. also Johnson, 223.

Most commentators agree, therefore, that the NIV paraphrase (found in almost all modern English translations) gets at the sense: the person is being told to sit on the floor next to the footstool.[11] In any case, the situation is clear enough: Christians in positions of some authority in the community (the verb "show special attention" is in the plural) are fawning over the rich and treating the poor with disdain and contempt.

4 In the second part of his conditional sentence, James now characterizes the conduct he has described in vv. 2-3. He gives his verdict in two clauses, each in the form of a question that expects a "yes" answer. (Greek uses the particle *ou* to indicate this kind of a question; we accomplish the same thing in English by using the word "not"). Logically, then, the questions are equivalent to assertions (cf. TEV: "you are guilty of creating distinctions among yourselves and making judgments based on evil motives"). James's first accusation uses a form of the verb *diakrinō,* which has two meanings that would make sense in this context: "separate, make distinctions" and "doubt, waver." The NIV, along with most other modern translations and commentators, adopts the former meaning: *have you not discriminated among yourselves?* (see also NRSV; NASB; REB; NLT; TEV; NJB).[12] This meaning of the verb is certainly attested in the NT (see, most clearly, Acts 15:9) and obviously fits the context. But it does not advance James's argument very far, since this conclusion was obvious on the face of the matter. The second interpretation might then be the better option. The verb frequently refers to an internal attitude of doubt in the NT (e.g., Matt. 21:21; Mark 11:23; Acts 10:20; Rom. 4:20; 14:23; Jude 22). More importantly, James has already used the verb with just this meaning (1:6) to introduce a key motif in his letter: the warning to Christians not to have a divided heart in their relationship to God and to one another. "Among yourselves" would then be translated "in yourselves," James's point being that the discrimination exhibited in the community is another manifestation of a wavering, divided attitude toward God.[13] The improper "division" being made between rich and poor reflects the improper "divisions" harbored in the minds of the believers. Consistently *Christian* conduct comes only from a consistently *Christian* heart and mind.

Christians who discriminate in the manner James has depicted in vv. 2-3, second, are *judges with evil thoughts.* The reference to "judges" might suggest that the "meeting" that James describes is some kind of judicial setting (see the notes in the introduction to this section). But James

11. See esp. Mayor, 84.

12. Mayor, 85; Dibelius, 136-37; Tasker, 58; Laws, 102; Davids, 110.

13. See esp. Ropes, 192-93; Hort, 50; Mussner, 119; Johnson, 223.

may also be influenced by the apparent OT source for his imagery, Lev. 19:15, which condemns partiality in the context of a judicial dispute. He may also be using the very word "judges" with a pejorative sense. In 4:11-12, he condemns Christians who speak against other believers of taking upon themselves the rights of a "judge" that only God can legitimately exercise. When Christians show favoritism toward people in the assembly, they implicitly claim God's own right to stand in judgment over other people. But James's addition of the phrase *with evil thoughts* leaves no doubt about the negative nature of this "judging." The NIV rendering suggests that the judges are characterized by evil motives (see NLT; TEV). This is a perfectly acceptable rendering, since the Greek word involved *(dialogismos)* often refers to "thoughts" in the NT (Matt. 15:19; Mark 7:21; Luke 2:35; 5:22; 6:8; Rom. 1:21; 1 Cor. 3:20). But the "thought" would refer more definitely to the sinful standards that the judges are using to make their decisions (cf. REB; NJB)[14] or even to the verdicts that the judges reach.[15]

5 *Listen, my dear brothers* signals a shift in focus and emphasizes the importance of what James is about to say (see, e.g., Deut. 6:3; Isa. 1:10; Mark 4:3; 7:14; Acts 2:22; 7:2; 13:16; 15:13). Having illustrated and condemned in vv. 2-4 the discrimination that he prohibits in v. 1, James now explains why such favoritism is wrong.

First, favoritism toward the rich is wrong because it contradicts God's own attitude, as revealed in his gracious election to salvation. A full discussion of NT election is quite unnecessary in order to understand this text. Suffice it to say that James joins other NT writers in attributing the Christian's status to God's choice (the verb James employs here is used in this sense also in 1 Cor. 1:27, 28; Eph. 1:4). James assumes that his readers are well aware of the many poor people who have embraced Jesus as their Messiah. Their conversion is powerful evidence of God's deep regard for poor people. In a stark reversal of status, poor people have become *rich in faith.* "In" here designates the sphere in which the wealth of these believers now is to be found. Expanding on the meaning of this spiritual wealth, James adds that they will also *inherit the kingdom that he promised to those who love him.* The one who has promised the kingdom — *he* — is probably God, the subject of the sentence. But it is possible that James also has in mind Jesus' beatitude: "Blessed are you poor, for yours is the kingdom of God" (Luke 6:20; cf. Matt. 5:3). The kingdom, or reign, of God is central to the preaching of Jesus. He presented himself

14. Turner, 213.

15. BAGD, noting that the word has this meaning in secular Greek, suggest this as a possibility; cf. also BDF ¶165; Laws, 102.

as the one through whom God's reign was even then being realized (Matt. 12:28; Mark 1:15; Luke 17:21). But the fullness of its power and the riches of its blessings are still future: it is "when the Son of man comes in his glory, and all the angels with him," that faithful servants receive their "inheritance, the kingdom prepared . . . from the foundation of the world" (Matt. 25:31, 34). NT writers followed Jesus' lead, often using the language of "inheriting the kingdom" to describe this final establishment of God's kingly power in the lives of his people (1 Cor. 6:9, 10; 15:50; Gal. 5:21; Eph. 5:5). Christians, however poor in material possessions they may be, possess spiritual wealth presently and anticipate greater blessings in the future. It is from this spiritual vantage-point, not the material, that Christians should judge others. Whether believers or unbelievers, people should not be evaluated by Christians according to the standards of the world.

James's general point in this verse, then, is clear enough: God's choice of poor people to inherit his kingdom is evidence of his regard for them and shows how wrong Christians are to discriminate against these very poor people. But this argument raises a serious question. Is James condemning one form of discrimination by replacing it with another? That is, does James picture God here as one who discriminates in his election in favor of the poor and, therefore, implicitly, against the rich? This question introduces one of the most controversial aspects of the theology of James. The reader should consult the Introduction for a general discussion of this issue, but we must assess here the specific contribution of this text. Two matters are especially important: the connotation of the word "poor" and the breadth of James's assertion.

The Greek word *ptōchos* has a range of meaning in biblical Greek. Clearly, it often designates simply people who are poor in a strict material sense: those who do not have much money. But its use in the OT to translate the Hebrew word *'anaw* (and esp. its plural, *'anawim*) introduces a second nuance. For the Hebrew words refer to people who are "poor" in a spiritual sense: humble and meek, recognizing their utter dependence on the Lord and trusting him for deliverance (see esp. Ps. 69:32; Isa. 29:19; 61:1; Amos 2:7, all of which use *ptōchos* in the LXX). The word *ptōchos,* in other words, has both a material and a spiritual meaning. In the former sense, its antonym is "wealthy"; in the latter sense, its antonym is "wicked." Jesus' teaching exhibits this duality of meaning, as is seen most clearly in the two forms of the beatitude: "Blessed are the poor" (Luke 6:20); "Blessed are the poor in spirit" (Matt. 5:3). In many NT texts, it is very difficult to decide which of these meanings — or, more often, which combination of these meanings — we should give the term. The illustration of vv. 2-3 makes clear that the word in v. 5 must have some degree of material significance. But the qualification James adds to the word raises the possibility of other nuances. Just what this qualification is must first be established, because the text is uncertain. Many good manuscripts have the genitive of the word *kosmos,* "world," leading to the translation "of the world," or "of this world" (see KJV; NASB; TEV). But other, probably slightly superior, manuscripts have a dative form of the same word, which gives rise to two possible renderings: "in the world" (NRSV; NLT);[16] or "in the eyes of the world" (NIV; see also REB).[17] This latter text, translated in the way the NIV does, should probably be accepted. It is according to the evaluation of the world, non-Christian people hostile to God, that these people are accounted "poor." While certainly not eliminating the material sense from the word "poor," this interpretation does suggest that the word also has a spiritual sense.[18]

Second, how broadly are we to take James's claim that *God has chosen those who are poor in the eyes of the world to be rich in faith?* Some interpreters, particularly advocates of liberation theology, suggest a very broad interpretation: God chooses only poor people for salvation, while wealthy people are excluded.[19] But this interpretation is possible only if we ignore the many NT passages — including one, we have argued, in James itself (1:10-11) — that include wealthy people in the church. It also reads into the text a word — "only" — that James simply does not use. James writes to a Christian community that is made up largely of poor people; and for them it was evident on every side that God was choosing poor people to be saved. But to infer from James's positive assertion about poor people a negative verdict on rich people — God does not choose rich people to have faith — is unwarranted. Balance is perilously difficult to maintain on this issue. If liberation theologians err on one side, it is all too easy for me and other Western Christians to err on the other. For James's claim that God chooses the poor to receive his kingdom echoes a rather persistent NT theme. The coming of Messiah, Mary announces, echoing OT language, will mean a reversal of fortunes for the people of the world:

> "he has scattered those who are proud in their inmost thoughts.
> He has brought down rulers from their thrones
> but has lifted up the humble.
> He has filled the hungry with good things
> but has sent the rich away empty." (Luke 1:51b-53)

16. This translation assumes that the dative indicates sphere.

17. This translation takes the dative as a dative of reference or "ethical" dative (see Turner, 238; Ropes, 193-94; Martin, 64).

18. Davids, 111-12; Martin, 64-65. See also Penner, 270-73.

19. See, e.g., Tamez, 31-32.

Luke sounds this reversal theme throughout his Gospel. Similarly, Paul reminds the Corinthians:

> Brothers, think of what you were when you were called. Not many of you were wise by human standards; not many were influential; not many were of noble birth. But God chose the foolish things of the world to shame the wise; God chose the weak things of the world to shame the strong. He chose the lowly things of this world and the despised things — and the things that are not — to nullify the things that are, so that no one may boast before him. (1 Cor. 1:26-29)

God, the NT suggests, delights especially to shower his grace on those whom the world has discarded and on those who are most keenly aware of their own inadequacy. James calls on the church to embody a similar ethic of special concern for the poor and the helpless.

6 The beginning of v. 6 is the continuation of the argument of v. 5. God shows his regard to the poor by choosing them for his kingdom (v. 5); *but you have insulted the poor.* "Insulted" could also be translated "dishonored" (NASB; NRSV; TEV), which provides in some ways a better contrast with v. 5. Those whom God "honors" the church "dishonors."

James's first reason, then, for prohibiting discrimination against the poor is that it manifests an attitude contrary to that of God. His second reason, found in vv. 6b-7, takes the form of three parallel questions, each expecting a positive answer. These questions appear at first to be suggesting a very pragmatic, *quid pro quo* kind of ethic. Don't give any favor to the rich, James seems to be saying, because they don't deserve it. They have mistreated you, and you would be foolish to repay such actions with kindness. But James is not counseling the Christians not to be kind to these rich people; he is simply arguing that they should not give undue deference to them at the expense of the poor. Perhaps some believers were calculating that excessive flattery of rich people who visited the assembly might gain favor for them. If so, James suggests, their calculations are far off.

James therefore first asks, *Is it not the rich who are exploiting you?* James, as we have seen, treats the majority of the Christians to whom he writes as poor. Contributing to this poverty, he now suggests, are the immoral and perhaps illegal practices of rich people. The strongly marked socioeconomic class distinction presupposed here corresponds closely to what we know of conditions in the first-century Middle East. A small group of wealthy landowners and merchants accumulated more and more power, while large numbers of people were forced from their land and grew even poorer. Most of James's readers probably belonged to this class of poor agricultural laborers. The scenario is one that would be very familiar to readers of the OT. The prophets frequently denounce (even using the same verb James uses here, *katadynasteuō*) rich people who "oppress" the poor (Amos 4:1), including orphans and widows (Ezek. 22:7).

The second accusation James makes against the rich — *they . . . are dragging you into court* — is closely related to the first. These rich people were undoubtedly using their wealth and influence with the courts to secure favorable verdicts against the poor. Practices familiar in every age, such as forcing people to forfeit their land for late payment of mortgages, insisting on ruinous interest rates for any monetary help, and the like, are probably in view.

7 The third example of the oppressive practices of the rich moves from the economic sphere to the religious: the rich *are slandering the noble name of him to whom you belong*. Indeed, the two may not have been clearly separated, as religious differences may have played a role in the decisions of the rich to oppress the poor and defenseless Christian community. The "slander" directed against Christians may have taken several different forms. The word James uses is *blasphēmeō,* from which we get the word "blaspheme." In its deepest sense, the word connotes a violation, usually in speech, of God's own person (see, e.g., Matt. 9:3; 26:65; Mark 3:28-29). But it can be extended to include any slander that involves God, even indirectly — such as criticism directed against Christian behavior by other believers (1 Cor. 10:30; Rom. 14:16) or abuse heaped on believers by unbelievers over differences in morality (1 Pet. 4:4). Because James supplies so little information, we can only speculate about the exact situation here. It may have been Gentiles profanely mocking the God whom believers claimed to worship. It may have been Jews criticizing Christian claims about Jesus. Or, more generally, it may have involved unbelievers making fun of Christian morality and worship practices (such as the Lord's Supper).

The specific object of the unbelievers' slander is *the noble name of him to whom you belong.* The NIV is a good paraphrase for a Greek construction impossible to translate directly into English: "the good name which has been called upon you." The construction, which is not good Greek either, betrays its Semitic origins (see, e.g., Amos 9:9, quoted in Acts 15:17). To have a name "called" on someone suggests the idea of ownership; hence the NIV rendering. Whose is the "good" or "honorable" (Gk. *kalos*) name bestowed on believers? One possibility is "Christian" (cf. 1 Pet. 4:14, 16), but the concept of ownership that is suggested by the language makes this possibility unlikely. Probably James intends either God or, more likely, Christ (in light of v. 1). Some see an allusion here to the baptismal ceremony, in which the name of Christ was solemnly pronounced over and, in a sense, "transferred" to the believer. But this is not clear.

2. *Discrimination Is Wrong Because It Violates the Kingdom Law of Love (2:8-13)*

8 If you really keep the royal law found in the Scripture, "Love your neighbor as yourself," you are doing right. 9 But if you show favoritism, you sin and are convicted by the law as lawbreakers. 10 For whoever keeps the whole law and yet stumbles at just one point is guilty of breaking all of it. 11 For he who said, "Do not commit adultery," also said, "Do not murder." If you do not commit adultery but do commit murder, you have become a lawbreaker.

12 Speak and act as those who are going to be judged by the law that gives freedom, 13 because judgment without mercy will be shown to anyone who has not been merciful. Mercy triumphs over judgment!

In vv. 5-7, James has argued that favoritism toward the rich at the expense of the poor is wrong because (1) it contradicts God's regard for the poor; and (2) it makes no sense. The former reason is theological, while the second is more (but not completely) pragmatic. But the attention James devotes to the matter suggests that his third argument against such favoritism is the most important: it violates the law of love (vv. 8-13). The main point comes at the beginning, in vv. 8-9: partiality is sinful because it violates the love command. Verses 10-11 justify James's assertion that committing one sin, such as showing favoritism, can turn one into a "lawbreaker" by insisting on the indivisibility of the law. Some of James's readers might be questioning the importance that he gives to obedience to the law in these verses. So, in the concluding verses of this paragraph, James insists that believers will have to account for their actions against the standard of God's law. This emphasis on obedience as the criterion in the judgment both returns to the "true religion" theme with which this section opened (1:21-27) and anticipates the "true faith seen in works" argument of 2:14-26.

8 The connection between v. 8 and the preceding verses is forged with a Greek word *(mentoi)* that could be translated either *really* (NIV; NRSV; the NLT "indeed" is similar) or "however" (NASB; REB). A decision is difficult because usage favors the latter rendering while context favors the former. The word in question has an adversative meaning in all seven of its other NT occurrences (John 4:27; 7:13; 12:42; 20:5; 21:4; 2 Tim. 2:19; Jude 8). But it is not easy to give v. 8 an adversative relationship to its context. The best we can do is to think that v. 8 contrasts with v. 6a: "you have insulted the poor . . . *however,* if you fulfill the royal law, you do well."[20] This connection is pretty distant, however. So, since the sense of

20. Defenders of an adversative sense here include BDF ¶450(1); Davids, 114; Mayor, 89; Mussner, 123.

"really" or "indeed" is attested for the word,[21] we should probably prefer this alternative.[22]

James makes his point in vv. 8-9 by contrasting two conditional sentences:

If you really keep the royal law . . .	*you are doing well.*
But if you show favoritism	*you sin. . . .*

The concept of "keeping the law" is, of course, very common in the OT, Judaism, and the NT (although the actual verb James uses [*teleō*] occurs with this sense only in Luke 2:39 and Rom. 2:27); and almost always with reference to the law of Moses. And since James quotes a commandment from the Mosaic law to illustrate his point, we might well conclude that a reference to that law here is clear. But several other considerations suggest that the reference may be more nuanced.

First, we note the use of the adjective "royal." The word could also be translated "supreme" or "governing"; and some take it to introduce the following love command. James would then be claiming that his commandment was the specific "law" that governs, or takes precedence, over all others.[23] This interpretation is enshrined in the NJB translation: "Well, the right thing to do is to keep the supreme Law of scripture: 'you will love your neighbor as yourself.'" However, while the interpretation squares well with Jesus' teaching about the love command, the Greek word used here can probably not bear the meaning "governing" or "supreme." This term means "belonging to the king." Philo, commenting on Num. 20:17, strikingly compares the "royal road" mentioned in that verse to the law of God. He argues that the road is "royal" both because it belongs to God and because it leads to him, and claims that the law has the same properties (*Posterity and Exile of Cain* 101-2). NT usage, while sparse, similarly suggests the simple meaning "royal" (John 4:46, 49; Acts 12:20, 21). Even with this meaning, James could intend to identify the "royal law" with the love commandment that follows.[24] But this view has against it the fact that "law" in the NT usually refers to an entire body of commandments rather than to a single commandment. And the argument of vv. 10-11 would seem to assume this broader application of the term. More important for our immediate question is the proximity of "royal" to the related word "kingdom" *(basileia)* in v. 5. Combined with Jesus' focus on the love command of Lev. 19:18 (Matt. 22:34-40 and par.),

21. See LSJ, 1102.
22. So most commentators.
23. Hort, 53.
24. Laws, 108-9.

this suggests that James intends "royal" to connote the law pertaining to the kingdom of God. As with the phrase "the perfect law that gives freedom" in 1:25, then, "royal law" might be James's way of referring to the sum total of demands that God, through Jesus, imposes on believers: "the whole law as interpreted and handed over to the church in the teaching of Jesus."[25] Understood in this sense, the "royal law" may well extend beyond the Mosaic law as fulfilled and reinterpreted by Jesus to include the teaching of Jesus.

The NIV translation poses a difficulty for the view that "royal law" denotes broadly all the commandments incumbent on Christians. For the phrase *found in Scripture* seems to identify the royal law with the love command. However, the NIV rendering may not be justified. The Greek phrase uses the preposition normally translated "according to" (*kata;* cf. the more literal renderings in NASB and NRSV). What James might be suggesting, then, is that completing the sum total of God's will for his people (the moral law) takes place in accordance with conformity to the central demand of that law, love for the neighbor.[26]

James's suggestion that the love command stands at the heart of the NT ethical code goes back, of course, to Jesus' teaching. When asked to identify the "greatest commandment" in the law, he responded:

> "'Love the Lord your God with all your heart and with all your soul and with all your mind.' This is the first and greatest commandment. And the second is like it: 'Love your neighbor as yourself.' All the Law and the Prophets hang on these two commandments." (Matt. 22:37-40)

Jesus' teaching on this point had an enduring impact on the way the early Christians understood their new covenant obligations, especially in relationship to the OT law (Gal. 5:13-14; Rom. 13:8-10). In the OT, the *neighbor (rēʿa)* means particularly the fellow Israelite, but Jesus expands the application to include everyone with whom a person might come into contact, including foreigners (Luke 10:25-37) and enemies (Matt. 5:44). James is in line with that teaching as he argues that love for the neighbor, the heart of "the royal law," forbids the church from discriminating against any who might enter its doors. And James's application of this love command to the problem of favoritism finds a solid contextual basis in Leviticus 19, where a prohibition of partiality occurs just three verses before the command to love the neighbor (compare Lev. 19:15 and 19:18).[27]

9 James's encouragement to believers to "do well" by completing

25. Davids, 114. See also Johnson, 230; Frankemölle, 400-402.
26. See Johnson, 230-31, for a similar view.
27. See esp. Johnson, "Leviticus 19," for this point.

the royal law, epitomized in the love command, has no clear connection to its context. But that verse, as we have seen, does not function by itself; it is the first part of an argument that is completed in v. 9. And the return to the subject of favoritism in this verse shows that James has not left the topic that he introduced in v. 1. Implicit in the logic of James's argument is the assumption, perhaps drawn from Leviticus 19, that favoritism violates the demand of love for the neighbor. And so he can accuse those who show favoritism of committing sin and label them "lawbreakers." *Show favoritism* translates a verb, used only here in the NT, that comes from the same root as the word "favoritism" in v. 1. *You sin* is the NIV abbreviation of a longer clause in Greek, lit., "you are working sin." Johnson notes that, while James views "works" very positively, he uses the verb "work" only in a negative sense (cf. also 1:20: "man's anger does not bring about ['work'] the righteous life that God desires"). Love for the neighbor, extended by Jesus to all people, including those different from us (Luke 10:25-37; Matt. 5:43-47), requires that poor, shabbily dressed people be given as much respect and attention as the well-dressed and prominent. And extending James's principle, the love command also requires that we enthusiastically welcome into our church meetings people from other races, and that we give as much deference to people with no status in the community as we do to famous politicians, actors, or athletes. In Christ, as Paul puts it, "there is neither Jew nor Greek, slave nor free, male nor female" (Gal. 3:28). In obedience to their king, Jesus, Christians are to build among themselves a genuine counterculture, in which the values of the kingdom of God rather than the values of this world are lived out.

Since favoritism violates the command of love, the heart of kingdom law, the final conclusion James draws in this verse follows as a matter of strict logic: believers who show favoritism are *convicted by the law as lawbreakers.* The verb translated "convict" *(elenchō)* often means "reprove" (a sinner; cf. Matt. 18:15) or "refute" (opponents; cf. Tit. 1:9), but sometimes (as here) it has the legal sense of "convict" (of wrongdoing; cf. also John 8:46; 16:8; 1 Cor. 14:24; Jude 15). It is the law that does the convicting, since its standards are violated when favoritism is shown. Such believers are, indeed, "lawbreakers," or "transgressors" (NASB; NRSV) — the technical NT term for a person who directly disobeys a positive command (see also v. 11; Rom. 2:25, 27; Gal. 2:18; and note the use of the related term "transgression" in Rom. 2:23; 4:15; 5:14; Gal. 3:19; 1 Tim. 2:14; Heb. 2:2; 9:15).

10 In vv. 10-11 James justifies *(for)* the last clause of v. 9 by showing that the breaking of even one commandment incurs guilt for the law as a whole. We are presented with a chain of reasoning that leads at the end of

v. 11 to the same accusation James has already leveled in v. 9 — Christians who show favoritism are "transgressors of the law." James's assertion of the law's unity is nothing new, for Jews and even pagans had frequently made the same point. The Roman moralist Seneca, for instance, claims in his treatise *De beneficiis* that "he who has one vice has all."[28] But it is of course the Jewish version of this teaching that is most relevant for James. See, for instance, the response of the pious Eleazar when commanded to eat forbidden food: "Do not suppose that it would be a petty sin if we were to eat defiling food; to transgress the law in matters either small or great is of equal seriousness, for in either case the law is equally despised" (4 Macc. 5:20-21; see also *b. Horayot* 8b; *b. Shabbat* 70b; 1QS 8:16; *T. Asher* 2:5-10; Philo, *Allegorical Interpretation* 3.241). Paul reflects the same tradition in Gal. 5:3: "I declare to every man who lets himself be circumcised that he is obligated to obey the whole law." But especially significant, as is usually the case for James, is Jesus' teaching: "I tell you the truth, until heaven and earth disappear, not the smallest letter, not the least stroke of a pen, will by any means disappear from the Law until everything is accomplished. Anyone who breaks one of the least of these commandments and teaches others to do the same will be called least in the kingdom of heaven" (Matt. 5:18-19).

James signals that he is citing proverbial truth in vv. 10-11 by interrupting the second person plural direct address of vv. 8-10 and 12-13 with the third person singular style of "customary" or "gnomic" truth *(whoever . . .).* The hypothetical nature of the situation makes it unnecessary to follow Johnson in giving a conative sense to the verb "keep" (e.g., "undertakes keeping the whole law"). James is not suggesting that anyone is in reality fulfilling every demand of the law; he simply puts forth a "suppose it were so" assumption. That person, were he to "stumble" (i.e., fail to obey; cf. 3:2; Rom. 11:11; 2 Pet. 1:10) at even one "point" (or commandment), is *guilty of breaking all of it.* The NIV rendering here is very appropriate. Some versions simply translate "have become a transgressor of the law" (NRSV), but leave out the notion of judicial guilt that the word James uses here seems to have (*enochos;* cf. six of the seven other NT occurrences: Matt. 5:21, 22; 26:66; Mark 3:29; 14:64; 1 Cor. 11:27; Heb. 2:15 is less clear).

11 James now explains why the law is an indivisible unity. As Johnson puts it, "Critical to the argument is that the commandment is not just a text but 'someone speaking'."[29] If we view the law as a series of individual commandments, we could assume that disobedience of a partic-

28. M. O'Rourke Boyle, "The Stoic Paradox of James 2:10," *NTS* 31 (1985) 611-17.
29. Johnson, 232.

ular commandment incurred guilt for that commandment only. But, in fact, the individual commandments are part and parcel of one indivisible whole, because they reflect the will of the one Lawgiver. To violate a commandment is to disobey God himself and render a person guilty before him.

The commandments James uses to illustrate his point come, of course, from the Decalogue. He reverses the order in which they are found in the OT (see Exod. 20:13-14; Deut. 5:17-18), but they do occur in this order in at least one important manuscript of the Septuagint (Vaticanus, B; see also Luke 18:20; Rom. 13:9). However, James may not intend to follow the order of any text but rather the dictates of his own logic. The prohibition of "murder," on this line of reasoning, is cited not haphazardly as a well-known example but because James finds it to be particular apropos to the situation of his readers. Martin suggests the possibility of a literal application, on the assumption that James's readers were embroiled in the internecine Jewish strife that preceded the war of rebellion against Rome.[30] But this scenario is unlikely (see the Introduction). It is more likely that James's reference to the prohibition of murder presumes the "deepening" of its sense that Jesus gave it (Matt. 5:21-26). Anger, Jesus taught, is also "covered" in his reinterpretation of the commandment; and James may see the favoritism being shown in the community as an instance of this kind of anger, or disregard of others, and so tantamount to "murder." Perhaps, then, he intends to single out people in his community who may be priding themselves on their avoidance of "sins of the flesh" (adultery) all the while they are discriminating against poor people and de facto committing murder.[31] While a very attractive interpretation, we must admit that the text does not provide the evidence we would need to commit ourselves to it. James may, after all, simply be citing these two commandments as representative examples (as did, e.g., Paul [Rom. 13:9]).

As we have noted above, then, the logic of these verses is thoroughly Jewish. But just how "Jewish" is James? Pressed to its logical conclusion, James's argument would require obedience to every single commandment of the law, including the requirements concerning ceremonial observances. Is this what James intends? Nothing in his letter would suggest that he holds so strict a view. And he does give us a hint within vv. 10-11 that this is not the case. Generally when Jewish theologians made the point that James makes in v. 11, they cited a "light" commandment to set beside a "heavy" one. Thus Eleazar, in the 4 Maccabees text quoted

30. Martin, 70.
31. See Hort, 55.

above, asserts that eating defiling food (a "small" matter) is equally as serious as disobedience of a "great" commandment. But James cites two Decalogue commandments, of supposedly equal "weight." He therefore suggests that he is thinking only of some parts of the OT law in vv. 10-11. Corroboration of this suggestion comes from early Christianity, where the love command was closely associated with the "fellowman" commandments of the second table of the Decalogue (see Matt. 19:18-19; Rom. 13:8-10). Therefore, while employing logic drawn from the OT and Jewish orthodoxy, James applies it to a new situation. It is not the OT law per se that he urges perfect compliance with, but "the royal law" (v. 8), "the law of liberty" (v. 12; cf. 1:25). This "law" takes up within it the OT law, but as understood through Jesus' fulfillment of it. And so just as Jesus' apparent unqualified endorsement of the law (Matt. 5:18-19, quoted above) is tempered in the context by his claim to be the fulfiller of the law (v. 17), so James applies this standard point about the law's unity to the law as reinterpreted by Jesus (see v. 8 and our comments there).

12 After a detour to solidify his claim that people who show favoritism are "lawbreakers" (vv. 10-11), James now takes up his exhortation once again: *Speak and act as those who are going to be judged by the law that gives freedom.* Both "speak" and "act" are in a Greek tense that stresses the continuing nature of these actions: "be constantly speaking," "always be acting." And the Greek text puts even more emphasis on the need for Christians to regulate their conduct with an eye on the judgment to come; literally rendered, it says, "Speak in such a manner and act in such a manner as those who are about to be judged by the law of liberty." With these commands, James returns to the dominant theme in this section of the letter: the need for believers to validate the reality of their "religion" by "doing" the word (1:22). But a new twist is added here. For the first time, James warns about eschatological judgment and suggests that conformity to the demands of the law will be the criterion of that judgment. He therefore anticipates the controversial teaching of 2:14-26, where he argues that "doing" ("works") is necessary if one wants to experience God's justifying verdict.

This teaching about judgment according to the law might seem theologically difficult. Hort is not the only commentator who tries to get around the perceived problem: ". . . the sense would seem to be not that the law of liberty is the standard or the instrument by which they are to be judged, but that they are to be judged as men who have lived in an atmosphere, as it were, of a law of liberty. . . ."[32] But the preposition James uses here (Gk. *dia,* translated *by* in the NIV) cannot refer merely to the "atmosphere" of the

32. Hort, 56.

law. Its normal instrumental sense fits perfectly well in the verse; and we find the preposition used in similar contexts with this meaning elsewhere: for example, Rom. 2:12b: "all who sin under the law will be judged by the law." We do need to remember, as we have shown repeatedly in this section (see the notes esp. on 1:25 and 2:8) that the law in question here is not the OT law as such, but the OT as reinterpreted and imposed by Christ on his followers. And the idea that Christians will be judged on the basis of conformity to the will of God expressed in Christ's teaching is found in many places in the NT. Jesus warned that he would judge "all the nations" at his return and reward only those who showed compassion to others (Matt. 25:31-46). John says, "Those who obey his commands live in him" (1 John 3:24). And even Paul, so often set in opposition to James on these kinds of points, affirms that "we must all appear before the judgment seat of Christ, that each one may receive what is due him for the things done in the body, whether good or bad" (2 Cor. 5:10). God's gracious acceptance of us does not end our obligation to obey him; it sets it on a new footing. No longer is God's law a threatening, confining burden. For the will of God now confronts us as a *law of liberty* — an obligation we discharge in the joyful knowledge that God has both "liberated" us from the penalty of sin and given us, in his Spirit, the power to obey his will. To use James's own description, this law is an "implanted word," "written on the heart," that has the power to save us (Jas. 1:21).

13 James reinforces the commands of v. 12 with a further warning, probably again the citation of a proverbial truth (as in vv. 10-11, note the shift to the third person singular). The "retribution" formula, in which people get, in effect, exactly what they have done to others, was extremely popular in the ancient world. So James warns that *judgment without mercy will be shown to anyone who has not been merciful.* The connection between the verses shows that James views mercy as included within the law by which we are to be judged. The OT, of course, repeatedly requires God's people to be merciful to others. Especially worth quoting, because of the connection between mercy and concern for the poor and powerless, is Zech. 7:9-10: "This is what the LORD Almighty says: 'Administer true justice; show mercy and compassion to one another. Do not oppress the widow or the fatherless, the alien or the poor.'" Jewish writers from about James's time echo this idea: "You also, my children, have compassion toward every person with mercy, in order that the Lord may be compassionate and merciful to you" (*T. Zebulun* 8:1). But more relevant, as usually is the case in James, is the teaching of Jesus. Particularly apropos is the parable about the unmerciful servant (Matt. 18:21-35). But James also, in effect, transforms Jesus' beatitude — "Blessed are the merciful, for they will be shown mercy" (Matt. 5:7) — into its opposite: "Cursed are those are not merciful, for they will not be shown mercy." Being "merciful," as these texts suggest, is not merely a feeling of concern, but involves actively reaching out to show love to others. The discrimination that James's readers are practicing is the opposite of such mercy; and if they continue on this path, they will find at the end of their lives a judgment "without mercy."

But James does not end the paragraph on this negative note, but with a word of hope: *Mercy triumphs over judgment!* The assertion is short, even (again!) proverbial; and, for this reason, difficult to interpret. The reference to "judgment" is clear enough from v. 12: the negative verdict of condemnation that God will pronounce over evildoers in the last days. But whose "mercy" is it that triumphs over judgment? Some commentators think that James refers to the mercy of God himself. While setting forth a strict standard, conformity to his holy law, as the basis of judgment, God is ultimately a God of mercy, who also provides in his grace a means of escaping that judgment. As Hort describes the image, "κρίσις [judgment] comes so to speak as the accuser before the tribunal of God, and ἔλεος [mercy] stands up fearlessly and as it were defiantly to resist the claim."[33] This gracious note is, of course, sounded very often in the NT, and James may well refer to it here.[34] But the "mercy" that James has been referring to in this context is human mercy, not God's (v. 12). We therefore think it more likely that he is making a point about the way in which the mercy we show toward others shows our desire to obey the law of the kingdom and, indirectly therefore, of a heart made right by the work of God's grace.[35] The believer, in himself, will always deserve God's judgment: conformity to the "royal law" is never perfect, as it must be (vv. 10-11). But our merciful attitude and actions will count as evidence of the presence of Christ within us. And it is on the basis of this union with the one who perfectly fulfilled the law for us that we can have confidence of vindication at the judgment.

D. Saving Faith Reveals Itself in Works (2:14-26)

This paragraph is the most theologically significant, as well as the most controversial, in the Letter of James. Taking the right approach to the unit as a whole is very important, so we preface our detailed exegetical comments by investigating several broader issues.

33. Hort, 57.
34. See esp. Martin, 72-73.
35. See, e.g., Dibelius, 148; Laws, 117-18.

First, the structure of the passage. The outline below will help us to visualize the sequence of argument.

Introduction of topic: faith without works cannot "save" (v. 14)
(What good is it?)
A. Illustration (vv. 15-16) *(What good is it?)*
  Conclusion: ***faith by itself, if it is not accompanied by action, is dead*** (v. 17)
B. An objector: faith and deeds are separable (v. 18a)
  James:
    faith can only be shown by deeds (vv. 18b-19)
    faith without deeds is useless (v. 20)
      Abraham was considered righteous by a deed (v. 21)
      (Explanation of Abraham's faith and deeds [vv. 22-23])
        So: justification requires faith and works (v. 24)
      Rahab also was considered righteous by a deed (v. 25)
    faith without deeds is useless (v. 26)

The passage opens with a direct address to the readers ("my brothers"), raising the question of the efficacy of a faith unaccompanied by deeds. As he did in 2:2-4, James begins his response with an illustration involving poverty (vv. 15-16) followed by a concluding observation (v. 17). The question "What is the good of it?" frames vv. 14-16. James then utilizes a device very popular in an ancient literary form of argument, the "diatribe," by introducing an imaginary interlocutor with whom James can carry on a "conversation" as a means of instructing his readers. The objector protests that faith and deeds need not always go together (v. 18a). James's first response is practical: only by deeds can faith truly be demonstrated (vv. 18b-19). The second response begins with a renewed address to the interlocutor ("You foolish man"). James makes the point of this response clear by beginning and ending with the same emphasis (an *inclusio*): "faith without works is useless/dead" (vv. 20 and 26). The examples of Abraham and Rahab occupy the next inner "ring" of the argument (vv. 21-23 and 25), while the center of the structure is highlighted with another direct address of the readers: "You [plural] see that a person is justified by what he does and not by faith alone" (v. 24).

James leaves us in no doubt about the theme of this paragraph, announced three separate times in the course of the argument:

- faith by itself, if it is not accompanied by action, is dead (v. 17)
- faith without deeds is useless (v. 20)
- faith without deeds is dead (v. 26)

In what way is such faith "dead"? In the sense that it does not attain its purpose: it cannot save (v. 14) or justify (v. 24). Critical to understanding the argument of the section and integrating it successfully into a broader biblical perspective is the recognition that James is not arguing that works must be *added to* faith. His point, rather, is that genuine biblical faith will inevitably be characterized by works. Trying to add works to a bogus faith is an exercise in futility, for only by "accepting the implanted word" (1:21) and experiencing the inner transformation that it brings can one produce works pleasing to God. James, in a sense, proposes for us in these verses a "test" by which we determine the genuineness of faith: deeds of obedience to the will of God.

This insistence that true faith produces deeds is related to its context in at least three ways. The most immediate connection is with vv. 12-13. James's warning that believers will be judged according to the "law of liberty" naturally raises the question, at least in the minds of some Christians, "What judgment? — we thought that we were saved by faith and that we did not have to worry about the judgment." And so James makes clear just what kind of faith it is that will provide security in the judgment. A second, more remote connection is with the argument of 2:1-13. As the example of vv. 15-16 reveals, believers' treatment of poor people is still very much in James's mind. The call for a faith that leads to deeds echoes the idea of v. 1 and gives further basis for the warning against favoritism.[36] Some commentators, indeed, emphasize this dimension of the paragraph to the extent that they make it the primary theme; Davids, for instance, titles this section "Generosity Is Necessary."[37] But doing so unfairly diminishes the third, and broadest, connection that 2:14-26 has to the argument of the letter. For this paragraph is the capstone on James's presentation of "true religion," begun in 1:21. Obedience to the word, James has insisted, is a necessary mark of authentic Christianity. Taken by itself, however, such an emphasis could lead to an externalistic interpretation of Christianity, as if all that mattered was outward conformity to the demands of Scripture. And so 2:14-26 adds a necessary corrective: "true religion" begins with faith — but a faith that works. In this sense the "true religion" of 1:26 is nothing more than the genuine faith of 2:14-26, and the faith vs. works antithesis of this paragraph corresponds almost exactly to the "hearing the word"/"doing the word" antithesis of 1:22.[38]

But the occasion of the "true faith" emphasis of this paragraph

36. See, e.g., Martin, 80; Frankemölle, 421-24.

37. Davids, 119.

38. Johnson, 238; cf. also Verseput, "Faith and Deeds," 100-101.

goes beyond the argumentative demands of the letter itself. James's polemical style, with quotations of and rebukes directed against an imaginary interlocutor (vv. 18 and 20), strongly suggests that he is writing in this context to oppose what he thinks are false views circulating among his readers. And the criticism in v. 24 of a "faith only" view of justification suggests further that these false views have some relationship to the apostle Paul. To be sure, a connection is not altogether clear, for this kind of view might well have been circulating in Jewish circles independent of Paul and early Christianity.[39] But it is more likely, considering the distinctively Pauline vocabulary of v. 24, that the teaching of the Apostle to the Gentiles is lurking here in the background. What, then, is the connection? Many commentators follow the tack taken by Luther and insist that James directly sets himself in opposition to the view of justification taught by Paul and current in the Pauline churches.[40] Some even think that the "foolish man" of v. 20 is Paul himself! Such a view presumes that James and Paul present irreconcilable views on justification. In the course of our exegesis, we will attempt to show that this is unlikely; and we deal broadly with the whole issue also in the Introduction. But, to confine ourselves to the historical question, such a view also presumes a certain dating of James that we think is unlikely. If, as we argued in the Introduction, James was written in the mid-40s, then he of course could not know about Paul's teaching from his letters; and it is even unlikely that he would be acquainted with his teaching directly from other sources. When we add to this the fact that James's polemic does not really touch the basic Pauline perspective, the scenario that makes best sense is to think that he is writing to oppose a misunderstood form of Paul's teaching. The readers of the letter, scattered by persecution into areas near Antioch, have become acquainted with a perverted form of the Pauline viewpoint, with the slogan "faith alone justifies" as its hallmark.[41] James writes, then, to counter this false view of the relationship between faith, works, and salvation. James and Paul, when properly interpreted in their own contexts, are not opposed to one another on this point. They give the appearance of a conflict because they are writing from very different vantage points in order to combat very different problems.

39. See esp. Davids, 131-32.

40. See, e.g., G. Luedemann, *Opposition to Paul in Jewish Christianity* (Minneapolis: Fortress, 1989), 144-49.

41. See the Introduction; cf. also Martin, 95-96 (though he puts the letter at a later date). This understanding of the historical context apparently goes back as far as Augustine (cf. *Enarrationes in Psalmos* 31/II, 3, 6) (cf. P. Bergauer, *Der Jakobusbrief bei Augustinus und die damit verbundenen Probleme der Rechtfertigungslehre* [Vienna: Herder, 1962], 51-52).

14 What good is it, my brothers, if a man claims to have faith but has no
deeds? Can such faith save him? 15 Suppose a brother or a sister is without
clothes and daily food. 16 If one of you says to him, "Go, I wish you well;
keep warm and well fed," but does nothing about his physical needs, what
good is it? 17 In the same way, faith by itself, if it is not accompanied by ac-
tion, is dead.

18 But someone will say, "You have faith; I have deeds."

Show me your faith without deeds, and I will show you my faith by
what I do. 19 You believe that there is one God. Good! Even the demons be-
lieve that — and shudder.

20 You foolish man, do you want evidence that faith without deeds is use-
less? 21 Was not our ancestor Abraham considered righteous for what he did
when he offered his son Isaac on the altar? 22 You see that his faith and his ac-
tions were working together, and his faith was made complete by what he did.
23 And the scripture was fulfilled that says, "Abraham believed God, and it
was credited to him as righteousness," and he was called God's friend. 24 You
see that a person is justified by what he does and not by faith alone.

25 In the same way, was not even Rahab the prostitute considered righ-
teous for what she did when she gave lodging to the spies and sent them off
in a different direction? 26 As the body without the spirit is dead, so faith
without deeds is dead.

14 Verse 14 is formally unconnected to its context (grammarians call this "asyndeton"); and the direct address "my brothers" (see the note on 1:2) suggests a topic shift. James announces the new topic in two related rhetorical questions: *What good is it, my brothers, if a man claims to have faith but has no deeds? Can such faith save him?* "Good" translates a word *(ophelos)* that could also be rendered "profit" or "gain"; cf. 1 Cor. 15:32: "If I fought wild beasts in Ephesus for merely human reasons, what have I gained?" (lit., "what is the gain?") (the only other NT occurrence of the word is in v. 16). The "if" clause in this first question is put in a hypothetical form (*ean* with the subjunctive mood); and the identification of the person making the claim is equally vague: *man* (or "someone" [*tis*]; it is gender-neutral). This does not mean, however, that James gives here a general warning without any real basis among the readers of the letter. Verses 20 and following make clear that the situation is far more than hypothetical. James presumably uses this form of question because he wants to put the matter to his readers as a general rather than a specific occurrence. The use of the verb *claim* (lit. "says") suggests at the outset that James questions the reality of the faith.

The word translated "deeds" in the NIV is a critical word throughout this argument. It is the plural form of the very common Greek word *ergon,* which means simply "work," "action," "accomplishment." The plural form we find here occurs often in the NT to denote behavior with ethical and religious consequences. The "works" can be evil, leading to condemnation, or good, leading to commendation from God (contrast John 3:19-20 with 3:21). Particularly significant for the NT use of the word is the Jewish emphasis on "works" done in obedience to torah as the necessary response to God's election of the people of Israel. Paul's phrase "works of the law" (Gal. 2:16; 3:2, 5, 10; Rom. 3:20, 28) clearly echoes this Jewish emphasis. James uses "works" in a general sense to refer to actions done in obedience to God. Some modern versions tend to avoid the translation "works" in favor of "deeds" (NIV) or "actions" (NLT; TEV; REB), probably out of concern that "works," through the influence of some well-known verses in Paul (e.g., Eph. 2:9), might have a negative connotation.

James's second rhetorical question is put in a form showing that it expects the answer "no" (the Greek particle *mē* signifies this); in sense, then, it is tantamount to an assertion: "That kind of faith can't save anyone" (NLT). The interpretation of this sentence must steer carefully between two extremes. On the one side is the view that renderings such as the KJV "Can faith save him?" could lead to: that James is denying that faith can save a person at all. This is clearly not James's viewpoint, since he emphasizes in this very paragraph that the right kind of faith does, indeed, save (see vv. 21-26). What the KJV misses, and what almost all modern English translations recognize, is that the Greek article used with "faith" has an anaphoric significance — that is, it "refers back" to a previous use of the same word (note "*that* faith" in NASB; NRSV; REB; TEV; NJB). What James is contesting, then, is that the particular faith he has just mentioned can save. This faith is what a "man" who does not have works *claims* to have. James's main point is that this "faith" is, in biblical terms, no faith at all.

The opposite error is made by those who, with the best intentions, want to guard against precisely the kind of theological error we have just been discussing. They avoid the potential difficulty by insisting that the word "save" does not refer here to eschatological deliverance, but to some kind of rescue from earthly danger or trial.[42] They note that "save" (Gk. *sǭzō*) apparently has this meaning in 5:14. But the word does not seem to have this meaning elsewhere in James (1:21; 4:12; 5:20). Especially important is the occurrence in 1:21, since the present discussion is part of the argument begun in that verse; and 1:21 speaks definitively

42. For example, Z. Hodges, *The Gospel under Siege* (Dallas: Redención Viva, 1981), 26-27.

about the "salvation of souls." Moreover, "save" is also used here in a context that is discussing rescue at the judgment (vv. 12-13) and justification (vv. 21-25). Clearly, we must give the verb the full theological force that it normally has in the NT epistles (of the 30 occurrences of "save" outside of James in the NT epistles, 29 clearly refer to eschatological deliverance, the possible exception being Heb. 5:7).[43]

15 The two questions in v. 14 that set the agenda for the rest of the passage move from the general to the particular. The "good" or "benefit" of faith without works in the first question becomes salvation in the second. In his elaboration of this concern in the rest of the passage, James similarly moves from the general to the particular. Thus, in vv. 15-17, he elaborates on the lack of "benefit" generally that one gains from faith without works. Then, after the transition in vv. 18-19, he attacks specifically the lack of saving power (using "justify") in the "dead" faith that produces no works.

James makes clear that the illustration of vv. 15-16 applies to the first question he raises by repeating at the end of v. 16 the same question with which v. 14 began: "What good is it?" The illustration functions much like the one James used in vv. 2-3, in which a specific incident from the life of the church is used to give concrete expression to the point he is trying to make. How realistic is this incident? A few commentators think that James cites an actual circumstance that he has learned about.[44] But the Greek construction James uses to describe the incident (*ean* with the subjunctive mood) suggests (though it does not require) that James is giving a hypothetical example. And the hypothetical nature of the situation is underscored by the indefiniteness of *brother or sister.* Nevertheless, the fact that James again chooses an example of mistreatment of the poor in the Christian community makes clear that the illustration represents a pattern of behavior that is all too typical for James's readers.

James begins by describing the desperate condition of a member of the community (*brother or sister;* the latter is rare in the NT as a description of a fellow Christian [cf. also 1 Cor. 7:15; 9:5; Rom. 16:1; Phlm. 2; 1 Tim. 5:2]): *without clothes and daily food.* The Greek word represented in the NIV by "without clothes" is *gymnos,* "naked" (the word from which we derive "gymnasium," so called because Greek men competed naked in sporting events). The word can, of course, denote complete lack of clothing, but it can also designate a person wearing only an inner layer of clothing; see John 21:7, where Peter puts on this "outer garment" be-

43. See esp. G. Z. Heide, "The Soteriology of James 2:14," *Grace Theological Journal* 12 (1992) 69-97.

44. For example, Martin, 84.

cause, John explains, he was "naked" (NIV: "he had taken it off"). Probably, then, we are to envisage a person inadequately dressed for the conditions; he or she is "in rags" (REB), in need of clothing (NLT; TEV; NJB). Nakedness or lack of clothing can symbolize both poverty (Rev. 3:17) and shame (Rev. 3:18). The believer is also in need of food "for the day" (a literal rendering of the Greek word here). This word might mean that the believer lacked food for that particular day,[45] but it probably means that he or she was habitually underfed, constantly falling short of the "daily supply" of food required to sustain life and health.[46] The picture James paints comes to life for us in the homeless of our society.

16 Faced with an obvious and immediate need, the community member *(one of you)* responds with pious words but without giving any concrete aid. *I wish you well* is more literally translated "Depart" or "go" in peace, a common biblical blessing (e.g., Judg. 6:23; 1 Sam. 20:22; 2 Kgs. 5:19; Mark 5:34; Luke 7:50; 8:48; 24:36; John 20:19; Acts 16:36). "Peace" in this formula, reflecting the common biblical use of the term, is the well-being and blessedness that God gives those who walk with him. Therefore, as Johnson remarks, "It is not the form of the statement that is reprehensible, but its functioning as a religious cover for the failure to act."[47] The same thing can be said about *keep warm and well fed*. The NIV translation (which appears to assume that the verbs are middle in voice) suggests that the uncaring believer is vaguely encouraging the brother or sister to find clothing and food. But they could also be translated "be warmed and be filled" (NASB, taking the verbs as passive), perhaps a prayer that God would supply their need. In either case, the point is the same: confronted with a need among his own brothers and sisters, this "believer" does nothing but express his good wishes. *What good is it?* James asks. Within the sense of the illustration, this "good" refers to the situation of need that has gone unprovided for: words, however well meant, have not profited these needy people much. But some allusion to the second question of v. 14 is probably also intended: failure to provide for an obvious need not only harms those who are in need, but also raises question about the spiritual state of the one who fails to act to relieve the need. While this illustration undoubtedly reflects conditions among his readers, James may also make allusion here to the teaching of Jesus in the Matthean parable of the "Sheep and the Goats." God, says Jesus, will grant entrance into the kingdom on the basis of works of charity, but dismiss from his presence those who fail to relieve the needs of the destitute.

45. Laws, 120-21.
46. Adamson, 122.
47. Johnson, 239.

Jesus, quoting one of those in need, says: "For I was hungry and you gave me nothing to eat, I was thirsty and you gave me nothing to drink, I was a stranger and you did not invite me in, I needed clothes and you did not clothe me, I was sick and in prison and you did not look after me" (Matt. 25:42-43).

17 *In the same way* introduces the "moral" of the illustration: *faith by itself, if it is not accompanied by action, is dead.* This conclusion suggests that vv. 15-16 have two functions in James's argument. On the one hand, they give a concrete example of the kind of unconcern for the poor that James deplores among his readers. But, on the other hand, they also serve to provide a genuine illustration by way of analogy to the theological point that is the real burden of James at this point: the words of an uncaring believer who fails to act to help a person in need are as useless as the profession of faith of a believer who does not have deeds. "Action" is an NIV stylistic equivalent for "deeds" (v. 14); the Greek word is the same *(erga).* The problem with this kind of faith, James says, is that it is "by itself." Some English translations give the impression, with the way they handle this phrase, that the problem with faith that James focuses on here is that it is unaccompanied by works. It is, as the TEV puts it, "alone." But, granted James's argument in this passage, a more likely sense of this phrase is not so much "by itself" as "in itself." James, in other words, is arguing that the kind of faith he has just described is "not merely outwardly inoperative but inwardly dead."[48] The Greek phrase involved *(kath' heautēn)* has a similar meaning in Josephus's statement about the law: "The greatest miracle of all is that our Law holds out no seductive bait of sensual pleasure, but has exercised this influence *through its own inherent merits*" (*Against Apion* 2.284). Faith that lacks works, James concludes, is likewise, through its own inherent defect, useless, inactive, inert (the meaning of *nekros* in a context like this; cf. Rom. 7:8; Heb. 6:1; 9:14). Once again, then, we must underscore the point: James is not really contrasting faith and works, as if these were two alternative options in one's approach to God. He is, rather, contrasting a faith that, because it is inherently defective, produces no works and a faith that, because it is genuine, does result in action.

18 James moves on to a new stage in his argument by engaging in a discussion with another person whom he here quotes: *But someone will say.* But who, exactly, is James quoting? How far does the quotation extend? And what is the position that the person is adopting vis-à-vis James? These questions are difficult to answer; indeed, Martin Dibelius, one of the classic commentators on James, claims that vv. 18-19 is "one of

48. Mayor, 99.

the most difficult New Testament passages in general."[49] The problem arises from two factors. First, ancient Greek manuscripts, with a few exceptions, did not use punctuation marks. We therefore have no clear indication of where quotations in the NT begin and end. It is obvious in this case that the quotation begins immediately after the introductory formula *someone will say;* but where does it end? Second, whatever view one adopts, one is left with difficulties. No solution found in the literature provides a fully satisfactory explanation for every datum of the text. We will have to rest content with accepting the interpretation that has the fewest difficulties. But which interpretation this might be is, as one might expect, a very subjective decision. As a result, interpreters differ strongly on the sense to be given the verse. But the three main possibilities are the following.

1. James might be citing the opinion of an "ally" of his on the question of faith and works. James would cite this supporter in order to highlight even more clearly the questionable faith of the person whom he has described in vv. 14-17. A paraphrase will bring out just what the ally's point is: "You [the false believer of the illustration] say that you have faith; and I have works. But you cannot show me your faith because you do not have works; I, on the other hand, can show you my faith by my works."[50] The undoubted strength of this interpretation is that it maintains consistency in the use of pronouns throughout the verse. "You" is always the person who claims to have faith but does not have works (i.e., the "man" of vv. 14-17); "I" is always James or his ally, who insists that faith must be evidenced in works. But the view also suffers from a serious handicap: it does not give a very natural interpretation to the introductory quotation formula, "But someone will say." The strong adversative "but" (Gk. *alla*) suggests that the view that James is about to quote is in disagreement with his own. Moreover, "someone" *(tis)* seems to function like the same word in v. 14, to introduce on the scene a person with whom James will disagree. This "someone" also is most naturally identified with the "you" of v. 20 — and James quite plainly does not consider him to be an ally — "O foolish man." Adding considerable strength to this adversative reading of the introductory formula is the recognition that James is employing here a well-known device in ancient argumentation. A key component of the diatribe style was the frequent quotation of an imaginary interlocutor to advance one's own argument. The author would use such an interlocutor to pose questions or to raise objections to the view the author was himself propounding as a method of presenting

49. Dibelius, 154.
50. Mayor, 99-100; Adamson, 124-25, 135-37; Mussner, 136-38.

the issues to the reader in a clear and striking manner. Paul employs this device throughout Romans, as he raises questions sparked by his teaching that he will go on to answer (see, e.g., 3:1, 5, 9, 27; 4:1; 6:1, 15; 7:7, 13; 9:19, 30; 11:1, 11). But 1 Cor. 15:35 is the closest parallel to Jas. 2:18. In the midst of his defense of the resurrection body, Paul interjects: "But someone may ask, 'How are the dead raised?'" The person asking this question is not necessarily hostile to Paul's viewpoint; but neither here nor in the other examples of the diatribe style within the NT and in secular literature is the person who is introduced with this formula simply an "ally."

2. The person whom James quotes may be an objector who is casting doubt on the reality of James's faith. Three specific forms of this general approach deserve mention.

a. The objector's words might be confined to the very first words of v. 18, construed as a question: "Do you [James] really have faith?" James then responds: "I do have works; and while you cannot show me your faith at all, since you lack works, I can show you my faith *by* those works."[51] But standing in the way of this interpretation is the strained interpretation that must be given the Greek word *kagō,* "and I," which comes immediately after the question (on this view). It is very unlikely that that word could introduce a response to a question.

b. The objector's words might occupy all of vv. 18-19: "You [James] claim to have faith, and I can just as well claim to have works. But you cannot show me your faith apart from works, whereas I, if I wanted, could show you my faith from my works. Your [James's] faith is no better than that of the demons!" James's response would then begin in v. 20.[52] This view retains the natural force of the opening phrase, but, like the first option, it suffers from a strained interpretation of the phrase "and I have works." Furthermore, the objector would here seem to be taking the same stance that James has, claiming to be able to demonstrate his faith through his works.

c. The difficulty of the current text has led a few to suggest an alternate text. Zane Hodges proposes the adoption of some variants in the Byzantine textual tradition, resulting in the following paraphrase (variants are reflected in the italicized words): "You have faith and I have works. Show to me your faith *from your* works, and I will show to you, from my works, *my* faith. You [James] believe that God is one. You do well. But the demons also believe [as you do] and tremble [for fear of

51. Hort, 60-61; H. Neitzel, "Eine alte crux interpretum im Jakobusbrief 2.18," *ZNW* 73 (1982) 286-93; Klein, 71-72; Cargal, 122-25.

52. Cf. C. E. Donker, "Der Verfasser der Jak. und sein Gegner. Zum Problem der Einwandes in Jak. 2:18-19," *ZNW* 72 (1981) 227-40.

judgment]." According to Hodges, the opponent of James is sarcastically challenging the idea that anyone could demonstrate one's faith (a hidden matter of the heart) through works. Faith must always be a matter of confession, the opponent claims; and James's view of faith is therefore deficient.[53] However, quite apart from its dubious textual basis,[54] the irony necessary to sustain this view is simply not evident.

3. The objector's words are confined to the words quoted in most modern English versions, *"You have faith; and I have works,"* but the pronouns are not intended to identify James and the opponent specifically. Rather, they are used more generally to distinguish two different people, or two different positions: "One person has faith; another has works"; or "There is faith on the one hand; there is works on the other." The REB adopts this view in its translation: "One chooses faith, another action."[55] With either construal, the objector's point would be that faith and works are separate entities; separate "gifts" even. Did not Paul say that the Spirit sovereignly distributed such gifts (1 Corinthians 12)? And did he not say that faith itself was one such gift (1 Cor. 12:9; cf. Rom. 12:3)? How can James, then, demand that all Christians possess *both* faith and works? To this reasoning James responds that faith and works are not special gifts that a Christian may or may not have — neither is an "option" for any Christian. Only where works are seen is genuine, saving faith present. The difficulty with this view is that "you" and "I" in the quotation do not have their natural function, specifying definite individuals. To be sure, a few parallels to the generalized use of the pronouns in this way (equivalent to "someone" . . . "another one") have been noted,[56] but these are very much the exception.

Each view, then, has its difficulties; but, on the whole, we think the third view has the fewest. It gives a natural sense to the introductory formula, maintains the perspective on faith and works that James keeps throughout this paragraph, and fits naturally into the flow of the argument. James uses the device of the imaginary objector to further his argument for the inseparability of faith and works. In contrast to this objector,

53. Z. C. Hodges, "Light on James Two from Textual Criticism," *BibSac* 120 (1963) 341-50.

54. The key variant, reading *ek* in place of *chōris* (see the "from" in the translation above), is confined almost entirely to the Byzantine text, a family of mss. generally considered to be inferior to others by modern scholars. (Hodges, however, is also an advocate of this general textual tradition.)

55. This view is clearly becoming the majority view among scholars. See esp. Ropes, 208-14; and S. McKnight, "James 2:18a: The Unidentifiable Interlocutor," *WTJ* 52 (1990) 355-64.

56. Ropes (p. 209) mentions a passage in the works of the Cynic Teles (3d cent. B.C.).

who argues that a person can have genuine faith without works, James insists that the two are always found together.

On the view we have adopted, James's response to the objector is found in vv. 18b-19. He begins with a challenge: *Show me your faith apart from deeds, and I will show you my faith by what I do.* The verb "show" is usually taken to mean "make visible"; cf. NLT: "I can't see your faith if you don't have good deeds." This is the normal meaning of the verb *(deiknymi)* in the NT, so the interpretation is quite acceptable. But the verb can also mean "prove, demonstrate" (e.g., Matt. 16:21; Acts 10:28), and the only other occurrence in James has this meaning: "Let [the wise person] demonstrate on the basis of his good conduct that his works are done in the humility of wisdom."[57] James, then, may not be challenging the objector to reveal faith by actions, but to prove that he has faith by what he does — something that James himself is fully prepared to do.

19 James caps his response to the objector (*you* is singular), by comparing his faith to the faith of demons. What James says here is similar to his point of departure in v. 14. In both situations, faith involves a verbal profession that does not go beyond words. Differences in the manuscript tradition make it unclear whether the verbal profession here is "There is one God" (NIV; KJV; REB; NLT; TEV; a confession of monotheism) or "God is one" (NRSV; NASB; a confession of God's unity). The latter, being similar to the famous Jewish confession, the *Shema* (Deut. 6:4), may be preferable. For James is writing to Jewish Christians for whom the *Shema* would have been among the most basic of beliefs (the confession is appropriated by early Christians; cf. 1 Cor. 8:4-6; Gal. 3:20; Eph. 4:6; 1 Tim. 2:5). Proclaiming that "God is one" in that context would have been similar to churchgoers today loudly proclaiming their belief in the deity of Christ. *Good!* (lit., "you do well") is James's response. James may want us to read a bit of sarcasm into his reply; Johnson notes an implicit contrast with the same phrase in 2:8. But James may also intend it as a straightforward commendation. In either case, the problem lies not with the confession itself, but from the implication that it does not go beyond the verbal to touch the heart and the life. As Mitton puts it, "It is a good thing to possess an accurate theology, but it is unsatisfactory unless that good theology also possesses us."[58] The warning applies especially to people like me who study and teach theology day in and day out. C. S. Lewis is said to have warned new Christians about going into the ministry for fear that constant contact with "holy things" would render them commonplace. Those of us in ministry must beware the danger that our

57. BAGD classify both verses in James under the heading "explain, prove."
58. Mitton, 110.

theology — accurate and well stated as it might be — degenerate likewise into a verbal exercise.

The demons perfectly illustrate the poverty of verbal profession in and of itself. They are among the most "orthodox" of theologians, James suggests, agreeing wholeheartedly with the *Shema* (the NIV *that* has nothing corresponding in the Greek, but some kind of object for the verb seems to be required). Yet what is their reaction? They *shudder.* This verb, used only here in the NT, refers to the reaction of fear provoked by contact with God or the supernatural. It occurs particularly frequently in the papyri to describe the effect that a sorcerer aims to produce in his hearers.[59] Since ancient people often regarded the very pronouncing of the name of a god as having the power to provoke fear and terror, the verb is particularly appropriate in this context. What the word contributes to James's argument is not so clear. It may be just an "add-on" without any real importance in James's argument — as the NIV suggests by setting it off from the main sentence with a dash. But James might also want to suggest an ironical contrast between the demons and people who have faith without works: at least the demons display some kind of reaction to their "faith"![60] Another nuance might also be seen. The word "shudder" can also be applied to the dread experienced by sinful people who know they are deserving of judgment to come (e.g., Philo, *The Worse Attacks the Better* 140). So, James might be implying, as demons, knowing something of the true God, yet lacking true faith, shudder in fear of judgment, so also ought people whose verbal profession is not followed up with actions.

20 James continues to address the interlocutor he introduced in v. 18. But the paragraph break in the NIV recognizes that this verse belongs more to what follows than to what precedes. It introduces the subject that will occupy James in the rest of the chapter. In v. 17, James asserted that "faith, by itself, if is not accompanied by action, is dead." He now takes up this point to provide support for it. This support takes the form of OT evidence for the positive role of works (vv. 21-25). James then draws the section to a close by restating the key point: *faith without deeds is dead.*

You foolish man is the kind of direct address of an fictitious opponent typical of the diatribe style (see, in the NT, Rom. 2:1; 9:20). While, therefore, the view that James here attributes to this "foolish man" was undoubtedly present among his readers, we need not assume that he has a particular person in mind as he writes. (Still less is there any reason to

59. MM.
60. Laws, 127-28.

think, as a few radical scholars have suggested, that the "foolish man" is Paul.) "Foolish" translates a Greek word that means, literally, "empty." The word is seldom applied to people in biblical Greek (cf. only Judg. 9:4 and 11:3 [in MS B]). But secular authors sometimes used it in this kind of context; and it is probably roughly equivalent to other terms used in similar ways in the NT (cf. esp. *mōros* in Matt. 23:17; *anoētos* in Luke 24:25 and Gal. 3:1; and *aphrōn* in 1 Cor. 15:36). These all connote a lack of understanding, and usually with the implication that the intellectual failure has moral bases or implications. A stubborn, "hard-hearted" ignorance is the general idea. The "fool" of Proverbs may be something of a parallel, although with perhaps greater focus on moral failure. Addressing this person directly (the verb is singular), James asks, *do you want evidence that faith without deeds is useless?* The NIV *want evidence* is a fair (though somewhat paraphrastic) rendering of the verb, which is the customary Greek verb meaning "know." James is asking if this foolish man wants to "come to know," "be shown," that faith without deeds is useless. *Useless* is again a sufficient translation, but misses a wordplay in the Greek that is impossible, without great awkwardness, to capture in English. (The KJV "dead" rests on an inferior textual variant.) The Greek word for "deeds" is *erga,* whereas the word for "useless" is *argos,* literally "not-working" (Jesus applies it to workers who were "idle" [Matt. 20:3, 6]). Faith that does not "work," James is saying, "does not work" — it does no "good" (v. 14), is "dead" (vv. 17 and 26) and useless.

21 James's appeal to the OT to prove the importance of a "faith that works" is natural in a letter written to Jewish Christians. Equally natural is the appeal to Abraham. For, as James puts it, Abraham is "our father," or *ancestor* (NIV; the word *patēr* can mean both one's immediate father and one's more remote ancestor). It was the fulfillment of God's promise to him (initially given in Gen. 12:1-3) that created Israel as a nation; "descendants of Abraham" became a standard way to designate the people of God (e.g., Ps. 105:6; Jer. 33:26; cf. Gal. 3:16; Heb. 2:16). But Abraham's significance for Israel led also to Jewish elaboration of his great moral virtue. "Abraham was perfect in all his deeds with the Lord, and well-pleasing in righteousness all the days of his life" (*Jub.* 23:10); Abraham "did not sin against thee" (Pr. Man. 8); "no one has been found like him in glory" (Sir. 44:19). Reference to Abraham to prove the importance of "works" would obviously strike a chord with Jewish Christians.

But James is not content simply to mention Abraham's "works" in general: he makes particular reference to one of the most famous episodes in Abraham's life, the offering of his son Isaac (Genesis 22). In a "test" of Abraham's willingness to obey the Lord, God called on Abraham to offer in sacrifice his only son, the son indeed whom God had already promised would be the foundation of Abraham's line of descent. Just as Abraham is about to culminate the sacrifice by slaying his son on the altar he had built, his hand is stayed, and Isaac's life is spared. This incident has been the subject of intense speculation among both ancient and modern writers. James's reference to this specific story undoubtedly owes something to its use among the Jews of his day. Philo labels the "offering of Isaac" the greatest of Abraham's "works" (*Abraham* 167). Even more pertinent is the tradition reflected in 1 Macc. 2:51-52: "Remember the deeds of the fathers, which they did in their generations; and receive great honor and an everlasting name. Was not Abraham our father found faithful when tested, and it was reckoned to him as righteousness?" This text, in addition to the specific similarities to Jas. 2:21 — "our father" and the "was not . . ." question form — alludes to three key ideas in James: Abraham's "deeds"; "testing" (see 1:2-4, 12); and the "reckoned as righteousness" of Gen. 15:6 (quoted in v. 22). Furthermore, the "test" in the Maccabees text is almost certainly a reference to the offering of Isaac. James's argument here, then, takes its origin from a widespread Jewish tradition. But vv. 22-23 show that James qualifies the tradition in a critical manner: he introduces faith as the ultimate cause of the works through which Abraham was justified.

But this does not change the fact that in v. 21 James makes Abraham's "deeds" (*erga,* paraphrased in NIV as "what he did") a cause or instrument (*ex,* the Greek preposition translated "for" in NIV has this sense here) of his being "justified." Thus arises the famous tension between James and Paul, who appears to contradict James on two key points. First, Paul appeals to Gen. 15:6 to prove that Abraham's *faith* was "credited" to him for righteousness (Gal. 3:6; Rom. 4:1-9). Second, Paul insists that Abraham, and people generally, are justified by faith and not by works (e.g., Rom. 3:28). Resolution of the tension between the two writers, we think, is possible when all the relevant factors are taken into account. We will lay the groundwork for this resolution in the exegetical details as we move verse by verse through this section. In the Introduction, we place the resolution that we argue for here in a broader context (see the section under "Theology" on "Faith, Works, and Justification"). Two issues from the text require scrutiny here: the meaning of "justify" for James, and the relationship between Abraham's "deeds," said to be the basis for his justification, and the offering of Isaac.

Most Christians take their understanding of the verb "justify" from the writings of Paul; and naturally enough, for he gives the term a theological prominence that is foundational for biblical theology, and for soteriology. Specifically, Paul uses "justify" (Gk. *dikaioō*) to denote God's initial judicial verdict of "innocence" pronounced over the sinner who trusts Jesus Christ in faith. But we must not assume that James, writing before Paul, uses the word in the same way. In fact, the evidence for the use of this verb in the OT, in Judaism, and in the teaching of Jesus suggests the contrary. When this evidence is considered, two meanings for the verb appear more likely for James.

First, *dikaioō* might mean "vindicate in the judgment." The verb occurs 44 times in the LXX, usually in legal settings. Especially relevant are those texts in which God is pictured as the judge before whom one pleads one's case (1 Sam. 12:7; Isa. 43:26; Mic. 7:9) and who passes judgment on the lives of men and women. In these texts, it is one's actual conduct that forms the basis for God's "vindication." For example, in Mic. 6:11, the Lord warns that he will not acquit *(dikaioō)* the man "with dishonest scales." In Solomon's prayer at the time of the Temple dedication, he pleads with God: "When a man wrongs his neighbor and is required to take an oath and he comes and swears the oath before your altar in this temple, then hear from heaven and act. Judge between your servants, condemning the guilty and bringing down on his own head what he has done. Declare the innocent not guilty *(dikaioō),* and so establish his innocence" (1 Kgs. 8:31-32). The general thrust of the OT, therefore, is that "men are declared to be in the right *on the facts, i.e.* because in general or in a specific matter they *are* upright, and innocent."[61] And this declaration is naturally closely related to the final judgment (Isa. 43:9; 45:25; 50:8; 53:11[?]).

Judaism maintained the same basic viewpoint: a person's "righteousness" (Gk. *dikaiosynē,* a word from the same root that "justify" is from) is related to correct conduct, as defined by God's law, and the verdict of justification was pronounced over those who faithfully observed the covenant stipulations.[62] Matthew's Gospel reflects this Jewish usage.[63] While entrance into the kingdom is dependent on commitment to Jesus ("following Jesus"), "righteousness" is mainly, if not exclusively, the conduct expected of the disciple (Matt. 5:20) and "justify" refers to the verdict pronounced over a person's life at the last judgment, a verdict based on what a person has done. See especially Matt. 12:37: "For by your words you will be acquitted ['justified'], and by your words you will be condemned."

If James uses the verb with this sense, then he will be claiming that

61. J. A. Ziesler, *The Meaning of Righteousness in Paul: A Linguistic and Theological Inquiry* (SNTSMS 20; Cambridge: Cambridge University Press, 1972), 18.

62. See, on this and the whole subject, esp. L. Morris, *The Atonement: Its Meaning and Significance* (Leicester, Eng.: Inter-Varsity Press, 1983), 177-202.

63. See esp. B. Pryzybylski, *Righteousness in Matthew and His World of Thought* (SNTSMS 41; Cambridge: Cambridge University Press, 1980), 37-76.

the ultimate vindication of the believer in the judgment is based on, or at least takes into account, the things that person has done. So "justify" in Paul refers to how a person gets into relationship with God, while in James it connotes what that relationship must ultimately look like to receive God's final approval.[64]

But a second meaning of *dikaioō* should also be considered. In a few passages, the verb has the sense "demonstrate to be right," "vindicate." Clearest, perhaps, is Matt. 11:19 (par. Luke 7:35): "Wisdom is proved right by her actions"; in other words, the existence and value of wisdom are demonstrated in the actions that arise from it (cf. also Luke 10:29; 16:15). While not nearly as well attested as the former meaning, this sense of "justify" is often attributed to the verb in James. On this reading, James would be claiming that Abraham was "shown to be right" by his actions: his prior acceptance by God (Gen. 15:6), the "righteousness" that he had already attained by faith, was demonstrated in his deeds of obedience.

Harmony with Paul is quite clear if this second meaning is adopted. But we question whether it is the most likely. Not only is "show to be right" a fairly rare use of the verb, but the meaning does not fit the context as well. To be sure, advocates of the "show to be righteous" interpretation can point to v. 18, where James challenges his opponent to "show" him his faith. But, as we commented on that verse, "show" probably has the sense "prove" rather than "reveal." More important is the overall thrust of this passage, established by the broader context, in which the issue is what constitutes the "true religion" that will survive the judgment of God (1:21-27; 2:12-13) and by the specific question raised in v. 14: will "that kind of faith" save a person? Tentatively, then, we adopt the former meaning of the verb, according to which James is asserting that Abraham was granted a positive verdict in the judgment by God on the basis of his pious acts.

But this interpretation appears to conflict with another aspect of the text, raising the second exegetical issue we need to examine here. For James, according to the NIV translation (and many others), says that Abraham was justified *when* he offered Isaac — not at the last judgment. However, the word "when" in the NIV has nothing directly corresponding to it in the Greek text; it reflects an interpretation of the participle *(anenenkas)* "offering." That participle might just as well be translated "having offered," in which case the verdict of justification would come at

64. Another possibility is that James views the crediting of righteousness to Abraham as the approval expressed by God during his lifetime and a consequence of his obedience (R. T. Rakestraw, "James 2:14-26: Does James Contradict the Pauline Soteriology?" *Criswell Theological Review* 1 [1986] 33).

some indeterminate time after the offering. Another possibility, perhaps more likely, is to take the participle as specifying one of the "deeds" of Abraham; see the REV: "Was it not by his action, in offering his son Isaac on the altar, that our father Abraham was justified?"

22 James continues in this verse to address the imaginary interlocutor first introduced in v. 18 (*you see* is singular). He instructs his readers by letting them listen in to his debate, as he proves to him that "faith without deeds is useless" (v. 20). Verse 21, as we have noted, must be interpreted in light of this expressed purpose, keeping us from imagining that James cites Abraham as an example of works apart from faith. And this point is now confirmed in v. 22, which comments on v. 21: *You see that his faith and his actions were working together, and his faith was made complete by what he did.* Abraham's faith, James now makes clear, is presupposed throughout the argument. Moreover, he has probably had Gen. 15:6 in mind from the outset. James focuses in v. 21 on Abraham's works because it is this aspect of the patriarch's life that he needed to highlight for his rhetorical purposes. Indeed, some of his readers might have cited Gen. 15:6 to stress Abraham's faith and then interpreted that faith, as some Jews did, in an intellectual sense, his turning from idolatry "to the worship of the one god" (cf., e.g., Philo, *Virtues* 216; Josephus, *Antiquities* 1.154-57; *Jub.* 11-12).[65] James is intent on demonstrating that Abraham's faith went much further than mere intellectual assent.

The NIV translation obscures another wordplay in the Greek, captured well in the NASB: "you see that faith was working with [*synērgei*] his works [*ergois*]." Instead of the translation "works with," a few commentators suggest that the verb here means "assist," "help." The point, they suggest, is that Abraham's faith sustained his works by enabling him to produce them.[66] But the verb usually has the meaning "work with" in the NT (1 Cor. 6:16; 2 Cor. 6:1; [Mark 16:20]; Rom. 8:28 is debated; cf. also one of the two occurrences in the LXX [1 Esdr. 7:2]). So the usual translation should probably be accepted. James's point is not so much that Abraham's faith produced his works as that his faith and works cooperated together. The end of that cooperation is not stated in this verse, but we can assume from v. 21 and v. 23 that it is justification. Both the NASB and NIV *(were working together)* bring out the continuous force of the tense that James uses with this verb (the imperfect). He therefore emphasizes that Abraham's faith was not confined to a mental reorientation at the time of his "conversion" or to an occasional verbal profession but that it was an active force, constantly at work along with his deeds.

65. See Davids, 128-29.
66. Tasker, 69; Cranfield, 341.

James's second assertion about Abraham's faith in this verse stands in careful balance with the first: "faith cooperates with works" — "works complete faith." A chiastic pattern of faith — works — works — faith is also evident.[67] But in what sense can it be said that works "complete" faith? Is faith in James's view a quality that is incomplete until actions follow from it? To avoid this kind of conclusion, Calvin suggests that the idea here might be that works revealed Abraham's faith to be perfect. But the word never has this sense elsewhere. The verb *(teleioō)* means "complete a task or mission" (e.g., John 17:4; 19:28; Acts 20:24), to "bring to perfection or maturity" (Phil. 3:10; Heb. 2:10). No NT text has the same combination of words that James uses here (the verb *teleioō* with the preposition *ek*), but Philo uses them together at least twice, each time describing Jacob: he "was perfected as the result of discipline" (*Husbandry* 42); "was made perfect through practice" (*Confusion of Tongues* 181; cf. also *Preliminary Studies* 35 [with *dia*]). Jacob, these texts suggest, grew in maturity as a result of the challenges he faced in life. But, because the subject is inanimate, the closest parallel to James's usage (despite a slightly different construction) is 1 John 4:12: "if we love one another, God lives in us and his love is made complete in us." Clearly our love does not "complete" God's love in the sense that the love of God is inadequate or faulty without our response. It is rather that God's love comes to expression, reaches its intended goal, when we respond to his grace with love toward others. So also, Abraham's faith, James suggests, reached its intended goal when the patriarch did what God was asking him to do.

23 The "and" connecting this verse to the previous one does not indicate much about their relationship. But, judging from content, we can surmise that James sees in v. 23 the result of the dynamic cooperation between Abraham's faith and works that he described in v. 22 (note the "thus" in NRSV; "and so" in NLT). These results were two: the Scripture about Abraham's faith being credited to him as righteousness (Gen. 15:6) was "fulfilled"; and he was called "the friend of God." *Scripture,* in the singular, can denote the whole OT canon (e.g., Gal. 3:22) but more often refers to a specific text from the OT (cf., e.g., Mark 12:10; Luke 4:21; John 19:24) — in this case, of course, Gen. 15:6. Granted the Jewish tradition that James depends on in these verses, it is likely that Gen. 15:6 has been in his mind from the beginning of his discussion of Abraham. In this famous OT text, Abraham's faith is specifically his complete trust in God with reference to the Lord's promise that he would have a natural descendant (vv. 4-5). In response, God "credits" Abraham's faith to him as righteousness. Some Jewish interpreters thought that this crediting

67. See, e.g., J. C. Lodge, "James and Paul at Cross-Purposes," *Bib* 62 (1981) 201.

meant that Abraham's faith was his righteousness: a response that earns God's favor.[68] But the specific wording of the text suggests rather that this "crediting" of righteousness to Abraham meant "to account to him a righteousness that does not inherently belong to him."[69] Paul's citation of this text in Galatians 3 and Romans 4 picks up on this idea, as the apostle uses Abraham to show that God graciously accords the forensic status of righteousness to sinners who do not deserve it (see esp. Rom. 4:3-5).

James, however, uses Gen. 15:6 with a very different — some would even say contradictory — purpose. For he sees this verse "fulfilled" in the cooperation of Abraham's faith and works. James's use of the word "fulfill" *(plēroō)* requires consideration. We sometimes automatically assume that "fulfilling the Scripture" refers to the accomplishment of what had been predicted in OT prophecy; and, of course, the word is often used in this way. James may therefore read Gen. 15:6 as a prophecy "fulfilled" when Abraham offered Isaac.[70] But the word is also used much more broadly than this. It means, basically, "to fill" or "fill up" and can be used of fishing nets (Matt. 13:48) and houses (John 12:3). When applied to the OT, then, it has the general sense "bring to ultimate significance," and can be applied to OT history (e.g., Matt. 2:18) and law (Matt. 5:17). It would make better sense if James were to be using the word in this broader sense. What he is suggesting is that Abraham's faith, in its relationship to righteousness, found its ultimate significance and meaning in Abraham's life of obedience. When Abraham "put faith in" the Lord, God gave him, then and there, the status of a right relationship with him: *before* he had done works, *before* he was circumcised. This is Paul's point about Abraham (Rom. 4:1-17). But the faith of Abraham and God's verdict of acquittal were "filled up," given their ultimate significance, when Abraham "perfected" his faith with works. It is after the greatest of those works, cited by James in v. 21, that the angel of the Lord reasserted God's verdict: "now I know that you fear God" (Gen. 22:12).

How, then, does James understand "righteousness" in this text? Ziesler gives it a "moral" interpretation: Abraham's "faith-completed-by-works is righteousness."[71] But an ethical understanding of the word, while well attested in the NT, does not fit either the original sense of Gen. 15:6 or the context (compare "justify" in vv. 21 and 24). We have very little

68. See, e.g., Ziesler, *Righteousness,* 181-85.

69. O. P. Robertson, "Genesis 15:6: New Covenant Exposition of an Old Covenant Text," *WTJ* 42 (1980) 265-66. See also G. von Rad, "The Anrechnung des Glaubes zur Gerechtigkeit," *TLZ* 76 (1951) cols. 129-32; Morris, *The Atonement,* 187.

70. Ropes, 221.

71. Ziesler, *Righteousness,* 132.

evidence that the term "justify" can have this meaning. In light of word usage and context, then, James probably assumes a forensic meaning for the term, indicating the status of "rightness" that Abraham attained with God. When did Abraham attain this status? Perhaps this is to ask the wrong question of James. It is not the timing, but the fact of God's declaration of Abraham's righteousness that James is concerned with. Abraham's works, especially his offering of Isaac, reveal the character of his faith, a faith that is crediting for righteousness. When that righteousness is conferred is simply not an issue for James here.[72]

James is therefore not using Gen. 15:6 in a way contradictory to that of Paul. They address different issues from different backgrounds and need to make different points about Abraham's paradigmatic experience with the Lord. And so, without necessarily disagreeing about the basic sense of the verse, they set Gen. 15:6 in different biblical-theological contexts and derive different conclusions from their contextual readings. Paul seizes on the chronological placement of Gen. 15:6 and cites it as evidence of the initial declaration of righteousness that Abraham attained from God solely on the basis of faith. James views the same verse more as a "motto," applicable to Abraham's life as a whole.

The second result of the cooperation between Abraham's faith and works is that *he was called the friend of God.* The NIV, along with most translations, closes the quotation marks after the citation of Gen. 15:6, implying that these words are not an OT quotation. And this is certainly appropriate, because the words are nowhere found in the OT. James probably derives the title "friend of God" for Abraham from Jewish tradition, where it was fairly widespread (see, e.g., *Jub.* 19:9; 20:20; Philo, *Sobriety* 56; *Abraham* 273; and *T. Abraham,* passim). But the ascription has its roots in the OT, where Abraham is called the "beloved" of God (2 Chron. 20:7; Isa. 41:8; see also Isa. 51:2; and Dan. 3:35 in the Septuagint). James cites it as an indication of the privileged status Abraham was given on account of his deep faith and practical obedience. He therefore stands for James "as the supreme example of what it means to have 'friendship with God' rather than 'friendship with the world'" (Jas. 4:4).[73]

24 This verse is the center of James's discussion of faith, works, and justification (vv. 21-25). Its importance is indicated by the shift from the indirect argument of vv. 21-23, where he engaged in debate with an imaginary interlocutor, to the direct appeal to his readers in v. 24: *You* [plural] *see.* In vv. 21-23, James has shown from the life of Abraham that works are intimately connected with faith and that they are also involved

72. See, e.g., Rakestraw, "James 2:14-26," 5.
73. Johnson, 244.

in what he calls "justification." He now brings these three key concepts together in a terse theological summary: *a person is justified by what he does and not by faith only.* By speaking generally of a "person" (Gk. *anthrōpos*), James highlights the programmatic character of this assertion (for parallels, see Matt. 4:4; Acts 4:12; Rom. 3:28; Gal. 2:16). The NIV "what he does" is yet another variant translation of the term "works" *(erga)* that James highlights throughout this passage. "Justify" will have the same meaning that it did in v. 21: God's final declaration of a person's "innocence" before him at the time of the judgment. The present tense — "is justified" — is used not because the activity is ongoing at the present time but because James is presenting a timeless truth.

If this verse represents the heart of James's teaching about justification, it is also the lightning rod in the theological controversy between James and Paul. The tension between Paul and James is evident when we set beside each other key statements about justification from each author:

Jas. 2:24:	A person	is justified	by works	and not by faith alone
Rom. 3:28:	A person	is justified	by faith	and not by works of the law

An obvious point of difference is that James speaks simply of "works," while Paul refers to "works of the law." Many scholars see in this difference a promising approach to resolve the apparent contradiction between Paul and James. James, just about everyone agrees, using the word to denote anything done in service to God (with special emphasis, some claim, on works of charity). But is this also what "works of the law" in Paul refers to? Theologians in the past sometimes asserted that "works of the law" referred to the ceremonial practices of the Jewish faith.[74] Therefore Paul would allow works done by Christians in response to God's grace to have some kind of instrumental role in justification, and Paul and James could be brought into harmony. But very few contemporary scholars think that "works of the law" can be confined to ceremonial observances only — and rightly so. Paul seldom refers to the ceremonies of the Jewish faith, and the contexts in which the phrase occurs show that the meaning is far broader. But another restricted meaning of the phrase is advocated by a great many (and growing) number of scholars in our own day. Noting that the word "law" in the phrase must refer to the Jewish law, the torah, they claim that Paul intends in verses such as Rom. 3:28 to deny only that works done in the context of torah observance can justify. However, while these scholars are undoubtedly correct to identify "law" with

74. See, e.g., the fourth-century monk (and opponent of Augustine) Pelagius; and the seventeeth-century English divine George Bull (cf. his *Harmonica Apostolica* [1670]).

torah, the conclusions they draw from this identification are not probable. Paul refers specifically to torah because he is discussing the issue of works in a Jewish context, where actions done in obedience to God were defined by the Mosaic law. But the context in which he uses the phrase shows that it is to be seen as a subset of the larger category "works" (compare Rom. 3:28 with Rom. 4:1-8).[75] Rom. 3:28, then, excludes works of any kind from justification.

A more profitable approach is to compare the word "faith" in Paul with the phrase "faith alone" in James. The addition of "alone" shows clearly that James refers to the bogus faith that he has been attacking throughout this paragraph: the faith that a person "claims" to have (v. 14); a faith that is, in fact, "dead" (vv. 17 and 26) and "useless" (v. 20). This faith is by no means what Paul means by faith. He teaches that faith is a dynamic, powerful force, through which the believer is intimately united with Christ, his Lord. And since faith is in a *Lord,* the need for obedience to follow from faith is part of the meaning of the word for Paul. He can therefore speak of "the obedience of faith" (Rom. 1:5) and say that it is "faith working through love" that matters in Christ (Gal. 5:6). This is exactly the concept of faith that James is propagating in this paragraph. Once we understand "faith alone," then, as a neat summary of the bogus faith that James is criticizing, we can find no reason to expect that Paul would have any quarrel with the claim that "faith alone" does not justify.

However, we are still left with an apparent contradiction between James and Paul: the former claims that works are a necessary basis or means of justification; the latter denies that works can have any place in justification. As we suggested in our interpretation of v. 21, resolution of the tension can come only when we recognize that James and Paul use "justify" to refer to different things. Paul refers to the initial declaration of a sinner's innocence before God; James to the ultimate verdict of innocence pronounced over a person at the last judgment.[76] If a sinner can get into relationship with God only by faith (Paul), the ultimate validation of that relationship takes into account the works that true faith must inevitably produce (James). As Calvin puts it, ". . . as Paul contends that we are

75. The meaning of "works of the law" in Paul (used in Gal. 2:16; 3:2, 5, 10; Rom. 3:20, 28) is at the center of the controversy over the "new perspective" on Paul and has therefore received an enormous amount of attention in current scholarship. See, e.g., D. J. Moo, "'Law,' 'Works of the Law,' and Legalism in Paul," *WTJ* 43 (1983) 73-100; idem, *The Epistle to the Romans* (NICNT; Grand Rapids: Eerdmans, 1996), esp. 211-17.

76. For this general approach, see esp. G. Eichholz, *Glaube und Werke bei Paulus und Jakobus* (Munich: Kaiser, 1961), esp. 24-37; J. Jeremias, "Paul and James," *ExpTim* 66 (1954-55) 368-71; T. Laato, "Justification according to James: A Comparison with Paul," *TrinJ* 18 (1997) 43-84.

justified apart from the help of works, so James does not allow those who lack good works to be reckoned righteous."[77]

25 At first sight, the transitional phrase *in the same way* suggests that v. 25 will furnish a further proof for the principle that James has set forth in v. 24. But it might also go back beyond v. 24 to the illustration of Abraham in vv. 21-23. Two considerations support this more remote connection. First, v. 25 and v. 21 are formulated in precisely parallel fashion:

v. 21 Was not our ancestor Abraham considered righteous for what he did
v. 25 was not even Rahab the harlot considered righteous for what she did
v. 21 (cont.) when he offered his son Isaac on the altar?
v. 25 (cont.) when she gave lodging to the spies and sent them off in a different direction?

Second, while the high point of vv. 20-26 from a conceptual point of view, v. 24 is an interruption from a rhetorical point of view. The passage is cast in the form of a dialogue with an imaginary interlocutor; and v. 25, because of its similarity in form to v. 21, probably carries on this dialogue. It is as if, in v. 24, James suddenly interrupted his dialogue to turn to his readers and make his point clear to them, only to resume the dialogue thereafter.

We need not repeat here our conclusions about those words and forms that v. 25 has in common with v. 21. *Considered righteous,* or "justify" *(dikaioō),* will again mean "vindicate in the judgment"; and the final clause introduced by the NIV with *when* should rather be taken as an example of the *action,* or "works," mentioned earlier (see again REB: "Was she not justified by her action in welcoming the messengers into her house and sending them away by a different route?").

Rahab's story is told in Joshua 2. She was an inhabitant of Jericho who became convinced through the tales of God's mighty acts on behalf of Israel that "the LORD your God is God in heaven above and on the earth below" (v. 11). Therefore, when the spies from Israel came into Jericho, Rahab put them up, hid them when the king sought them, and eventually helped them escape by lowering them on a rope from the roof of her house. The OT text identifies her as a "prostitute" (both Hebrew and Septuagint; other versions, however, have "innkeeper" [see the footnote in NIV]). James's appropriation of the story is quite straightforward. He unambiguously identifies Rahab as a "prostitute" *(pornē);* although he differs from the Septuagint of Joshua 2 in referring to the "spies" as "messengers" or "envoys" *(angeloi).* While James does not specifically mention

77. Calvin, *Institutes* 3.27.2.

Rahab's "faith," it can certainly be inferred both from the OT itself and from the parallel with Abraham.

A larger question is why James chooses Rahab for his illustration when other, more illustrious examples were ready to hand. Ancient traditions suggest two possible explanations. Certain Jewish writers viewed both Abraham and Rahab as classic types of the proselyte: the foreigner who identifies with the people of Israel. Rahab, of course, fits the pattern perfectly; but Abraham also left his home in Ur in response to the call of God to identify with the people of Israel. However, it is not entirely clear that this tradition was current in James's day (the tradition is apparently found only in post-NT rabbinic texts, although it is very widespread). Moreover, it is not clear why the status of proselyte would be important for James's argument.

More to the point is a second tradition, found especially clearly in the late first-century Christian writing *1 Clement*. In this letter, both Abraham and Rahab are presented as models of faith and hospitality: Rahab because she welcomed the "spies" into her home, Abraham because he received the three "men" who, according to Genesis 18, visited him and brought predictions about his family (this latter incident is frequently mentioned in Jewish tradition). James may then intend the reader to see in the faith of Abraham and Rahab a direct contrast to the "dead" faith of the man in vv. 15-16 who refuses to give aid to those in need.[78] One wonders, however, if this tradition influenced James, why he does not mention the Genesis 18 incident. A simpler, though perhaps sufficient answer, is that James wanted variety. So alongside the famous and celebrated ancestor of the Jewish people, a man, "the friend of God," he places an obscure Gentile woman of low moral character. Thus he implies that anyone is capable of acting on his or her faith — whether a patriarch or a prostitute.

26 James rounds off the passage by reiterating its central point: faith without works is dead. This final reminder harks back to the similar assertions in vv. 17 and 20. From a literary standpoint, though, the connection with v. 20 is particularly important, these two verses creating a "frame" around the faith/works/justification dialogue. The comparison of faith without works to *the body without the spirit* is intended by James as a general analogy. This point is missed by some who "milk" more from the illustration than James intended. Zane Hodges, for instance, argues that James identifies faith with the "body," and that good works are therefore the invigorating force behind faith.[79] But James's point, as the

78. See particularly R. B. Ward, "The Works of Abraham: James 2:14-26," *HTR* 61 (1968) 283-90.

79. Hodges, *Dead Faith*, 8-9.

repeated emphasis of the passage shows, is simpler. The *spirit* here is the life principle that animates the body (cf. Gen. 2:7; Luke 8:55; 23:46; 1 Cor. 7:34) — without the spirit the body ceases to be. In the same way, James suggests, faith that is not accompanied by works ceases to be. It becomes mere profession and has no claim to be biblical faith. We again emphasize that James is not arguing that works be "added" to faith, but that one possess the right kind of faith, a "faith that works."

Somewhat ironically, no one has captured the basic message of Jas. 2:14-26 more forcefully than Luther (from his preface to *Romans*):

> O it is a living, busy active mighty thing, this faith. It is impossible for it not to be doing good things incessantly. It does not ask whether good works are to be done, but before the question is asked, it has already done this, and is constantly doing them. Whoever does not do such works, however, is an unbeliever. He gropes and looks around for faith and good works, but knows neither what faith is nor what good works are. Yet he talks and talks, with many words, about faith and good works.

James 3

IV. THE COMMUNITY DIMENSION OF SPIRITUAL WHOLENESS: PURE SPEECH AND PEACE, PART 1 (3:1–4:3)

James 1:19–2:26 is the only larger section of the letter that has a fairly obvious conceptual unity, focused on the need to practice true religion by doing the works that the word of God requires. No such theme binds together the following paragraphs. James warns about the considerable and potentially destructive power of human speech (3:1-12); contrasts the "wisdom from above" with the "wisdom from below" (3:13-18); rebukes his readers for quarreling (4:1-3); issues a strongly worded call to repentance (4:4-10); and tells his readers to stop criticizing one another (4:11-12). However, while James is obviously not consistently elaborating a single theme, two considerations suggest that these paragraphs are joined in a loose relationship. First, the passage begins (3:1-12) and ends (4:11-12) with warnings about the misuse of speech, especially in the context of the community (cf. the "teachers" of 3:1 and the "one another" of 4:11). Second, the topics that James treats in these paragraphs are also sometimes found together in both secular and Jewish moral exhortation. Johnson has demonstrated the similarity of 3:13–4:10 to the ancient *topos* ("topical discussion") "On jealousy," which often traced violent behavior (4:1-3) to jealousy.[1] But the same exhortations regarding jealousy sometimes include rebukes about sinful speech as well. One of the second-temple Jewish books that contains many themes similar to those we find in James is

1. L. T. Johnson, "James 3:13–4:10 and the *Topos* ΠΕΡΙ ΦΘΟΝΟΥ," *NovT* 25 (1983) 327-47.

The Testaments of the Twelve Patriarchs. This book contains some of the closest parallels to James's discussion of envy and violence. But in some of these same contexts hateful, critical speech is also denounced (cf. *T. Gad* 4–5). Moreover, James himself brings "quarreling" right into the center of his appropriation of this popular moral *topos* (4:1). These factors strongly suggest that James views 3:1-12 and 4:11-12 as part of this larger discussion.[2]

Since the topics in this section are only loosely related, a common theme that could serve as a heading is difficult to identify. But the heart of James's concern seems to be the violent quarrels that are shaking the community. All that James says in this section can be loosely related to this concern:

> Teachers, especially, should not use the tongue in a destructive way (3:1-12)
> > True wisdom is humble and peaceable (3:13-18)
> > > Quarreling comes from envy (4:1-3)
> >
> > Repent from worldliness; submit to a jealous God (4:4-10)
>
> Community members should stop slandering each other (4:11-12)

While we have presented the material in something of a chiastic pattern, we don't think a genuine chiasm is evident here. The opening and closing sections clearly relate to one another; and the main point comes in the middle. But for a genuine chiasm to be present, 3:13-18 and 4:4-10 would have to relate to one another. But only a few superficial contacts exist between the two. Indeed, the call to repentance in 4:4-10 stands out in many ways as a critical section in the letter, which James intends, we think, to encompass all the exhortations of the letter. We signal this central role by isolating the unit as a section in its own right.

A. Control of the Tongue Manifests the Transformed Heart (3:1-12)

> 1 *Not many of you should presume to be teachers, my brothers, because you know that we who teach will be judged more strictly.* 2 *We all stumble in many ways. If anyone is never at fault in what he says, he is a perfect man, able to keep his whole body in check.*
>
> 3 *When we put bits into the mouths of horses to make them obey us, we can turn the whole animal.* 4 *Or take ships as an example. Although they*

2. See also Cargal, 138-39.

are so large and are driven by strong winds, they are steered by a very
small rudder wherever the pilot wants to go. 5 *Likewise the tongue is a*
small part of the body, but it makes great boasts. Consider what a great for-
est is set on fire by a small spark. 6 *The tongue also is a fire, a world of evil*
among the parts of the body. It corrupts the whole person, sets the whole
course of his life on fire, and is itself set on fire by hell.

7 *All kinds of animals, birds, reptiles and creatures of the sea are being*
tamed and have been tamed by man, 8 *but no man can tame the tongue. It*
is a restless evil, full of deadly poison.

9 *With the tongue we praise our Lord and Father, and with it we curse*
men, who have been made in God's likeness. 10 *Out of the same mouth come*
praise and cursing. My brothers, this should not be. 11 *Can both fresh wa-*
ter and salt water flow from the same spring? 12 *My brothers, can a fig tree*
bear olives, or a grapevine bear figs? Neither can a salt spring produce
fresh water.

This section relates to the preceding discussion in the letter in two ways. First, the concern about "words" in this paragraph is loosely connected to the concern about "works" in 2:14-26; as Tasker puts it, "words are also works." And very significant "works" — in a saying that has probably influenced James's argument in 2:14-26, Jesus claims that one's words will be the basis for God's eschatological judgment (Matt. 12:37). A movement from the importance of works to the crucial "work" of human speech is therefore a natural progression. Second, this long section on the problem of the tongue picks up James's identification of the control of the tongue as one of the clearest examples of "true religion" (1:26; cf. 1:19-20).

Verse 1 raises the question of the occasion and specificity of James's warning about sinful speech. Why does James single out the teacher in the opening of his exhortation? Two answers are commonly given. Most commentators, without ignoring v. 1, nevertheless do not think that James is concerned only, or even especially, with teachers throughout the paragraph. They suggest that James singles out teachers at the outset because they provide a convenient "jumping off point" for the general warning about the tongue. Others, however, think the reference sets the direction for the passage as a whole. Without denying that it has application to the problem of human speech generally, they argue that the paragraph is directed to the problem of Christian leaders who are using the tongue improperly. The illustrations James chooses are directed to this specific context, they argue. "Blessing" and "cursing" (v. 9) probably have a worship setting in view; and the small things that control big things (vv. 3-5) have at least partial reference to the leaders who control the church.[3] However, while James has obvious concern about the application of his teaching to Christian leaders (cf. also v. 13), we doubt that he writes as directly as this to those leaders throughout the paragraph. Verse 1, after all, is directed not to Christian leaders, but to any Christian who might want to become a teacher. The general address to the readers in 4:1 and 4:11 certainly demonstrates that the problem of sinful, critical speech involved more than the leaders. And James gives little indication that the admonitions of vv. 2-12 have special reference to leaders. So, on the whole, we prefer the former view: a concern about people wanting to teach leads James into a general warning about the tongue.

The paragraph unfolds in four stages. (1) In vv. 1-2 James introduces the issue by warning people who want to be teachers about the peculiar difficulty of controlling the tongue. (2) The incredible power of the tongue is the theme of vv. 3-6, summarized in v. 5a: "the tongue is a small part of the body, but it makes great boasts." (3) Powerful as it is, the tongue is extremely difficult to keep under control (vv. 7-8). (4) Verses 9-12 end the passage on a note typical for James throughout the letter: the tongue reveals its evil nature by manifesting that "doubleness" which is so typical of sin.[4]

These verses, more than any others in the epistle, reveal the breadth of James's background. The problem of uncontrolled speech is a frequent theme among secular moralists and in OT and Jewish Wisdom literature. Especially is this motif prominent in Proverbs, which constantly singles out speech habits as a key marker of godliness (see, e.g., 10:8, 11, 21; 11:9; 12:18, 25; 13:3; 16:27; 17:14; 18:7, 21; 26:22). The illustrations that James uses in this section reflect knowledge of all these sources. They do not mean that James must have been deeply steeped in Greco-Roman moral philosophy, for all of them are of a type that would have been widely known among those with even a minimal acquaintance with Hellenistic culture. The picture of James that emerges is of a reasonably well-educated Jew who knows his OT thoroughly and who is well acquainted with Hellenistic-Jewish culture, language, and literature.

1 Instead of launching immediately into the main topic of the paragraph — the destructive potential of human speech — James begins by discouraging his readers from becoming teachers. *Teachers (didaskaloi)* were prominent in the life of the early church from the beginning. The office of teacher was roughly the equivalent of the rabbi in the Jewish community (cf. Matt. 23:8; John 1:38). Paul ranked the gift of teaching very high on the list of gifts the Spirit bestows on the church (1 Cor. 12:28; see

3. See Martin, 103-7, for a good explanation and defense of this approach.

4. See Frankemölle, 478-81.

also Acts 13:1; Rom. 12:7; Eph. 4:11). Unlike the prophet, who transmitted to the community revelations received from the Lord (cf. 1 Cor. 14:30), the teacher had the task of expounding the truth of the gospel on the basis of the growing Christian tradition (cf., e.g., 2 Tim. 2:2). The rough equivalent to the rabbi would have meant that a teacher in the early Jewish-Christian church would have had considerable prestige. Particularly would this have been the case in a society where few people could read and where people in the lower classes had fewer opportunities for advancement in status. We can understand, then, why James might have to admonish believers about seeking too eagerly the role of teacher. Since James may allude again in 3:13 to a certain arrogance among the leaders of the community, we can surmise that the problem actually had arisen among his readers.[5] Too many were seeking the status of teacher without the necessary moral (and perhaps also intellectual) qualifications. Perhaps, indeed, unfit teachers were a major cause of the bitter partisan spirit (cf. 3:13-18), quarreling (4:1), and unkind, critical speech (4:11) that seemed to characterize the community. James therefore begins his admonition about the tongue with a practical illustration of the problem uncontrolled speech can create.

The second part of v. 1 grounds the command in the beginning of the verse. Christians should not be too eager to become teachers, James argues, *because you know that we who teach will be judged more strictly.* James's shift to the first person plural — "we" — reveals that he considers himself a teacher. And by identifying himself with those whom he warns, James also creates a more effective platform for his warning. The affectionate address *my brothers* (e.g., James's fellow believers) has the same purpose. The translation of the NIV, quoted above, is similar to that found in most English versions. But the KJV suggests a different interpretation: "we shall receive the greater condemnation." The Greek, if anything, favors this meaning, since the word *krima,* used here, usually refers to the negative outcome of judgment, for example, "condemnation," in the NT (cf., e.g., Mark 12:40 [= Luke 20:47]; Luke 23:40; Rom. 2:2; 3:8; 5:16). However, the word can also have a neutral sense, referring to the act of judgment without regard to the outcome (John 9:39; 1 Cor. 6:7; Heb. 6:2). The translations prefer this alternative because of context: it would seem overly harsh for James to be claiming that teachers will receive a more severe penalty in the judgment than other believers. Not many, to be sure, would clamor to become teachers were that the case! But the logic of James's argument, as we follow it into v. 2, suggests a third interpretation of the "greater judgment": teachers, be-

5. Martin, 107, against, e.g., Johnson, 255. The Greek construction used here (*mē* + present imperative) does not settle the case one way or the other.

cause their ministry involves speech, the hardest of all parts of the body to control, expose themselves to greater *danger* of judgment. Their constant use of the tongue means they can sin very easily, leading others astray at the same time.

Teachers, because they bear so much responsibility for the spiritual welfare of those to whom they minister, will be scrutinized by the Lord more carefully than others. Jesus warned: "From everyone who has been given much, much will be demanded; and from the one who has been entrusted with much, much more will be asked" (Luke 12:48). God has given to teachers a great gift and entrusted to them "the deposit" of the faith (cf. 2 Tim. 1:14). He will expect a careful account of the stewardship. Paul reflects just this sense of responsibility as he addresses the elders of the church at Ephesus. He stressed that he had been faithful to his task as a herald of the gospel: "I declare to you today that I am innocent of the blood of all men. For I have not hesitated to proclaim to you the whole will of God" (Acts 20:26-27). If Paul serves as a positive example, many of the Jewish teachers of Jesus' day exhibited the other side of the picture: because of their insincerity and desire for gain, Jesus announced that "they will receive the greater condemnation" (Mark 12:40, NRSV). Those of us who teach God's word regularly need to follow James's example and apply the warning of this verse to ourselves. When we undertake to guide others in the faith, we must be especially careful to exhibit the fruit of that faith by the way we live. Our greater knowledge brings with it a greater responsibility to live according to that knowledge. Of course, James is not trying to talk people who have the appropriate call and the gift out of becoming teachers. But he does want to impress upon us the seriousness of this calling and to warn us about entering into the ministry with insincere or cavalier motivations.

2 The NIV does not explicitly indicate a connection between vv. 1 and 2. But James again here uses *gar,* "because," "for" (NASB; NRSV), indicating that v. 2 explains or gives the basis for v. 1. The probable logic of the argument is: Teachers are more susceptible to judgment than others *because* they regularly engage in that activity which is hardest to keep from sin — one's speech. James begins by acknowledging that *we all stumble in many ways.* The Greek word translated "many ways" in the NIV *(polla)* could also refer to the large number of sins (cf. NRSV: "all of us make many mistakes"). But the context favors the NIV interpretation, James's argument requiring reference not to the number but to the variety of sins. The Greek word for *stumble (ptaiō)* always has a metaphorical sense in the Bible: "be ruined, defeated" (usually in the LXX); or "make a mistake," "sin" (in the NT; see also 2:10; Rom. 11:11; 2 Pet. 1:10 [although this last occurrence could belong in the first category]). The word is not used often enough to be sure about its precise nuance, but it may suggest a minor or inadvertent sin. This sense would fit both occurrences in James, where in each case James highlights the fact or significance of even the smallest deviation from the will of God (see also 2:10). And, while the Greek verb is different, this seems to be the sense of a text that might have influenced James here, Sir. 19:16: "A person may make a slip without intending it. Who has never sinned with his tongue?"

James uses this same verb in the second assertion of the verse, *If anyone is never at fault in what he says, he is a perfect man, able to keep his whole body in check.* As we all know to our chagrin, words have a way of escaping our mouths before they are carefully considered — sometimes with unfortunate results. The problem is one that Proverbs highlights repeatedly. See, for instance, 18:6-7: "A fool's lips bring him strife, and his mouth invites a beating. A fool's mouth is his undoing, and his lips are a snare to his soul." But Philo provides the closest parallel: "But if a man succeeded, as if handling a lyre, in bringing all the notes of the thing that is good into tune, bringing speech into harmony with intent, and intent with deed, such an one would be considered perfect and of a truly harmonious character" (*Posterity and Exile of Cain* 88).[6] Indeed, the ease with which people sin in speech and the dire results of this sin are staple themes in both Jewish Wisdom literature and in Hellenistic moral exhortation broadly. James, then, is hardly saying anything new in claiming that a person (Gk. *anthrōpos*) who did not sin in speech would be perfect. Indeed, James adds, that person would surely be able to control the whole body as well. So difficult is the mouth to control, so given is it to utter the false, the biting, the slanderous word, so prone to stay open when it were more profitably closed, that the person who has it in control surely has the ability to "keep in check" other, less unruly, members of the body. The word for *keep in check* here means, literally, "bridle." The word both harks back to 1:26 (the only other occurrence of the verb in the NT) and anticipates the metaphor of v. 3 (the word "bit" is cognate in Greek to the word "bridle" here).

Since James continues to include himself in what he says in this part of the verse — "*we* all stumble in many ways" — his focus may still be on teachers. And some commentators think that the "body" language may carry on this focus. The possessive pronoun after "body" — "his" in the NIV — has nothing corresponding to it in the Greek. Therefore, while some reference to the human body is required by the metaphor, it is possible to think that "controlling the whole body" might have a secondary reference to exercising influence over the church, "the body of Christ."[7]

6. Cf. Johnson, 256.
7. See, e.g., Reicke, 37; Martin, 110.

Teachers who can speak well and appropriately have great power to direct the life of the congregation. While obviously true enough, this extended sense is improbable. For one thing, James gives no evidence that he, or his readers, would be familiar with the application of "body" language to the church. Of course, we cannot exclude the possibility; for, while appearing in its full theological splendor in Paul, the imagery has roots in the teaching of Jesus (e.g., John 2:20-22). But all James's uses of the word "body" (see also 2:16, 26; 3:3, 6) are sufficiently explained without any hint of this ecclesiological application. Second, James's use of "all" in the second part of this verse strongly suggests that he is reverting to the subject of v. 1a — "many of you," the readers of the letter in general.

3 Our words, James has now made clear, have an enormous impact on our spiritual condition. But has not James perhaps exaggerated the issue? Can our speech really have that big an impact? James anticipates this objection and now launches into a series of illustrations to reinforce his belief that a comparatively small "member," such as the tongue, has influence out of all proportion to its size. James compares the tongue to the bit that controls the horse (v. 3), the rudder that steers the ship (v. 4), and the spark that causes a forest fire (v. 5). Each of these illustrations is found quite widely in the ancient world, sometimes in conjunction with one another. James again reveals himself as a pastor concerned to bring home his message to his readers by selecting images from his world and the literature of the time.

The NIV introduces v. 3 with "when," a stylistic equivalent in this context to the word "if" found in other translations (cf. NASB; NRSV; REB also has "when"). The KJV, however, has "behold." The difference reflects variant readings in the Greek manuscripts: some have *ide* (or *idou*), an imperative form of the verb "see," while others have *ei de,* "now if." The similarity in spelling between the two explains how one reading could easily have evolved from the other. And *ei de* is more likely to be the original text, for two reasons: (1) it has stronger manuscript support; and (2) it could easily have been changed by an early scribe who, perhaps unconsciously, assimilated the beginning of v. 3 to the opening of v. 4 (*idou,* "behold").

James's reference to "bridling" in v. 2 may well have suggested to him the imagery of the horse and bit that he uses in v. 3. But the use of the horse to illustrate how something small can control something large was widespread in the ancient world. The fifth-century-B.C. playwright Sophocles has one of his actors say, "I know that spirited horses are broken by the use of a small bit" (*Antigone* 477). To be sure, James does not specifically mention the small size of the bit. But the readers, of course, would know this, and James's reference to *the whole animal* probably suggests it by contrast. By putting bits into the mouths of horses, James points out, we can *make them obey us* (lit., "persuade them for our benefit" [taking *hēmin* as a dative of advantage]). And, as a result, we can *turn the whole animal.* The slightly paraphrastic NIV rendering conceals what might be another important connection between vv. 2 and 3. For the NIV "animal" translates the Greek word *sōma,* "body." The phrase "the whole body" is then something of a catch-phrase that creates a link between the two verses. The point is important because some commentators suggest that here again "body" does not means just the physical body of the horse, but alludes also to the spiritual "body of Christ" — the church. Favoring this interpretation, these interpreters argue, is the poor fit between the illustration, taken literally, and the point that James wants to make. For the tongue does not "control" the body the way that a bit controls a horse. "James' intention is to show that the tongue is the means by which a body of great size . . . — namely, the church — is controlled by a separate part of much smaller size, namely, the teachers who are decisively influential out of proportion to their number, as they control . . . the direction of the whole body."[8] But our reason for rejecting this interpretation applies just as much here as in v. 2: James has not prepared his readers for any such theological application of the word "body." Probably, then, it is not so much "control" that James intends to illustrate but "direction": as the bit determines the direction of the horse, so the tongue can determine the destiny of the individual. Believers who exercise careful control of the tongue are able also to direct their whole life in its proper, divinely charted course: they are "perfect" (v. 2). But when that tongue is not restrained, small though it is, the rest of the body is likely to be uncontrolled and undisciplined also.

4 James's second illustration makes exactly the same point as the first: very small things can direct very large things. James invites us to consider ships — not specific ships (as the NASB, "Behold the ships also," might suggest) but ships in general (the article in Greek is probably generic). The NIV *Or take ships as an example* is paraphrastic but captures the sense very well. James did little to reinforce the contrast in size between bit and horse that is central to these illustrations. But he makes the point very clear in this second image. First, James explicitly contrasts ships, which are "very large" (NIV *so large*), with rudders, which are *very small* (the superlative adjective *elachistou* is probably elative). Second, he points out that the rudder controls the huge ship in the midst of *strong winds.* "Strong" translates a Greek word *(sklēros)* that means "hard," "rough," "cruel" (other NT occurrences are Matt. 25:24; John 6:60; Acts

8. Martin, 110; see also Reicke, 37-38.

26:14; Jude 15). Applied to winds (cf. Prov. 27:16 [LXX] and Isa. 27:8), the word must mean "violent," "rough" (REB translates "gales"). Another difference between this image and the first is the explicit reference to the ultimate "will" or "impulse" (Gk. *hormē*) that controls the rudder and hence the ship: the *pilot.* James thus sets up the application that he will make of these images in v. 5, with all three key components in place: "the guiding desire (the steersman), the means of control (the rudder), and that which is controlled (the ship), corresponding in turn to human desire, the tongue, and the body."[9]

The imagery of the small rudder that steers a huge ship was widespread in the ancient world. Aristotle, for instance, contrasted the small size of the rudder, turned by one man, with the "huge mass" of the ship it controls (*Quaestiones Mechanica* 5). But what is especially interesting is that a number of writers used the same combination of illustrations that we find in James. The rule of God over the world is compared to the charioteer's guidance of the horse through reins and bit and to the pilot's steering of a ship (e.g., Pseudo-Aristotle, *De mundo* 6; frequently in Philo). We also find texts that refer in the same context to the charioteer, the helmsman, and the taming of the animal world (cf. v. 7) (Philo, *Creation* 83–86). Still others combine the images of horse, ship, and fire — as James does in vv. 3-5. The best example is perhaps a passage in Philo, in which he talks of the power of the mind to direct the senses:

> Mind is superior to Sense-perception. When the charioteer is in command and guides the horses with the reins, the chariot goes the way he wishes. . . . A ship, again, keeps to her straight course, when the helmsman grasping the tiller steers accordingly. . . . Just so, when Mind, the charioteer or helmsman of the soul, rules the whole living being as a governor does a city, the life holds a straight course. . . . But when irrational sense gains the chief place, . . . the mind is set on fire and is all ablaze, and that fire is kindled by the objects of sense which Sense-perception supplies. (*Allegorical Interpretation* 3.224)

The moralist Plutarch even uses the imagery of a runaway ship and a fire to illustrate the destructive and uncontrollable nature of loose speech (*De garrulitate* 10). The point in citing these parallels is not to argue that James depends on any one of them directly. So widespread were the images of horse, ship, and fire in the literature that they must have been common sources for illustrations in the everyday world of James's environment. And, indeed, all three were so common that they would have been natural sources for illustrations.

9. Johnson, 258.

5 James wraps up the opening section of his discourse on the tongue by explicitly applying the illustrations of vv. 3-4. The bit and the rudder, small though they may be, are comparable to the *tongue, a small part of the body* that nevertheless *makes great boasts.* For the first time in this passage we find the word "tongue," used by metonymy for human speech. Although the Greek word for *boast (aucheō)* is found only here in the NT, the idea of "boasting" is often negative, involving arrogant presumptuousness before God. James's only other reference to boasting has just this nuance (4:16-17). Here, however, it is used more neutrally: the tongue can legitimately make the claim to have considerable power. Phillips paraphrases, "the human tongue is physically small, but what tremendous effects it can boast of!"

The imagery of the spark and the forest fire in the last part of v. 5 provides a further illustration of the "great boasts" that small things can make (v. 5a). At the same time, the point being illustrated shifts slightly, since the nuance of destructiveness is now added. A slight break therefore comes between vv. 5a and 5b, with the latter introducing the image of fire that will dominate vv. 5b-6.[10] The beginning of the half verse also suggests a bit of a break. James uses the same word he used in v. 4 — "behold" or "see" *(idou)* — but in this case without the connective conjunction (*kai,* translated "or" in NIV). The NIV's *consider* captures the sense of the word well. What James wants us to consider is *what a great forest is set on fire by a small spark.* Impossible to convey in English translation is a striking rhetorical feature of this sentence: the words "great" and "small" translate the same Greek word. The word in question *(hēlikos)* "expresses magnitude in either direction" (Hort). By giving it contextually marked opposite meanings, James accentuates the contrast between the small initial "fire" (NIV *spark;* the Greek word is just the usual word for "fire" [*pyr*]) and the huge resulting conflagration.[11] "Forest" translates a Greek word that means "wood." James might then be referring not so much to a "forest" (a rare feature of Near Eastern topography in James's day) but to the brush that covers so many Palestinian hills and which, in that dry Mediterranean climate, could so easily and disastrously burst into flame.[12]

10. See, e.g., D. F. Watson, "The Rhetoric of James 3:1-12 and a Classical Pattern of Argumentation," *NovT* 35 (1993) 58-59; and note the paragraph breaks at this point in the REB and the TEV.

11. The word has a similar function in Philostratus, *Life of Apollonius* 2.11.2: "for it seems to me a super-human feat for such a tiny [*tēlikoud*] mite to manage so huge [*tēlikouto*] an animal."

12. L. E. Elliott-Binns, "The Meaning of *'YLH* in Jas. III.5," *NTS* 2 (1995) 48-50; see also the note in Hort, 104-7.

The appeal to fire to illustrate the point James is making is not unexpected. First, as we noted in v. 4, other authors used the images of horse, ship, and fire together to illustrate a point. Second, a raging, out-of-control fire is a natural way to illustrate disastrous consequences. We speak of a disease, for instance, "spreading like wildfire." In the ancient world, the rapid and damaging spread of fire was frequently used to convey a warning about the effect of unrestrained passions. Some authors apply just this imagery to human speech. The OT compares the speech of a scoundrel to "a scorching fire" (Prov. 16:27), and a Jewish writer from the intertestamental period claims that the tongue "will not be master over the godly, and they will not be burned in its flame" (Sir. 28:22). As these references suggest, and as we would naturally expect in any case, comparing something to fire focuses on its destructive effects. We find in this half verse, therefore, an advance in James's argument: not only does the tiny tongue — like the bit and the rudder — possess power all out of proportion to its size; it also has the potential to bring disaster — like the spark in a dry forest.

6 James now abandons simile — the tongue is *like* the bit, the rudder, the spark — in favor of straightforward metaphor: *The tongue also is a fire.* The "also" of the NIV is a possible translation of the word James uses here *(kai);* but a more likely rendering in this context is "and" (found in most of the other English versions). "Also" makes little sense in this context, since James has already identified (implicitly) the tongue with fire in v. 5b. His point in v. 6, rather, is to sharpen the point about the tongue being a fire; we might paraphrase: "And yes, the tongue really is a fire."

How we are to translate the continuation of this assertion is not clear. The difficulty is that James uses a series of five nouns, all in the nominative case, with only one indicative verb. Interpreters and translator have to decide just how to combine these words in a way that makes the best grammatical and logical sense. And, since every conceivable combination has difficulties, the choice among the options is not easy. In fact, so difficult is the text that a few scholars suggest conjectural emendations. They think that a very early scribe miscopied the verse, so that all our existing manuscripts now have it wrong. We need to correct this early mistake by modifying the wording. However, while such a scenario cannot be completely ruled out, the abundant and early evidence about the NT text that we possess always makes such emendation a last resort. Slightly different is the suggestion that we follow one of the ancient translations (the Syriac Peshitta) and render "the tongue, also, is a fire; the sinful world [is] wood."[13] But we are still resorting to an interpreta-

13. Adamson, 142.

tion that has no basis in any Greek text of Jas. 3:6. Better to work with the text that we have, despite the difficulties.

We can start by clarifying the meaning of a crucial phrase, rendered in the NIV *a world of evil.* Since the word translated "world" (Gk. *kosmos*) can also mean "adornment" (as in 1 Pet. 3:3), a few scholars think that James might be suggesting that the tongue is the "adornment" of evil, or unrighteousness *(adikia)*.[14] On this view, he would be thinking of the way people can use fine-sounding phrases to make evil acts appear to be not only acceptable but even beneficial. But this interpretation, not very well represented among the commentators, must be rejected. It gives to *kosmos* a meaning that is very rare in the NT and does not fit the metaphor of fire very well at all. Also to be rejected is the interpretation suggested in the Latin Vulgate, which takes *kosmos* to mean "sum total" or "mass" (the NLT may reflect this interpretation: "It is full of wickedness"). This understanding also depends on a rare meaning of *kosmos* (never does the word clearly have this meaning elsewhere in the NT). The most common meaning of *kosmos* in the NT is "world," often with the nuance of the fallen, sinful world-system. This is the meaning the word has in its three other occurrences in James (1:27; 4:4). The word "unrighteousness" or "evil" will then be added to make clear this negative nuance of the word; we can translate "the unrighteous world." (A close parallel to this construction is found in Luke 16:9, "mammon of unrighteousness," translated in the NIV as "worldly wealth.") Almost all modern English translations adopt this general meaning (NRSV: "a world of iniquity"; REB: "the whole wicked world"; TEV: "a world of wrong"; NJB: "a whole wicked world").

With the meaning of this key phrase settled, we are now in a position to decide on the translation of the sentence as a whole. Three options are possible (the renderings are my own, literal translations of the Greek):

1. "The tongue is a fire, the world of unrighteousness. It [the tongue] is appointed among our members as that which stains the whole body, setting on fire the course of our existence." This option, represented among translations by the NASB and argued by the great pietist scholar Bengel, rests on three key decisions. It (a) understands the phrase "world of unrighteousness" as an appositive qualifier of "fire"; (b) puts a punctuation break after this phrase; and (c) takes the phrase "which stains the whole body" as the predicate of the verb "is appointed."

2. "The tongue is appointed as a fire, indeed, as the world of unrighteousness in our members; it stains the whole body, sets on fire the course of our existence. . . ." Proposed by Mussner, this interpretation, in agree-

14. Chaine, 81.

ment with the first alternative, (a) puts "world of unrighteousness" in apposition to "fire"; but (b) places a punctuation break between "members" and "which stains"; and (c) takes "fire" as the predicate of the verb "is appointed."

3. "And the tongue is a fire. The tongue is appointed among our members as the world of unrighteousness, staining the whole body, setting on fire the course of existence. . . ." This alternative is the most popular of the three, represented (essentially) in most English translations (NIV; NRSV; REB; NJB; NLT) and defended by most commentators. It (a) does not place "world of unrighteousness" in apposition to "fire," but (c) makes it the predicate of the verb "is appointed"; and (b) puts a punctuation break between the initial assertion and the further elaboration. The clause "which stains . . ." then begins a further elaboration of "the tongue."

The majority view is probably to be followed. The form of the word we have translated "stain" (a feminine participle, *spilousa*) makes it very difficult to turn into the predicate of the verb "is appointed," as in the first alternative. But the second alternative is equally problematic, because too many words (in the Greek text) come between the verb "is appointed" and its predicate, "fire." The third option avoids these difficulties and gives, on the whole, the most natural reading of the Greek text. A problem with this view, however, is James's use of the verb we have translated "is appointed" *(kathistatai)*. The translations that adopt this basic rendering reveal the problem by rendering the verb, variously, "is placed" (NRSV); "represents" (REB); "occupying" (TEV); and "is" (NJB). If the verb is passive, the translation of the NRSV is accurate enough; and the understood subject of the verb may even be God, who, for the testing of humans, has himself appointed the tongue to have this role.[15] But James uses the same form of this verb in a similar construction in 4:4, where it is middle and has the meaning "makes oneself." This interpretation fits perfectly the idea of the tongue's arrogant boasting (v. 5). Though a small member of the body, it "appoints" itself as the "unrighteous world"; that is, the tongue, by virtue of being the most difficult of all parts of the body to control, becomes the conduit by which all the evil of the world around us comes to expression in us. As Calvin puts it, "a slender portion of flesh contains the whole world of iniquity." Jesus made similar claims about the tongue. He taught that it is "what comes out of [a man's] mouth" that makes him "unclean"; and, elaborating, noted that the mouth expresses the heart, in which are found "evil thoughts, murder, adultery, sexual immorality, theft, false witness, slander" (Matt.

15. Baker, 126-27.

15:11, 18-19). No other "member" of the body, perhaps, wreaks so much havoc on the godly life.

James ends v. 6 with a series of three parallel participles that further decry the baneful effects of the tongue. The NIV preserves the parallelism nicely by rendering them as indicative verbs:

> It corrupts the whole person,
> sets the whole course of his life on fire,
> and is itself set on fire by hell.

By "corrupting" or "staining" *(spilousa)* the whole person, the tongue destroys "true religion" — which, James has told us, requires that we keep ourselves from being polluted, or "stained" *(aspilon)* by the world. "Person" is a good rendering of Gk. *sōma* here, which refers in this context not just to the physical body but to "our whole being" (TEV). The second and third clauses return to the imagery of fire that dominates vv. 5b-6, as James identifies the extent and the source of the devastation that the tongue creates in a person's life. The NIV's "whole course of his life" translates a Greek phrase that means, literally, "the wheel of origin, or existence." The same phrase was used in certain ancient pagan religions to describe the unending cycle of reincarnations from which one could seek deliverance by adherence to the religion. Some commentators (e.g., Ropes) think that the occurrence of this technical religious phrase here demonstrates that the author of the letter must have been familiar with such religious currents and is therefore unlikely to have been a Palestinian Jew like James the brother of the Lord. But such a conclusion is unnecessary. The word "wheel" was fairly widely used among Jews in the Hellenistic period to characterize the regular "turn" of fortune. And the phrase "wheel of existence" itself may, like so many originally technical expressions, have become fairly widespread as a way of describing the "ups and downs" of life.[16] ("Existence" translates the same word [*genesis*] that James used in 1:23 to qualify "face"; see our notes on this word there.) A Palestinian Jew acquainted with the wider Hellenistic world could easily have used such a phrase with this sense. The NIV translation *the whole course of life* therefore captures the sense of the phrase quite well. Not only does the tongue corrupt the whole person; it also "sets on fire," wreaks havoc, throughout one's life. But where does this enormously destructive potential come from? From *hell,* says James. "Hell" translates the Gk. *gehenna,* which is a transliteration of two Hebrew words that mean "Valley of Hinnom." This valley, just outside Jerusalem, gained an

16. See, for discussion and examples, Dibelius, 196-98; and Johnson, 260.

evil reputation in the OT and intertestamental period. Pagan child sacrifices were carried out there (cf. Jer. 32:35), and trash was often burned in it. Jesus used the word to refer to the place of ultimate condemnation. James again betrays his connection to Jesus, since only in the teaching of Jesus do we find this word elsewhere in the NT (11 times). The power of Satan himself, the chief denizen of hell, gives to the tongue its great destructive potential.

James does not elaborate the ways in which the destructive power of the tongue can make itself felt. But he undoubtedly would have thought of those sins of speech that are enumerated in Proverbs: thoughtless "chattering" (10:8; cf. 12:18; 29:20); lying (12:19); arrogant boasting (18:12); gossiping (10:18). Think what enormous, sometimes irreversible, harm can be caused to people by unsubstantiated, often false, rumors. Such a rumor can be harder to stop than any forest fire (v. 5). We know from bitter experience that the childhood taunt, "Sticks and stones may break my bones, but words will never hurt me," reverses the truth of the matter. Far easier to heal are the wounds caused by sticks and stones than the damage caused by words.

7 Having established the considerable and potentially destructive power of the tongue in vv. 3-6, James goes on in vv. 7-8 to remind us that the tongue is extremely difficult to bring under control. The same point was already touched on in v. 2, where James attributed perfection to any person who is able to avoid sinning in speech. The verses are formally introduced (note the *for*) as evidence that the tongue is, indeed, "set on fire by hell" (v. 6). How else, James's logic appears to run, can we explain human inability to train the tongue? But James sets up this point by way of contrast, commenting first on how human beings have been able to train *all kinds of animals, birds, reptiles and creatures of the sea.* "Animal" translates a Greek word that can refer to virtually any kind of animal (in Acts 28:4, 5, a snake), but often, as apparently here, specifically to a quadruped.[17] Although the words are not exactly the same, this fourfold division of the animal kingdom clearly reflects the Genesis creation account: "Then God said, 'Let us make man in our image, in our likeness, and let them rule over the fish of the sea and the birds of the air, over the livestock, over all the earth, and over all the creatures that move along the ground'" (Gen. 1:26). This way of summarizing the nonhuman creaturely world became common in Jewish (e.g., Philo, *Special Laws* 4.110-16) and Christian (e.g., Acts 11:6) writings. Allusion to creation shows that James is making a general theological assertion about the nature of the world. Human ability to "tame" the animal world, suggests James, is inherent in

17. BAGD, 361.

the image of God and the divine mandate to "subdue" the world. The NIV obscures a detail in the text that adds weight to this point. For the verse begins with a reference to every "species" (NIV *kind*) of animal and concludes with a reference to the "species" of humankind. The "human species," James is saying in brief, is subduing every animal "species." Moreover, James uses the verb "tame" twice: once in the present tense to stress the continuing process by which human beings are subduing creatures, and again in the perfect tense — *have been tamed* — to show that this process is rooted in the state of affairs created by the divine mandate. Highlighting the intractable nature of the tongue by contrasting reference to human dominion over nature makes good sense in and of itself. But James may again owe the imagery to Jewish tradition, which could illustrate human control over the world by comparing man to the driver of a chariot (v. 3) or the pilot of a ship (v. 4).[18]

8 In the Greek of this verse, *the tongue* comes first for contrast: human beings may subdue animals — but *the tongue* no one can tame. All the major English translations, including the NIV, translate something like *no man* here. But what James says is, literally, "no one . . . of (or among) people." Why this awkward addition? James may simply be continuing the focus on human beings as a species that was so important in v. 7. But Augustine thought that James was making a more subtle point: ". . . he does not say that no one can tame the tongue, but no one of men; so that when it is tamed we confess that this is brought about by the pity, the help, the grace of God."[19] If this is James's intent, he would be holding out hope to us that we could, through the powerful work of the Spirit, bring our speech into perfect conformity with the will of God. Such a person, James has indicated, would be "perfect" or "complete" (Gk. *teleios*) (v. 2). In addition, then, to the exegetical question (can James's wording really bear this sense?), we must also consider the theological question: does James and/or the NT as a whole envisage the possibility of Christians attaining perfection in this life? We have answered this question in the negative (see our comments on 1:4). We therefore doubt that Augustine's interpretation is correct. James does, indeed, suggest that the ultimate taming of the tongue is impossible. Should this lead us to abandon all efforts to bring our speech under control? Of course not. The realiza-

18. Verse 7 is virtually a summary of Philo's argument in *Creation* 83-88. The Jewish philosopher argues for the dominion of man over the world by noting the way humans have subdued all kinds of creatures, including the horse (by means of the bit), and concludes that "the Creator made man after all things, as a sort of driver and pilot, to drive and steer the things on earth, and charged him with the care of animals and plants, like a governor subordinate to the chief and great King."

19. *On Nature and Grace* 15; cf. Knowling, 78.

tion that perfection in something is unattainable should not dampen in the least our enthusiasm to become as good at it as possible. We may never reach the point where the tongue is perfectly controlled; but we can surely advance a long way in using our speech to glorify God.

At the end of v. 8, James adds two more characterizations of the tongue to show just why we find it so hard to subdue: it is *a restless evil, full of deadly poison.* (Other versions take these as "ejaculative" nominatives — "a restless evil, full of deadly poison" [NRSV][20] — but the difference is slight.) The word "restless" translates the same word that James used in 1:8 to describe the "double-minded man, *unstable* in all he does." The LXX uses the same word with reference to sins of speech in Prov. 26:28: "A lying tongue hates those it hurts, and a flattering mouth works *ruin.*" Note also the early Christian document, Hermas, *Mandate* 2.3: "Slander is evil; it is a restless *(akatastaton)* demon, never at peace" (cf. Jas. 4:1). The nature of this "restless evil" is not entirely clear. On the one hand, James might be reiterating how hard it is to control the tongue: it is, as Phillips paraphrases, "always liable to break out." On the other hand, James could be thinking of the "instability and lack of single-mindedness" that characterize the tongue.[21] The former idea fits well with the emphasis on the difficulty of taming the tongue in vv. 7-8. But the latter anticipates the argument of vv. 9-12 and matches the other occurrence of the word in James (and this is the only other occurrence in the NT). James concludes the verse with a description of the tongue taken directly from the OT: *full of deadly poison.* See, for instance, Ps. 140:3: "They [evil men] make their tongues as sharp as a serpent's; the poison of vipers is on their lips." (Paul quotes the same verse to illustrate the manifold sins of the non-Christian world [Rom. 3:13].)

9 James brings his critique of the tongue to a conclusion by attributing to it the "doubleness" that he so frequently deplores in his letter. The "double-minded man" (1:8; cf. 4:8), inconsistent in his faith, trying to please both God and the world at the same time, epitomizes the concern that James has for his readers. Such a person tries to combine faith in Jesus Christ with denigration of Christ's people (2:1-13). They claim to have faith in God while failing to exhibit the works that true faith always produces (2:14-26). And now, we find, they use the same tongue both to *praise our Lord and Father* and to *curse men, who have been made in God's likeness.* This matter of the doubleness of the tongue is the theme of vv. 9-12. These verses are not tied to the preceding context in any explicit manner (i.e., no particle or conjunction is found at the beginning of v. 9). But a log-

20. Cf. Martin, 117.
21. Davids, 145.

ical connection seems clear: the inconsistency of the tongue is a very clear indication of the "restless evil" (v. 8) that it is.

James could choose no stronger contrast to illustrate the duality of the tongue than its use in "praising" God and "cursing" human beings. The NIV's *praise* could also be rendered "bless" (Gk. *eulogeō*). The blessing of God was a basic part of Jewish devotion. "The Holy One, blessed be he" is one of the most common designations of God in rabbinic literature, and the "eighteen benedictions," a liturgical formula cited daily, concluded each of its sections with a blessing of God. The early Christians, of course, were equally concerned to bless God in prayer and praise (cf. 2 Cor. 1:3; Eph. 1:13; 1 Pet. 1:3). The exact combination "Lord and Father" as a designation of God occurs only here in the Bible, but in several places we find these two titles used closely together. And it may be significant that most of these instances involve a person expressing praise or supplication to God (see Isa. 63:16; 64:8; Matt. 11:25 [= Luke 10:21]). Blessing, or praising, God is one of the most important and positive forms of human speech. James might be thinking specifically of the worship of the community, in which believers united their voices in singing and asserting the praise of God. But if praising God is one of the highest forms of speech, cursing people is one of the lowest. The opposing nature of "blessing" and "cursing" is rooted in God's own speech. In the most famous biblical example of such speech, God repeatedly sets before Israel these two alternatives as the result of its reaction to his law (see, e.g., Deut. 30:19). Partly as a result of these warnings and partly as the result of a general understanding of the nature of speech, people in the ancient world attributed great power to the curse. The ancient curse was far more than abusive language; it called on God, in effect, to cut a person off from any possible blessing and to consign that person to Hell. Jesus prohibited his disciples from cursing others; indeed, they were to "bless those who curse you" (Luke 6:28; cf. Rom. 12:14). As James emphasizes, what makes cursing especially evil is that the one whom we pronounce damned has been made *in God's likeness.* James has already alluded in this context to God's creation utterance, as he designated the various kinds of creatures over which God has given man dominion (v. 7; cf. Gen. 1:26). Here he alludes again to the same passage (see also 1:27) to remind us of the special likeness that human beings bear to God himself. James is probably here again reflecting common Jewish tradition; the rabbis taught that one should not say "'Let my neighbor be put to shame' — for then you put to shame one who is in the image of God" (*Genesis Rabbah* 24 [on Gen. 5:1]).

10 James now draws the moral from v. 9: *Out of the same mouth come praise and cursing. My brothers, this should not be.* In the passage thus far, James has referred to the "tongue" as the organ of speech. His shift in this verse to "mouth" and the language, natural to this metaphor, of "come out" probably reflects his dependence once again on the teaching of Jesus. Accused of allowing his disciples to transgress the customary Jewish laws about ritual cleanness, Jesus took occasion to identify those things that truly defile a person:

> "What goes into a man's mouth does not make him 'unclean,' but what comes out of his mouth, that is what makes him 'unclean.' . . . Don't you see that whatever enters the mouth goes into the stomach and then out of the body? But the things that come out of the mouth come from the heart, and these make a man 'unclean.' For out of the heart come evil thoughts, murder, adultery, sexual immorality, theft, false testimony, slander. These are what make a man 'unclean'; but eating with unwashed hands does not make him 'unclean.'" (Matt. 15:11, 17-20)

Jesus also pointed to the seriousness of what comes out of the mouth by making it a standard of judgment: "by your words you will be acquitted, and by your words you will be condemned" (Matt. 12:37). James also views what comes out of the mouth as a barometer of spirituality. Though a small member, the tongue "makes great boasts" (v. 5) and represents in our bodies "a world of evil" (v. 6). And nowhere does the tongue reveal its evil power more than in its doubleness. Such a concern about the tongue is not new; James again reveals his indebtedness to certain Jewish moral traditions. Note, for instance, *T. Benjamin* 6:5: "the good set of mind does not talk from both sides of its mouth: praises and curses, abuse and honor, calm and strife, hypocrisy and truth, poverty and wealth, but it has one disposition, uncontaminated and pure, towards all men." See also Sir. 5:14–6:1: "Do not be called a slanderer, and do not lie in ambush with your tongue; for shame comes to the thief, and severe condemnation to the double-tongued. In great or small matters do not act amiss, and do not become an enemy instead of a friend; for a bad name incurs shame and reproach; so fares the double-tongued sinner."[22]

James's bottom line is: "it is not necessary that these things should happen in this way" (a literal rendering). This assertion "wonderfully captures the moralist's sense of outrage at 'what ought not to be.'"[23] Christians who have been transformed by the Spirit of God should manifest the wholeness and purity of the heart in consistency and purity of speech.

22. See also Ps. 62:4; Sir. 28:12 ("If you blow on a spark, it will glow; if you spit on it, it will be put out; and both come out of your mouth"); Philo, *Decalogue* 93. Strictures against being "double-tongued" were taken up elsewhere in early Christianity (see *Did.* 2:4; *Barn.* 19:7).

23. Johnson, 262.

11 James hammers home the point that a pure heart and impure and "double-tongued" speech are incompatible with three illustrations (vv. 11-12). The first two are cast in the form of a rhetorical question that expects a negative answer (explicit in Greek with the use of the particles *mēti* and *mē*); the third is a straightforward negative statement. Each points out how absurd it would be for one thing to produce something of a completely different kind. And each exhibits James's pastoral ability to put truth in a form understandable to his readers by using some of the most common of all ancient Near Eastern objects. The importance of the *spring (pēgē)* in dry Palestine can hardly be overestimated. Many a village owed its origins to the discovery of a spring, and depended on its reliable production of potable water for its continuing existence. It was obviously vital that a spring continue to yield *fresh* (or "sweet" [Gk. *glykos*]; cf. Rev. 10:9, 10) *water.* To be sure, some streams and springs produced a mixture of fresh and salt water that was unusable. But springs did not pour forth fresh water one day and salt water the next. Such a thing just did not happen. And so, James implies, it is also inconceivable to think of a mouth pouring forth praise to God one moment and curses against fellow human beings the next. The word that the NIV translates "salt" is, as the NIV margin indicates, from a Greek word that means "bitter" *(pikros).* We might have expected James to use the common Greek word for "salt" here *(alykos),* as he does in v. 12. Perhaps James employs the more unusual term because it is found in several OT and intertestamental Jewish texts as a description of the wrong kind of speech (Ps. 64:3; Prov. 5:4; Sir. 29:25). By comparing the tongue to a spring that produces bitter water, James reinforces his warning that the tongue is, indeed, "full of deadly poison" (v. 8).

12 James's next two illustrations, drawn from the agricultural world, not only touch on the everyday life of his readers but also resonate with ancient moral teaching. For the idea of the plant producing according to its peculiar nature was widespread. The Greek writer Epictetus, for instance, asked: "How can a vine be moved to act, not like a vine, but like an olive, or again an olive to act, not like an olive, but like a vine? It is impossible, inconceivable" (*Discourses* 2.20.18-19). Even more relevant, however, may be the famous saying of Jesus about good trees producing good fruit and vice versa. See especially Matt. 7:16: "Do people pick grapes from thornbushes, or figs from thistles?" James's point is the same one that he has made with the illustration of the spring in v. 11: as the fig tree cannot produce olives or the grapevine figs, so the pure heart cannot produce false, bitter, harmful speech.

In the last part of v. 12, James returns to the imagery of fresh and bitter water from v. 11, but now makes a slightly different point: *Neither can a salt spring produce fresh water.* Several important Greek manuscripts add the word equivalent to our "so also" at the beginning of this sentence. This word is the same one that James has used repeatedly to introduce comparisons (*houtōs;* see 1:11; 2:17, 26; 3:5); if adopted here, we would translate: "And in the same way, neither does a salt spring produce fresh water." But the fact that James has used the word quite a lot makes us wonder if an early copyist accidentally added it (particularly because it is similar to the Greek word for "neither" [*oute*] that now stands first in the sentence). And the text makes good sense as is. Because he has changed the grammatical construction a bit (from a rhetorical question to an assertion), James uses the word "neither" to add yet a third illustration of the point that he makes in these verses.

The phrase "salt spring" in the NIV translates a single Greek word *(alykos)* that means "salt." (It is a different Greek word from the one translated "salt" by the NIV in v. 11.) The idea that "salt" or "salt water" (so most English translations) could produce "fresh water" makes no sense, and a number of ancient manuscripts and translations have different wording that smooths out the difficulty. The KJV follows one of these variants and so translates: "so can no fountain both yield salt water and fresh." But variants of this kind are usually suspected of being later attempts to make a difficult text easier; and we should probably therefore work with the text that we have. The best alternative, therefore, is to assume that the Greek word here can have the meaning "salt spring," a sense that is attested for a word closely related to the one that is used here.[24]

However, whatever the precise wording, James's point is obvious: bad things don't produce good things. And so a person who is not right with God and walking daily in his presence cannot consistently speak pure and helpful words. One who is double and inconsistent with regard to the things of God in his heart (*dipsychos,* 1:8 and 4:8) will be double and inconsistent in his speech. We have noted that James's imagery of like things producing like probably depends to some extent on Jesus' well-known proverb about the good tree bearing good fruit. If taken strictly, and without regard for other biblical teaching, such imagery could suggest that a person who is once made "good" by God through Christ and the Holy Spirit will inevitably live the right kind of life in all respects. But we must not make the mistake of pressing a helpful comparison between trees and the spiritual life beyond its intent. As theologian Hendrikus Berkhof trenchantly reminds us, "A man is after all not a tree."[25] The au-

24. See BAGD; the related word is *alykis,* and refers to a salt spring in Strabo 4.1.7. See also Dibelius, 205.

25. H. Berkhof, *The Christian Faith* (Grand Rapids: Eerdmans, 1979), 452.

tomatic natural processes of plant life cannot be exactly compared to the willing, deciding processes of human life. But, whatever its limits, the imagery conveys an important warning: only a renewed heart can produce pure speech; and consistently (though not perfectly) pure speech is to be the product of the renewed heart.

B. True Wisdom Brings Peace (3:13–4:3)

> 13 *Who is wise and understanding among you? Let him show it by his good life, by deeds done in the humility that comes from wisdom.* 14 *But if you harbor bitter envy and selfish ambition in your hearts, do not boast about it or deny the truth.* 15 *Such "wisdom" does not come down from heaven but is earthly, unspiritual, of the devil.* 16 *For where you have envy and selfish ambition, there you find disorder and every evil practice.* 17 *But the wisdom that comes from heaven is first of all pure; then peace loving, considerate, submissive, full of mercy and good fruit, impartial and sincere.* 18 *Peacemakers who sow in peace raise a harvest of righteousness.*
>
> 4:1 *What causes fights and quarrels among you? Don't they come from your desires that battle within you?* 2 *You want something but don't get it. You kill and covet, but you cannot have what you want. You quarrel and fight. You do not have, because you do not ask God.* 3 *When you ask, you do not receive, because you ask with wrong motives, that you may spend what you get on your pleasures.*

Most commentaries and English translations follow the chapter division and place a significant break between the last paragraph of chap. 3 (3:13-18) and the first of chap. 4 (4:1-3 or 4:1-10). Good reasons can be found for positing such a break: 4:1 is asyndetic (i.e., no particle or conjunction formally connects the verse to chap. 3); the key vocabulary changes; and the contrast between two kinds of wisdom in 3:13-18 does not appear to have much to do with the rebuke of quarreling in 4:1-3. But a closer look reveals significant connections between the two paragraphs. James is especially concerned about the unrighteous and misguided "zeal" or "envy" (Gk. *zēlos*) that people characterized by "earthly" wisdom are displaying (3:16); and it is this same envy (*zēloō;* translated "covet" in NIV) that is leading to bitter arguments in the community (4:2). Nor is this word a minor one in the argument. As we noted in the introduction to 3:1–4:12, James depends in this section of his letter on a widespread Hellenistic-Jewish moral *topos,* or traditional "topic," that traced social ills back to jealousy *(zēlos)* and envy *(phthonos).* The closest parallels to James come in *The Testaments of the Twelve Patriarchs,* a Jewish pseudepigraphical work most of which was written around 100 B.C. In this book, slander (*katalalia, T. Gad* 3:3), violence *(polemos),* and murder (*T. Simeon* 4:5) are all traced to jealousy. And these, of course, are just the issues attacked by James in 4:1-12. Moreover, the *Testaments* frequently highlight as a basic spiritual problem "double-mindedness," striking another familiar chord for the reader of James (cf. 1:8 and 4:8). Direct dependence of James on the *Testaments* is unlikely. James, we may surmise, knows of the kind of tradition found in the *Testaments* because it was so common in the ancient world. He presses it into use here in order to rebuke his readers for jealous and selfish attitudes that are manifesting themselves in disunity and bitter disputes.

The common thread running through both paragraphs is peace. After the initial rhetorical question setting up the issue of wisdom (v. 13a), James calls on his readers to demonstrate the reality of their wisdom in humility and good works (v. 13b). This leads into the contrast between two kinds of wisdom that dominates the paragraph. The wrong kind is characterized by envy, selfishness, and disorder (vv. 14-16) — the opposite of peace. The right kind of wisdom, on the other hand, is above all "peace loving" (the first specific "fruit of wisdom" listed in v. 17). And James underscores this virtue with his concluding blessing on peacemakers (v. 18). The absence of peace, on the other hand, is obviously the main issue in 4:1-3. The community is marked by quarrels and arguments — some of them perhaps even violent. And James traces these disputes to the characteristics of false wisdom that he pointed out in 3:14: envy (v. 2) and selfishness (v. 3).

Since James opens this section by asking "Who is wise and understanding among you?" he might be returning here to his rebuke of the leaders of the community that seems to be the focus of vv. 1-2. Indeed, some commentators (e.g., Martin) think that James has never left this focus, arguing that the entire discussion of the tongue has particular relevance to teachers. On this view, all of 3:1–4:3 can be seen as a rebuke directed especially (though not only) to the leaders of the church, who are using false and abusive speech in pursuit of their theological agenda and are, as a consequence, splitting the church into factions. However, we have argued above that 3:1-12 is directed to the entire community; and we think it likely that 3:13–4:3 is also. Certainly it would often be church leaders who prided themselves on a superior degree of wisdom and who were in a position to create significant disunity. But ordinary members of the congregation could create similar difficulties by opposing the leadership or engaging in bitter partisan fights for their own views. James seems to have the whole community in view in 3:13–4:3.

13 James begins his critique of envy and the disputes it engenders with a rhetorically effective invitation: *Who is wise and understanding among you?* James asks people who think that they have special understanding and insight in spiritual matters, in effect, to step forward so that he can analyze the legitimacy of their claim. As we noted above, many commentators think that this question has in view especially teachers (see v. 1). But neither "wise" *(sophos)* nor "understanding" *(epistēmōn)* is regularly used as a title for the teacher. They occur together several times in the Septuagint, once with reference to the qualities leaders should possess (Deut. 1:13, 15) but also with application to all of Israel (Deut. 4:6; Dan. 5:12 applies them to the prophet). James has already emphasized that "wisdom" is a quality that all believers should seek to attain (1:5). Moreover, even 3:1 is not really directed to teachers, but to those who would *become* teachers. We therefore think that James invites any of his readers who might pride themselves on their wisdom to consider seriously what he is about to say.

Those people who respond to James's invitation in v. 13a quickly find themselves the object of searching and perhaps unwanted scrutiny. For James assesses these people's claim to wisdom not in theological terms — how much doctrine do they know, how many Greek verbs can they parse — but in practical terms: *Let him show it by his good life, by deeds done in the humility that comes from wisdom.* The NIV rendering takes several liberties with the Greek, although all are justified in order to bring out the sense that James apparently intends. For the Greek is very awkward here, reading, literally, "let him show on the basis of good conduct his works in the humility of wisdom." The "let him show"[26] challenge reminds us of James's challenge in 2:18 to the "believer" who thinks works and faith can be separated: "Show me your faith without deeds." Indeed, the test of true wisdom that James applies here picks up key ideas he touches on earlier in the letter: the importance of humility (1:21)[27] and good works (2:14-26). "Good conduct," James insists, is the basis on which one can demonstrate wisdom. This phrase, or similar ones, occurs several times in the letters of Peter in a general way to denote a lifestyle that pleases God. See especially 1 Pet. 2:12: "Live such good lives [lit., 'have good conduct'] among the pagans that, though they accuse you of doing wrong, they may see your good deeds and glorify God on the day he visits us." (See also 1 Pet. 1:15; 3:1, 2, 16; 2 Pet. 3:11.) As we will see in the latter stages of James's letter especially, James and Peter share a num-

26. Martin (129) uses a false interpretation of the aorist tense to argue here that James requires a sudden change in lifestyle. But the aorist simply states the fact of the command and gives us no ground for inferences about the nature or frequency of the "showing."

27. Hoppe (51) finds a number of significant parallels between 3:13-18 and 1:17-20.

ber of key words, phrases, and topics. The idea that "good deeds" are to be shown on the basis of good conduct is a little unusual, but clear enough: it is our acts of obedience to God, performed consistently day after day, that make up the "good conduct" of the wise person. But more difficult to understand is the loose addition "in the humility of wisdom." What James appears to mean, however, is that the good works are to be done in a spirit of humility — a humility that itself is the product, or result, of wisdom (taking the genitive *sophias* as a genitive of source). James is clearly trying to say two things here: true wisdom produces good works and true wisdom produces humility. The results of false wisdom that James highlights in v. 14, envy and selfishness, are in clear contrast to this humility, suggesting that it is especially this quality that James is concerned to emphasize here. Humility, or "meekness" (Gk. *praütēs*) was not usually prized by the Greeks. They thought it signaled a servility unworthy of a strong and confident person. But a different picture emerges in the NT. Jesus himself claimed to be "meek" (Matt. 11:29; cf. Matt. 21:5) and blessed those who were meek (Matt. 5:5). This Christian meekness, or humility, comes from understanding our position as sinful creatures in relationship to the glorious and majestic God (note James's elaboration of this point in 4:7). It recognizes how unable we are in and of ourselves to achieve spiritual fulfillment or to chart our own course in the world. And this humility before God should then translate into humility toward others (see, e.g., Gal. 6:1; Eph. 4:2; Col. 3:12; 2 Tim. 2:25; Tit. 3:2; 1 Pet. 3:2, 16).

James's insistence that wisdom is to be tested by the kind of life one lives is in keeping with the idea of wisdom in the OT. Wisdom, we remember, begins with the fear of the Lord (Prov. 1:7), enables us to discern what is "right and just" (Prov. 2:9), and leads us to "walk in the ways of good men and keep to the paths of the righteous" (Prov. 2:20). In stark contrast to this biblical perspective were certain Greek ideas of wisdom, which prized intellectual ability and knowledge of divine secrets — sometimes to the detriment of the moral life. Paul seems to have encountered such notions of wisdom in Corinth (see 1 Cor. 1:18–2:16 especially). A few commentators think that James's teaching also presupposes such false ideas of wisdom, but this is not clear.[28] His rebuke of false wisdom is not so much directed against a particular view of wisdom as against a failure of people to live out in the ways they should the implications of wisdom. Throughout his discussion, James's conception of wisdom remains relatively undeveloped, following quite closely the lines laid down in the OT.

28. Klein, e.g., thinks that James in this paragraph might be polemicizing against a Pauline-like christological wisdom teaching (154-61).

14 This verse is set in antithesis to James's challenge in v. 13b. If a person *harbors bitter envy and selfish ambition* in the heart, that person is, in effect, living a lie: claiming to be wise but conducting himself in a way that denies that claim. The reason that James can draw this conclusion is that *bitter envy and selfish ambition* are contrary to humility. If, then, humility marks the wise person, these negative qualities exclude a person from being considered wise. The word translated "envy" is an important and theologically significant word, *zēlos.* It has two basic senses: a neutral or even positive sense, "zeal," "jealousy"; and a negative sense, "envy." The former meaning is seen in those many texts that describe God as "jealous": demanding that his people serve him alone, renouncing allegiance to any other god or "idol." This meaning, then, is applied to human beings who display a similar concern to protect God's people or institutions from any hint of compromise or defilement. Phinehas, who killed Israelites because they were compromising the holiness of God's people by sleeping with foreigners, is the OT prototype of the "zealot" (Num. 25:11-13; see Ps. 106:30). Jesus displayed the same "zeal" or "jealousy" for God's Temple by chasing the moneylenders out of it (John 2:17; in the NT, see also Rom. 10:2; 2 Cor. 7:7, 11; 9:2; 11:2; Phil. 3:6; Heb. 10:27). The Jewish terrorists of James's day, who pursued a campaign of violence against the Romans in order to restore the purity of Israel as a theocracy, were given the name "Zealots." But this word can also take on a negative sense, referring to a self-oriented desire to possess things that are not really ours (see Acts 5:17; 13:45; Rom. 13:13; 1 Cor. 3:3; 2 Cor. 12:20; Gal. 5:20). The qualification "bitter" (*pikros;* used in v. 11 of water) makes clear that James has the bad kind of "jealousy" in mind here. Particularly, as the context suggests, he is thinking of the kind of jealousy or envy that people display when other people challenge their own ideas and gain some hearing for them (this sense is evident in the NT in Acts 5:17 and 13:45).

What makes this nuance of "envy" particularly likely here is the word that it is paired with, "selfish ambition" *(eritheia).* The word occurs only here in the NT, but is sometimes related to a similar word that Paul uses three times in conjunction with "jealousy," "strife" *(eris).* Note KJV: "But if ye have bitter envying and strife in your hearts. . . ." But most modern English translations follow the NIV in rendering *selfish ambition,* and this is probably the right decision. The only attested pre-NT occurrence of the word comes in Aristotle, who uses it to describe the narrow partisan zeal of factional, greedy politicians in his own day. This meaning makes excellent sense here in James. Some who pride themselves on their wisdom and understanding are displaying a jealous, bitter partisanship that is the antithesis of the humility produced by true wisdom.

James warns people characterized by these negative traits not *to boast about it or deny the truth.* The word for "boast" *(katakauchaomai)* is a compound form of a verb used especially often in Paul *(kauchaomai).* The simple form of this verb is also translated "boast" — probably the best translation of a word that usually has the dual sense "take pride in" and "put confidence in." Its sense is best gained from the OT verse that provides a key background for its use in the NT, Jer. 9:23-24: "This is what the LORD says: 'Let not the wise man boast of his wisdom or the strong man boast of his strength or the rich man boast of his riches, but let him who boasts boast about this: that he understands and knows me. . . ." The compound form of the verb that is used here usually has the sense of "boast over against" something or somebody (see the other three NT occurrences, Rom. 11:18 [twice] and Jas. 2:13). But James does not indicate any object for the verb here. The literal sense of the verb would require that the object be the other people who are claiming to be wise. James's point would be that they should not put themselves over these others. But James does not actually introduce such a person here, so it is probably better to supply an object from the immediate context. This object could be "truth" (see NEB) or "wisdom" (see TEV, "don't sin against the truth by boasting of your wisdom"). The latter is the better alternative, since James goes on to speak about false wisdom in v. 15. To boast about wisdom when one is displaying jealousy and selfish ambition is, in effect, to give the lie to the truth about what wisdom is and does. For wisdom must always be accompanied by humility. Rather than the "or" of the NIV, then, the connective between the two clauses should be "and" or even "and so" (see NASB).

15 To be sure, James now goes on to note, people such as those he has described in v. 14 do possess "wisdom" — but it is not biblical wisdom. *Such "wisdom" does not come down from heaven.* The quotation marks around "wisdom" in the NIV effectively convey the idea that one can only speak of the self-oriented learning of these people who claim to be "wise" as a phantom wisdom — a false representation of the real thing. The Greek does not make clear whether James is denying that this wisdom comes down from heaven or that this wisdom can be identified with the wisdom from heaven (see NASB: "This wisdom is not that which comes down from above").[29] But the difference in meaning is slight. The NIV "from heaven" (see also TEV) is a legitimate paraphrase for the Greek, which is literally "from above." James has used the same word in 1:17 to identify the realm from which all good gifts come. This is God's

29. The ambiguity is whether to take *hautē* as attributive — "this wisdom" — or predicative — "this is not the wisdom."

realm, who delights to give his children what they ask for — especially wisdom (see 1:5). True wisdom comes not (or, at least, not only) through intellectual effort or study; it is the gift of God (cf. Prov. 2:6).

But the "wisdom" that people who are selfish and partisan have has just the opposite nature and origin. It is *earthly, unspiritual, of the devil.* The word "earthly" has as its opposite "heaven" (see esp. John 3:12; 1 Cor. 15:40; 2 Cor. 5:1; Phil. 2:10). The word does not always have a negative connotation, sometimes simply denoting that which is typical of, and belongs to, the earthly sphere (e.g., John 3:12; 1 Cor. 15:40; 2 Cor. 5:1; Phil. 2:10). But when used in the sense of thinking or behavior, "earthly" has a negative nuance, suggesting a narrow perspective that fails to consider God's realm and will (cf. Phil. 3:19): "earthbound" is a good rendering.[30] The second word James uses to describe this false wisdom can also have a neutral sense. It is the Greek word *psychikos,* an adjective derived from the Greek word for "soul." Greek writers used the word to contrast bodily functions and appetites with the life of the inner person; and it occurs in the Apocrypha to denote an emotion that is sincere, "from the soul," or, as we would say, "from the heart" (2 Macc. 4:37; 14:28). But the word always has a negative sense in the NT, in all five of its occurrences being placed in explicit opposition to "spirit" or "spiritual" (see also 1 Cor. 2:14; 15:44, 46; Jude 19). It has to do with that part of man "where human feeling and human reason reign supreme."[31] This consistent contrast between "soulish" and "spiritual" justifies the NIV rendering "unspiritual" (see also NRSV; TEV; NLT). James has arranged his three descriptions of false wisdom in ascending order of strength: "earthbound," "unspiritual," and, climactically, "demonic." This latter word (Gk. *daimoniōdēs,* lit. "pertaining to demons") occurs only here in the Bible. It may mean that the wisdom is demonic either in nature or, more probably, in origin. For such a nuance would make a neat opposition with what James has said earlier in the verse. The false wisdom that some in the community are boasting about is not "from above"; it is "from the demons." In sum, then, this false wisdom, which does not lead to good works and humility (v. 13), is characterized by "the world, the flesh, and the devil." In each of these ways, it is the direct antithesis of "the wisdom that comes from above" — heavenly in nature, spiritual in essence, and divine in origin.

16 With the "for" that connects this verse to v. 17, James indicates that what he now says justifies the harsh verdict about false wisdom that he has issued in v. 16. The earthbound, unspiritual, and even demonic

30. Johnson, 272.
31. Knowling, 87.

character of this wisdom is evident from the effects it has in the life of the church. In order to make this point, James reiterates the two character traits displayed in the lives of those who are (wrongly) claiming to be "wise" (v. 14): *envy and selfish ambition.* When people hold such attitudes, the result can only be *disorder and every evil practice.* The Greek word translated "disorder" *(akatastasia)* is another form of a word that James has used in 1:8 and 3:8 to describe the "double-minded" person and the "double-speaking" tongue. These words are rendered, respectively, "unstable" and "restless" in the NIV. The noun that James uses connotes a restless, unsettled state. Luke uses it to describe the "tumults," the uprisings and revolutions, that will typify the period preceding the *parousia* (Luke 21:9). And Paul, pleading with the Corinthians to refrain from an unbridled, unorganized display of individual spiritual gifts in the assembly, reminds them that "God is not a God of disorder *(akatastasis)* but of peace" (1 Cor. 14:33; cf. also 2 Cor. 6:5 and 12:20). The same "disorder" is bound to break out in churches where people are pursuing their own selfish concerns and partisan causes rather than the good of the body as a whole. While what James says here applies to any Christian who prides himself or herself on being "wise and understanding," he may especially have in mind the leaders of the community.[32] For envy and selfish ambition among the leaders have tremendous potential to damage the unity and order of the church as a whole. When those who are being looked to for direction and wise counsel act on the basis of a personal agenda or in a spirit of "one-upmanship" toward one another, great damage to the church ensues. In addition to "disorder," this damage takes the form of "every evil practice." The word "every" (Gk. *pan*) might here have the nuance "every kind of" (cf. NRSV; REB; TEV; NLT; NJB). A few commentators have sought to identify a specific evil practice that James might have in mind here (e.g., Johnson suggests that lawsuits may be in view), but the wording seems deliberately vague. The wrong kind of wisdom brings about just about every kind of evil practice that one could name.

17 James has told us what the "wisdom that comes from above [NIV *heaven*]" is not (v. 15); now he tells us what it is. Or, more accurately, he lets us know what the *wisdom that comes from heaven* does. For James quite clearly continues to operate with the biblical understanding of wisdom as a basic, God-given orientation that has profound practical effects on the way a person lives. Like true faith (2:14-26), true wisdom is identified by the quality of life that it produces.[33] But James's description of the

32. Martin, 132.

33. On the importance of 2:14-26 and 3:13-18 in the theology of James, see esp. Hoppe, 9.

qualities produced by wisdom from heaven also resembles another NT text, Paul's delineation of the "fruit of the Spirit" (Gal. 5:22-23). To be sure, verbal resemblance between the two lists is minimal; but humility, peaceableness, and upright behavior are the focus in both texts. In a general sense, what Paul claims that the Spirit produces, James claims true wisdom produces. When we add to this resemblance the fact that James never mentions the work of the Spirit, we can understand why some scholars claim that wisdom in James is equivalent to the Spirit in Paul.[34] Support for such an identification, moreover, might be found in Jewish literature, where the two are frequently associated. Nevertheless, we should probably be cautious about suggesting any real theological equivalence between the two. James, we must remember, is writing before Paul wrote his letters and before he was familiar with the apostle's theology. So we certainly cannot speak of any sort of "replacement" of one concept with the other. Nor is it clear that a theology of the Spirit had been well worked out by the time James wrote. Probably, then, the similarity between the lists is quite indirect. The OT and Jewish writings provide a general profile of the character of the godly person. James, following OT and Jewish antecedents, attributes these qualities to the presence and power of wisdom; Paul, developing more fully the implications of new covenant fulfillment, attributes them to the Spirit. In other words, equivalence in effect between wisdom in James and the Spirit in Paul does not mean equivalence in the two entities themselves.

The first, and preeminent, attribute that wisdom produces is purity. The word *pure (hagnos)* connotes innocence and moral blamelessness. The summarizing nature of the term can be gleaned from Paul's expressed desire to present the church as a "pure [*hagnos*] virgin" to Christ (2 Cor. 11:2; cf. also 2 Cor. 7:11; Phil. 4:8; 1 Tim. 5:22; Tit. 2:5; 1 Pet. 3:2; 1 John 3:3). The seven qualities that follow in the list are specific dimensions of this overall purity. James has arranged them into three groups. The first three words all begin with the same letter and have similar endings as well: *eirēnikē* ("peace loving"), *epieikēs* ("considerate"), *eupeithēs* ("submissive"). James sets off the middle two character traits ("mercy" and "good fruit") by subordinating them to the word "full of." Alliteration is again used to group the last two words, each beginning with an "a" sound. Moreover, the two have an almost rhyming, metrical similarity: *adiakritos* ("impartial"), *anypokritos* ("sincere").

The literary arrangement James has used does not necessarily indicate a conceptual arrangement as well. But we are probably justified

34. See on this Kirk, "The Meaning of Wisdom in James," 24-38, and the section on "Wisdom" in the Introduction.

in thinking that James has carefully brought together the first three qualities to make a general overall point. For the believer who is characterized by these three traits — *peace loving, considerate, submissive* — is the exact opposite of the envious, selfish, and ambitious person who is driven by demonic wisdom (vv. 15-16). "Peace loving" is especially important, coming at the head of the list of specific virtues and being picked up for further emphasis in v. 18. Moreover, it is just this concern for peace that a community marked by serious dissensions (4:1-2) is badly in need of. "Peace loving" (also REB; NLT) is a fair English rendering of *eirēnikē,* usually rendered "peaceable" (e.g., KJV; NASB; NRSV; NJB; the only other NT occurrence is Heb. 12:11). The connection between peace and wisdom is not new; the OT makes the same point (Prov. 3:17). The next two traits are probably subordinate to the first: it is the person who is *considerate* and *submissive* who will be *peace loving.* "Considerate" *(epieikēs)* indicates a willingness to yield to others and a corresponding unwillingness "to exact strict claims" (Hort). With such an attitude, the believer, motivated and empowered by wisdom, will follow in the footsteps of his or her Lord, who also was characterized by "meekness and gentleness [*epieikeia*]" (2 Cor. 10:1). Significantly, Paul requires "overseers" to be people who are "gentle" (1 Tim. 3:3; cf. also Acts 24:4; Phil. 4:5; Tit. 3:2; 1 Pet. 2:18). Although the NIV translates the third word in this opening triad with *submissive,* the Greek word is not from the word-group that is normally rendered "submissive" in the NT *(hypotag-).* The word *(eupeithēs;* its only NT occurrence) means, literally, "easily persuaded." What is meant is not a weak, credulous gullibility, but a willing deference to others when unalterable theological or moral principles are not involved.

In the second group of virtues, James now notes that wisdom from heaven is also *full of mercy and good fruit.* Jesus frequently highlighted mercy *(eleos)* as a key indicator of the godly person (Matt. 5:7; 18:21-35; 23:23; Luke 10:37). James provides his own definition of "mercy": love for the neighbor that shows itself in action (2:8-13). It is not surprising, then, that James couples *mercy* so closely with *good fruit* — acts of mercy are those "fruits" that genuine wisdom, like genuine faith, must produce.

Rounding out James's "fruit of wisdom" are two qualities that may also have much in common with each other. But one must decide first on the meaning of the former word, *adiakritos* (used only here in the NT). The *a-* at the beginning of the word functions like our prefix *un-* in English, negating the quality that follows. The word *diakritos* comes from a verb that means "doubt"/"waver" or "make a distinction." So in this context *adiakritos* might mean "undoubting," in the sense of "simple" or "straightforward" (REB);[35] or "not making distinctions," "impartial" (NIV; cf. KJV; NRSV; TEV).[36] Each of these meanings can find some support from James's teaching elsewhere. James has stressed the incompatibility of Christianity and partiality (2:1-4) and mentions mercy in that context, as he does here. But he uses the verb *diakrinō* to mean "be divided" in 1:6 and 2:4; and one of James's central pleas is for "undivided" loyalty to God — not least in this general context (see "double-minded" in 4:7). Furthermore, the idea of being undivided in loyalty fits well with the next word, "sincere" *(anypokritos).* This word has the literal sense "not playing a part." The person characterized by wisdom from heaven will be stable, trustworthy, transparent — the kind of person consistently displaying the virtues of wisdom and on whom one can rely for advice and counsel.

18 As the capstone to his portrait of two contrasting "wisdoms," James returns to emphasize what seems to be his key concern in all this: the peace that genuine (as opposed to fraudulent) wisdom can bring to the community. There is therefore a clear connection with James's rebuke of dissensions in what follows (4:1-2). But connections with the previous context are also clear, via the concern with "peace" (cf. v. 17; and note also the repetition of the word "fruit"). Nevertheless, the verse fits into its context a bit awkwardly and has a simple proverbial style, both of which suggest that James may here be quoting a saying current in the early church.[37] The originally independent nature of the saying may also help explain why a decision about its precise sense is difficult. Most translations, like the NIV, understand the verse as a statement about what peacemakers *produce: Peacemakers who sow in peace raise a harvest of righteousness* (see also NASB, REB, TEV). But it is also possible to take the verse as a promise about what peacemakers will receive for their efforts; see the NRSV: "And a harvest of righteousness is sown in peace for those who make peace." The latter rendering has a stronger grammatical basis and is supported by a good number of commentators.[38] But the former translation, with its reference to the great benefits that peacemakers produce, fits the context better; note especially what would then be a perfect

35. Dibelius, 214; Hort, 86; Johnson, 275.

36. Laws, 164; Martin, 134. And note *T. Zebulun* 7:2: "without discrimination be compassionate and merciful to all."

37. See esp. Dibelius, 215.

38. The issue is the significance of the dative *tois poiousin* ("those who make"). A dative of advantage ("for," "for the benefit of") is more common than a dative of agency ("by"; this sense is presumed in the [somewhat paraphrastic] NIV rendering). Favoring the dative of advantage are, e.g., Mayor, 133; Dibelius, 215; Martin, 135. See also the grammars, BDF 191 (4); Turner, 238.

contrast with the manifold evil practices that are the result of demonic wisdom (v. 16). So we slightly incline toward the NIV interpretation.[39]

What is this *harvest of righteousness* that peacemakers sow? A literal rendering is "fruit of righteousness," and this can mean either (1) "the fruit that righteousness produces" (*dikaiosynēs* as a genitive of source), or (2) "the fruit that is righteousness" (*dikaiosynēs* as an epexegetic genitive). The phrase is quite common in the LXX, where it almost always means the latter. And this rendering makes good sense in this context, since James has not prepared us for the idea of "righteousness" as a status or relationship that might lead to a godly life. A couple of commentators want to define "righteousness" here more precisely, Laws arguing that James is referring to wisdom itself[40] and others that peace is the reference. But James gives us no basis to introduce such fine distinctions here. *Righteousness* in Jas. 1:20 meant that conduct which is pleasing to God, and this is the "fruit" intended here also. It includes all the virtues listed in v. 17 and is the opposite, as we have suggested, of "every evil practice" (v. 16). This righteousness cannot be produced in the context of human anger (1:20); but it *can* grow and flourish in the atmosphere of peace. Those who create such an atmosphere are assured by their Lord of their reward: "Blessed are the peacemakers, for they shall be called sons of God" (Matt. 5:9).

39. See, e.g., Ropes, 250-51; Tasker, 82-83; Mussner, 175; Davids, 155; Johnson, 275.

40. Laws, 166. She links Prov. 11:30, where "fruit of righteousness" is connected with "tree of life," and Prov. 3:17, where "wisdom" is associated with "tree of life."

James 4

1 As we noted in the introduction to this section, most commentators and translations place a significant break in James's argument between chap. 3 and chap. 4. Many think that 4:1-10 forms a unit of thought with emphasis on the need for repentance from evil human desires.[1] Others expand the unit to include vv. 11-12 and accordingly put more emphasis on the issue of sinful speech and quarreling.[2] And a good case can be made for a shift in argument at the chapter break. The question *What causes fights and quarrels among you?* appears to be parallel to the question in v. 13 and to change the subject from wisdom to community dissension. When, however, one looks more closely at the content of vv. 13-18 and 4:1-3, one discovers that James is, in fact, pursuing a common theme through both paragraphs. Key to this continuity is the recognition that James's discussion of wisdom in vv. 13-18 is very specifically focused. He is not really interested in talking about wisdom per se, but in that fruit of wisdom which brings order and peace to the church. Seen in this light, vv. 13-18 prepare the way perfectly for James's rebuke of quarreling in the church.

The beginning of chap. 4, then, does not introduce a new topic, but a shift of focus within discussion of the same topic. James's commendation of peacemakers in v. 18 flows naturally into a discussion of the community problems that created so strong a need for peacemakers. Just what these community problems were is a matter of considerable debate. In this verse and in v. 2 James refers to *fights and quarrels* and in v. 2 to killing

1. E.g., Laws, 167.

2. E.g., Mussner, 175-76. Frankemölle notes many connections between 4:1-12 and the initial statement of the letter's theme in 1:2-18 (573-74).

and to coveting. But it must initially be noted that the word translated *quarrels* in the NIV *(machai)* means "battles" or "strife" of any kind. When it is combined with the first word *(polemoi)*, which almost always refers to literal wars or battles, and the use of the word "kill" in v. 2, a good case can then be made that James is deploring actual violence among the members of the community. While we might consider such a situation unlikely at first sight (not even the Corinthian church was that bad!), one can, in fact, make a pretty good case for it. Martin, for instance, reminds us that James is writing at a time when the Jewish Zealot movement was very influential. Some of the believers may well have been former Zealots, and, granted this, "the taking of another's life is not out of the realm of possibility for the church members as a response to disagreement."[3] Martin is quite right to insist that the religious climate of James's context was very different from ours. But we still must wonder whether James would have been content with the little that he says here had the believers to whom he is writing actually been killing one another. And while it is true that the Greek words translated "fights" and "kill" in the NIV normally refer to physical violence, the word *machai* points in a different direction. It, too, can refer to violent conflicts (e.g., Josh. 4:13), but most of its occurrences in the LXX and all three of its other occurrences in the NT (2 Cor. 7:5; 2 Tim. 2:23; Tit. 3:9) denote verbal quarrels or inward anxiety. Particularly noteworthy is the prominence of the word in OT (Proverbs) and Jewish (Sirach) wisdom books, which have so much in common with James's teaching at this point in his letter. And while the former word in James's question *(polemos)* usually denotes physical violence, it, too, occasionally has a metaphorical meaning. Particularly striking, in light of Jas. 3:1-12 and 4:11-12, is *Pss. Sol.* 12:3, which teaches that slanderous lips "kindle strife [*polemos*]." Both words, then, resemble their English counterparts, "battle," "fight," in that they can refer to verbal disputes as well as armed conflicts (e.g., "the United Nations fought over the meaning of the treaty clause"; "Churchill always loved a parliamentary battle"). We think that this metaphorical meaning is likely here, despite the presence of the word "kill" in v. 2 (for which see below). Particularly significant is the fact that the problem of community strife fits perfectly into the larger topic that James develops in this part of the letter. For disputes are almost always accompanied by harsh words, criticism, and slander — the misuse of the tongue that James castigates (3:1-12; 4:11-12; 5:9).

The quarrels of James's day have too often marred the Christian

3. Martin, 144; cf. also M. J. Thompson, "James 4:1-4: A Warning against Zealotry?" *ExpTim* 87 (1976) 211-13.

church. The seventeenth-century Jewish philosopher Spinoza observed: "I have often wondered that persons who make boast of professing the Christian religion — namely love, joy, peace, temperance, and charity to all men — should quarrel with such rancorous animosity and display daily towards one another such bitter hatred, that this, rather than the virtues which they profess, is the readiest criteria of their faith."[4] Some battles, to be sure, need to be fought. But even then they must be fought without sacrificing Christian principles and virtues. We do not know what the disputes that James refers to were about.[5] The fact that James does not comment directly on the issues involved suggests that his concern was more with the selfish spirit and bitterness of the quarrels than with the rights and wrongs of the various viewpoints.

The source of these quarrels, James now goes on to note, is *your desires that battle within you. Desires* translates the Greek word *hēdonē,* which means simply "pleasure," but often with the connotation of a sinful, self-indulgent pleasure (we get our word "hedonism" from it). It consistently has this negative meaning in the NT (Luke 8:14; Tit. 3:3; 2 Pet. 2:13). James was not the first to identify "desires" as the source of sin; note 4 Macc. 1:25-26: "in pleasure *(hēdonē)* there exists even a malevolent tendency, which is the most complex of all the emotions. In the soul it is boastfulness, covetousness, thirst for honor, rivalry, malice; in the body, indiscriminate eating, gluttony, and solitary gormandizing." James would have undoubtedly added to this list jealousy (see 4:2) and selfish ambition (see 3:16). The military imagery with which the verse opens is carried over into this assertion as well, as James describes desires as "battling," "waging war" "in your members" (NIV substitutes "within you" for this phrase). The "members" (Gk. *melē*) might be the "parts" of the individual human body[6] or the "parts" of the Christian church: believers.[7] The former is a bit more likely when we consider the close parallel to this language in 1 Pet. 2:11: "Dear friends, I urge you, as aliens and strangers in the world, to abstain from sinful desires, which war against your soul."

2 The first part of v. 2 expands on the nature of these sinful desires that are creating such havoc in the community. The NIV *you want something* conceals a verbal link with the end of v. 1. For the verb here is *epithymeō,* another word that means "desire" (James probably changed

4. *Tractatus Theologico-Politicus,* chap. 6.

5. Mussner (169, 188-89) suggests that the place of the torah among Christians may have been the issue. But if so, it is surprising that James writes so unreflectingly about the law (1:25; 2:8-11; 4:11-12).

6. Crotty, 55-56; Laws, 168; Davids, 157.

7. E.g., Martin, 144-45.

from the *hēd-* root because the verb from that root is rare[8]). Just what James is saying about "desire" in this verse is disputed. The problem is to determine the relationship among the series of verbs that occur in the first part of the verse. Two main alternatives exist.

1. A three-clause structure:
   a. "You want something but don't get it."
   b. "You kill and covet, but you cannot have what you want."
   c. "You quarrel and fight" (NIV; see also KJV).[9]
2. A two-clause structure:
   a. "You want something and do not have it; so you commit murder."
   b. "And you covet something and cannot obtain it; so you engage in disputes and conflicts" (NRSV; see also REB; NASB; TEV; NLT; NJB).[10]

The former rendering takes the sequence of positive-negative verbs as key to the structure, so that each of the first two clauses describes frustrated desire. James then indicates the results of that frustration in the third clause. A key problem for this punctuation of the verse is the apparently anticlimactic position of "you kill." Martin tries to solve this problem by taking the next verb, "covet," closely with "you kill": "you kill out of jealousy." James would then be pointing out to his readers that their campaign of violence has not succeeded in achieving its goal; quite the contrary, it has led to a continual and escalating cycle of violence.[11] But taking the two verbs as mutually interpreting is not the most natural reading of the text.

In favor of the second punctuation is especially the parallelism that is created: "you kill" and "you quarrel and fight" occupy the same logical place in James's argument. The struggles that are wracking the community, James would be suggesting, are the product of their envious desire to get what they don't have. This fits better into the context, since James has been at pains to show that disorder and evil in the community stem from "bitter envy and selfish ambition" (3:14-16). Moreover, this second punctuation produces a sequence that fits exactly into the Hellenistic moral tradition that James is borrowing from at this point in his letter.[12]

8. The verb form corresponding to *hēdonē* is never used in the NT; and Tit. 3:3 shows that *hēdonē* and *epithymia* were often interchangeable.

9. Among commentators, see Dibelius, 218; Davids, 157-58; Martin, 140-41.

10. Most commentators also support this rendering. See esp. Hort, 89; Mayor, 136; Ropes, 254.

11. Martin, 146.

12. See again esp. Johnson, "James 3:13–4:10."

According to this tradition, "envy" *(phthonos)* and "jealousy" (*zēlos;* cf. 3:14 and 16; and the verb *zēloō* in this verse) inevitably lead to hostile acts, such as quarrels, murder, and wars. An excellent example of this pattern is found in *T. Simeon.* The whole section is titled "Concerning Envy [*phthonos*]." It describes how envy led Simeon to seize and attempt to murder his brother Joseph. Speaking now at the end of his life, Simeon warns his children that "envy dominates the whole of man's mind" and "keeps prodding him to destroy the one whom he envies" (3:2-3). The same pattern is exemplified in the writings of Epictetus, a second-century-A.D. moralist. He implies an organic relation between envy and violence when he notes that Caesar can free people from "wars and fightings" *(polemoi kai machai)* but not from "envy" *(phthonos).*[13] In the NT, the chief priests' decision to deliver Jesus to Pilate is attributed to "envy" *(phthonos)* (Mark 15:10), while the persecution suffered by the early church is often attributed to "jealousy" or "zeal" *(zēlos)* (Acts 5:17; 13:45; Phil. 3:6). While James uses the root *zēlos* rather than *phthonos* (which is more often found in these traditions), the two were often interchangeable (1 Macc. 8:16; *T. Simeon* 1:6; 4:5), and *zēlos* is found in these traditions also.

For these reasons, therefore, we should follow the majority of modern translations and punctuate as in the second option above.[14] Frustrated desire, James makes clear, is what is breeding the intense strife that is convulsing the community. But just how intense was this strife? Here we must tackle the difficult "you kill" *(phoneuete).* As we have seen, some commentators take the verb quite seriously: James's readers, following the violent traditions of their Zealot background, are murdering one another. Giving a word its normal meaning is a sound exegetical procedure. But sometimes the context makes the normal meaning difficult, if not impossible. We think this is the case here. James makes clear that the problems he is describing were within the community ("among you" [v. 1]). It strains credulity to suppose that James would pass so quickly over so serious a matter within the community. Nor would a zealot impulse lead to violence against fellow religionists, however strong the differences of opinion might be. But if we do not give "you kill" its normal sense, what alternatives are there? A few have followed the emendation of Erasmus, who thought that an early scribe might have changed an original *phthoneite,* "you are envious," into *phoneuete.* But emendation (which has no textual basis) is always a last resort in interpreting a text as rich in

13. *Discourses* 3.13.9.

14. The major difficulty with this punctuation is the *kai* ("and") at the beginning of the second clause. But *kai* can occur in such a context to introduce a second, parallel, sentence.

manuscript evidence as is the NT. Another alternative, attractive because James so often depends on the teaching of Jesus, is to interpret "you kill" in a spiritual way: "you are murderously angry" (see Matt. 5:21-26; 1 John 2:15).[15] However, nothing in James's context prepares us for such an interpretation. Perhaps, then, the best alternative is to take "you kill" in its normal, literal, sense, but as a hypothetical eventuality rather than as an actual occurrence. As we have seen, the tradition to which James is indebted often portrayed murder as the end product of envy. James is warning his readers about just where their envious desires might lead them if not checked in time. James's readers are not yet killing each other. But "fightings" and "wars" *are* already in evidence among them; and, if covetous zeal goes unrestrained, the danger of actual violence is real. With penetrating insight, then, James provides us with a powerful analysis of human conflict. Verbal argument, private violence, or national conflict — the cause of them all can be traced back to the wrongful lust to want more than we have, to be envious of and covet what others have, whether it be their position or their possessions.

With "you quarrel and fight" James returns to the point at which he began in v. 1. We therefore have something of a chiasm in vv. 1-2a:

A Fights and quarrels (v. 1a)
  B come from wrong desires (v. 1b)
  B′ Frustrated desire (v. 2a) leads to
A′ quarrels and fights (v. 2b)

The end of v. 2 therefore goes with v. 3, as James explains why his readers' desire to "have" has met with failure rather than success. *You do not have, because you do not ask God.* What is it that James's readers want to have? He nowhere says in these verses, but the context suggests an answer: the kind of wisdom that will enable them to gain recognition as leaders in the community. James has rebuked his readers for wanting to become teachers (3:1) and for priding themselves on being "wise and understanding" (3:13). They apparently want to lead the church, but don't have the right kind of wisdom to do so. Moreover, James's language here reminds us inevitably of his earlier encouragement: "If any of you lack wisdom, he should ask God" (1:5). James attributes the failure of these people to gain the power and prestige they want to their failure to do just this: ask God.

15. Davids (158-59) notes that James accuses the rich of murdering the poor in 5:6 and that the biblical tradition characterized a failure to meet the needs of the poor as murder. However, 5:6 comes in a denunciation of those who are clearly outside the community and is not parallel to 4:1-3.

3 To be sure, James notes, *you ask.* But *you do not receive, because you ask with wrong motives, that you may spend what you get on your pleasures.*[16] The Greek is more indefinite than the NIV translation: "you do not receive, because you ask wrongly, in order to spend freely on your pleasures." "Spend freely" (the verb is *dapanaō*) can have a neutral sense (Mark 5:26; Acts 21:24; 2 Cor. 12:15), but the meaning here is negative, as in Luke 15:14, where the prodigal son is said to have "freely spent" all of his father's inheritance. Jesus had promised, "Ask, and it will be given you" (Matt. 7:7). But clearly Jesus had in mind that asking which has as its focus and motive God's name, God's kingdom, and God's will (Matt. 6:9-10) — not an asking that had the purpose of the indulgence of those "pleasures" *(hēdonai)* that are at war with our souls (cf. v. 1). Hort comments: "God bestows not gifts only, but the enjoyment of them: but the enjoyment which contributes to nothing beyond itself is not what He gives in answer to prayer; and petitions to Him which have no better end in view are not prayers."

V. A SUMMONS TO SPIRITUAL WHOLENESS (4:4-10)

> 4 *You adulterous people, don't you know that friendship with the world is hatred toward God? Anyone who chooses to be a friend of the world becomes an enemy of God.* 5 *Or do you think Scripture says without reason that the spirit he caused to live in us envies intensely?* 6 *But he gives us more grace. That is why Scripture says: "God opposes the proud but gives grace to the humble."* 7 *Submit yourselves, then, to God. Resist the devil, and he will flee from you.* 8 *Come near to God and he will come near to you. Wash your hands, you sinners, and purify your hearts, you double-minded.* 9 *Grieve, mourn and wail. Change your laughter to mourning and your joy to gloom.* 10 *Humble yourselves before the Lord, and he will lift you up.*

16. The Greek text of vv. 2b-3 presents a striking shift in the voice of the verb *aiteō* ("ask"), as James moves from the middle — "you do not ask God" — to the active — "When you ask" — back to the middle again — "you ask with wrong motives." Scholars have suggested all manner of explanations for this variation. Mayor thought that the active (v. 3a) denoted "the word without the spirit of prayer," while Hort argued that the active suggests the asking of a person, while the middle connotes asking for something. In three of the four other NT instances where the same verb shifts voice, however, it is difficult to discern any difference in meaning (cf. also A. T. Robertson, *A Grammar of the Greek New Testament in the Light of Historical Research* [Nashville: Broadman Press, 1934], 626). Probably, then, we should see no difference in meaning in the two forms of the verb.

The abrupt and harsh *you adulterous people* marks the beginning of one of the most strongly worded calls to repent that we find anywhere in the NT. James warns his readers about flirtation with the world and its consequences for their relationship to God (v. 4). He reminds them of God's jealousy for his people and the availability of his grace (vv. 5-6). And on the basis of this, he urges his readers to repent (vv. 7-10). Throughout the section James depends heavily on the OT, quoting it twice and reflecting its vocabulary and themes in every verse. As we noted in the introduction to the last section (3:13–4:3) and in our notes on 4:1, most commentators include vv. 4-10 with vv. 1-3 as one continuous section. The call to repentance in vv. 4-10 would then relate particularly to the selfish envy and divisiveness that James has analyzed in 4:1-3. And James's criticism of his readers for praying selfishly (v. 3) might be the specific trigger for his denunciation of their generally idolatrous attitudes.[17] But we think that 4:4-10 has a much broader scope. Indicative of its relative independence from the immediate context is the disappearance — for the moment — of the vocabulary and themes of Hellenistic moral exhortation that so strongly mark 3:1–4:3 (and esp. 3:13–4:3). These are replaced with language and ideas drawn from OT prophetic denunciations of Israel. In the midst of his exhortation about speech, envy, and divisiveness, James breaks out in a passionate summons to his readers to turn away from their worldly ways and submit themselves wholeheartedly once again to their gracious but jealous God. James gathers up all the specific issues that he deals with in his letter into one all-embracing demand. Here, if anywhere, we find the heart of James's letter.

4 After the many times that James has called his readers "brothers" (1:2; 2:1, 14; 3:1, 10, 12) or even "my dear brothers" (1:16, 19; 2:5), his address *you adulterous people* really catches our attention. The Greek word James uses is actually feminine; see "adulteresses" in the NASB. Some manuscripts, indeed, have both the feminine and masculine forms (hence KJV: "adulterers and adulteresses"), but this reading is pretty obviously an attempt to avoid the problem of the feminine form. A literal reading would suggest that James is accusing his female readers of engaging in adulterous sexual activity.[18] But this is unlikely. Nothing in the context would suggest such an accusation, and James goes on in vv. 5-10 to castigate his readers quite generally. The clue to the feminine form and to the accusation that James is making here is found in the OT, especially the prophetic books.[19]

17. For example, Laws, 173; Johnson, 278.

18. So Hort, 91-92.

19. Another suggestion is that James is influenced by the presentation of the "adulterous woman" in Proverbs (see J. Schmitt, "You Adulteresses: The Image in James 4:4," *NovT* 28 [1986] 327-37).

The prophets frequently compare the relationship between Yahweh and his people to a marriage relationship. See, for instance, Isa. 54:5-6: "'For your Maker is your husband — the LORD Almighty is his name — the Holy One of Israel is your Redeemer; he is called the God of all the earth. The LORD will call you back as if you were a wife deserted and distressed in spirit — a wife who married young, only to be rejected,' says your God." As this text suggests, the Lord is consistently portrayed as the husband and Israel as the wife in this imagery. Accordingly, therefore, when Israel's relationship with the Lord is threatened by her idolatry, she can be accused of committing adultery; see Jer. 3:20: "'But like a woman unfaithful to her husband, so you have been unfaithful to me, O house of Israel,' declares the LORD" (see also Isa. 57:3; Ezek. 16:38; 23:45). But it is in Hosea that this imagery reaches its pinnacle. The Lord commands Hosea to marry a prostitute so that her unfaithfulness might poignantly and painfully reveal the tragic dalliance of Israel with foreign gods. Israel, God claims, has "been unfaithful," going after other lovers, Baal and other false gods (Hos. 2:5-7). This marital imagery for the covenant relationship between God and Israel is picked up by Jesus, who called those who rejected him "a wicked and adulterous generation" (Matt. 12:39; 16:4).

James, following this tradition, uses "adulteresses" to label his readers as unfaithful people of God. By seeking *friendship with the world,* they are, in effect, committing spiritual adultery. As Johnson points out, the ancient view of friendship sheds light on the seriousness of the charge that James is making here. We speak rather casually of "friends" in our day, but in the Hellenistic world friendship "involved 'sharing all things' in a unity both spiritual and physical."[20] We can therefore understand why James insists that *Anyone who chooses to be a friend of the world becomes an enemy of God.* "Enemy," especially in light of the OT background we have cited, must involve hostility of God toward the believer as well as that of the believer toward God.

We have no evidence that James's readers were overtly disclaiming God and consciously deciding to follow the world instead. But their tendency to imitate the world by discriminating against people (2:1-13), by speaking negatively of others (3:1-12), by exhibiting "bitter envy" and "selfish ambition" (3:13-18), and by pursuing their own destructive pleasures (4:1-3) amounted to just that. James, as it were, wants to raise the stakes so that his readers see their compromising conduct for what it really is. God tolerates no rival. When believers behave in a worldly manner, they demonstrate that, at that point, their allegiance is to the world rather than to God.

20. Johnson, 279.

5 James's striking application of the OT imagery of God as the spouse of his people in v. 4 is the key to understanding this verse. Verse 5 explains why flirtation with the world is so serious a matter by bringing to mind the jealousy of the Lord, which demands total, unreserved, unwavering allegiance from the people with whom he has joined himself. But this reading of the verse is by no means the only one possible. Indeed, Jas. 4:5 is one of the most difficult verses in the NT. The degree of difficulty is revealed in the fact that our major English translations provide quite distinct interpretations. The NRSV, NASB, and NLT follow the line we have laid out above; but the NIV, REB, and TEV take the verse to refer to the jealous longings of human beings. Several matters in the text call for careful attention: the identity of the Scripture that James refers to in the opening words; the reference of the term "spirit" *(pneuma);* the meaning and object of the verb *epipothei* (translated variously as "desire," "yearn," "long"); and the meaning of the term *phthonon* (divine "jealousy" or human "envy"?). Since the identity of the Scripture reference is entirely dependent on the translation of the "quotation," we will begin with this latter issue.

As we suggested above, two major interpretations are possible, although other minor differences yield a bewildering variety of alternatives.

1. James is referring to God's jealousy for his people: "God yearns jealously for the spirit that he has made to dwell in us" (NRSV).[21]
2. James is referring to the human tendency to be envious: *the spirit he caused to live in us envies intensely* (NIV).[22]

The English reader may well wonder how such diametrically opposite translations could come from the same Greek text (for no textual variants are involved). The problem boils down to three key ambiguities in the Greek.

1. The Greek word for "spirit," being neuter, can function either as the subject of the verb *epipothei* or as its object.[23] So, in the second alternative, "spirit" is taken as the subject and interpreted to mean the natural spirit of every human being. In the first alternative, however, "spirit" is made the object of the verb and understood as the spirit that God breathed into man to make him a living creature (Gen. 2:7), or, alterna-

21. See, e.g., Hort, 93-94; Dibelius, 224; Ropes, 261, 264-65; Mussner, 181-82; Davids, 164; Frankemölle, 602-5; Martin, 145; Klein, 112-15.

22. See, e.g., Laws, 177-78; Adamson, 171-73; Johnson, 280-82.

23. In other words, *pneuma* can be either nominative or accusative.

tively, to the Holy Spirit that God has implanted in believers (cf. NLT).[24] But if "spirit" is the object of the verb, then we must supply a subject for the verb; and advocates of the first alternative naturally supply "God" as the most likely identification of the one who caused the spirit to dwell in us.

On the whole, this issue is most naturally resolved in favor of the "divine jealousy" interpretation. It makes best grammatical sense to take "God" as the subject of both the main verb — *epipothei,* "desire," "yearn" — and the subordinate verb — *katǫkisen,* "cause to dwell." But if God is the subject of "desire," then this desire must obviously be a positive yearning; and this means, in turn, that *phthonos* must mean "jealousy" rather than "envy."

2. But this last decision brings us to the second major issue creating such ambiguity in the Greek text: the meaning of the word *phthonos.* And this issue undoubtedly favors the "human envy" interpretation. For *phthonos* always has a negative connotation in biblical Greek and is naturally never used with reference to God. Moreover, as we have seen, *phthonos* is a key word in the tradition that James has used in 3:13–4:3, and in this tradition the word always describes a sinful human attitude.

3. Closely related to our decision about the meaning of *phthonos* is the third key issue: the meaning of the verb *epipothei,* in combination with the preposition *pros.* If James is referring here to human envy, the combination will have to mean something like "tend toward." "Toward" is a perfectly acceptable rendering of *pros,* but "tend" is not the most natural translation of the verb. The "divine jealousy" interpretation suffers from almost exactly the opposite problem. It can give the verb its normal meaning of "desire," "yearn," but must interpret the preposition in a somewhat unusual way, as an adverbial construction: "in a jealous manner." Similarly indecisive is the evidence for the general use of the verb *epipotheō.* It is never used with reference to God in biblical Greek; and this obviously favors the "human envy" view. But it also always has a positive meaning in the NT; and this pattern, of course, favors the "divine jealousy" view.

The three key exegetical details therefore point in different directions. The grammar of the sentence (point one) favors the "divine jealousy" view; the meaning of *phthonos* (point two) the "human envy" interpretation; and favoring neither clearly is the third issue, the construction *epipotheō pros.* Advocates of the "human envy" view often argue that the

24. A variant of this interpretation takes *pneuma* as the subject of the verb, but views it as the Holy Spirit within the believer, who jealousy yearns for the Christian (as in NLT).

evidence from the meaning of *phthonos* is so overwhelming that it decisively tips the scales in favor of this interpretation. But we are not so sure of this. Since *phthonos* and *zēlos* are sometimes interchangeable (cf. 1 Macc. 8:16; *T. Simeon* 4:5; *T. Gad* 7:2), and the latter was frequently used of the "jealousy" of God, it is not impossible to ascribe *phthonos* to God. Moreover, *phthonos* was occasionally used by Greek writers of the jealousy of the Olympian gods. Therefore, while unusual, James's uses of *phthonos* with respect to God's desire for his people is not impossible.

Since, therefore, in our view the exegetical data of the verse are not conclusive, context becomes a key deciding factor. A reference to human envy can, of course, fit into this general context, for James has warned them about this sin three times (3:14, 16; 4:2). And it could be argued that a statement about human sin in v. 5 provides a more natural contrast with the "greater grace" of God in v. 6. But the immediate context provides strong, and, in our opinion, decisive, support for the "divine jealousy" interpretation. Verse 5 clearly substantiates a point made in v. 4. And v. 4 focuses on the spiritual adultery that James's readers are committing by following the world in distinction from their only true "spouse," the Lord. A reminder of God's desire that his people be wholly and unreservedly his provides a beautifully appropriate substantiation of the warning against any flirtation with the attitudes and the values of the world in v. 4.

As we mentioned above, it is not clear whether James thinks of "the spirit that he has made to dwell in us" as the Holy Spirit given to believers, or as God's creative spirit by which he has invigorated humankind (Gen. 2:7). Perhaps the latter is slightly more likely, however, since James never elsewhere refers to the Holy Spirit. In either case, the phrase reminds us that God has a claim on us by virtue of his work in our lives.

We are now in a position to return to the beginning of the verse and identify the "Scripture" to which James refers. The difficulty is that the words that James "quotes" do not reproduce any OT text — or even any noncanonical Jewish text, for that matter. Many scholars therefore suppose that James is citing a lost apocryphal text.[25] But *scripture (graphē)* is limited to references to the canonical OT in the NT. If we interpret the verse, as we have argued, as a reference to the jealousy of God, OT support is, of course, abundant (e.g., Exod. 20:5; 34:14; Zech. 8:2). Some insist that the singular "scripture" must introduce a single OT text. But this is not clear; "scripture" in John 7:37-39 refers to an allusive reference or

25. Some popular suggestions are *Apocalypse of Moses* 31; the lost *Book of Eldad and Modad* (see esp. D. Deppe, "The Sayings of Jesus in the Epistle of James" [Ph.D. dissertation, Free University of Amsterdam, 1989)], 38-42); and an unknown book (see Adamson, 170-71, for a list of suggestions).

theme (and cf. also, possibly, Matt. 2:23, Gal. 3:22). This being so, we can identify that which *graphē* speaks about as the biblical theme of God's jealousy for his people.[26]

6 Our decision about the meaning of v. 5 will determine the nature of the mild contrast that introduces v. 6a: *But he gives us more grace.* If v. 5 refers to the sinful longings of the human spirit, then the *more* or "greater" *(meizona) grace* will suggest the ability and willingness of God to overcome sinfulness: "he gives us grace potent enough to meet this and every other evil spirit" (Phillips). If, however, as we have argued, v. 5 depicts God's jealousy for his people, then James here is reminding us that God's grace is completely adequate to meet the requirements imposed on us by that jealousy. Our God is "a consuming fire," and his demand for our exclusive allegiance may seem terrifying. But our God is also merciful, gracious, all-loving, and willingly supplies all that we need to meet his all-encompassing demands. As Augustine has said, "God gives what he demands."

But, in keeping with his strong emphasis on exhortation throughout the letter, James does not let this word of grace stand by itself for long. God's grace demands response: the response of humility. James introduces this note via his quotation from Prov. 3:34: *"God opposes the proud but gives grace to the humble."* (This text is quoted also in 1 Pet. 5:5, another example of the close relationship between James and 1 Peter.) The humility introduced in this quotation becomes the dominant motif in the commands in vv. 7-10.[27] God's gift of sustaining grace is enjoyed only by those willing to admit their need and accept the gift. The *proud,* on the other hand, meet only resistance from God. God's opposition toward the arrogant person is a recurring motif in the OT (see, e.g., Ps. 18:27; 34:18; 51:17; 72:4; 138:6; Isa. 61:1; Zeph. 3:11-12). Worth mentioning is that "pride" *(hyperēphania)* is often associated with jealousy and envy in Hellenistic writings.[28] Perhaps James would want us to see here an implicit condemnation of these jealous and selfish people whom he has criticized in 3:13–4:3.

26. Laws argues that James implies a reference to verses like Ps. 42:1 and 84:2, which speak of the soul's "longing" *(epipotheō)* for the Lord. She punctuates the sentence as a question — "Is pious longing the proper manner of the soul's desire?" — and suggests that these verses provide the answer (Laws, 174-79; and, in greater detail, "Does Scripture Speak in Vain? A Reconsideration of James IV.5," *NTS* 30 [1974] 210-15; see also Adamson, 170-73; Schlatter [249] had already mentioned Ps. 42:1 in connection with this verse). But the interpretation demands too allusive a scriptural reference.

27. Penner (149-68), indeed, argues that the verse serves to introduce the entire last major section of the letter (4:6–5:12). In this section, James both commends the humble (4:7-10) and chastises the "proud" (4:11–5:12). Penner is right to note some verbal parallels with 4:6 in the rest of the letter; but he pays too little attention to the tight connections between vv. 4-5 and 6-10 on the one hand and 4:11-12 and 3:1-12 on the other.

28. See the texts cited in Johnson, 283.

7 Verses 7-10 contain a series of commands that flow directly from the quotation of Prov. 3:34 in v. 6. If God gives the grace to meet his claim on our lives to those who are humble, then we must become humble if we expect to enjoy that grace. James sounds this call for humility in v. 7a and 10: *submit yourselves to God/humble yourselves before the Lord.* The Greek verb in v. 10 — *tapeinoō* — comes from the same root as the Greek word for "humility" *(tapeinos)* in the Proverbs quotation. This verbal link effectively ties the series of commands to the promise of grace in the quotation of v. 6. And, while not related verbally (the Greek verbs are different), *submit yourselves to God* and *humble yourselves before the Lord* are conceptually similar, forming an *inclusio.* Between these two "bookends" we find a carefully structured series of commands that spell out some of the aspects and implications of the overall call to "submit to God."

> *Resist the devil, and he will flee from you.* (7b)
> *Come near to God and he will come near to you.* (8a)
>
> *Wash your hands, you sinners,*
> *and purify your hearts, you double-minded.* (v. 8b)
>
> *Grieve,*
> *mourn,*
> *and wail.* (v. 9a)
>
> *Change your laughter to mourning*
> *and [change] your joy to gloom.* (v. 9b)

What James writes in vv. 6-10 is strikingly similar to 1 Pet. 5:5-9. Peter also quotes Prov. 3:34 (v. 5b), following it with commands to "Humble yourselves, therefore, under God's almighty hand, that he may exalt you in due time" (v. 6) and resist the devil (v. 9). These parallels suggest that what James says here may reflect a widespread early Christian call to repentance.

To *submit* to God means to place ourselves under his lordship, and therefore to commit ourselves to obey him in all things. The Greek verb *(hypotassō)* means to "put in order under," and suggests the existence of a hierarchy of authority — such as God institutes in human government (Rom. 13:1, 5; 1 Pet. 2:13) and in marriage (Eph. 5:21; Col. 3:18; Tit. 2:5; 1 Pet. 3:1, 5). The essence of unbelief is failure to "submit" to God's law (Rom. 8:7) and his righteousness (Rom. 10:3). Submission language occurs particularly often in the NT in conjunction with the frequently quoted Ps. 8:6: "You made him [man, or 'the son of man'] ruler over the works of your hands; you put everything under his feet" (the LXX uses the verb *hypotassō,* "submit"). The verse is applied to Christ, the one, as "man" par excellence, who "fulfills" this expectation (1 Cor. 15:27; Eph. 1:22; Heb. 2:5-8), but Christ's lordship over creation lasts only until the redemptive plan is finished. Then, Paul reminds us, Christ will himself "be made subject" to God, who will be "all in all" (1 Cor. 15:28). Christians, James suggests, are even now to recognize God's lordship and to place ourselves in glad submission under his wise rule.

The commands in the first couplet — *resist the devil* and *draw near to God* — unpack the significance of "submitting" to God. Placing ourselves under God's authority means, negatively, that we firmly refuse to bow to the devil's authority. The verb translated "resist" means to "stand against," and can also be translated "oppose" or "withstand" (see, e.g., Acts 6:10; Rom. 9:19; Eph. 6:13). The word "devil" translates Gk. *diabolos,* which is used in the Septuagint to translate *śṭn,* the Hebrew root that gives us the title "Satan." The two titles are thus identical in meaning (cf. Rev. 20:2), both suggesting that one of the devil's primary purposes is "to separate God and man."[29] When we resist the devil's purposes, he will, James promises, *flee from you.*[30] Whatever power Satan may have, the Christian can be absolutely certain that he has been given the ability to overcome that power.

8 Parallel to the negative command plus promise in v. 7b is the positive command plus promise in v. 8a: *Come near to God and he will come near to you.* The verb "come near" (Gk. *engizō*) often refers to approaching God in worship in the OT (e.g., Lev. 21:3, 21, 23; Isa. 29:13; 58:2; 65:5; Ezek. 40:46, etc.) and has this meaning once also in the NT (Heb. 7:19). But a call to draw near to God in worship does not fit this context well, since James goes on to use the same verb of God's drawing near to us. So he is probably using the verb much as it is used in Hos. 12:6: "But you must return to your God; maintain love and justice and wait for [LXX *engize,* "come near"] your God always." See also *T. Dan* 6:2, where the command to "draw near to God" is preceded by the exhortation to "be on your guard against Satan and his spirits." James is urging that we repent of our sins and seek God as an important aspect of his overall call to "submit" ourselves to God (v. 7). The promise that God will come near to those who come near to him does not, of course, apply to the salvation of unbelievers[31] but to the restoration to fellowship of Christians. Like the father of the prodigal son, God stands always ready to welcome back his children who turn from their sinful ways.

29. W. Foerster, *TDNT* 2:73.

30. In addition to being in 1 Peter, this idea is found in pre-Christian Judaism; see *T. Naph.* 8:4; *T. Iss.* 7:7.

31. A few 12th-century theologians held this view; cf. McGrath, *Iustitia Dei* 1:84.

At the end of v. 8, James issues two more commands that unpack in more detail the general exhortation to "come near to God." Together, they call for a radical repentance that embraces the total person. The two commands are formulated in perfect parallelism: imperative verb plus object, climaxed with a pejorative address to the readers. And enhancing both the parallelism and the sharpness of the commands is the omission of any articles or possessive pronouns. A literal rendering would be:

wash hands, sinners;
and purify hearts, double-souled!

The strongly negative descriptions of the readers pick up the similar denunciation that opens this paragraph: "you adulterous people" (v. 4). As we noted in our comments on v. 4, these blunt addresses gain all the more strength from their contrast with James's typical address "brothers" or "beloved brothers." Clearly, he sees his readers as both Christian and in need of a wake-up call that will bring home to them the seriousness of their departure from godly attitudes and behavior. "Double-souled," NIV *double-minded* (Gk. *dipsychos*), captures a key motif of the letter as a whole. James used this word (which, as we noted, may have been coined by him) in 1:8 to depict the person whose faith wavers and vacillates. Its repetition here underscores especially James's accusation that his readers are attempting to be "friends" with both God and the world at the same time (v. 4): a conflict of basic allegiance that our jealous God will simply not tolerate (v. 5). The Christian, living in the "overlap" of the ages, is pulled between the kingdom of Christ and the kingdom of Satan, the realm of Spirit and the realm of "flesh." To allow "the world" to entice us away from total, single-minded allegiance to God is to become people who are divided in loyalties, "double-minded" and spiritually unstable. James's readers, by exhibiting a jealousy and selfishness typical of this world (cf. 3:15), by failing to act on what they hear and say (1:19–2:26), in their "double" use of the tongue (3:9-10), and in their violent disputes with one another (4:1-2), are guilty of this "double-minded" attitude. They must repent of both this external behavior — *wash your hands* — and the internal attitude that leads to such behavior — *purify your hearts.* The imagery of both "washing" and "purifying" stems from the OT provisions for priestly purity in ministering the things of the Lord (the verbs have this sense in the three verses where they occur together: Num. 31:23; 2 Chron. 29:15; Isa. 66:17). But both verbs had come to be applied more broadly to ethical purity as well. James also reflects the OT in using "hands" and "heart" to denote both deed and disposition. The psalmist required "clean hands and a pure heart" for those who would stand before the Lord (Ps. 24:3-4); James asks the same of those who would "come near to God."

9 In v. 8b James used language drawn from the requirements for cultic purity to issue his call to repentance; in v. 9 he turns to the prophets for his imagery. *Grieve, mourn and wail* are all used by the prophets to denote reactions of those who suffer God's judgment (e.g., Isa. 15:2; Jer. 4:13; Hos. 10:5; Joel 1:9-10; Mic. 2:4). But even more to the point are those places where they use such language to call God's people to repentance from sin. Joel, warning of the nearness of the day of the Lord, pictures the Lord as inviting his people to "'return to me with all your heart, with fasting and weeping and mourning'" (2:12). James, like Joel, is convinced that the eschatological judgment is "imminent" (5:8); therefore, like Joel, he calls on God's people to exhibit a heartfelt sorrow for sin that is the mark of true repentance — what Paul called a "godly sorrow . . . that leads to salvation and leaves no regret" (2 Cor. 7:10). Paul also called on Christians to "mourn" for their sin (1 Cor. 5:2). And Peter expresses his sorrow at betraying the Lord by "weeping" (Luke 22:62). The biblical writers therefore suggest that all persons will inevitably "mourn" for their spiritual state. They can wait to mourn until it is too late, when God has brought his judgment on the earth. Or they can mourn now, turning sorrowfully from their sin so that they will have no occasion to mourn when the Lord returns.

James reinforces the need to take sin seriously by adding, *Change your laughter to mourning and your joy to gloom.* "Laughter" is often the mark of the "fool" in the OT and Jewish literature, the person who scorns the idea of right living and blithely goes along in a life of indolence and pleasure (see, e.g., Prov. 10:23; Eccl. 7:6; Sir. 27:13). Jesus reflected this tradition when he said, "Woe to you who laugh now, for you will mourn and weep" (Luke 6:25b). A carefree, "devil-may-care" attitude is typical of those who are "friends with the world." They live the hedonist philosophy "eat, drink and be merry, for tomorrow we die," a worldview that ignores the terrifying reality of God's judgment. But even the committed Christian can slip into a casual attitude toward sin, perhaps presuming too much on God's forgiving and merciful nature. James's words in this passage directly counter any such attitude. He wants us to see sin for what it is — a serious breach in our relationship with a loving heavenly father, a breach that, if not healed, can lead to both temporal and spiritual disaster. James's insistence that we turn our "joy into gloom" might sound strange in light of Paul's injunction to "rejoice in the Lord always" (Phil. 4:4). But the joy Paul speaks about is the joy that comes when we realize that our sins are forgiven in Christ; the joy James warns about is the fleeting and superficial joy that comes when we indulge in sin. True

Christian joy can never be ours if we ignore or tolerate sin; it comes only when we have squarely faced the reality of our sin, brought it before the Lord in repentance and humility, and experienced the cleansing work of the Spirit.

10 The final command in this paragraph, *humble yourselves before the Lord,* returns to the note on which the commands began: *submit yourselves to God.* It also brings us back to the quotation from Prov. 3:34 that serves as the springboard for the series of commands. If God gives grace "to the humble," then humbling ourselves before God is obviously the way to experience that grace. To "humble ourselves before the Lord" means to recognize our own spiritual poverty, to acknowledge consequently our desperate need of God's help, and to submit to his commanding will for our lives. This humility is beautifully exemplified in the tax-collector of Jesus' parable, who, deeply conscious of his sin, called out to God for mercy. In response, Jesus pronounces him justified, and summarizes: "everyone who exalts himself will be humbled, and he who humbles himself will be exalted" (Luke 18:14). This saying (parallel to others where humility before other people is the point: Matt. 23:12; Luke 14:11) was taken up as a popular motto in the early church (cf. 2 Cor. 11:7; 1 Pet. 5:6). It reminds us that we gain spiritual vitality and victory not through our own strength or effort but through giving ourselves completely to the Lord. When we try to "exalt ourselves" by relying on our own abilities, status, or money, we meet with inevitable failure and even condemnation — God humbles us. James makes this same basic point earlier in his letter when he encourages the "humble" brother to boast in his "exaltation" and the rich brother to boast in his "humiliation" (1:9-10).

VI. THE COMMUNITY DIMENSION OF SPIRITUAL WHOLENESS: PURE SPEECH AND PEACE, PART 2 (4:11-12)

A. Critical Speech Is a Presumptuous Violation of the Law (4:11-12)

> 11 *Brothers, do not slander one another. Anyone who speaks against his brother or judges him speaks against the law and judges it. When you judge the law, you are not keeping it, but sitting in judgment on it.* 12 *There is only one Lawgiver and Judge, the one who is able to save and destroy. But you — who are you to judge your neighbor?*

Verses 11-12 form a single argument about the sinfulness of critical speech. But the connection between these verses and their context is not easy to determine. Several interpreters attach the verses to what follows. Cargal, for instance, while suggesting that the verses are transitional, nevertheless thinks that they introduce the last main section of the letter, extending to 5:20. He notes that the commands of 4:11 and 5:19 form a kind of contrasting *inclusio:* believers are not to judge one another (4:11), but to restore those who have gone astray (5:19).[32] Others who take vv. 11-12 with what follows do not think this new section extends so far. Johnson argues that 4:11-12, 4:13-17, and 5:1-6 all rebuke a form of arrogance,[33] while Martin sees in both 4:11-12 and 4:13-17 a rebuke of arrogant speaking.[34] Other interpreters, however, take vv. 11-12 with what has come before them. Davids, for instance, thinks that these verses end a larger segment on community conflict.[35] We think that this latter view is closest to the truth. "Speaking evil" *(katalalia)* of others is a manifestation of the pride that God resists (4:6) and which is to be avoided by humility before God (4:10). And "speaking evil" is often linked to "jealousy" *(zēlos)* (2 Cor. 12:20; 1 Pet. 2:1), "selfishness" (2 Cor. 12:20), quarrels (*polemas* in *Pss. Sol.* 12:3) and pride (*T. Gad* 3:3), and is said to be a manifestation of double-mindedness (Hermas, *Similitude* 8.7.2; see *Mandate* 2). Finally, the prominence of "the law" and "judging" in vv. 11-12 corresponds to the theme of 2:8-13. Just as Lev. 19:18 (the love command) was quoted there, so Lev. 19:16, which prohibits slander, may be in James's mind here; the shift from "brother" to "neighbor" in v. 12 makes this especially plausible. These several connections suggest that vv. 11-12 form a basically independent section that picks up a number of James's favorite themes. But the prominence of the tradition that links "speaking evil" to the sins of jealousy, quarreling, and pride, which have been the focus of 3:13–4:10, suggests that they belong generally to this larger discussion. Perhaps vv. 11-12 should be seen as a brief "reprise" of the larger discussion of sins of speech that opened the section (3:1-12). We would then have an *inclusio* on speech that frames the section 3:1–4:12.

11 The harsh, denunciatory address of 4:4 — *adulterous people* — and of 4:8 — *sinners* and *double-minded* — gives way here to James's more familiar *brothers.* He therefore signals a shift from the call to repentance that acts as the center of the letter (4:4-10) back to exhortations relating to specific forms of behavior. He begins with a prohibition of *slander.* This

32. Cargal, 170-71.
33. Johnson, 291-92.
34. Martin, 160-61.
35. Davids, 169.

word translates a Greek word *(katalaleō)* that means, literally, "speak against." It denotes many kinds of harmful speech: questioning legitimate authority, as when the people of Israel "spoke against God and against Moses" (Num. 21:5); slandering someone in secret (Ps. 101:5); bringing incorrect accusations (1 Pet. 2:12; 3:16). James warns his readers never to indulge in such slanderous speech.[36] While we cannot know for sure just why slander was a problem in the community, the divisions that were wracking the church (3:13–4:3) may provide the best explanation. Quarrels over most issues usually end up including personal attacks and judgmental attitudes.

James's reason for prohibiting slander is interesting: *Anyone who speaks against his brother or judges him speaks against the law and judges it. Speak against* in the NIV is simply a translational variant of "slander" earlier in the verse; the Greek word is the same. But James's addition of the "judging" idea takes the argument a step further. He suggests that our criticism of a fellow believer involves standing in judgment over that believer. The *law* is probably the OT law, especially since there may be an allusion here to Lev. 19:16: "Do not go about spreading slander among your people." This verse comes just before the "love command" (Lev. 19:18), which James singles out as the heart of the "royal law" (2:8); and James's concern with partiality may pick up a motif in the same context (cf. 19:15). But, as we have noted in our interpretation of 1:25 and 2:8, James implies a new covenant context for the love command and its related exhortations. When James speaks of the law here, then, we are probably justified in thinking that he refers to the OT law insofar as it has been taken up into the "law of the kingdom" that Jesus laid upon his followers.

But how can James claim that criticism of a fellow believer is tantamount to criticism of the law? Clearly a part of the argument is missing; but James's shift to the word "neighbor" at the end of v. 12 implies what we need to supply. That word must be a reminiscence of the love command — confirming the suspicion that James might have Leviticus 19 in mind throughout. So James assumes that criticism of a fellow believer contradicts the demand that we love our neighbors. Therefore, we fail to keep the law when we slander and stand in judgment over one another. And in failing to keep the law, James says, we also "judge" it. The last part of the verse explains: *When you judge the law, you are not keeping it, but*

36. The form of the prohibition is *mē* + present imperative. Many grammarians have thought that this construction indicates that an action in progress is to stop: e.g., "stop slandering one another." But this does not seem to be the case. The present tense may well suggest continuous action, but there is no reason to think that the action must already be in progress. It is better to see the prohibition as globally prohibiting involvement in the action.

sitting in judgment on it. Since James contrasts "judging" the law with "keeping" it, he apparently thinks that failure to do the law implies a denial of the law's authority. However high and orthodox our view of God's law might be, a failure actually to do it says to the world that we do not *in fact* put much store by it. Again we see coming to the surface James's understanding of Christianity as something whose reality is to be tested by the measure of obedience.

12 But there is another reason why slandering another is so wrong: it also involves an infringement on the unique right of God himself: *There is only one Lawgiver and Judge, the one who is able to save and destroy.* Jews sometimes called Moses the "lawgiver" (e.g., Philo, *Moses* 2.9), but James, following the LXX (Ps. 9:20; the verbal form appears in, e.g., Exod. 24:12), applies the word to God. And the Scriptures, of course, regularly portray God as the only ultimate judge of the world. In order to make clear the nature of the "judging" that James has in view here, he adds a final description of God: *the one who is able to save and destroy.* As Jesus reminded us, it is God alone who is able "to destroy both soul and body in hell" (Matt. 10:28). James therefore is thinking of "judging" in terms of determining the ultimate spiritual destiny of individuals. And the believer has no right to make any such determination: *But you — who are you to judge your neighbor?* As we noted earlier, the introduction of *neighbor* here reveals that an implicit anchor for James's rebuke is the love command, with its demand that we love "the neighbor" (Lev. 19:18; cf. Jas. 2:8).

In light of the argument of these verses, therefore, we should note that James is not prohibiting the proper, and necessary, discrimination that every Christian should exercise. Nor is he forbidding the right of the community to exclude from its fellowship those it deems to be in flagrant disobedience to the standards of the faith, or to determine right and wrong among its members (1 Corinthians 5 and 6). James rebukes jealous, censorious speech by which we condemn others as being wrong in the sight of God. It is this sort of judging that Paul condemned among the Roman Christians, who were apparently questioning the reality of one another's faith because of differing views on the applicability of some ritual laws (Rom. 14:1-13; see esp. vv. 3-4 and 10-13). It is entirely possible that some situation like this was responsible for the problems James addresses. A bitter, selfish spirit (3:13-18) had given rise to quarrels and disputes about certain matters in the church (4:1-2). These disputes were apparently conducted, as they usually are, with a notable absence of restraint in the use of the tongue (3:1-12), including perhaps cursing (3:10) and denunciations (4:11-12) of one another. Such behavior is nothing more than a manifestation of a worldly spirit (3:15; 4:1, 4). It must be replaced by "the wisdom from above," with its meekness, reasonableness, and peaceableness (3:17). This flirtation with the world must be seen to be incompatible with God's jealous desire to have his people's wholehearted allegiance (4:4-5). Yet God is willing to turn and bestow his favor if sinful pride can give way to deep-felt repentance and sincere abasement before him (4:6-10).

VII. THE WORLDVIEW OF SPIRITUAL WHOLENESS: UNDERSTANDING TIME AND ETERNITY (4:13–5:11)

The conceptual flow of James's letter at this point is not easy to discern. We have argued that 3:1–4:12 exhibits a general unity of thought, centered on the problem of community divisiveness and extending to its cause — selfish, envious attitudes — and its manifestation — sinful, critical speech. As we noted in the introduction to the previous section, many commentators think the shift to a new focus occurs at 4:6 or 4:11, with the problem of arrogance bringing a general unity to the material right through 5:6 or even 5:12. We think, however, that it is more natural to locate the transition at 4:13. First, the rebuke of critical speech in 4:11-12 forms an *inclusio* with the treatise on the tongue in 3:1-12. These texts expose one of the most serious manifestations of the selfishness and resultant bickering that James rebukes in 3:13–4:3. Second, the form of address in 4:13 — "Now listen, you who say" — obviously parallels the introduction to 5:1-6: "Now listen, you rich people." These paragraphs, James implies by this literary device, belong together. But the similarities are more than literary: both paragraphs rebuke the attitude of well-to-do people who arrogantly suppose that they can think and act without reference to God and to eternity. Arrogant selfishness is the problem in both paragraphs.

If, then, 4:13 initiates a new section that extends to at least 5:6, where should we place the end of the unit? An obvious possibility would be to include only the two generally parallel paragraphs, 4:13-17 and 5:1-6. But the call for patient endurance that begins in 5:7 is closely related, especially in light of the biblical background, to 5:1-6 (and, to a lesser extent, 4:13-17 as well). In 5:7-11, James delineates the response that faithful Christians should have to the arrogant selfishness he has rebuked in the previous verses.

The underlying issue that brings loose unity to 4:13–5:11 is a clash of worldviews. We find, on the one hand, a worldview that largely leaves God out of account, marked by boastful self-reliance (4:13-17) and selfish indulgence (5:1-6). The reality of God and his ultimate judgment is ignored or scorned. Faithful Christians, James urges, must respond with a resolute reaffirmation of the biblical worldview, marked by God's constant providential ordering of events (4:15) and the reality of a coming day on which God will reward the faithful and punish the sinful (5:1, 3, 5, 7).

A. Arrogant Planning Ignores God's Providence (4:13-17)

> 13 *Now listen, you who say, "Today or tomorrow we will go to this or that city, spend a year there, carry on business and make money."* 14 *Why, you do not even know what will happen tomorrow. What is your life? You are a mist that appears for a little while and then vanishes.* 15 *Instead, you ought to say, "If it is the Lord's will, we will live and do this or that."* 16 *As it is, you boast and brag. All such boasting is evil.* 17 *Anyone, then, who knows the good he ought to do and doesn't do it, sins.*

Underlying the boastful arrogance of the people both in this paragraph and in the next one is wealth. To be sure, the people James chastises in 4:13-17 are never said to be rich; but the extensive travel plans and desire to "make money" suggest that they belong to the relatively well-to-do merchant class. But are these well-off merchants Christians or not? James leaves this matter up in the air. The "rich" whom James condemns in 5:1-6 are probably not Christians (see the notes there). The parallels between that text and this one — especially the similar address — might lead us to suppose that both passages describe the sin and fate of the wicked rich. On the other hand, James chastises these merchants for failing to look at life from a Christian perspective (v. 14), urges them to acknowledge the Lord's sovereignty and providence as they make their plans (v. 15), and suggests that they know what they ought to do in this matter (v. 17). James would hardly address non-Christians in this way. It is just at this point that 5:1-6 differs from 4:13-17: James pronounces a verdict of condemnation on the "rich" of 5:1 with no hint that their fate might be avoided. In 4:13-17, then, James returns to the theme of 1:10-11, encouraging rich believers to avoid boasting in their own worldly accomplishments and to put their trust in the Lord.[37]

13 *Now listen* is a fair paraphrase of the Gk. *age nyn,* which means "come now." It is a stock form of address in the diatribe style that James uses elsewhere (see esp. 2:18-21).[38] James's tone is brusque and admoni-

37. See, e.g., Frankemölle, 634-35; Blomberg, 156.

38. James does not intend it to be a true imperative, as is evident from the singular form of the verb *(age),* which disagrees with the plural subject (*hoi legontes,* "you who say").

tory, a tone reinforced by *you who say* that immediately follows. Coming in place of James's usual address to his readers as "brothers," this tone might suggest that he intends here to turn his attention to people outside the church — letting the Christians listen in so that they can learn from the admonition. But we have already noted that the content of the paragraph seems to presuppose a Christian address. The tone James adopts suggests, however, that he regards the attitude of these Christians as unworthy of who they really are. We are reminded of a father forced to rebuke his children for behavior not in keeping with family values.

James's quotation of the merchants that he addresses here is, of course, fictional — as the language *this or that city* makes clear. What he does is to put words on their lips that pointedly bring to expression the underlying attitude that they are adopting in the plans that they make. Here are people, says James, who are deliberate and self-confident planners. They decide where they will go, when they will go, and how long they will stay.[39] Moreover, they are quite sure about the outcome of all these plans: they will *make money.* The picture James paints here would be familiar to his first-century readers. This period was marked by growing commercial activity, and especially in the Hellenistic cities of Palestine (such as those in the Decapolis). Jews were especially active in these ventures; many had left Palestine to settle in cities throughout the Mediterranean world in pursuit of financial gain. And, of course, the picture is equally familiar to us in the modern world. Modes of transportation and distances have changed, but the "bottom line" has not.

However, we need to guard against a misinterpretation at this point. It would be terribly tempting (and some interpreters have succumbed to the temptation) to find here a rebuke of those who are out to make a profit at all. The economic system we call capitalism, in other words, might be the real target of James's polemic. But, whatever we might think about the compatibility of Christianity and the profit motive of capitalism, it would be wrong to find any critique here. As the following verses make clear, James is not rebuking these merchants for their plans or even for their desire to make a profit. He rebukes them rather for the this-worldly self-confidence that they exhibit in pursuing these goals — a danger, it must be said, to which businesspeople are particularly susceptible. And we should guard here against another kind of misinterpretation: the idea that James is forbidding Christians from all forms of planning or of concern for the future. Taking out life insurance and saving for

39. The Greek for the last idea, *poiēsomen ekei eniauton* (lit., "we will make there a year") is colloquial for "we will spend a year there" (cf. similar constructions in Acts 15:33; 18:23; 20:3; 2 Cor. 11:25).

retirement, for instance, are not condemned by James; these may very well be a form of wise stewardship. What James rebukes here, as v. 16 will make clear, is any kind of planning for the future that stems from human arrogance in our ability to determine the course of future events.

14 James now tries to bring these self-confident merchants back to a proper sense of their place in the world. He reminds them of the kind of people they really are. James makes this point subtly right at the beginning of the verse. The NIV attempts to capture the nuance with its introductory *Why.* The basis in the Greek text for this nuance is the word *hoitines* at the beginning of the verse. This word bears a qualitative sense: "people such as you." James is asking, in effect: How can you, being the kind of creatures that you are, presume to dictate the course of future events? The fragility of human life and the consequent uncertainty of all human plans is the main point of the verse. But what is not clear is just how James goes about establishing this point. The NIV (along with the KJV, RSV, and NEB) divides the first part of the verse into two parts: a statement, *you do not even know what will happen tomorrow;* and a question, *What is your life?* The other main option, represented in the NASB, is to take all these words as part of one longer statement: "you do not know what your life will be like tomorrow" (NASB; cf. also TEV; NJB; NLT).[40] The situation is complicated because the Greek manuscripts contain a number of alternate textual forms. The most important of these is the introduction of a conjunction after "tomorrow," which would almost require that we break up the words into two parts (it seems to be presumed by the KJV translators; hence their "*For* what is your life?").[41] But this word should probably not be included in the text. On the other hand, most Greek manuscripts do have the Greek word equivalent to "for" as the introduction to the last statement in the verse (cf. TEV: "For you are like a thin fog . . ."). The point, then, is this: the placement of the "for" in the best Greek manuscripts (with the last assertion only) favors the NASB rendering. But favoring the NIV punctuation is the placement of the word "what" *(poios)* so late in the verse (after "tomorrow"). This makes it difficult to take it as the object of "you know" *(epistasthe),* as the alternative requires.[42] On the whole, we think this latter consideration outweighs the

40. See, e.g., Johnson, 295-96. The punctuation behind the NASB rendering is found in the standard Greek texts (the 27th ed. of Nestle-Aland and the 4th ed. of the UBS text). We must remember, however, that the punctuation of the Greek text is largely the decision of modern editors.

41. For detailed evaluations of the variants, see Metzger, 683-84, and Ropes, 278-79.

42. In the NT *poios* always occurs closely with a verb of knowing when it is its object. It is separated from it only by the subject of the verb (see Matt. 24:42 and 43; Luke 9:55; 12:39; Rev. 3:3).

significance of the "for." We should adopt the NIV-style rendering, with an assertion followed by a question.

The NIV rendering of James's initial assertion captures the idea conveyed by a compact Greek construction (the object of "you know" in Greek is simply "that of tomorrow" [*to tēs aurion*]). The question then follows quite abruptly (the absence of a connecting word in the best Greek manuscripts is unusual); but the abruptness is rhetorically effective. The answer to the question about "life" comes at the end of the verse: *You are a mist that appears for a little while and then vanishes.* "Mist" translates a relatively rare word within biblical Greek *(atmis),* which can also be rendered "smoke" (see TEV; cf. Acts 2:19 [the only other NT occurrence]; cf. also Gen. 19:28) or even "vapor" (NASB; cf. Hos. 13:3[?]). But whichever word we choose, the point is clear enough: human life is insubstantial and transitory, here one minute and gone the next. Illness, accidental death, or the return of Christ could cut short our lives just as quickly as the morning sun dissipates the mist or as a shift in wind direction blows away smoke.

The transitory nature of life that James reminds us of here is a recurring biblical theme. Proverbs 27:1 warns: "Do not boast about tomorrow, for you do not know what a day may bring forth." Job 7:7, 9, 16 and Ps. 39:5-6 describe life as a "breath." But, as is so often the case, especially close to James's teaching are some words of Jesus. In Luke 12:15, he warns the crowds about covetousness and reminds them that "a man's life does not consist in the abundance of his possessions." In a brief parable, he illustrated his point with a rich man who, like James's merchants, made definite plans for acquiring more goods, but who was prevented from executing his plans by his death (Luke 12:16-20). This passage contains several themes that James utilizes both here and in 5:1-6, and it is quite possible that it has furnished the stimulus for his own exhortations.

15 *Instead* connects this verse to v. 13 rather than to v. 14: "Come, you who are saying [v. 13] . . . instead of saying . . ."[43] James urges these confident and presumptuous merchants to add a key qualifier to their planning: *"If it is the Lord's will."* This explicit expression of dependence on the Lord has come to be known as the "Jacobean condition" *(conditio Jacobaea),* although the sentiment is, of course, widespread in the NT (most famously in the Lord's Prayer [Matt. 6:10]; cf. also Matt. 26:42; Acts 18:21; 21:14; Rom. 1:10; 15:32; 1 Pet. 3:17). It is not enough, James suggests, to recognize that one's own life is uncertain and transitory (v. 14). Such a recognition, after all, is not even specifically religious. What these merchants need to go on to reckon with is that their lives are also in the hands of God. This world is not a closed system; what appears to our

43. See Johnson, 296.

senses to be the totality of existence is in fact only part of the whole. This life cannot properly be understood without considering the spiritual realm, a realm that impinges on and ultimately determines the material realm in which we live day to day. Of course, such a worldview is not specifically Christian. Few of the people who lived in James's day would have been agnostic or atheistic; most recognized the existence of some form of divine being. And so it is not surprising that phrases such as "if God wills" (Latin *Deo volente*) or "if the gods will" are found in many kinds of ancient literature.[44] And the fact that James quotes such a widespread proverbial saying might lend support to the idea that he is writing to non-Christian merchants, using language familiar to them to gain a point of contact for a more specifically Christian perspective.

On the other hand, it might be significant that James encourages them to say not "if God wills" but "if the Lord wills." The title "Lord" *(kyrios)* conveys a more distinctive Jewish-Christian perspective than the title "God" would have done. The "Lord" could be Jesus, since James applies the title to him elsewhere in the letter (1:1; 2:1; 5:7, 8). But he usually applies the title to God the Father, the OT Yahweh, and this is probably the case here as well. Thus, James takes a common expression of general religious sentiment and "baptizes" it in the service of his distinctive biblical vision of a biblical worldview of history and its sovereign ruler.

The Greek manuscripts of this verse offer two basic ways of understanding the words that James urges these merchants to adopt. Some read a form of the verb "live" (a subjunctive) that would make it a part of the protasis (the "if" clause): "If the Lord wills and we continue to live, then we will do this or that." But the better manuscripts have the indicative form of the verb, and all modern English translations have followed this reading, which makes "live" a part of the apodosis (the "then" clause): "If the Lord wills, then we will live and do this or that."[45] Appropriately in the light of James's reminder that our lives are a "mist" (v. 14), James thus makes the continuance of life itself contingent on the will of the Lord. But he also, in light of v. 13, reminds us that our plans must also be subject to the same condition. This Paul did, as he frequently expressed his submission to the Lord's will in his plans for missionary work (Acts 18:21; Rom. 1:10; 1 Cor. 4:19; 16:7; cf. Heb. 6:3). And, more significant yet for James's background, Jesus himself exhibited the same sub-

44. See Dibelius (233-34) for a wide selection of examples.

45. A remaining difficulty with this reading of the verse is the presence of the *kai* (usually translated "and") before the verb *poiēsomen* ("we will live"). But *kai* can, due to Semitic influence, introduce an apodosis (cf. BDF 442[7]). It is also possible to take the two occurrences of *kai* together in a "both . . . and" construction (Davids, 173; Martin, 167).

mission to the Lord's will at the great crisis of his own life in Gethsemane. However, as Calvin pertinently observes, Jesus, Paul, and the other apostles do not always *state* this condition when they plan for the future. What was important is not the verbalization but that "they had it as a principle fixed in their minds, that they would do nothing without the permission of God." James attributes no magical significance to the words themselves. "If the Lord wills" can become nothing more than a glib formula without any real meaning. James, rather, wants us to adopt the attitude expressed by the words as a fixed perspective from which to view all of life. This perspective should add an element of contingency to all our planning — "if the Lord allows this to happen." But it should also force us to evaluate our planning from a biblical ethical perspective — "if this kind of plan is in accordance with the Lord's will expressed in Scripture for his people."

16 This verse contributes significantly to our understanding of the problem that James addresses in these verses. Taken by itself, the quotation that James places on the lips of the merchants in v. 13 could appear quite unobjectionable. Indeed, one could find many places in Scripture where prophets and apostles state their plans in very similar terms. But the problem, as James now makes clear, is the attitude underlying this planning. *As it is* (Gk. *nyn,* "now") brings us back to James's own present and to the problem that he is addressing. And the root problem is arrogance: *you boast and brag.* Where the NIV uses two indicative verbs, the Greek text in fact has an indicative verb followed by the preposition *en* ("in") with a plural object: "you boast in your arrogances." Many other English versions adopt the interpretation presumed in the NIV, taking "arrogances" generally as a modifier of "boast." The NIV (cf. also REB and TEV) suggests this idea by using two mutually interpreting indicative verbs — "boast-and-brag" — while other translations make the same point in a more literal rendering; see NRSV: "you boast in your arrogance." Some such qualification is probably necessary since the verb "boast" *(kauchaomai)* need not have a negative connotation. This verb is distinctively Pauline in the NT; Paul uses it thirty times, and James twice (see also 1:9). It combines the ideas of "put confidence in" and "rejoice in," with the slightly archaic "boast" still probably the best single English equivalent. The point of importance here is that "boasting" is not itself a negative activity or attitude: the question is what it is that one is boasting in (see the notes on 1:9). And so James must qualify the verb to indicate that he uses it to depict a boasting that arises from misplaced pride in one's own ability to chart the future. But the prepositional phrase, rather than describing the manner of the boasting, might qualify "boast" in a different way. In every other NT occurrence of the combination "boast" *(kauchaomai)* and "in" *(en),* the object of "in" indicates the object in which one boasts. And the fact that James uses the plural form of the noun here (*alazoneiais,* "arrogances") might suggest the same thing. Phillips captures the meaning that results from this interpretation very well: "'you get a certain pride in yourself in planning your future with such confidence."[46] The only other occurrence of the Greek word for "arrogance" in the NT might indicate that this interpretation is moving in the right direction: "For everything in the world — the cravings of sinful man, the lust of his eyes and the *boasting* of what he has and does — comes not from the Father but from the world." It is this "pride of life," this arrogant sense of self-sufficiency so characteristic of the world, that James condemns in this passage. *All such boasting is evil,* James concludes.

The Greeks called this boastful pride *hybris,* and Homer in *The Iliad* depicted in imaginative detail the havoc it wreaked when Achilles succumbed to it. People not only leave God out of account in planning their lives; they brag about it as well, proclaming in effect their autonomy and independence from the Lord. On the view we have taken of this paragraph, we must remember, James is rebuking not people of the world but Christians. He warns, therefore, of the tendency of the world to "press us into its mold" by leading us, perhaps very subtly, to begin assuming that we control the duration and direction of our lives. Such an attitude is simply inconsistent with a Christian worldview in which there is a God who sovereignly directs the course of human affairs.

17 The teaching about "sins of omission" in this verse appears to be rather awkwardly added to the end of this paragraph. Most commentators, in fact, think that the content of the verse was a traditional saying that James has added at this point. Dibelius, following his overall view of James as a letter composed of often unrelated traditional teachings, does not think the verse fits into its context at all. However, James does explicitly connect the verse to its context, with a "therefore" *(oun).* While the saying may well have been traditional, then, we should presume that James had good reason to include it at this point in his argument. Laws suggests a rather complex, "intertextual" explanation for the inclusion of the saying. She notes that Prov. 3:27-28 prohibits any delay in doing good to a neighbor — and in the Septuagint this prohibition is grounded in the consideration that "you do not know what the next day will bring forth." This language, of course, reminds us immediately of Jas. 4:15; and James has steered our attention to Proverbs 3 already by quoting from it in 4:6. The connections are, to be sure, intriguing, and scholars are increasingly cognizant of these kinds of verbal and conceptual "echoes" of the OT in

46. See also Martin, 167-68.

the NT. But this suggested echo seems a little too farfetched to be accepted. The wording of v. 17 in James gives little basis for a connection with Proverbs.

Other commentators suggest another rather specific tie-in to the context: that James is rebuking the merchants for failing to do good with their money (a motif that is implicit in 5:1-6). But James is not yet talking about the problem of wealth per se. So probably we are to posit a more general connection between v. 17 and what James has commanded us to do in v. 15. He has urged us to take the Lord into consideration in all our planning. We therefore have no excuse in this matter: we know what we are to do. To fail now to do it, James wants to make clear, is sin. We cannot take refuge in the plea that we have done nothing positively wrong. As Scripture makes abundantly clear, sins of *omission* are as real and serious as sins of *commission.* The servant in Jesus' parable who fails to use the money he was entrusted with (Luke 19:11-27); the people who fail to care for the outcasts of society (Matt. 25:31-46) — they are condemned for what they failed to do. Another teaching of Jesus reminds us very forcibly of James's words here: "That servant who knows his master's will and does not get ready or does not do what his master wants will be beaten with many blows" (Luke 12:47). James's reminder here is an important one. For we have a tendency, when we think of sin, to think only of those things we have done that we should not have done. I know my own confessions before the Lord tend to focus on these kinds of sins. But I should also consider those ways in which I have failed to do what the Lord has commanded me to do. Perhaps I did not reach out to help a "neighbor" in need; or perhaps I failed to bear witness to a co-worker when I had the opportunity. These also are sins for which I must seek God's forgiveness.[47]

47. See the excursus in Tasker, 106-8.

James 5

B. Misusing Wealth and Power Brings God's Judgment (5:1-6)

1 *Now listen, you rich people, weep and wail because of the misery that*
is coming upon you. 2 *Your wealth has rotted, and moths have eaten your*
clothes. 3 *Your gold and silver are corroded. Their corrosion will testify*
against you and eat your flesh like fire. You have hoarded wealth in the last
days. 4 *Look! The wages you failed to pay the workmen who mowed your*
fields are crying out against you. The cries of the harvesters have reached
the ears of the Lord Almighty. 5 *You have lived on earth in luxury and self-*
indulgence. You have fattened yourselves in the day of slaughter. 6 *You*
have condemned and murdered innocent men, who were not opposing you.

As we noted in the introduction to 4:13–5:11, this paragraph is closely related to 4:13-17 in both style and content. Both paragraphs begin with the stock formula of address *age nyn,* "come now" (NIV "Now listen"). And both paragraphs condemn a pursuit of wealth that fails to take into account the reality of God and his will for humanity. For this reason, as we noted, many commentators think that both sections must deal with the same kind of people. The usual argument is from 5:1-6 to 4:13-17: since the former depicts the wicked rich, the latter must also be directed to non-Christians. But the opposite tack is also sometimes taken. Frankemölle, for instance, thinks that the merchants attacked in 4:13-17 are Christians; and so the "rich" in 5:1-6 must also be believers.[1] He argues that the severe language of the passage is intended to awaken these

1. Frankemölle, 630-32.

rich, complacent, believers to the terrible reality of judgment that awaits those who abuse wealth. But his view is difficult to maintain. For the differences between 4:13-17 and 5:1-6 are greater than the similarities. The former is written in the dialogical style of the diatribe, with questions, answers, and exhortations to repent. James 5:1-6, however, has none of that. James's style is that of the prophets pronouncing doom on pagan nations. He unrelievedly attacks these people, with no hint of exhortation.

The "rich" whom James attacks in the paragraph are wealthy landowners, as v. 4 reveals. This was a class of people frequently criticized in the OT, Jewish literature, and the wider Greco-Roman world for their greedy acquisition of land and their exploitation of those forced to work on the land for them. The socioeconomic conflict between these two classes was acute in the first-century world, and James accurately reflects the situation.[2] And, in so forthrightly denouncing the "rich," James has become a key biblical spokesperson for the liberation theology movement. However, as we pointed out in the exposition of 1:10-11, the term "rich" must be carefully defined in the biblical context. It bears not only an economic sense but a theological one as well; and sorting out the degree to which one or the other of these nuances is present in any given occurrence of the word is not easy. What can be said about the "rich" in this passage, however, is that they are condemned not simply for their wealth; they are condemned for their sinful use of wealth. Applying the text to all wealthy people, then, would be a misreading of the passage. On the other hand, we cannot avoid the serious reminder about money and possessions that we confront in this text. One of the sins for which God condemns these people is their selfish accumulation of money and things (vv. 2-3). In the Western world, where amassing material wealth is not only condoned but admired, we Christians need to come to grips with this point in James and ask ourselves seriously: When do we have too much?

The structure of the paragraph is clear enough. Governing the passage is James's announcement of condemnation on the "rich" (v. 1). He then explains why these rich people are destined for condemnation: (1) they have selfishly hoarded wealth (vv. 2-3); (2) they have defrauded their workers (v. 4); (3) they follow a self-indulgent lifestyle (v. 5); and (4) they oppress "the righteous" (v. 6). A final point calls for attention: Why does James preach this message of denunciation of non-Christians in a letter addressed to the church? Calvin appropriately isolates two main purposes: James "has a regard to the faithful, that they, hearing of

2. See, e.g., R. MacMullen, *Roman Social Relations: 50 B.C. to A.D. 284* (New Haven: Yale University Press, 1974), esp. 5-27, 88-120.

the miserable end of the rich, might not envy their fortune, and also that knowing that God would be the avenger of the wrongs they suffered, they might with a calm and resigned mind bear them."[3]

1 James sets the tone of the rebuke that follows by repeating the brusque form of address from 4:13: *Listen now. You rich people,* as we have argued in the introduction to this section, are not among the (Christian) readers of the letter. They are, rather, wealthy non-Christians who are oppressing the Christian community.

The condemnation that James pronounces over them is issued in the tones of the OT prophets. *Weep (klaiō)* and *wail (ololyzō,* an onomatopoeic word, sounding like what it describes) occur frequently in the prophets to depict the reaction of the wicked when the day of the Lord arrives, although only here in the Greek Bible are they used together. See, for example, Isa. 13:6: "Wail, for the day of the LORD is near; it will come like destruction from the Almighty"; cf. also, e.g., Isa. 15:3; Amos 8:3). In fact, *ololyzō* ("wail") is found only in the prophets in the OT and always in the context of judgment (Isa. 10:10; 13:6; 14:31; 15:2-3; 16:7; 23:1, 6, 14; 24:11; 52:5; 65:14; Jer. 2:23; 31:20, 31; Ezek. 21:17; Hos. 7:14; Amos 8:3; Zech. 11:2). This background makes clear that *the misery that is coming upon* the rich refers not to earthly, temporal suffering, but to the condemnation and punishment that God will mete out to them on the day of judgment. The word for "misery" in Greek is in the plural (cf., e.g., NRSV), probably accentuating the degree of misery that will come with the judgment (the word occurs elsewhere in the NT only in Rom. 3:16).

As we have pointed out in the Introduction and earlier in the commentary (see the notes on 1:9-11 and 2:5), James's denunciation of the rich picks up and develops a pervasive biblical theme. God's concern for the poor is reflected in many of the Mosaic laws that give direction to the people of Israel as they live in covenant relation with their God. In Israel's later history, these laws were often ignored, and the poor were oppressed and taken advantage of by wealthy, powerful officeholders and landholders. As a result, the term "rich" can occasionally be used as a synonym for "the unrighteous" (cf. Prov. 10:15-16; 14:20). The prophets take up the theme, frequently denouncing the socioeconomic oppression being practiced by the wealthy (see Amos especially). Intertestamental Jewish writers continue and expand this social critique (see esp. *1 Enoch* 94–105), and it finds a secure place also within the NT. Jesus, especially in Luke's Gospel, issues many serious warnings about the threat of riches to genuine discipleship. In a saying particularly close to James's teaching,

3. Calvin, 342. Wessel suggests, further, that the preaching may represent a prophetic attempt to reach non-Christians who were frequenting Christian assemblies (965).

Jesus pronounced a woe upon the rich and warned that their "consolation" in this world would be replaced by "mourning" and "weeping" in the next (Luke 6:24-25). Revelation 18:10-24 is a lengthy "woe" directed to the merchants of the earth who "weep and mourn" over the devastation of the great city, Babylon. In all this, it is not always easy to determine the basis on which the rich are being judged. But although some traditions appear to condemn the rich merely because they are rich, in the NT, at least, condemnations of wealthy people are almost always attributed to a *misuse* of wealth. Certainly James's enumeration of the sins of the rich people that he condemns shows that this is the case here. It is particularly obvious that James does not intend to pronounce judgment on all rich people if, as we have argued, Jas. 1:10 implies the presence of rich Christians among James's readers. The designation *you rich* in verse 1, therefore, essentially means, as so often in Scripture, the *unrighteous* rich. But, having said this, we must caution against a tendency for Western Christians (most of whom are "wealthy" in comparative terms) to dismiss as entirely irrelevant the teaching of a paragraph like this. We cannot overlook the fact that "the rich" and "the unrighteous" are so easily associated. Scripture warns that wealth can be a particularly strong obstacle to Christian discipleship. Not for nothing did Jesus warn, "I tell you the truth, it is hard for a rich man to enter the kingdom of heaven" (Matt. 19:23).

2-3 James underscores the prophetic-style condemnatory tone of this paragraph by using a rapid-fire series of short clauses and sentences that lack connecting conjunctions or particles. Verses 2 and 3 exemplify this pattern particularly clearly. Two simple clauses bound together in a compound sentence and depicting the transitory nature of material possessions make up v. 2: *Your wealth has rotted, and moths have eaten your clothes.* Verse 3 (with no connecting word) continues the theme and extends it. The fleetingness of wealth is again the point in the opening clause: *Your gold and silver are corroded.* James then applies the point he has established in these first three clauses with another sentence composed of two simple clauses: *Their corrosion will testify against you and eat your flesh like fire.* The argument concludes with the enigmatic *You have hoarded wealth in the last days.* Although we have no explicit grammatical connection to go by, it is clear enough that these verses together provide the first reason for the condemnation that the "rich" of v. 1 stand under: they have used their wealth for their own selfish purposes.

A few commentators think that James might refer to the three main categories of material wealth in the ancient world: agricultural products *(wealth), clothes,* and precious metals *(gold and silver).* But *wealth* (Gk. *ploutos*) is a very general word, covering money or possessions of any kind; and we have insufficient basis to give it a restricted meaning here. To be sure, a literal interpretation would restrict James's reference to those possessions that are capable of "rotting." But the occurrences of this verb in the LXX (it does not occur elsewhere in the NT) show that it can be applied metaphorically to anything that is transitory. See, for example, "every work *decays* and ceases to exist, and the one who made it will pass away with it" (Sir. 14:19; cf. also Job 16:7; 19:20; 33:21; 40:12; Ps. 37:6; Ezek. 17:9; Ep. Jer. 1:71). *Moths have eaten your clothes* reminds us of Jesus' similarly worded warning about the the fragility of "treasures on earth" that are consumed by moths (Matt. 6:19; cf. also Job 13:28: "So man wastes away like something rotten, like a garment eaten by moths"). More unusual is James's claim that *Your gold and silver are corroded.* The word "corroded" translates a Greek word *(katioō)* that means "rust"; yet, of course, gold and silver are metals that cannot rust. A few commentators think that James, because of his lower-class origins, might simply be ignorant about the properties of gold and silver. But, in fact, "rust" was already being attributed to silver and gold (see, e.g., Sir. 29:10; Ep. Jer. 10). The word seems to have taken on a general sense of "decay" (see also Ezek. 24:6, 11, 12). Together, then, the three clauses in v. 2 and v. 3a remind the rich people whom James condemns that the money and material possessions in which they place so much stock will not last. In fact, the perfect tense that James uses in all three clauses *(sesēpen, gegonen, katiōtai)* suggests that the material possessions of these rich people are already in the state of being "rotted," "moth-eaten," "rusted." Of course, this was not strictly true; and some commentators, therefore, suggest that James uses the perfect tense here in a way similar to the prophets' use of an equivalent Hebrew tense: to underscore the certainty of a prediction about the future.[4] But we have noted that the images James uses were being used metaphorically to characterize material possessions as both transitory and unreliable. So the normal meaning of the perfect tense in Greek — to state a condition — makes perfect sense here.[5] Although the rich people do not, or cannot, see it, their great wealth has already lost its luster. It stands already under the doom of the things of this world that will fade away and can provide no foundation for the life to come.

And not only will wealth bring no lasting benefit to its possessors; it will even stand as a witness against them. The Greek of *testify against you* could also be taken in a positive sense: "testify on your behalf" (the Greek

4. E.g., Mayor, 154; Dibelius, 236; Davids, 175; Johnson, 299. Cf. Robertson, *Grammar,* 898.

5. See, e.g., M. Mayordomo-Marin, "Jak 5,2.3a: Zukünftiges Gericht oder gegenwärtiger Zustand?" *ZNW* 83 (1992) 132-37.

word is *eis*). But such a rendering would run counter to the denunciatory tone of the whole paragraph as well as to the imagery of this verse. For *eat your flesh like fire* is an image of God's judgment. See the similarly worded Jdt. 16:17: "Woe to the nations that rise up against my people! The Lord Almighty will take vengeance on them in the day of judgment; he will send fire and worms into their flesh; they shall weep in pain forever." Why does the transitory nature of their wealth spell doom for these rich people? James does not make clear the logical connection, but we can easily infer it from biblical teaching elsewhere. The very fact that they have accumulated so much suggests that these rich people have been guilty of focusing on "earthly treasure" at the expense of "heavenly treasure," showing plainly just where their "heart" really is (Matt. 6:19-21). See, for example, Ezek. 7:19: "They will throw their silver into the streets, and their gold will be an unclean thing. Their silver and gold will not be able to save them in the day of the LORD's wrath. They will not satisfy their hunger or fill their stomachs with it, for it has made them stumble into sin." But an additional idea, consonant with James's concern throughout the epistle, may also be present. Sirach, an intertestamental Jewish book that has many parallels with James, suggests a connection between wealth and failing to help the poor in language very similar to that of James: "Help a poor man for the commandment's sake, and because of his need do not send him away empty. Lose your silver for the sake of a brother or a friend, and do not let it rust under a stone and be lost. Lay up your treasure according to the commandments of the Most High, and it will profit you more than gold" (Sir. 29:9-11). A similar perspective is found in the Lucan version of Jesus' words about treasure: "Sell your possessions and give to the poor. Provide purses for yourselves that will not wear out, a treasure in heaven that will not be exhausted, where no thief comes near and no moth destroys" (Luke 12:33). People who hoard wealth are not only demonstrating utterly false priorities; they are also depriving others of their very life.[6] Here we find another application for the proverb about failing to do good that James quotes in 4:17. As Calvin comments, "God has not appointed gold for rust, nor garments for moths; but, on the contrary, he has designed them as aids and helps to human life." In this sense, James may intend the decay of the goods described in vv. 2-3a to be understood, at least in part, literally: the actual evidence of disuse will stand as a witness against the rich.

The last clause of v. 3 is again short and abrupt: *You have hoarded wealth in the last days.* The NIV rendering fails to bring out the striking metaphor that James employs here. For the verb that he uses *(thēsaurizō)*

6. See most clearly Dibelius, 236; Tasker, 110-11; Davids, 176.

means "lay up treasure" and normally has, as we would expect, a positive sense. James might, therefore, simply mean that the rich people are investing their money for "their last days," for example, their retirement. But the shift to judgment imagery in the previous sentence, as well as the NT use of the phrase "the last days," forbids this neutral interpretation. Following on the OT prophets' prediction of a period of time, "the last days," when God would intervene decisively to bring deliverance to his people and judgment to his enemies, the early Christians use this phrase in a theological sense (see Acts 2:17; 2 Tim. 3:1; Heb. 1:2; 2 Pet. 3:3). But the two comings of Messiah also make clear that this decisive intervention of God comes in two separate stages. "The last days" could, then, refer to the time of judgment to come. In this case, James, like Paul in Rom. 2:5, would be using "store up treasure" in an ironic sense: these rich people are "storing up" wrath for the day of judgment that is coming (cf. NRSV ["for"] and, very explicitly, the NLT: "This treasure you have accumulated will stand as evidence against you on the day of judgment"). But the preposition James uses before "last days" *(en)* is more naturally translated "in," and all other occurrences of the phrase "the last days" in the NT refer to the present time of fulfillment. The application of this expression to their own time testified to the early Christians' belief that they were living in an era of indefinite duration immediately preceding the climax of history. James shares this perspective, as his conviction about the nearness of the *parousia* makes clear (5:8). What James is saying, then, is that those who are avidly accumulating wealth in his day are particularly sinful because they utterly disregard the demands made upon people by the display of God's grace in Christ, and especially foolish because they ignore the many signs of the rapidly approaching judgment. The REB captures the idea very well: "You have piled up wealth in an age that is near its close." Like the rich fool, they failed to reckon with sudden judgment (Luke 12:15-21). "It is in *the last days* that you are laying up treasure!" As those who live in these "last days," we, too, should recognize in the grace of God already displayed and the judgment of God yet to come a powerful stimulus to share, not hoard, our wealth.

4 The first accusation that James levels at the unrighteous rich is, as we have seen, muted and somewhat indirect. Not so the second: they have cheated their workers of their pay. James's *Look* (Gk. *idou*) draws attention to this accusation. But its precise wording is unclear. Most Greek manuscripts have the verb *apostereō,* which means "defraud," "rob" (Mark 10:19; 1 Cor. 6:7, 8; 7:5; 1 Tim. 6:5). But two of the best manuscripts read *aphystereō,* "withhold" (cf. NASB; the word does not occur in the NT; and only in Neh. 9:20 and Sir. 14:14 in the LXX). A decision between the two is difficult; but we would have expected James to have used the former word, since it taps into a rich biblical tradition that informs his treatment of the poor and helpless throughout his letter. See especially Mal. 3:5: "'So I will come near to you for judgment. I will be quick to testify against sorcerers, adulterers and perjurers, against those who defraud [*apostereō* in the LXX] laborers of their wages, who oppress the widows and the fatherless, and deprive aliens of justice, but do not fear me,' says the LORD Almighty." Granted the significance of the "love command" (Lev. 19:18; cf. 2:8) in James and other possible allusions to this chapter on the law in the letter, Lev. 19:13 is another important background text: "'Do not defraud your neighbor or rob him. Do not hold back the wages of a hired man overnight." Note also Deut. 24:14-15: "Do not take advantage of a hired man who is poor and needy, whether he is a brother Israelite or an alien living in one of your towns. Pay him his wages each day before sunset, because he is poor and is counting on it. Otherwise he may cry to the LORD against you, and you will be guilty of sin." As this text in James makes clear, such admonitions were still needed in the first century. This period witnessed an increasing concentration of land in the hands of a small group of very wealthy landowners. As a result, many farmers were forced to earn their living by hiring themselves out to their rich landlords. Jesus' parable about the workers in the vineyard (Matt. 20:1-16) is cast against this familiar rural background, and it is significant that the workers expect their pay at the end of the day. Prompt payment would have been very important for the laborer, who often got by at a barely subsistence level and who needed a steady income to provide "daily bread" for himself and his family. In a society where credit was not readily available, the failure to pay workers promptly could jeopardize life itself.

In an echo of Deut. 24:15, which describes defrauded workers "crying out" to the Lord against their employers, James claims that the wages themselves *are crying out against you.* The imagery reminds us of Cain's blood crying out to God for justice (Gen. 4:10). When God's people utter "cries" (Gk. *boai*) in the Bible, they are often pleading with God for deliverance from danger and for justice (see, e.g., Exod. 2:23; 1 Sam. 9:16; 2 Chron. 33:13; cf. also 3 Macc. 5:7). What the rich think they do in secret, and without danger of prosecution, is not hidden from *the Lord Almighty. Almighty* captures the sense, if not the form, of the Greek here, which has *sabaōth* (transliterated in KJV; NASB), the transliteration of a Hebrew word that means "army." The title *Lord of hosts* pictures God as the powerful leader of a great army. Sometimes this army is an earthly one, as when David expresses his confidence in the outcome of his fight by claiming to come "in the name of the LORD Almighty, the God of the armies of Israel, whom you have defied" (1 Sam. 17:45). More often it is the heavenly host that God is pictured as leading. Isaiah saw "the LORD of hosts" in his famous vision (Isaiah 6), and the title became a favorite of his. He uses it often in descriptions of the judgments that God will bring upon Israel and the nations; and sometimes, as in Isa. 5:9, this judgment is linked specifically to oppression of the poor. Therefore, when James affirms that the wrongdoing of the rich has become known to God, he makes clear that this God is holy, powerful, and determined to judge those who infringe his commandments.

5 James continues the abrupt, disjunctive style of the passage as he introduces yet a third explanation for the "misery that is coming upon" the rich. Judgment will overtake them because they have *lived on earth in luxury and self-indulgence.* James uses two separate verbs to get his point across: *tryphaō* and *spatalaō.* The former verb need not have a negative connotation; it occurs in Neh. 9:25 (LXX) to describe the ease of life that God granted the Israelites for their obedience in conquering the land: "They ate to the full and were well-nourished; they reveled in your great goodness" (cf. also Isa. 66:11). But the cognate to this verb has a negative connotation in the NT (Luke 7:25; 2 Pet. 2:13), and James clearly uses it here to depict a sinful, self-indulgent lifestyle. The second verb is more exclusively negative. Its only other biblical occurrences are in 1 Tim. 5:6 — "But the widow who lives for pleasure is dead even while she lives" — and Ezek. 16:49, where the people of Sodom are condemned for being "overfed and unconcerned" and for not helping "the poor and needy." The easily overlooked phrase *on earth* contributes to these negative connotations, suggesting a contrast between the pleasures the rich have enjoyed in this world and the torment that awaits them in eternity. Although the wording is not the same, a very similar nuance occurs in Abraham's words to the rich man in Jesus' parable: "Son, remember that in your lifetime you received your good things, while Lazarus received bad things, but now he is comforted here and you are in agony" (Luke 16:25).

Indeed, this parable stands as a key witness to a widespread eschatological teaching in the Bible: that the ease of the rich and the suffering of the poor in this life would be reversed in the life to come. James's hint at this tradition in the phrase "on earth" provides an important clue to the correct interpretation of the difficult last sentence of the verse: *You have fattened yourselves in the day of slaughter. Day of slaughter* could refer to any time when the poor suffer horribly while the rich are indulging themselves; as Dibelius paraphrases the idea, "You can live riotously while it goes badly for the pious." But the "reversal of fortunes" theme we have mentioned, along with the parallel between v. 5b and "you have hoarded wealth in the last days" (v. 3), suggests rather that *the day of slaughter* is a specific eschatological point in time. Reflecting a growing tendency in eschatological interpretation, A. Feuillet has argued that the reference may be to the judgment that fell on Jerusalem and the Jews in the Roman conquest of A.D. 70.[7] But James seems to connect this day of judgment with the *parousia* of the Lord (5:7); and that word becomes virtually a technical term to denote the return of Christ in glory at the end of history. It is, therefore, far more likely that *the day of slaughter* is a vivid description of the day of judgment. While not found in the Septuagint, the phrase has an equivalent in the Hebrew text of Isa. 30:25 (v. 24 in the MT), where the day of the Lord is pictured. The pseudepigraphical *1 Enoch* also uses the phrase to describe the judgment (90:4) and in a context that has many parallels to Jas. 5:1-6. Moreover, the Bible often uses the imagery of a slaughter in battle to describe the day of judgment (see, e.g., Ezek. 7:14-23; Rev. 19:17-21). James's point then, as in v. 3, is that the rich are selfishly and ignorantly going about accumulating wealth for themselves and wastefully spending it on their own pleasures in the very day when God's judgment is imminently threatened. The "last days" have already begun; the judgment *could* break in at any time — yet the rich, instead of acting to avoid that judgment, are, by their selfish indulgence, incurring greater guilt. They are like cattle being fattened for the kill.

6 James has accused the "rich" of hoarding wealth (vv. 2-3), cheating workers (v. 4), and living self-indulgently. Now, in the climax of his denunciation, he accuses them of condemning and murdering *innocent men.* The NIV rendering here is interpretive; the Greek has simply "the righteous one" *(ton dikaion).* The singular construction, with the definite article, has led a number of scholars to surmise that James is thinking of the murder of a particular righteous individual. One identification, which can be traced back fairly early in Christian tradition, is that the "righteous one" is Jesus himself.[8] But nothing in the context has prepared us for the introduction of Jesus at this point. If the letter is pseudonymous, another possibility is opened up: that "the righteous one" is James himself, whose martyrdom might well stand for the readers as a particularly poignant expression of persecution.[9] But, in addition to the problem with pseudonymous authorship (for which see the Introduction), the

7. A. Feuillet, "Le sens du mot Parousie dans l'Evangile de Matthieu — comparison entre Matth. xxiv et Jac. V,1-11," in *The Background of the New Testament and Its Eschatology,* ed. W. D. Davies and D. Daube (Cambridge: Cambridge University Press, 1964), 261-88. He ties the interpretation of this passage in James to a similar view of the Olivet Discourse.

8. Johnson cites Oecumenius, Bede, and Cassiodorus (304 [he himself does not hold this view]). Among modern scholars, see Feuillet, "Le sens du mot Parousie," 276-77.

9. See Mayor, 160; Frankemölle, 662-64 (but as paradigmatic); and, as possible, Dibelius, 240; Martin, 182.

context demands a more general reference. "The righteous one" is the typical follower of God, experiencing persecution at the hands of the wicked rich. James's use of the word "condemn" (Gk. *katadikaō*) points to some kind of judicial verdict — and this reflects OT and intertestamental teaching directed to situations in which rich people use their wealth and influence to deprive the righteous poor of their rights and of their living. For instance, in Wis. 2:6-20, the desire of the wicked who live luxuriously in this life, with no thought for tomorrow, is to "oppress the righteous poor man" (v. 10) and to "condemn him to a shameful death" (v. 20). See also especially Amos 2:6; 5:12; Mic. 2:2, 6-9; 3:1-3, 9-12; 6:9-16; Ps. 10:8-9; 37:32; Jas. 2:5-7. But how can James claim that the rich have *murdered innocent men?* He probably has in mind the practical outcome of the actions that the rich take against the poor to cheat them of their land and take away their gainful employment: the poor starve to death. Sirach, for instance, makes just this connection: "to take away a neighbor's living is to murder him; to deprive an employee of his wages is to shed blood" (Sir. 34:22).

As does the NIV, virtually all modern translations (NASB; NRSV; REB; NJB; TEV; NLT) take the last clause of the paragraph as a statement: *who were not opposing you.* The NIV rendering suggests that the lack of opposition to the wicked rich came before the persecution; that the rich "went after" people who had done nothing wrong. But the verb is a present indicative, better translated, as in the NASB, "he does not resist you." The focus would then be on the nonresistance of the poor, afflicted righteous (cf. Matt. 5:39; Rom. 12:14), who refuse, or are unable, to oppose the power and influence of the rich. Nevertheless, the rather "lame" conclusion that such an interpretation brings to the paragraph has led to alternate suggestions for the interpretation of this sentence. Two are worth mentioning. Each takes these final words as a question. The former takes the implied subject of the verb to be "the righteous one," the "opposition" of the righteous consisting in his plea for vindication and judgment before God (cf. Rev. 6:9-11).[10] The latter assumes the implied subject to be God: "Does God not resist you?" or, with reference to the future judgment, "Will not God resist you?"[11] But the context forbids us from assuming "God" to be the subject, since he has not been mentioned since 4:15. Turning the clause into a question makes more sense, but we would have expected a future tense if James

10. See, e.g., Ropes, 292; Davids, 180.

11. See esp. Johnson, 305. L. A. Schökel supports this interpretation by appealing to the literary structure of this part of the letter. He sees 5:6 as an *inclusio* relating to 4:6, where God is the subject ("James 5,2 [sic] and 4,6," *Bib* 54 [1973] 74).

had in view the cries of the righteous for vindication. On the whole, then, the usual view is best: James, "on a note of majestic pathos," concludes the paragraph by reminding us that the righteous are helpless victims of the stratagems of the rich and powerful.[12]

C. Patiently Enduring Trials Earns God's Reward (5:7-11)

> 7 *Be patient, then, brothers, until the Lord's coming. See how the farmer waits for the land to yield its valuable crop and how patient he is for the autumn and spring rains.* 8 *You too, be patient and stand firm, because the Lord's coming is near.* 9 *Don't grumble against each other, brothers, or you will be judged. The Judge is standing at the door!* 10 *Brothers, as an example of patience in the face of suffering, take the prophets who spoke in the name of the Lord.* 11 *As you know, we consider blessed those who have persevered. You have heard of Job's perseverance and have seen what the Lord finally brought about. The Lord is full of compassion and mercy.*

In the first two paragraphs of this general section of the letter, James castigates people for arrogance and for abusing wealth and power. Overly self-confident Christian businesspeople are probably in view in 4:13-17, whereas the non-Christian rich are James's target in 5:1-6. But both paragraphs lack James's customary address to his readers, "brothers." This changes in 5:7-11 (vv. 7, 9, 10). James thereby signals his intention to focus explicitly on the attitudes that God's people need to adopt in light of a biblical perspective on this world and the coming judgment. And James leaves us in no doubt about what he thinks the basic attitude must be. Note the words "be patient" *(makrothymeō)* in v. 7 (twice) and v. 8; "patience" *(makrothymia)* in v. 10; "endure" *(hypomeinō)* and "endurance" *(hypomonē)* in v. 11. In light of the soon return of Christ as judge and deliverer (vv. 7, 8, 9), believers need to imitate the farmer (v. 7) and the prophets (v. 10) in displaying patience with their situation and with each other (v. 9) and to imitate Job in the endurance of difficult circumstances (v. 11).

The contribution of this paragraph to the argument of the letter as a whole is debated. A growing number of scholars, focusing on literary issues more than many earlier interpreters had done, are impressed by the number of similarities between this paragraph and the opening section of the letter (1:2-18). God's "blessing" on those who "endure" is the most obvious of these parallels (compare 5:11 and 1:12). These schol-

12. Tasker, 116.

ars accordingly view 5:7-11 as the opening part of the letter's conclusion.[13] Some connection with 1:2-18 is clear. But we think a more basic connection binds this paragraph to 5:1-6 as the flip side to the condemnation of the rich that we find there. This connection is implicit and grows out of the recognition that 5:1-11 fits a very widespread biblical pattern. One of the clearest examples of this pattern is found in Psalm 37. This psalm is a marvelous song of encouragement directed to the righteous. They are described as "poor and needy" (v. 14) and as suffering persecution at the hand of the wicked (vv. 12-15, 32-33). They are tempted to be envious of the prosperity and well-being of the wicked (vv. 1, 7) and, somewhat paradoxically, also to be impatient for the wicked to receive judgement. In this situation, the psalmist encourages the righteous to "be still before the LORD" (v. 7); to "refrain from anger" (v. 8), for God will certainly vindicate the righteous people, mainly poor, who were suffering from similar circumstances. James's advice is the same as the psalmist's: "be patient," for the "coming of the Lord," when the wicked will be judged (5:1-6) and the righteous delivered, "is near."

7 The *then* (Gk. *oun,* "therefore") shows that James views his admonition to believers (*brothers,* or "fellow members of the family of God") as a logical consequence of his denunciation of the wicked rich in 5:1-6. These rich people, James has made clear, while prospering in this life, face a certain prospect of condemnation on the day of judgment ("the day of slaughter" [v. 5]). Because of that prospect, believers who suffer at the hands of the "rich" should *be patient . . . until the Lord's coming.* The word "coming" translates the Gk. *parousia,* which means basically "presence" (see 1 Cor. 16:7; 2 Cor. 10:10; Phil. 2:12). It was applied in secular Greek to the "arrival" of a king or dignitary. It is probably from this background that the technical sense of the word in the NT developed, for the early Christians consistently used the word to refer to the "coming" of Jesus at the end of history to judge the wicked (e.g., Matt. 24:37, 39; 2 Thess. 2:8) and deliver the saints (e.g., 1 Cor. 15:23; 1 Thess. 2:19; 3:13; 4:15; 5:23). To be sure, the exact phrase that James uses here and in v. 8 — "the coming of the Lord" — occurs only one other time to depict the return of Christ (1 Thess. 4:15). And the "Lord" here could, of course, be God the Father (as in vv. 4, 10, and 11 in this context). But the frequency with which NT writers apply the language to the return of Christ suggests that *parousia* quite early took on among the early Christians virtually a technical sense. James certainly intends, and his readers would certainly have understood, *the Lord's coming* to refer to Jesus' return as judge and savior.

Until this day comes, James urges his readers to adopt an attitude of

13. See, e.g., Frankemölle, 668.

patience.[14] As we noted in the introduction to this paragraph, the call for "patience" or "endurance" is the theme of these verses. "Patience" (from the root *makrothym-*) can sometimes be distinguished from "endurance" (from the root *hypomon-*), the former denoting the long-suffering attitude we are to adopt toward other people (1 Cor. 13:4; Eph. 4:2; 1 Thess. 5:14), the latter connoting the strong, determined fortitude with which we need to face difficult circumstances (Rom. 8:25; 2 Cor. 1:6; 2 Thess. 1:4). Or, to put it simply, we are *patient* with other people and *endure* difficulties. But this distinction does not appear to apply very neatly to James's use of these two word-groups in this paragraph. For the "patience" *(makrothymia)* of the prophets in v. 10 seems to be equivalent to the "perseverance" *(hypomonē)* of Job in v. 11. A similar overlap in meaning occurs in *T. Joseph* 2:7, where Joseph, after successfully resisting the temptation of Potiphar's wife, says "perseverance *(makrothymia)* is a powerful medicine and endurance *(hypomonē)* provides many good things" (see also Col. 1:11). James's combination of "be patient . . . until" helps pin down the sense of the word in this verse. *Until (heōs)* has a "pregnant" sense, suggesting the idea of a goal as well as a time period: "exercise patience as you wait for, and look for, the coming of the Lord." The attitude that James calls on us to adopt here, then, includes resignation in the face of suffering along with confident expectation of a day when the fortunes of this life will be reversed. And, negatively, James is probably also implicitly forbidding his readers from taking vengeance on their oppressors.[15] "Do not take revenge, my friends, but leave room for God's wrath, for it is written, 'It is mine to avenge; I will repay,' says the Lord" (Rom. 12:19).

In a style reminiscent of 3:1-12, James now adduces an example of the attitude he has just described (as in 3:4 and 5, the illustration is introduced with *idou,* "see"). The farmer who prepares a field, sows seed, and then waits for a crop is a very natural illustration of patience (see also 1 Cor. 9:7, 10; 2 Tim. 2:6). He can do little to effect the outcome but must wait and pray for the right rain at the right time. In Palestine, the farmer was particularly dependent on the rain that came in late autumn and early spring.[16] See, for example, Deut. 11:14, where God, in response to his people's obedience, promises "then I will send rain on your land in its

14. The Greek verb *(makrothymēsate)* is in the aorist tense, giving us no basis to draw any conclusions about a particular nuance in the command. As so often, the aorist is chosen as the simplest, more straightforward way of issuing the command.

15. See esp. Martin, 191, who again reads this text against the background of the growing Zealot movement in the 60s.

16. Actually, three-quarters of the average rainfall in Palestine falls in December-February, but it is the rain at the beginning and end of the growing season that is critical. See D. Baly, *The Geography of the Bible* (New York: Harper & Row, 1974), 50-51.

season, both autumn and spring rains, so that you may gather in your grain, new wine and oil." This is almost certainly the background for James's imagery in this verse, justifying two interpretive moves in the NIV rendering. First, the word "rains" does not occur in the best Greek manuscripts of this verse, but its addition in translation is appropriate. Second, the Greek words that James uses here mean simply "early" *(proimos)* and "later" *(opsimos)* (see NASB; NRSV), but the association of the terms with seasons of the year in the Septuagint justifies the NIV translation. A more interesting association may also be noted. Every reference to "early and later rains" in the OT occurs in a context affirming the faithfulness of the Lord (Deut. 11:14; Jer. 5:24; Hos. 6:3; Joel 2:23; Zech. 10:1). James's readers, being biblically literate, would have detected in the language of this verse an "echo" of this broader biblical theme and been thereby given a further reinforcement of the confidence they could place in the coming of the Lord to judge their enemies and deliver them.

8 James reiterates his call for patience, in imitation of the farmer *(too),* and adds to it an exhortation to *stand firm.* This NIV rendering is a bit paraphrastic, a literal translation of the Greek being "strengthen your hearts" (cf. NASB; NRSV). The very same language occurs in an eschatological context in 1 Thess. 3:13, where, however, the "strengthening of the heart" is accomplished by God himself: "May he strengthen your hearts so that you will be blameless and holy in the presence of our God and Father when our Lord Jesus comes with his holy ones." And similar uses of this verb in the sense of "be spiritually firm" occur in Luke 22:32; Rom. 1:11; 16:25; 1 Thess. 3:2; 2 Thess. 2:17; 3:3; 1 Pet. 5:10; 2 Pet. 1:12; Rev. 3:2. What is commanded, then, is firm adherence to the faith in the midst of temptations and trials. As they wait patiently for their Lord to return, believers need to fortify themselves for the struggle against sin and with difficult circumstances.

In v. 7, James urged believers to *be patient* in view of the *fact* of the Lord's coming. Now he bases his exhortation to patience and spiritual firmness on the *nearness* of the Lord's coming. The verb James uses, *engizō* ("is near"), occurs elsewhere in the NT in similar eschatological contexts. Jesus proclaimed at the beginning of his ministry that "the kingdom of God is near" (Mark 1:15; cf. also Matt. 3:2; 4:17; 10:7; Luke 10:9, 11); and Paul (Rom. 13:12) and Peter (1 Pet. 4:7), like James, reiterate the "nearness" of the end events. This theme, which, of course, is enunciated in many other places in the NT with different words and images, is one of the most controversial in the NT. Many scholars are convinced that Jesus himself predicted that he would return within the lifetime of the disciples, and that the earliest Christians shared this expectation of an immediate *parousia.* Gradually, however, as time went by and the *parousia* did not occur, Christians began to "postpone" the *parousia* to an indefinite time in the future. James, of course, would seem to share the earlier perspective. But this scenario raises an insistent issue for those, like me, who credit the NT with complete truthfulness: Jesus, Paul, Peter, James, and others were wrong about the timing of the *parousia*.

We cannot deal with the many texts and issues that would need to be examined to respond adequately to the so-called "delay of the *parousia*" hypothesis. But we need to say something about the "nearness" idea as we find it here in James. Not much help is gained from a consideration of the verb *engizō* itself — it denotes simply "nearness" in space (e.g., Acts 9:3) or time (usually in the NT). But what is crucial is to understand this "nearness" in the appropriate temporal framework: salvation history. With the death and resurrection of Jesus and pouring out of the Spirit, the "last days" have been inaugurated. This final age of salvation will find its climax in the return of Christ in glory. But — and here is the crucial point — the length of this age is unknown. Not even Jesus knew how long the "last days" would last (cf. Mark 13:32). What this means is that the return of Christ, as the next event in the salvation-historical timetable, is, from the time of the early church to our own day, "near," or "imminent." Every generation of Christians lives (or should live!) with the consciousness that the *parousia* could occur at any time and that one needs to make decisions and choose values based on that realization. So it was as true in James's day as it is in ours: we need to *be patient and stand firm, because the Lord's coming is near.*

9 At first glance, this verse does not have much in common with its context, beyond sharing an emphasis on the imminence of judgment. Typically, therefore, Dibelius views the verse as an isolated saying.[17] However, more careful consideration helps us understand why the verse in fact fits very well in its present context. In a general way, of course, James's prohibition of "grumbling" against one another fits with one of the most persistent motifs of the letter: the problem of sinful speech (cf. 1:27; 3:1-12; and esp. 4:11-12). But grumbling against those who are close to us is particularly likely to occur when we are under pressure or facing difficult circumstances. We vent the pressure from a stressful work environment or from ill health on our close friends and family. So it would be quite natural if James's readers, under the pressure of poverty and persecution (cf. 5:1-6), would turn their frustrations on one another. Moreover, the exhortation to be patient with the circumstances of suffering that the readers face could easily evoke the need for patience with fellow community members as well. Paul links patience with the need to "bear with one

17. Dibelius, 244.

another in love" (Eph. 4:2) and with a refusal to "pay back wrong for wrong" in 1 Thess. 5:14-15.

The word *grumble* translates a Greek word *(stenazō)* that elsewhere in the Bible occurs absolutely, usually with the meaning "groan," or "sigh" (26 occurrences in the LXX and five other NT occurrences [Mark 7:34; Rom. 8:23; 2 Cor. 5:2, 4; Heb. 13:17]; the same is true of the compound *katastenazō*). And the word typically connotes an expression of frustration from the people of God who are suffering oppression or even judgment. See, for example, Exod. 2:23: "During that long period, the king of Egypt died. The Israelites groaned in their slavery and cried out, and their cry for help because of their slavery went up to God." James clearly uses the verb to describe groaning or complaining against *(kata)* fellow community members. But the broader biblical use of the word again adds a nuance to the word, implying that the groans are the result of oppression.

As he did in 4:11-12, James connects the need to refrain from critical speech with judgment. In the former passage, however, he likened critical speech to judgment; here he warns that criticism of one another places a person in danger of judgment. This warning is similar to, and may be influenced by, Jesus' well-known prohibition: "Do not judge, or you too will be judged" (Matt. 7:1). To reinforce his warning, James reminds his readers again that this judgment is imminent: *the Judge is standing at the door!* Since James claims in 4:12 that "there is only one Lawgiver and Judge," he may refer here to God the Father.[18] But the parallelism between this statement and the references to the *parousia* in vv. 7-8 makes it more plausible to identify Christ as the judge.[19] Moreover, James again here probably alludes to the teaching of Jesus, who warned that "when you see all these things [e.g., the "signs"], you know that it [the *parousia*] is near, right at the door" (Matt. 24:32; par. Mark 13:29; and for the imagery of "standing at the doors," see also Rev. 3:20). We should note the striking shift in application of *parousia* language in these verses. James begins by alluding to the *parousia* as a time of judgment on the wicked in order to comfort and encourage struggling believers; but he then reminds those same believers that the *parousia* will also include a serious assessment of their own spiritual state and behavior. As Davids puts it, "The nearness of the eschatological day is not just an impetus to look forward to the judgement of 'sinners' . . . , but it is also a warning to examine one's behavior so that when the one whose footsteps are nearing finally knocks

18. Laws, 213.

19. So most commentators; see, e.g., Martin, 192; Johnson, 317; and note also Baker, 181.

on the door, one may be prepared to open. . . . The coming Lord is also the judge of the Christian."[20]

10 In vv. 10-11, James returns to the topic of vv. 7-8, as he reinforces and illustrates his exhortation to patience under duress. Reference to the fortitude of martyrs as a model for others to imitate became very popular in the wake of the Maccabean Revolt in the early to middle second century B.C. The refusal of pious Jews to renounce their faith at the insistence of the pagan king Antiochus IV of the Seleucid Empire was celebrated in books such as 2 Maccabees. James, like the author of Hebrews (see chap. 11, esp. vv. 35-37) at a slightly later date, adopts this martyrological tradition to encourage strength under trial in his own day. We find in James, however, only a snippet of this kind of tradition, as he briefly refers to the prophets (v. 10) and Job (v. 11).

James urges his readers to *take the prophets who spoke in the name of the Lord* as an *example of patience in the face of suffering.* The Greek word translated "example" *(hypodeigma)* reflects the Maccabean tradition we have mentioned above, being used three times in the literature to refer to the heroic example of the Jewish martyrs (2 Macc. 6:28, 31; 4 Macc. 17:23). It often refers to something or someone that spurs others to imitation (in the NT, see, in a positive sense, John 13:15; and, in a negative sense, Heb. 4:11; 2 Pet. 2:6; cf. also Heb. 8:5; 9:23). The NIV's *patience in the face of suffering* translates a difficult Greek phrase. In the Greek, the word order is reversed and the two terms are coordinated: literally, "suffering and patience" (NASB; NRSV). The phrase itself may again point to James's dependence on the Maccabean martyrologies, since a very similar phrase appears in 4 Macc. 9:8: "For we, through this severe suffering and endurance [*tēs kakopatheias kai hypomonēs*], shall have the prize of virtue and shall be with God. . . ." Most contemporary English versions follow the NIV in taking the two words as mutually interpreting (hendiadys is the grammatical term): "suffering that is qualified by patience"; for example, "patience under ill-treatment" (REB).[21] But the grammar, while allowing this rendering, does not favor it.[22] Another option, then, is to keep the two terms separate. "Example of suffering" would then refer to the prophets' willingness to undergo persecution for the sake of the call of God. It is also conceivable that the word translated "suffering" *(kakopatheia)* might have the extended meaning "endurance of suffering," as

20. Davids, 185.

21. See, e.g., BDF 442(16); Mitton, 188; Martin, 193.

22. The repetition of the article before *makrothymia* does not prevent us from taking the word closely with *kakopatheias* in a hendiadys; but we might have expected a single article governing both (as in 4 Macc. 4:8, quoted above), if this had been James's intention.

its cognate verb does in 2 Tim. 4:5 (cf. 2 Tim. 2:9).[23] But James uses this cognate verb himself in v. 13 with the simple meaning "suffer." We tentatively opt, then, for the rendering "example of suffering and patience."

James, of course, does not tell us what specific prophets he has in mind. But we naturally think of Jeremiah, who suffered so much at the hands of both pagan kings and, especially, his own people, in faithfulness to the message that God had given him to deliver. Intertestamental tradition, reflected in Heb. 11:37, asserted that the prophet Isaiah died a martyr by being sawed in two. In any case, James wants us to know that the prophets suffered in the cause of their God; they *spoke in the name of the Lord.* Doing God's will, James is suggesting, will often lead to suffering. What is needed is a willingness to bear up under the suffering, maintaining spiritual integrity and waiting patiently for the Lord himself to intervene to transform the situation. It may also be that James cites the prophets because they were people who not only suffered injustice but spoke out against it as well. Christians need to learn to suffer patiently as they await the Lord's vindication. But this is not to say that they cannot speak out against evil.[24]

11 At the opening of his book, after introducing Eleazar, his seven brothers, and their mother as his model martyrs, the author of 4 Maccabees says, "It is fitting for me to praise for their virtues those who, with their mother, died for the sake of nobility and goodness, but I would call them blessed for the honor in which they are held" (1:10). So James shows his dependence on this tradition once more in his opening words in this verse: *As you know, we consider blessed those who have persevered.* But another source, of far more general importance to James, also influences this saying, as well as James's reference to the prophets as models of suffering. For Jesus said, "Blessed are you when people insult you, persecute you and falsely say all kinds of evil against you because of me. Rejoice and be glad, because great is your reward in heaven, for in the same way they persecuted the prophets who were before you" (Matt. 5:11-12). Despite the tendency observed in some modern translations (e.g., REB; TEV), to be "blessed" is not the same as to be "happy." The latter speaks to the state of our emotions; the former to the objective state of our relationship with God. Only here and in Luke 1:48 does the verbal form "call blessed" (Gk. *makarizō*) occur in the NT; but the adjective "blessed" *(makarios)* and the noun "blessing" *(makarismos)* are, of course, very common. James's pronouncement of blessing here on those who persevere sounds very similar to what he said toward the beginning of the letter: "Blessed is the man who perseveres under trial, because

23. See W. Michaelis, *TDNT* 5:937; Mussner, 205.
24. See Blomberg, 158-59.

when he has stood the test, he will receive the crown of life that God has promised to those who love him" (1:12). Some commentators suggest that these verses have a formal literary relationship, the *inclusio* they form marking the letter opening and letter closing. But, as we noted in the introduction to this section, this specific literary relationship is unlikely. Nevertheless, the two verses do reveal the degree to which James pursues certain key motifs throughout his letter, giving it a general coherence that is sometimes missed.

James's shift from the vocabulary of "patience" *(makrothymeō* and *makrothymia)* in vv. 7-10 to "endurance" *(hypomonē)* in v. 11 may simply reflect the influence of 1:12 on James's language. But it is of course tempting to see more significance in the shift. Some think that James has used "patience" to speak mainly of the believer's response to other people, while he uses "endurance" to refer to the need to "bear up under" the trial.[25] But, as we suggested earlier, while this particular distinction has some lexical basis, we are not persuaded that this distinction, or any other proposed, really makes sense of the sequence of these verses. It is especially difficult to see any difference between the "patience" of the prophets as they underwent suffering (v. 10) and the "perseverance" of Job (v. 11). The "blessing" here in v. 11, then, brings to a pinnacle the paragraph as a whole, providing the ultimate encouragement for the attitude of "patient fortitude" that James is exhorting his readers to adopt in the face of their suffering.[26]

James adds one more example of "perseverance" under trial before he leaves the topic. And the example is a very curious one: Job. Few of us would single out Job as a model of faithful endurance in the midst of suffering. The canonical book rather pictures Job as a bit self-righteous, overly insistent on getting an explanation for his unjust sufferings from the Lord. The LXX does a little to change this picture, using the verb "persevere" *(hypomenō)* three times with reference to Job. But the Maccabean tradition we have seen James following makes no reference to Job; nor is he set forth as an example of endurance under suffering elsewhere in the NT or Jewish and rabbinical literature. However, we do find one exception to this omission: *The Testament of Job.* In this book, which presents Job as pronouncing a blessing on his children, Job proclaims that he is "fully engaged in endurance" (1:5) and encourages his children to be "patient";

25. See, e.g., Johnson, 319; and see esp. his fine analysis on p. 313.

26. Martin (193), following Adamson (192), curiously insists that the aorist form of *hyomeinantas* ("those who endure") shows that James is thinking only of those in the past who stood firm. In the context, of course, the main reference is past (cf. v. 10), but suggesting that the aorist tense demonstrates this betrays an unjustified insistence on temporal significance for tense in the participle.

for "patience is better than anything" (27:6-7; cf. 26:5).[27] The date of this book is not certain, and it may have undergone editing by Christian scribes.[28] But it probably comes from about the same time period as James and may at the least attest a Jewish tradition about Job's perseverance that James may also be picking up on. But we must also point out that James's singling out of Job's perseverance is not an unwarranted inference from the canonical book itself. For although Job did complain bitterly about God's treatment of him, he never abandoned his faith. In the midst of his incomprehension, he clung to God and continued to hope in him (see 1:21; 2:10; 16:19-21; 19:25-27). As Barclay says, "Job's is no groveling, passive, unquestioning submission; Job struggled and questioned, and sometimes even defied, but the flame of faith was never extinguished in his heart."[29]

If the readers have *heard of Job's perseverance,* they have also *seen what the Lord finally brought about.* A literal rendering of these words would be "you have seen the *telos* of the Lord." The word *telos* can mean either "purpose" or "end," and each of these meanings can be related to the word "Lord" (*kyriou,* a genitive) in a couple of different ways. The main possibilities are:

1. With the meaning "end":
   a. The "end" of the Lord's life (his death and resurrection)[30]
   b. The "end" of the Lord's ministry (the *parousia*)[31]
   c. The "end" that the Lord brought about in Job's situation, that is, the restoration of his fortune at the end of the book (NIV; REB; NLT; see TEV: "you see how the Lord provided for Job in the end").[32]
2. With the meaning "purpose": the "purpose" of refining Job that the Lord had in allowing his trials to come upon him (see NJB: you have seen "the Lord's purpose"; cf. also NASB; NRSV).[33]

27. See C. Hass, "Job's Perseverance in the Testament of Job," in *Studies on the Testament of Job,* ed. M. A. Knibb and P. W. van der Horst (SNTSMS 66; Cambridge: Cambridge University Press, 1989), 117-18.

28. See the discussion by R. Spittler in *The Old Testament Pseudepigrapha,* 1:829-37.

29. W. Barclay, *Letters of James and Peter* (2d ed.; Daily Bible Study; Glasgow: Saint Andrew Press, 1960), 147-48.

30. Augustine (*PL* 40:634).

31. A. Strobel, *Untersuchungen zum eschatologischen Verzögerungsproblem* (NovTSup 2; Leiden: Brill, 1961), 259; R. P. Gordon, "καὶ τὸ τέλος κυρίου εἴδετε (Jas. 5.11)," *JTS* 26 (1975) 91-95.

32. Adamson, 193; Laws, 216.

33. Mayor, 164; Ropes, 299; Martin, 195. See also Klein, who connects this phrase with "the crown of life" in 1:12 (79-80).

The first two interpretations have found little support and, indeed, have little lexically or contextually in their favor. But the other two (1c and 2) have almost equally good support. The word *telos* is one of the most discussed in the NT because of its use in the much debated Rom. 10:4: "Christ is the *telos* of the law." And, while the balance of uses is debated, it is agreed that the meanings "end" (in the sense of termination) and "goal" (as well as other nuanced combinations) are supported in the NT. (For the former, see, e.g., Matt. 10:22; Mark 3:26; 1 Cor. 1:8; Heb. 3:14; for the latter, e.g., 1 Tim. 1:5; 1 Pet. 1:9). And both interpretations also fit the contexts of Job and of James. In Job 42:5-6, Job confesses that he has finally learned his lesson about the majesty and sovereign goodness of God; and a reference to the "purpose" that God has in suffering would certainly be an important source of comfort for James's readers. On the other hand, the restorative "end" of Job's story is of course prominent in the canonical book and would be of equal comfort to James's readers. Your present suffering, James would be saying, is not the "end" of the story; God will transform your situation for good when Christ is revealed in glory. This latter interpretation should probably be adopted. The closest parallels to James's wording in intertestamental Jewish literature (*T. Gad* 7:4; *T. Benjamin* 4:1) and in the NT (Heb. 13:7) support this rendering, and it fits well with the overall message of the book of Job, one of whose purposes is to show how Job's integrity is rewarded in the end. And it also provides a natural lead-in to the final clause of the verse: the good end that God brought about in Job's situation shows that *The Lord is full of compassion and mercy.* Of course, James does not mean that patience in suffering will always be rewarded by material prosperity; too many examples in both the OT and the NT prove this to be wrong. But James does seek to encourage our faithful, patient endurance of affliction by reminding us of the blessing that we receive for such faithfulness from our merciful and compassionate God.

VIII. CONCLUDING EXHORTATIONS (5:12-20)

The debate about the flow of James's argument, intense at the beginning of the letter, surfaces here again. There are three interrelated problems. First, how does the prohibition of vows in v. 12 fit into the context? Does it go with the verses before it or the verses after it? Or is it simply an isolated saying? Second, what are the meaning and function of vv. 13-18? Is James encouraging prayer for spiritual restoration or physical healing? And is he dealing with a specific problem or is he giving general encouragement to pray? Third, where should we locate the beginning of the closing section of James's epistle? He does not conclude with the greetings, travel plans, and benedictions typical of many (especially Pauline) NT letters. The encouragement to minister to one another in vv. 19-20 certainly makes sense as a concluding exhortation. But what other material should we include with vv. 19-20 as the epistolary conclusion? Everything from v. 7 on? from v. 12 on? or from v. 13 on?

We will try to answer these questions in the exegesis that follows. Here we will content ourselves with an overview that anticipates some of these answers. The phrase *above all* in v. 12 marks the beginning of the epistolary conclusion. James wraps up his letter by touching on three issues that he considers critical for the community. And each of them involves speech.[34] First, in the last reprise of a key motif of the letter, James prohibits the wrong kind of speech — in this case, the taking of frivolous vows (v. 12). Second, James encourages mutual prayer for both physical and spiritual needs (vv. 13-18). And, finally, he exhorts his readers to take the teaching of the letter and apply it to those of their number who might be sinning in any of the matters that he has touched on (vv. 19-20).

A. Avoid Oaths (5:12)

> 12 *Above all, my brothers, do not swear — not by heaven or by earth or by anything else. Let your "Yes" be yes, and your "No," no, or you will be condemned.*

The NIV, like some other English translations (e.g., NRSV; NLT), includes v. 12 with the verses that come before it rather than those after it. And this reflects the view of a number of commentators, who think the prohibition of vows in v. 12 has its specific occasion in the distress that the community is experiencing (vv. 7-11). The *above all* might then suggest that the taking of vows is a similar, but more serious, sin of speech than grumbling against one another (v. 9).[35] Or it might indicate James's belief that the taking of vows is one of the worst manifestations of impatience.[36] But the connection between taking vows and persecution is not very obvious. Others, therefore, suggest a more general relationship to the letter as a whole. But can James really mean that the prohibition of oaths is the more important thing he wants to say in the letter?[37] More important

34. See esp. Johnson, 326, for this emphasis.
35. Tasker, 123-24; Adamson, 194-95.
36. Mayor, 165; Reicke, 56.
37. This is the suggestion of W. R. Baker, "'Above All Else': Contexts of the Call for Verbal Integrity in James 5.12," *JSNT* 54 (1994) 57-71.

than doing the word, than obeying the love command, than submitting to God's grace in Christ? Surely not. In fact, the difficulty of making sense of *above all* as an indicator of relative importance is one of the most important reasons to consider the possibility that the phrase has a purely, or at least primarily, literary function. Similar phrases occur in the epistolary conclusions of other Hellenistic letters.[38] And the phrase may function similarly to the common [*to*] *loipon* ("as to the rest," "finally") that Paul uses in his letter endings (see 2 Cor. 13:11; Phil. 3:1; 4:8; 1 Thess. 4:1; 2 Thess. 3:1; 1 Tim. 4:8). To be sure, the phrase that James uses here *(pro pantōn)* does not occur elsewhere in the NT to introduce a letter conclusion; unless, indeed, the closest parallel, 1 Pet. 4:8, is an epistolary conclusion.[39] For this reason, while taking the phrase as a literary marker that signals the beginning of the conclusion of the letter, we can probably not remove all contextual significance from the phrase.[40] James wants to highlight this prohibition — probably because he sees it as getting at the ultimate issue of personal integrity.

When James says *Do not swear,* it is not coarse or vulgar speech he prohibits but invoking God's name to guarantee the reliability of what a person says.[41] A person may take an oath to reinforce the truth of something he has said or to bind himself to a future course of conduct. The verb James uses here *(omnyō)* has this sense throughout the LXX and the NT (see, e.g., Mark 6:23; Acts 2:30; Rev. 10:6). Oaths, as we may also call them, are by no means consistently forbidden in Scripture. God himself takes oaths to guarantee the fulfillment of what he has promised (see, e.g., Heb. 3:11, 18; 4:3; 6:13, 16; 7:21). The OT law did not prohibit oaths but demanded that a person be true to the oath he had taken. Lev. 19:12 is both typical and potentially significant for James: "Do not swear falsely by my name and so profane the name of your God. I am the LORD." Its significance lies in its context: as we have seen, James makes the "love command" of Lev. 19:18 the heart of his "kingdom" law (2:8), and several other ethical issues that he tackles are also referred to Leviticus 19.[42] But concern about the devaluation of oaths through their indiscriminate use

38. See the examples in Mussner, 211.

39. Some scholars think that 4:7-11 marks the ending of an original letter to which another has been added in the course of transmission. At the least, however, the paragraph marks the conclusion to the body of the letter (see P. Achtemeier, *1 Peter* [Hermeneia; Minneapolis: Augsburg Fortress, 1996], 292-93).

40. See esp. the measured conclusion of Johnson, 327.

41. The Greek verb is in the present tense — *omnyete* — which, some grammarians argue, when used with *mē,* has the connotation of stopping an action one is already engaged in. But the evidence for this function of the tense is not very solid; and the simple translation "do not swear" is the most that the context justifies.

42. See, again, Johnson, "Leviticus 19," 397-98.

and a growing tendency to "weasel out" of oaths by swearing by less sacred things (cf. Matt. 23:16-22) led to warnings against using them too often (see Sir. 23:9, 11; Philo, *Decalogue* 84-95). Jesus, as it appears, went even further than this when he commanded his disciples not to swear "at all" (Matt. 5:34). Jesus' teaching in Matt. 5:34-37 is particularly important in understanding James' teaching, because it looks as if James is consciously reproducing that tradition. The similarity between the two passages is striking when they are set side by side:

Matthew 5:34-37	**James 5:12**
"Do not swear at all,	"Do not swear —
either by heaven . . .	not by heaven
or by the earth . . .	or by earth
or by Jerusalem . . .	or by anything else.
Do not swear by your head . . .	
Simply let your 'Yes' be 'Yes'	Let your 'Yes' be yes
and your 'No,' 'No';	and your 'No,' no,
anything beyond this	or you will be condemned."
comes from the evil one."	

Some argue that Matthew and James diverge on one crucial point: Matthew suggests a "substitute oath" — "yes, yes" and "no, no" — while James simply prohibits all oaths. But it is more likely that Jesus in Matthew is saying the same thing as James: our truthfulness should be so consistent and dependable that we need no oath to support it: a simple "yes" or "no" should suffice. "Our mere word should be as utterly trustworthy as a signed document, legally correct and complete."[43]

But does James (and Jesus before him) intend to prohibit *all* oaths? Many Christians in the Anabaptist tradition have concluded that this is the case and have refused by consequence to take oaths in the courtroom or anywhere else. However, it is doubtful that James intends to address the question of official oaths — oaths that others ask us to take for legal purposes. As the exhortation to let our "yes" and "no" suffice for themselves suggests, the issue seems to have been the voluntary oath — the oath taken to insure the truthfulness of what one had affirmed or promised. Christians committed to integrity in speech and personal relationships should never require an oath. But even this limitation does not go far enough, many argue. They suggest that James intends to prohibit only oaths that have the purpose of avoiding absolute truthfulness (this seems to be the issue, e.g., in Matt. 23:16-22). Indirect support for this further

43. Mitton, 193.

limitation comes from Paul's letters, where he frequently appears to take an oath to reinforce the truth of what he says (e.g., Rom. 1:9; 2 Cor. 1:23; 11:11; Gal. 1:20; Phil. 1:8; 1 Thess. 2:5, 10). Nevertheless, caution is required. While various suggestions have been made, we do not know the community situation that led James to issue this prohibition. We therefore have no evidence of the kind of polemical situation that informs Jesus' teaching. And Paul's "witness" formulas may not fit into the category of "oath."

B. Prayer and Healing (5:13-18)

13 *Is any one of you in trouble? He should pray. Is anyone happy? Let*
him sing songs of praise. 14 *Is any one of you sick? He should call the elders*
of the church to pray over him and anoint him with oil in the name of the
Lord. 15 *And the prayer offered in faith will make the sick person well; the*
Lord will raise him up. If he has sinned, he will be forgiven. 16 *Therefore*
confess your sins to each other and pray for each other so that you may be
healed. The prayer of a righteous man is powerful and effective. 17 *Elijah*
was a man just like us. He prayed earnestly that it would not rain, and it
did not rain on the land for three and a half years. 18 *Again he prayed, and*
the heavens gave rain, and the earth produced its crops.

An encouragement to pray is typical of the concluding sections of NT letters. Also typical of Hellenistic letters in general is a concluding "health" wish. James combines the two by encouraging prayer especially for physical ailments. Prayer is clearly the topic of this paragraph, being mentioned in every verse. James commends it to the individual believer, in the very different kinds of circumstances that he may face (vv. 13-14), and to the community as well (v. 16a). And he encourages such prayer by underscoring the powerful effects of prayer that flow from a righteous heart (vv. 16b-18). Some relationship to v. 12 may be perceived through the common theme of speaking with reference to God (bad speech, v. 12; and good, vv. 13-18), although the connection is muted at best. A more important context for the admonition to pray is the trials that the community is experiencing. The opening question of the paragraph, *Is any one of you in trouble?*, is lexically tied to the reference to the prophets' "suffering" in v. 10. James thus brings us full circle at the end of his letter, back to the "trials of many kinds" that he introduced as a basic community problem in 1:2.

13 James's exhortation to pray in vv. 13-18 stands out among similar such requests at the end of NT letters (Rom. 15:30-32; Eph. 6:18-20; Phil. 4:6; Col. 4:2-4; 1 Thess. 5:17, 25; 2 Thess. 3:1-2; Heb. 13:18-19) for its detail and length. The heading for the section, in v. 13, is similar to Paul's exhortations "pray in the Spirit on all occasions with all kinds of prayers and requests" (Eph. 6:18), and "pray continually; give thanks in all circumstances" (1 Thess. 5:17-18a). James, however, breaks down "all circumstances" into two contrasting situations. The former picks up the motif of trials with which the letter began (1:2) and which has been an undercurrent throughout 5:1-11: *Is any one of you in trouble?* The NIV *in trouble* translates the verbal form of the word James used in v. 10 to describe the "suffering" of the prophets. The word has the basic sense of "experience difficulty" and is used in the LXX with the meaning "take trouble," "work hard at" (Jon. 1:10; cf. also the noun form in 2 Macc. 2:26, 27; Mal. 1:13). But the sense "experience trouble" is found in the other NT occurrences of the verb (2 Tim. 2:9; 4:5). These other uses imply that the trouble being experienced is for the sake of the gospel, but it is not clear whether we should give the verb here in James so specific a sense.[44] The use of the noun form of this word in v. 10 would certainly point in this direction. But other elements in the context point to a broader meaning. The suffering that the righteous are experiencing at the hands of the wicked rich (5:6) involves economic oppression; and Job's suffering, of course, included economic disasters, illness, and the death of family members. Moreover, the "weakness" caused by physical illness that James goes on to talk about in vv. 14-15 is probably one specific example of the "trouble" the community is experiencing. Taken together, then, the data suggest that the word has a broad application, covering trials of all kinds.

How are those suffering in these various ways to respond? They are to *pray.* The Greek word here is *proseuchomai,* the most common word for prayer in the NT (over 80 occurrences). James uses the verb only in this paragraph (see also vv. 14, 17, and 18; the cognate noun, *proseuchē,* occurs only in v. 17 in James). Because the verb is so general in its meaning and application, no certainty about the content of the prayer that James calls for here can be attained. Perhaps James would include petition to God to remove the trial. But James's concern when he deals with trials elsewhere (1:2-4, 12; 5:7-11) is to encourage believers to endure the suffering with the right spirit and with a divine perspective on history. Presumably, then, the prayer that he encourages here is for the spiritual strength to endure the trial with a godly spirit.

The other situation that James mentions in the verse is not an exact opposite to being *in trouble.* For, as the NIV rendering *happy* suggests, the Greek word that James uses in his second question *(euthymeō)* connotes a state of the emotions rather than an outward circumstance. The verb oc-

44. As many commentators (e.g., Martin, 205) think.

curs elsewhere in the NT only in Acts 27:22 and 25, where it denotes the "peace of mind" that Paul encourages his fellow passengers to have despite the raging storm that was tearing apart their ship (the cognate noun has a similar sense in Acts 27:36 and 2 Macc. 11:26 [the verb does not occur in the LXX]). A reminder to turn to God is needed even more in times of cheer than in times of suffering. James specifically exhorts the community to *sing songs of praise.* The Greek verb here is *psallō,* from which we get the word "psalm." While the verb means simply "sing," all three of its other NT occurrences connote a song of praise to God (Rom. 15:9; 1 Cor. 14:15; Eph. 5:19; see the cognate noun in 1 Cor. 14:26; Eph. 5:19; Col. 3:16). So, especially coming from one who is doing well, the song here is almost certainly a song of praise to the Lord; see NLT, "continually sing praises to the Lord." The "continually" in the NLT rendering reflects the present tense of the verb *psalletō,* which often adds the nuance of a continual or repeated action. Giving praise to God, like our petitions for sustenance in times of trouble (*proseuchesthō,* "pray," is also present tense), should be a regular part of our lifestyle.

14 James now mentions a third circumstance in which prayer is especially needed: sickness. The Greek word behind the NIV's *is sick* is *astheneō,* "to be weak." This word and its cognate noun *(astheneia)* and adjective *(asthenēs)* are applied to all kinds of situations in the NT: mental ability (e.g., Rom. 6:19); spiritual condition (Rom. 5:6); general physical appearance (e.g., 2 Cor. 10:10); the conscience (e.g., 1 Cor. 8:7, 9; cf. Rom. 14:1, 2); or one's bodily constitution. In this last sense, the word means simply to be "sick" or "ill," and this is the sense almost universally given the word in this verse. But a few scholars have proposed an alternative meaning, "to be spiritually weak." The word can have this sense, and so can the word translated "sick" in the NIV of v. 15 (*kamnō;* see the notes there). Moreover, the language of v. 16 — "that you may be healed" — usually has a spiritual connotation in the NT. And other key words in the context, it is argued, point in the same direction: "save" (*sǭzō;* translated "make well" in the NIV) and "raise up" in v. 15. What James is describing, these scholars contend, is a person who is spiritually weak. The spiritual leaders of the church need to pray for this person so that his or her fervor for the Lord might be restored. An exhortation to pray for such a situation would fit very well at the end of a letter that has regularly chastised its readers for just such spiritual lassitude.[45]

45. See, for this general approach, M. Meinertz, "Die Krankensalbung Jak. 5.14f," *BZ* 20 (1932) 23-36; C. Armerding, "'Is Any among You Afflicted': A Study of James 5:13-20," *BibSac* 95 (1938) 195-201; C. Pickar, "Is Anyone Sick among You?" *CBQ* 7 (1945) 165-74; D. R. Hayden, "Calling the Elders to Pray," *BibSac* 138 (1981) 258-86.

But the usual view, adopted in virtually all modern English Bibles, that James is speaking here of physical illness, is overwhelmingly likely. When *astheneō* refers to spiritual weakness, this meaning is made clear by a qualifier ("in conscience" in 1 Cor. 8:7; "in faith" in Rom. 14:1, 2) or by the context. More importantly, in the NT material that has exercised the greatest influence on James's vocabulary and theology (the Gospels), *astheneō* always denotes physical illness (Matt. 10:8; 25:36, 39; Mark 6:56; Luke 4:40; John 4:46; 5:3, 7; 6:2; 11:1, 2, 3, 6). The same is true of the cluster of terms and concepts that we find here. The verb "save" is frequently used in the Gospels to denote the restoration of those who are ill (see the notes on v. 15); as is, as we might expect, the verb "heal" (v. 16). But perhaps the most striking parallel comes with the reference to "anointing with oil." Only once else in the NT is the practice mentioned, and then as a means of physical healing (Mark 6:13).

Unlike the first two general situations James mentioned in v. 13, the believer (note *one of you*) who is ill is not commanded to pray himself but to *call the elders of the church to pray over him.* Elders are mentioned in the book of Acts in connection with the church in Jerusalem (11:30; 15:2; 21:18) and the churches founded through Paul (14:23; 20:17). Although in his letters Paul refers to elders by name only in 1 Timothy (5:17) and Titus (1:5), "overseer" *(episkopos),* mentioned in the plural in Phil. 1:1 and in the singular (*episkopēs,* "office of elder") in 1 Tim. 3:1, is probably a different title for the same office. Both Peter (1 Pet. 5:1) and James assume the ministry of elders in the church, showing that the office was well established in the early church. The prominent role of the elders in Acts and the description of the office in the Pastoral Epistles suggest that elders were spiritually mature men who guided the spiritual development of local congregations. Since the Ephesian elders were to "shepherd," or "pastor," their flocks (Acts 20:28), and "pastors" are never mentioned along with elders in the NT, it is probable that the function of what we know as the pastor or minister was carried out by the elders. Hence, it is natural that the believer who is suffering from illness should summon the elders.

James's attribution of healing power to the prayer of local church ministers stands out in light of Paul's references to a "gift" of healing (1 Cor. 12:9, 28). Were there no "charismatics" who possessed this gift in James's churches? Is the power to heal confined by James to certain ecclesiastical officeholders? These questions are difficult to answer and involve us in the larger question of the relationship between "charismatic" and "organized" ministries in the NT. Briefly, however, it would seem that the early churches differed in the extent to which certain gifts were manifest. Indeed, the Corinthian church seems to be something of an exception in the NT, since only here do we read of such gifts as "healings" and "miracles" (contrast Rom. 12:6-8 and Eph. 4:11). Church organization does not depreciate or ignore gifts, but serves as a mechanism to recognize gifted individuals and channel their ministries for the edification of the body. Elders were those spiritual leaders who were recognized for their maturity in the faith. Therefore, it is natural that they, with their deep and rich experience, should be called on to pray for healing. They should be able to discern the will of the Lord and to pray with the faith that recognizes and receives God's gift of healing. At the same time, James makes clear that the church at large is to pray for healing (v. 16a). Therefore, while not denying that some in the church may have the gift of healing, James encourages all Christians, and especially those charged with pastoral oversight, to be active in prayer for healing.

Since the elders are summoned to the sick person, we may assume that the sickness is serious enough to restrict the mobility of the sufferer. The same conclusion might be suggested by James's use of the preposition *over* after the verb *pray*. Only here in biblical Greek does this combination occur, and it might picture the elders standing over the sick person. However, it might also be shorthand for laying hands on the person during the praying (see Matt. 19:13).

In addition to praying for the sick person, James also commands the elders to *anoint him with oil in the name of the Lord.* James might imply that the anointing is to precede the praying (since the participle *aleipsantes* is aorist),[46] but he probably intends them to be taking place at the same time (a contemporaneous aorist).[47] But more important than the timing of the act is its meaning: What does James think that the anointing will accomplish? The practice is mentioned only one other time in the NT: Mark says that the Twelve "drove out many demons and anointed many sick people with oil and healed them" (6:13). Unfortunately, Mark gives no more of an explanation for the anointing than does James. Theologians and scholars have debated the meaning of the practice for a long time. Interpretations can be divided into two main categories, with subdivisions in each.

1. A Practical Purpose

   a. Medicinal

   Oil was widely used in the ancient world both as a skin conditioner and as a medicine. A NT example is Luke 10:34, which describes the good Samaritan as coming to the aid of the man who had been beaten and robbed: "He went to him and bandaged his wounds,

46. See Schlatter, 281.
47. So most commentators.

pouring on oil and wine." Ancient sources testify to the usefulness of oil in curing everything from toothache to paralysis (the famous second-century physician Galen recommended oil as "the best of all remedies for paralysis" [*De simplicitate medicamentum temperatum* 2]). Considering this background, we might suppose that James is urging the elders to come to the bedside of the sick armed with both spiritual and natural resources — with prayer and with medicine.[48] Both are administered with the Lord's authority, and both together can be used by him in healing the sick.

b. Pastoral

As a different kind of practical purpose, others suggest that the anointing may have been intended as an outward, physical expression of concern and as a means to stimulate the faith of the sick person.[49] Jesus sometimes used physical props in his healings, apparently with just such a purpose.

2. A Religious Purpose

a. Sacramental

A sacramental understanding of this practice arose early in the history of the church. On the basis of this text the early Greek church practiced what they called the *Euchelaion* (a combination of the words *euchē*, "prayer," and *elaion*, "oil," both used in this text), which had the purpose of strengthening the body and soul of the sick. The Western church continued this practice for many centuries, as well as using oil for anointing on other occasions. Later, the Roman church gave to the priest the exclusive right to perform this ceremony and developed the sacrament of extreme unction (in A.D. 852).[50] This sacrament has the purpose of removing any remnant of sin and of strengthening the soul of the dying (healing is considered only a possibility). The Council of Trent (14.1) found this sacrament "insinuated" in Mark 6:13 and "promulgated" in Jas. 5:14. Since Vatican II, the rite has been called "the anointing of the sick." Clearly this developed sacrament has little basis in James's text: he recommends anointing for any illness and associates it with healing rather than with preparation for death. Nevertheless, the oil could have a sacramental function in that it acted as a "vehicle of divine

48. See esp. J. Wilkinson, *Health and Healing: Studies in New Testament Principles and Practices* (Edinburgh: The Handsel Press, 1980), 153; see also Ross, 79; Burdick, 204.

49. Tasker, 131; Mitton, 191; Hayden, "Calling the Elders to Pray," 265.

50. See K. Richter, "'Ist einer von euch krank . . .': Krankensalbungen in der frühen Kirche," *BK* 423 (1988) 13-16.

power."[51] Much as partaking of the Lord's Supper conveys to the believing participant a strengthening in grace, so anointing may be mandated by God as a physical element through which he works the grace of healing in the sick believer.

b. Symbolic

Anointing frequently symbolizes the consecration of persons or things for God's use and service in the OT. Typical is Exod. 28:41: "After you put these clothes on your brother Aaron and his sons, anoint and ordain them. Consecrate them so they may serve me as priests." The same usage is continued and expanded in the NT, where anointing is often a metaphor for consecration to God's service (Luke 4:18 [= Isa. 61:1]; Acts 4:27; 10:38; 2 Cor. 1:21; Heb. 1:9 [= Ps. 45:7]). If James has this background in mind, then he would be recommending that the elders anoint the sick person in order vividly to show how that person is being set apart for God's special attention in prayer.[52]

In order to reach a decision among these options, we need first to consider the force of the Greek word that James uses here. Scripture employs two Greek words that mean "anoint": *chriō* and *aleiphō.* James's choice of the latter word in v. 14 may shed light on the significance he attributes to the action. *Aleiphō* is used only twenty times in the Septuagint. Of dubious relevance are the seven times where the word refers to rubbing whitewash on a wall (all in Ezekiel, translating Heb. *tûh*). But the word frequently refers to the rubbing of oil on the face or body with a beautifying or hygienic purpose (nine times, usually with Heb. *sûk*). And the verb has a ceremonial significance in four verses. The precise meaning of Gen. 31:13 is unclear, but in Exod. 40:15 (twice) and Num. 3:3 *aleiphō* denotes the ceremonial anointing of the priests, whereby they were set apart for the service of God. This last usage is the regular significance of *chriō* in the Septuagint. In most of its seventy-eight occurrences, it designates the consecration of priests, sanctuary furnishings, or the king of Israel. Only three times does it refer to a cosmetic treatment. Sig-

51. Davids, 193; cf. also Calvin, 355-56; Dibelius, 252-54. There is evidence that oil was considered to have spiritual value (*Life of Adam and Eve* 36) and to aid in exorcising demons (*T. Solomon* 18:34). That the oil here had the purpose of exorcism, the illness being viewed as demon-inspired, is argued by Dibelius, 252, and W. Brunotte, *NIDNTT* 1:121. But anointing with oil is never done in conjunction with exorcisms in the New Testament; Mark 6:13, indeed, distinguishes between anointing the sick and casting out demons.

52. G. Shogren ("Will God Heal Us? A Re-Examination of James 5:14-16a," *EvQ* 61 [1989] 99-108) argues for a view very similar to this.

nificantly, neither word is used with reference to medicinal purposes in the Septuagint. The NT usage of *chriō* maintains this pattern and extends it. For the word never refers to a physical act but is always a metaphor for consecration (Luke 4:18 [= Isa. 61:1]; Acts 4:27; 10:38; 2 Cor. 1:21; Heb. 1:9 [= Ps. 45:7]). As in the Septuagint, *aleiphō* most often designates a cosmetic or hygienic anointing (Matt. 6:17; Mark 16:1; Luke 7:38, 46 [twice]; John 11:2; 12:3). It is possible, however, that the word has some symbolic overtones in the account of Jesus' anointing (John 11:2; 12:3).

The significance of these data for Jas. 5:14 is not clear. One could argue that James would have used *chriō* if he had intended the anointing to have symbolic significance, since this is the word that most often has this connotation in Scripture. On the other hand, considering NT usage, *aleiphō* was the only word James could have chosen if he wanted to signify an actual physical act of anointing.[53] And neither word has medicinal significance in Scripture (leaving aside for the moment the verses at issue, Mark 6:13 and Jas. 5:14). (In Luke 10:34, where oil [*elaion*] clearly has a medicinal use, the verb *epicheō,* "put on," is used.)

Lexicography does not, then, definitely rule in or out any of the four main options. But other factors suggest that James probably views the anointing as a physical action symbolizing consecration. Positively, as we have seen, this is by far the most common symbolic significance of anointing in the Bible. Negatively, each of the other views suffers from one or more serious difficulties. The medicinal view is problematic for two reasons. First, evidence that anointing with oil was used for *any* medical problem is not found — and why mention only one (albeit widespread) remedy when many different illnesses would be encountered? Second, why should the elders of the church do the anointing if its purpose were solely medical? Surely others would have done this already were it an appropriate remedy for the complaint.[54] The pastoral interpretation of the anointing has much to be said for it, and can be incorporated into the view we are arguing. But the value of the anointing does not lie in any physical connection between the action and the malady, as was the

53. See also Martin, 209.

54. Even if James does not specifically recommend medicinal measures here, we cannot draw the conclusion (as some sincere but misguided believers have) that reliance on medicine is a failure to have adequate faith. James would no doubt have shared the perspective of the Jewish wisdom book Sirach that he shares many ideas with: "Honor the physician with the honor due him, according to your need of him, for the Lord created him; for healing comes from the Most High, and he will receive a gift from the king. The skill of the physician lifts up his head, and in the presence of great men he is admired. He created medicines from the earth, and a sensible man will not despise them" (Sir. 38:1-4).

case with most of Jesus' healings (e.g., he rubs the eyes of a blind man [Mark 8:23-26] and places his fingers in the ear of a deaf person [Mark 7:33]). It lies, rather, in the symbolic connotations of the anointing. One's attitude toward the sacramental view will depend considerably on one's view of sacraments in general. But James's insistence in v. 15 that the sick person is healed through "the prayer of faith" suggests that the anointing itself does not convey the grace of healing power.

We conclude, therefore, that "anoint" in v. 14 refers to a physical action with symbolic significance. The verb *aleiphō* can have this meaning, being used equivalently to *chriō* in the Septuagint with reference to the consecrating of priests (Exod. 40:15; cf. *chriō* in 40:13; Num. 3:3). (Josephus can also use *aleiphō* with symbolic meaning, parallel to *chriō;* compare *Antiquities* 6.165 with 6.157.) And while *chriō* is usually used in these texts, James has probably chosen *aleiphō* because he refers to a physical action that the elders are to carry out. As the elders pray, they are to anoint the sick person in order to symbolize that that person is being set apart for God's special attention and care. Calvin, Luther, and other expositors think that the practice of anointing, along with the power to heal, was confined to the apostolic age.[55] But such a temporal restriction cannot be established. James's recommendation that regular church officers carry out the practice would seem to imply its permanent validity in the church. On the other hand, the fact that anointing a sick person is mentioned only here in the NT epistles, and that many healings were accomplished without anointing, shows that the practice is not a necessary accompaniment to the prayer for healing.

15 Anointing with oil, because its significance is so unclear, attracts a lot of attention in this passage. But anointing, whatever it signifies, is clearly subordinate to James's main concern in these verses: prayer. James makes this intention clear by picking up in v. 15 the prayer of the elders from v. 14. As we noted, James uses the normal NT word for prayer of any kind in v. 14 *(proseuchomai);* now, however, he uses *euchē,* which occurs only twice elsewhere in the NT, where it means "vow" (Acts 18:18; 21:23). Its cognate verb, however, refers to a fervent wish or petition in Acts 26:29; 27:29; Rom. 9:3. This prayer, James affirms, when offered *in faith, will make the sick person well; the Lord will raise him up.* The word for *make . . . well* in Greek is *sǭzō,* which is usually translated "save" and often refers to spiritual salvation in the NT (see all the other uses in James: 1:21; 2:14; 4:12; 5:20; and see the note on 2:14). Some interpreters, as we have seen, want to give the word this significance here, arguing

55. For example, Calvin, *Institutes* 4.19.18; and see the classic argument of B. B. Warfield, *Counterfeit Miracles* (reprint; London: Banner of Truth, 1972 [= 1918]).

that James is dealing in the passage with a believer whose faith is weak. And the Greek word behind *the sick person* might confirm this direction, since it can refer to spiritual disability (cf. Heb. 12:3). Others suggest that the salvation may include both a physical and a spiritual dimension.[56] Thus, even if the prayer of faith does not bring healing, it may bring salvation from sin. But this idea does not fit well in the text. For one thing, salvation is never seen to be the result of prayer in the NT. For another, giving two different, though related, meanings to "save" and "raise up" violates a cardinal principle of semantics: never give a word more meaning than the context requires. A physical restoration is all that the context requires, and we should be wary of adding an unnecessary reference to spiritual deliverance. Several elements of the text require a reference to physical healing; everything in the text makes sense as a description of physical healing. The verb *sǭzō* often refers to physical healing in the Gospels (cf. Matt. 9:21, 22; Mark 3:4; 5:23, 28, 34; 6:56; 10:52; Luke 7:50; 8:48, 50; 17:19; 18:42; John 11:12); and *kamnō* (NIV *sick person*) refers to physical distress in four of its six LXX occurrences (4 Macc. 3:8; 7:13; Wis. 4:16; 15:9). Similarly, James's promise that the Lord *will raise up (egeirō)* the sick person reflects the language of NT healing stories (Matt. 9:6; Mark 1:31; Acts 3:7). Thus the picture is of the elders praying "over" the sick person in his bed and the Lord intervening to *raise him up* from that bed.

To be sure, the last half of v. 15 might be cited as evidence that a spiritual interpretation is on the right track after all. Why else would James say that *if he [the sick person] has sinned, he will be forgiven?* In fact, however, the language reinforces the physical healing interpretation that we have been advocating. For sin and sickness were often closely associated in the ancient world. Certainly the book of Job, as well as Jesus (cf. John 9:2-3), makes it clear that drawing a direct relationship between illness and sin is impossible to do. But the NT continues to recognize that some illnesses are, in fact, the product of sin (Mark 2:1-12; 1 Cor. 5:5 [?]; 11:27-30). Recognizing this possible connection, James encourages the sick person to deal with any potential spiritual causes of the illness that he is experiencing. The "if" *(kan)* is therefore doubly important: it shows that James by no means assumes that sickness is caused by sin; and it makes a spiritual interpretation of the passage difficult, since it is difficult to imagine a condition of spiritual "weakness" that would not be a product of sin.

Before leaving this verse, we must turn back to ask about the apparently unconditional promise of healing that James issues here: *the prayer offered in faith* will *make the sick person well; the Lord* will *raise him up*. Some,

56. See, e.g., Johnson, 333 (commenting esp. on "raise up").

as we have noted, avoid the problem by confining the power of healing to the apostolic age; but nothing in the text suggests any such restriction. Others insist that the promise is infallibly answered, but in God's own timing. God may choose to heal in this age. But he will infallibly "heal" all believers in the age to come, on the day when the body is transformed and illness will no longer be a threat. And the verb *egeirō* ("raise up") might point in this direction, since it is regularly applied to resurrection in the NT. But this interpretation, though theologically appropriate, robs the present text of its real point. Believers who struggle with illness can, indeed, be confident that God will heal them in the end. But it does not require a special visit from the elders nor an anointing with oil to accomplish that. It is, as it were, part of their salvation itself, guaranteed them as a gift of grace by the Lord. James plainly envisages a much more immediate result of this special time of prayer for the sick believer.

A more fruitful approach is to focus attention on the qualification that James introduces: it is only the prayer *offered in faith* that brings healing. James's language here again has a point of contact with the opening section of the letter, where he insisted that the believer who asks God for wisdom "must believe and not doubt, because he who doubts is like a wave of the sea, blown and tossed by the wind" (1:6). Certain preachers and writers make a great deal of this call for faith, insisting that a believer simply needs to have enough faith in order to receive healing from the Lord. The devastating result of this line of thinking is that believers who are not healed when they pray must deal with a twofold burden: added to their remaining physical challenge is the assumption that they lack sufficient faith. But this way of looking at faith and its results is profoundly unbiblical. And, in James, at least, the prayer of faith that heals in v. 15 is offered not by the sufferer but by the elders (v. 14). Are the elders, therefore, at fault when their prayer for healing does not bring results in a reasonable amount of time? Would the healing have taken place if they had just believed enough?

Answering such a question involves us in the finely nuanced broader issue of the relationship between God's sovereignty and our prayers. But we can say this much. The faith exercised in prayer is faith in the God who sovereignly accomplishes his will. When we pray, our faith recognizes, explicitly or implicitly, the overruling providential purposes of God. We may at times be given insight into that will, enabling us to pray with absolute confidence in God's plan to answer as we ask. But surely these cases are rare — more rare even than our subjective, emotional desires would lead us to suspect. A prayer for healing, then, must usually be qualified by a recognition that God's will in the matter is supreme. And it is clear in the NT that God does *not* always will to heal the believer. Paul's own prayer for his healing, offered three times, was not answered; God had a purpose in allowing the "thorn in the flesh," that "messenger of Satan," to remain (2 Cor. 12:7-9).[57] Note also Titus 3:20, where Paul mentions that he "left Trophimus sick in Miletus." The faith with which we pray is always faith in the God whose will is supreme and best; only sometimes does this faith include assurance that a particular request is within that will. This is exactly the qualification that is needed to understand Jesus' own promise: "You may ask me for anything in my name, and I will do it" (John 14:14). To ask "in Jesus' name" means not simply to utter his name, but to take into account his will. Only those requests offered "in that will" are granted. Prayer for healing offered in the confidence that God will answer that prayer *does* bring healing; but only when it is God's will to heal will that faith, itself a gift of God, be present. As H. van der Loos puts it, "faith, forgiveness and healing are all three in essence dispensations of the grace of God. This implies that the relations between these three are not governed by the law of causality but by the will and intention of God."[58]

16 The *therefore* shows that the exhortation to mutual confession and prayer in this verse is the conclusion that the readers are to draw from the discussion of prayer in vv. 13-15. But the precise connection between this concluding exhortation and the earlier, more specific commands about prayer in vv. 13-15 is unclear. If vv. 14-15 are about the restoration of a spiritually weak person, then v. 16 will simply reiterate the need to pray for such a person, and the purpose of that prayer — *that you may be healed* — will have a spiritual significance. If, however, as we have argued, vv. 14-15 are about the need to pray for believers who are sick, then v. 16 might function in at least two different ways in relation to vv. 14-15. First, by understanding the purpose statement *that you may be healed* in a spiritual sense or in a combined spiritual/physical sense, we could view v. 16 as a generalization from the encouragement to pray for healing in vv. 14-15. Since the prayer for healing offered in faith accomplishes so much (v. 15a) and since God is anxious to forgive the sins of his people (v. 15b), the whole community should be encouraged to confess their sins to one another and to pray for one another. By so doing, the health (in the broadest sense) of the community will be insured.[59] Second,

57. Assuming that the "thorn in the flesh" is a physical ailment of some kind (see V. P. Furnish, *II Corinthians* [AB; Garden City, N.J.: Doubleday, 1984], 548-50; cf. also Wilkinson, *Health and Healing*, 112-42).

58. H. van der Loos, *The Miracles of Jesus* (NovTSup 9; Leiden: Brill, 1965), 263. On this whole matter, see, in more detail, D. J. Moo, "Divine Healing in the Health and Wealth Gospel," *TrinJ* 9 (1988) 191-209.

59. See, e.g., Cantinat, 254; Mussner, 227; Johnson, 335.

if we take *that you may be healed* in a physical sense, then v. 16 will conclude James's specific discussion about prayer for healing. Both confession of sins — precisely because sin can sometimes be responsible for illness — and prayer are necessary so that the healing of physical illnesses in the community can take place.[60] This last interpretation, tying v. 16 closely to the discussion of physical healing in vv. 14-15, is probably best. For the verb *heal (iaomai)* is consistently applied to physical afflictions. To be sure, it is used in the Septuagint to describe the "healing" of sin or faithlessness (cf. Deut. 30:3; Isa. 6:10; 53:5; Jer. 3:22). But in these contexts it is usually the case that sin has already been explicitly compared to a "wound," establishing a metaphorical "word game." In the NT *iaomai* is used in a spiritual sense only in quotations from these OT texts. When used independently, as here, it always is applied to a physical malady (Matt. 8:8, 13; 15:28; Mark 5:29; Luke 5:17; 6:18, 19; 7:7; 8:47; 9:2, 11, 42; 14:4; 17:15; 22:51; John 4:47; 5:13; 12:40; Acts 9:34; 10:38; 28:8; the only exception is Heb. 12:13, where sin has already been compared to a sickness).

On this reading of v. 16, James's encouragement to the community to *confess your sins to each other* will have particular reference to those sins that might be hindering physical healing. *Confess* translates a Greek verb *(exomologeō)* that means, basically, "agree with" (see Luke 22:6), but in the NT usually refers to a verbal acknowledgment of God's greatness (Matt. 11:25; Luke 10:21; Rom. 14:11; 15:9; Phil. 2:11) or of our own sins (Matt. 3:6; Mark 1:5; Acts 19:18). (The simple form of the verb *homologeō* has a similar range of usage.) This is the only verse in the NT that explicitly commands believers to confess their sins to one another, and it became the basis for the "rule" for small meetings in the eighteenth-century "methodist" movement. But how broadly are we to take this command? James might be requiring only that we confess our sin to those whom we have harmed by the particular sin (cf. Matt. 5:25-26). But the context of healing that we think carries over into v. 16 suggests rather that James thinks of sins that may have caused the illness for which prayers are being offered. We should note an important shift in emphasis in the passage: in v. 14 the elders are encouraged to pray for healing; now, however, the whole church body is to pray. As Davids says, James "consciously generalizes, making the specific case of 5:14-15 into a general principle of preventive medicine. . . ."[61] His focus is no longer on the specific case that he mentioned in v. 14 *(Is any one of you sick? . . .)* but on the general need for the community to be involved regularly (the present tense of the imperative verbs suggests this) in mutual confession and prayer as a way of

60. For example, Dibelius, 255; Davids, 195.
61. Davids, 195.

treating cases of sickness that might arise. At the same time, James's shift from elders to believers in general reminds us again that the power to heal is invested in prayer, not the elder. And while it is appropriate that those charged with the spiritual oversight of the community should be called to intercede for those seriously ill, James makes clear that *all* believers have the privilege and responsibility to pray for healing.

Verse 16 concludes with a reminder of the great power of prayer, providing a fitting capstone to the exhortations to pray in vv. 13-16a. The *righteous man,* or "person" (the Greek masculine form *dikaiou* is clearly generic), is simply the believer, the person who is "righteous" by virtue of receiving forgiveness through Jesus and is therefore part of the people of God. Prayer, James wants to make clear, is a powerful weapon in the hands even of the humblest believer; it does not require a "super saint" to wield it effectively. James employs yet a third Greek word for *prayer* here *(deēsis),* one that appropriately focuses attention on the petitionary aspect of prayer (see esp. those verses in which *deēsis* occurs with *proseuchē* [Eph. 6:18; Phil. 4:6; 1 Tim. 2:1; 5:5]). The NIV's *powerful and effective* translates the combination of adverb, verb, and participle in Greek: "is powerful to a great degree . . . being effective." The form of the participle *(energoumenē)* is ambiguous. It could be passive, in which case we could translate "prayer is very powerful when it is energized (by God or the Spirit)."[62] On this view, James would subtly introduce a qualification to the effectiveness of prayer: only when God "energizes" the prayer as it is offered in accordance with his will will it be effective. However, as theologically attractive as this interpretation might be, it probably reads too much into the text. The participle is probably a middle, with the sense "as it powerfully works" (as most English translations interpret).[63]

17-18 James caps off his encouragement to pray (vv. 13-16) with an example of a "righteous man" whose prayer was "powerful and effective": Elijah. Elijah, whose exploits were so spectacular and "translation" into the presence of the Lord so remarkable, was one of the most popular of all figures among Jews. He was celebrated for his powerful miracles and his prophetic denunciations of sin. Most of all, however, he was looked for as the helper in time of need, whose coming would pave the way for the Messianic age (Mal. 4:5-6; Sir. 48:1-10; Mark 9:12; Luke 1:17). But it is not Elijah's special prophetic endowment or unique place in history that interests James, but the fact that he was *a man just like us* (Gk. *homoiopathēs;* cf. Acts 14:15). As in v. 16b, James emphasizes that every believer has access to the kind of effectiveness in prayer that he is illustrating here.

62. Mayor, 177-79; Davids, 197.
63. See esp. Adamson, 205-12; cf. also Moule, 26.

Elijah, James reminds us, *prayed earnestly that it would not rain, and it did not rain on the land for three and a half years. Again he prayed, and the heavens gave rain, and the earth produced its crops.* "Prayed earnestly" is a good translation of the Semitic cognate construction, which literally rendered would read "prayed with prayer." The situation James describes is recorded in 1 Kings 17–18. God had proclaimed through Elijah that a drought would afflict the land as a means of punishing Ahab and Israel for their idolatry. Although the OT does not state that Elijah prayed for the drought, 1 Kgs. 8:42 does picture him praying for the drought to end, and it is a legitimate inference to think that he prayed for its onset also. Similarly, we should probably take the three and a half years specified by James (cf. also Luke 4:25) as a more specific figure for the rounded-off "three years" in 1 Kgs. 18:1. Perhaps the figure "three and a half" was suggested by its symbolic associations with a period of judgment (Dan. 7:25; cf. Rev. 11:12; 12:14).

A broader question is why James has chosen this particular illustration of effective prayer. As we have noted, the OT does not even mention the prayer, while several other outstanding illustrations of the power of prayer from the life of Elijah are close to hand: calling down fire to consume the sacrifice on Mount Carmel or raising to life the son of the widow (see Luke 4:25). One explanation for the unusual choice might be that James intends us to see an analogy between the sickness of a believer restored to health and the deadness of the land brought back to life and fruitfulness.[64] But the parallels are not very obvious, and James does nothing to drawn attention to what similarities do exist. Probably, then, James at least partly relies on Jewish tradition, where there is evidence for an association between the drought and Elijah's praying (Sir. 48:2-3; 2 Esdr. 7:109).[65]

C. A Concluding Summons to Action (5:19-20)

> 19 *My brothers, if one of you should wander from the truth and someone should bring him back,* 20 *remember this: Whoever turns a sinner from the error of his way will save him from death and cover over a multitude of sins.*

James does not conclude his letter with greetings and benedictions typical of epistolary endings, but with a summons to action. This kind of

64. Davids, 197; cf. also Martin, 213.

65. And Martin (213) notes many Jewish sources that attribute to Elijah great power in prayer.

ending is more typical of the more "formal" NT letters that read like published sermons; 1 John is an especially close parallel. James's letter has been full of specific rebukes and commands. Indeed, as we pointed out in the Introduction, there are more imperative verbs per word in James than in any other NT book. So it is fitting that he would in the end turn to the community with an encouragement to intervene on behalf of fellow Christians who may be having difficulty with the spiritual matters that James has been discussing.

19 For the last time James uses his favorite address, *brothers* (e.g., fellow members of the family of God, both male and female). But he does not here, as he has so often, call on his fellow believers to bring themselves into obedience to the gospel requirements. Rather, he encourages them to *bring back* any person among them who might have "wandered from the truth." *The truth* does not refer here to Christian doctrine in the narrow sense, but more broadly to all that is involved in the gospel. This truth is something that is to be done as well as believed (cf. Ps. 51:6; Gal. 5:7; 1 John 1:6). And for James, of course, correct doctrine cannot be separated from correct behavior. What the mind thinks, and the mouth confesses, the body must do — anything less is worldly, sinful "double-mindedness" (1:8; 4:8). The language of "wandering" that James uses here might suggest that he is thinking only of inadvertent or casual sins. But the Gk. *planaō* that we have here often refers to any deviation from the truth of the faith, whether inadvertent or intentional, minor or major. And, since James suggests in v. 20 that the "wandering" Christian is saved from spiritual death, the deviation from the faith here must be a very serious one, tantamount to apostasy.[66] Note the following verses, which illustrate the seriousness of sins that can be denoted by *planaō:* Matt. 22:29; 24:5; 2 Tim. 3:13; Titus 3:3; 2 Pet. 2:15. "Bring back" *(epistrephō)* can refer to a person's initial "turn" from sin to God in conversion (Acts 14:15; 15:19; 26:18; 1 Thess. 1:9). Here, however, James specifically refers to one *of you,* that is, a person who has at least outwardly identified with the Christian community. "Bring back" will mean, therefore, turning back to the faith from which one had strayed (cf. Mark 4:12 [= Isa. 6:10]; Luke 1:16; 22:32).

20 James has described a hypothetical situation in v. 19: a community member departs from the faith by becoming involved in sin of some kind and is brought back into the fold by a fellow believer. Now he describes the result of such an action: *Whoever turns a sinner from the error of his way will save him from death and cover over a multitude of sins. Error of his way* translates a Greek phrase *(planēs hodou)* that could also be rendered

66. See Martin, 218.

"wandering," or "erring" way (cf. REB; TEV; NJB). Believers are encouraged to take action to turn around a sinner who has taken a wrong and ultimately ruinous path by considering the wonderful results of such successful intervention: a soul is saved from death and many sins are covered. "Death" here, as commonly in James and almost always in the NT where sin is the issue, is ultimate "spiritual" death — the condemnation to eternal damnation that results from unforgiven sin (James uses the noun "death" [*thanatos*] in this sense the one other time it occurs in his letter [1:15]). James pictures death as the final destination on the path that the sinner has determined to take: when he is turned back from that journey, he has "saved" his life (see Ezek. 18:27; Rom. 6:23; and note the spiritual application of "save" [*sǭzō*] elsewhere in James: 1:21; 2:14; 4:12; in 5:15, we have argued, the word has a physical connotation).

But the Greek leaves somewhat ambiguous the question of whose "soul" is saved and whose sins are covered. While it is possible to understand the "soul" that is saved to be that of the person who does the converting, the referent of the pronoun *him* after *save* is almost certainly the sinner who has been converted. But James does not specify any personal object of the verb "cover," keeping to a very general, almost proverbial, phraseology. The words are an allusion to Prov. 10:12, where hate, which "stirs up dissension," is contrasted with love, which "covers all wrongs." "Cover" (*kalyptō* in both Proverbs and James) seems to refer here to the overlooking of slights and offenses against us in the interest of preserving peace. This meaning is unlikely in James, however, and 1 Pet. 4:8 shows that the phrase had become a traditional way of denoting God's forgiveness of sins (cf. Ps. 32:1). Many interpreters think that James intends to encourage the "converter" by reminding him that he can experience forgiveness for his own sins by his disinterested intervention in the lives of other people.[67] The notion that our efforts to bring others to repentance will bring benefit to our own spiritual standing is certainly biblical. The Lord promises Ezekiel that he "will save his life" if he is faithful in warning his people of their danger of judgment (Ezek. 3:21); and Paul tells Timothy that he will "save both himself and his hearers" if he takes heed to himself and his teaching (1 Tim. 4:16). The blessing given to the faithful believer must not, of course, be construed as a reward for his efforts. But the idea that God will treat us as we have treated others is inescapable in Scripture (Matt. 6:14-15; 18:23-35) and explicitly mentioned by James (2:12-13). Therefore, James may well be encouraging his readers to seek actively the conversion of those who are straying by reminding them that their efforts will be rewarded with God's forgiveness of their own sin. On

67. See, e.g., Dibelius, 258; Ropes, 315-16; Adamson, 204; Laws, 239; Mussner, 233.

the other hand, the sequence of thought in the verse makes it awkward to refer the covering of sins to a person different from the one whose salvation has been described. Furthermore, Scripture often associates salvation with the covering, the complete blotting out, of sins, so that the two phrases could be parallel descriptions of the blessing attained by the sinner who is brought back. Probably, then, James refers to the spiritual benefits enjoyed by the sinner who is turned from his sin in both descriptions at the end of v. 20.[68]

If James is indeed something of a sermon in epistolary form, these last two verses are an appropriate conclusion. Not only should the readers of James "do" the words he has written; they should be deeply concerned to see that others "do" them also. It is by sharing with James the conviction that there is indeed an eternal death, to which the way of sin leads, that we shall be motivated to deal with sin in our lives and in the lives of others.

68. For example, Mayor, 237-38; Davids, 201; Martin, 220; Johnson, 339.

Index of Subjects

Index of Authors

Index of Scripture References

Index of Early Extrabiblical Literature

Apocrypha and Pseudepigrapha

Dead Sea Scrolls

Rabbinic Literature

Philo